the haunted gallery

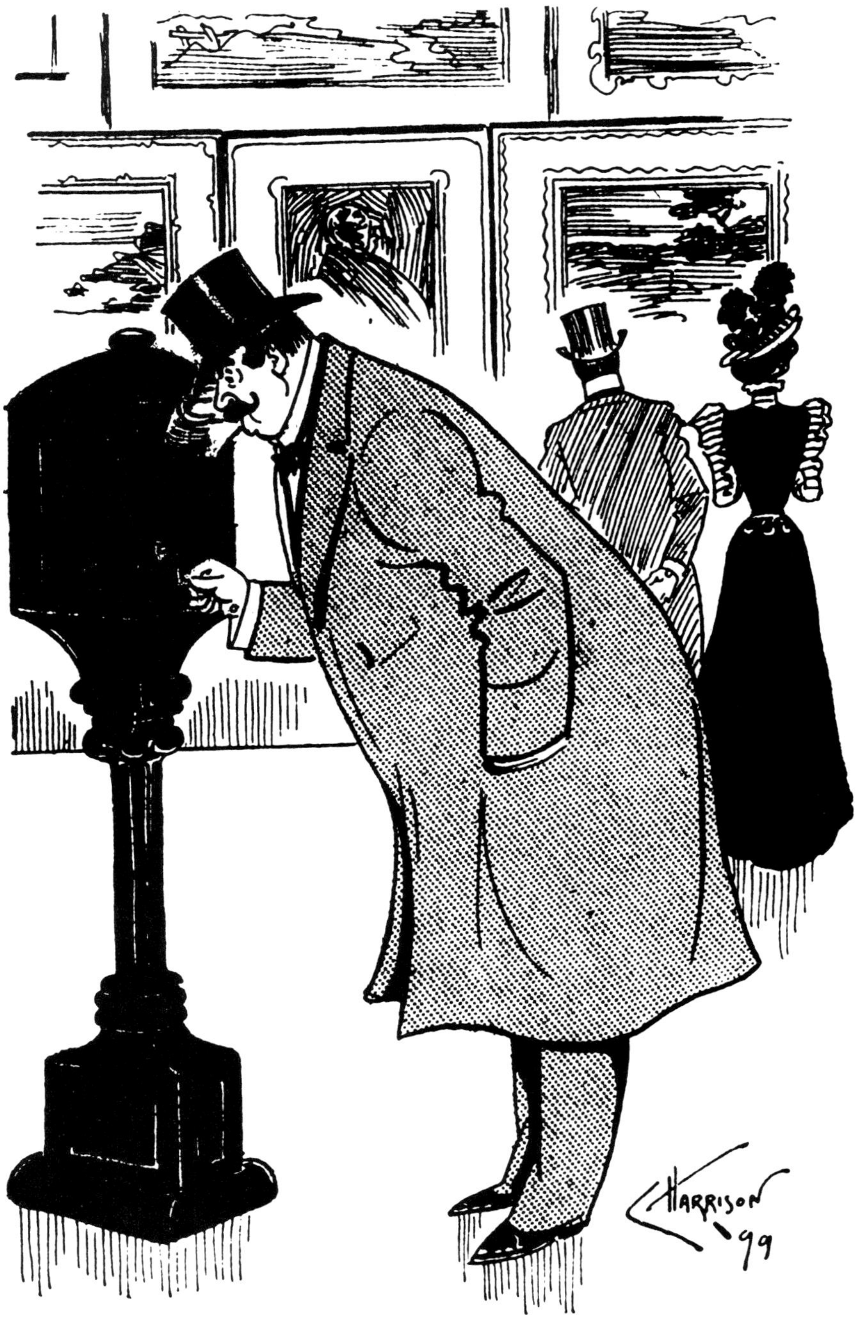
C HARRISON '99

Lynda Nead

The Haunted Gallery

PAINTING,

PHOTOGRAPHY,

FILM

c.1900

Yale University Press
NEW HAVEN AND LONDON

Designed by Gillian Malpass

Printed in China

Library of Congress Cataloging-in-Publication Data

Nead, Lynda.
The haunted gallery : painting, photography, film c.1900 / Lynda Nead.
p. cm.
Includes bibliographical references and index.
ISBN 978-0-300-11291-7 (cl : alk. paper)
1. Arts, Modern–20th century. 2. Motion in art. 3. Multimedia (Art) I. Title.
NX456.N43 2007
700.9'04--dc22

2006100420

A catalogue record for this book is available from The British Library

Frontispiece: 'A Mutoscope of the Pictures, for the use of visitors in a hurry. The Royal Academy "done" in five minutes', *Punch*, 10 May 1899, p. 255.

contents

acknowledgements

The research and writing of this book was made possible by a Leverhulme Major Research Fellowship. It is difficult to express my thanks to the Leverhulme Trust without appearing excessively fulsome. Without doubt, the period of the award was the most stimulating and challenging of my academic career, giving me time to familiarise myself with new disciplines and intellectual issues and to work and write in a sustained way.

I am also indebted to the generosity of a number of scholars in the field of nineteenth-century optical technologies and early film who shared their expertise and knowledge with me. In particular, I thank Simon Brown, Richard Crangle, Ine van Dooren, Frank Gray, Tom Gunning, Colin Harding, Stephen Herbert, Nico de Klerk, Luke McKernan, Simon Popple, Amy Sargeant and Vanessa Toulmin.

Thanks also to Tony Velinor for introducing me to ringcraft; to Valerie Nead for her sound advice; and most especially to the three Connor boys.

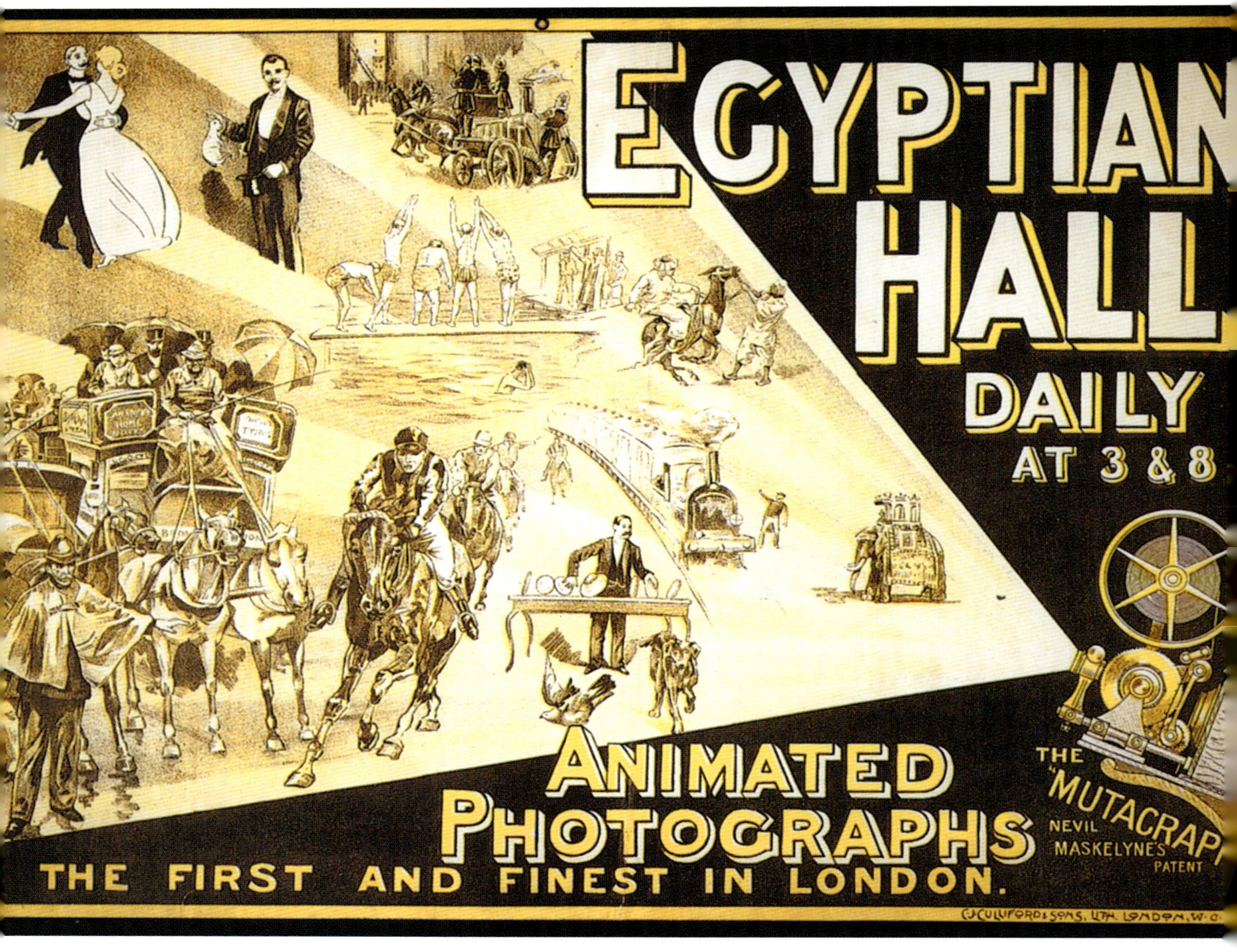
EGYPTIAN
HALL
DAILY
AT 3 & 8
ANIMATED
PHOTOGRAPHS
THE FIRST AND FINEST IN LONDON.
THE
"MUTACRAP
NEVIL
MASKELYNE'S
PATENT
C.J. CULLIFORD & SONS, LTD. LONDON, W.C.

introduction

The motif of haunting weaves through the pages of this book. The dream of motion haunts the visual arts from the classical period to the present day. Statues step down from their pedestals, portrait figures break free of their frames and enter the world of the living, flickers and glimpses of movement are perceived in the great paintings and sculptures of the Renaissance. The gallery, it is clear, is haunted by the possibilities of life and imminent movement. In the last years of the nineteenth century and the first years of the twentieth century, the transformation from stasis to movement and the varieties and velocities of motion possessed all forms of visual media, from high art and art criticism, to still photography and magic lantern slides, popular optical toys and projected film. To many writers and practitioners in this period it seemed as though motion was a condition of all the arts and that stillness was a state of impossibility.

The haunted gallery is a powerful metaphor for the uncanny magic of early film. Film was also possessed by cultural demons and phantoms and early film-makers returned to art again and again as the subject for their own productions, where they played with its values and transformed its images. If the work of art was just so many pencil or brushmarks on paper or canvas, if a photograph was just a trace of the world caught on sensitised paper, then film-makers would bring these inanimate images to life. They would create their own haunted gallery on the screens of the theatres and music halls that became the homes of this emergent medium in the late 1890s. There are, however, other kinds of hauntings and spectral manifestations in early film. Still frames are haunted by the photographic likenesses of those who are no longer living, who seem vivid and real in representation but are gone. Like the enchanted portrait, each time the projector is set in motion these figures also step out of their frames and come to life. In December 1895, the Lumières advertised their first public film exhibition with the words: 'For only one franc see lifesize figures . . . come to life before your very eyes.' It was an invitation to a séance in which the medium – in all senses of the word – was film.

The dictionary definition of 'medium' is simply a middle state; something that is intermediate between two qualities or degrees. It can also mean a person or an object that acts as an intermediary; an agent, channel or conduit of communica-

(facing page) 'Egyptian Hall Daily at 3 & 8. Animated Photographs. The First and Finest in London' (detail of plate 124).

tion and expression. The word thus describes the materials and techniques used in artistic creativity and the various forms of mass communication such as newspapers and radio. A medium conveys images and impressions to the senses; it is fundamentally concerned with the generation of representations and meanings. Within spiritualism, a medium is an intermediary agent between the living and the dead, communicating the appearances and desires of the past to the present. As a history of visual media around 1900, this book engages with all these definitions of 'medium'. It is also a study of intermediary spaces: between high art and mass culture; between residual and emergent forms of visual representation; between conditions of rest and rates of motion. It explores the years of extraordinary cultural production and innovation between 1895 and 1907, which marked the appearance and growth of public film shows before the formal institutionalisation of modern cinema. It is a period that offers the opportunity to develop new objects of historical analysis and different models of visual and cultural interpretation from those offered by conventional disciplinary methodologies.

In the main, publications on the visual arts in this *fin-de-siècle* period have taken the form of discrete studies of individual media. The history of fine art during these years has been treated separately from the development of other media in the period. Similarly, the development and early years of cinema have been separated out and isolated from the cross-fertilisation of aesthetic conventions and discourses that traversed painting, photography and film. The effect of this separation of visual media within academic disciplines and publishing has been to prevent a broader, intermedial understanding of how visual culture develops within a given historical time span: how new media draw on or differentiate themselves from older forms, how audiences are constituted, new forms of display and exhibition are created and so on. The polemical aim of *The Haunted Gallery* is thus to move beyond the established frameworks of interdisciplinarity – would not most art historians today describe their practice as 'interdisciplinary' to a greater or lesser degree? – and to formulate a different method of 'intermedial' study that focuses on the connections and spaces across media, that produces an integrated approach to visual media and that secures these forms within historical networks that include technology, magic, entertainment and desire. This model seeks to move substantially beyond the conventional notion of historical context; the folds of history will not permit simplistic accounts of images and their historical backgrounds.

Mediation means moving between things that are otherwise separated or opposed and it is the methodological principle adopted in this book. The chapters move across and between cultural forms and challenge existing orthodoxies such as the opposition of still and moving images, or the linear relationship of past and present. Rather than defining a historical period as a discrete stretch of time, laid out for the careful interpretation of the investigating scholar, it assumes a more dynamic, topological model of history.

At the end of the 1890s, in the first years of film, time seemed itself to haunt the new medium. The beam of light, created by the film projector, bore a new kind of historical archive – detailed, authentic and comprehensive – which seemed to fold time in on itself. If history was conceived as a linear progression, with key points or moments, located at fixed positions, then the film archive could capture the images of the past for the future and could draw the dead into a dynamic synthesis with the life of the present. Through time-lapse film, contemporaries witnessed the growth and development of a plant in a few moments and imagined a film record of a person's life, from cradle to grave, equally condensed into a matter of minutes. It seemed to one journalist writing in 1897 as though 'the flood of ages had been arrested and [was] returning into the exhaustless urn of time'.[1]

It is fascinating that this rich metaphor for the temporal and historical significance of film anticipates the topological images of history developed in the writings of Michel Serres. For Serres, historical time is imagined as folded, pleated and kneaded; it is spatial and topological, a dynamic volume, rather than a linear sequence.[2] Like the writer in 1897, Serres has compared time to the movement of water, a river that forks, changes its form and flow and folds over on itself. History is thus kinetic and cannot be separated into impermeable or isolated periods; it will continuously draw aspects of the past into its layers and folds and bring apparently diverse or distant phenomena into unpredictable proximity or unexpected networks. The rhythms of social life and visual representation in the years around 1900 were diverse and multi-temporal; self-conscious modernity went hand in hand with heritage and conservation, the viewer's attention was drawn to the streets and the stars and the image of the world was created equally by magic and technology.

If the haunted world of visual media in that era involved a temporal scrambling of past and present and a disregard for linear periodisations, then it was equally inattentive to place and national borders. Although this book focuses on the cultural and social landscape of Britain, this, too, was part of a much wider transnational network in which, for example, French film companies such as Pathé or Lumière sent their cameramen to film throughout the world, creating images that were then marketed, distributed and exhibited across Europe, America, Asia and Africa. With minor adjustments to titles and the addition or removal of lengths of celluloid, early films could quickly become global commodities that moved with ease round international commercial networks. All the media and forms discussed here display the qualities of adaptability and mobility. Paintings and performers went on world tours and were part of World Fairs; and lantern slides and films made distant places accessible, entertaining and profitable. Visual images moved across geographical boundaries in a way that redefines cultural categories of national schools and styles. There is, then, a folding of national identity and international networks in the material discussed in this book. Although in certain contexts visual media were recruited to specifically nationalistic discourses – the reinvention of the British countryside in the early 1900s, for example – this should not obscure the disregard for national boundaries that characterised their distribution and consumption.

The book is divided into three thematic parts. The first, 'Ghosts and Machines', examines the mechanisms and phantoms of movement in the visual media of the period. Chapter 1, 'Velocities of the Image *c.*1900', examines the developments in optical technology that made the idea of an absolutely still image a conceptual impossibility. Motion, in relation to the visual image, was diverse and varied; it was characterised by changes in speed and direction, by acceleration, arrest and reversal. In the realms of physiology and psychology, also, a new kinetic and embodied account of visual perception was being proposed. Like the image of the physical world produced by mechanical engineering, psychology's world of perception was full of movement, both within the beholder and beyond. Art critics and connoisseurs, versed in the experimental findings of psychological aesthetics, visited European art galleries and found movement everywhere. Paintings were writhing with life and made other visitors seem like ghosts in comparison.

Chapter 2, 'The Haunted Gallery', takes up the theme of ghosts and enchanted pictures. The transition from an inanimate to an animated state was a moment of immense cultural and psychic potency. It represented the slippage between the dead and the living, between image and reality. This chapter looks at the development of the haunted gallery as a space of cultural fantasy through art criticism and ekphratic writing and the visual representation of the Pygmalion myth. Projected images from the magic lantern and film created particularly compelling and terrifying effects. Early film-makers frequently turned to the subject of the animated painting, to the image or statue magically endowed with a mischievous life, for the theme was a metaphor for the new medium and its representational powers. It seemed to give inanimate forms life but its illusionistic capacities were inadequate, for the moving images were only shadows, ghosts of the real.

Part Two, 'Cameras and Cars', follows these two paradigmatic technologies of modern life onto the streets of the metropolis and the lanes of the countryside. The recent history of the city and the history of photography are utterly imbricated with each other. The development of hand-held cameras and roll film, discussed in the third chapter, 'Animating the Everyday', enabled a new kind of surreptitious photography that made the urban environment alive to the possibilities of becoming the unwitting subject of a photographic image. Individuals no longer had to give their consent to be turned into an image, which forced new definitions of the right to privacy within public space. The moving images of film also captured and animated the urban everyday but motion gave the streets duration and rhythm, creating a ghostly archive of urban passage, of faces, expressions and gestures from the past, caught within the silent, black and white frames of film.

Chapter 4, 'Paintings, Films and Fast Cars', focuses on the artist Hubert von Herkomer, in order to create a new history of the motor car and modernity and what I have called 'motorised vision' around 1900. Developing the argument made in earlier chapters concerning the diversity of speed in this period, it examines the historical experience of motor-car travel and the way in which it enabled the formation of a distinctive national identity based on rural life, nostalgia and conservation. Herkomer also stands as a symbol of intermediality in this period. An artist usually discussed solely in relation to the development of social realism, he moved with ease across media such as painting, theatre and film and sought to fold the aesthetic and moral values of art and film together into a new form of pictorial, narrative film art.

Part Three, 'Earthly and Astral Bodies', examines the pornographic and spiritual ambitions of visual media in this period. 'Strip', the fifth chapter, considers the implications of motion for the representation of the female body. In the context of the sexual innuendo and display of early strip films, the corporealised viewer, discussed in chapter 1, became a sexually motivated figure and writers, legislators and audiences were forced to reassess the role of popular, mass media within the unregulated environment of film in the first years of the twentieth century.

The tangible, corporeal bodies of film actresses and audiences are brought into contact with sublime, ethereal space travellers in the final chapter, 'Lumen and the Celestial Archive of Images'. Taking as its starting point the reproduction of astronomical photographs in the popular, scientific press in this period, it looks at the impact of late nineteenth-century astronomy on the visual imagination. What began as a terrestrial viewpoint moved quickly to a place somewhere else in the solar system or galaxy. Astronomy disrupted conventional notions of time and space. Viewers were conscious that the light that was seen through the telescopic lens or recorded on the photographic plate might have emanated from space thousands of light years before and that the forms and systems represented might already have changed, or disappeared entirely. The collapse of conventional notions of time and space in the astronomical image liberated the visual imagination and the entire histories of worlds and civilisations were conceived within the sublime archive of images carried in a beam of light and watched by astral space travellers.

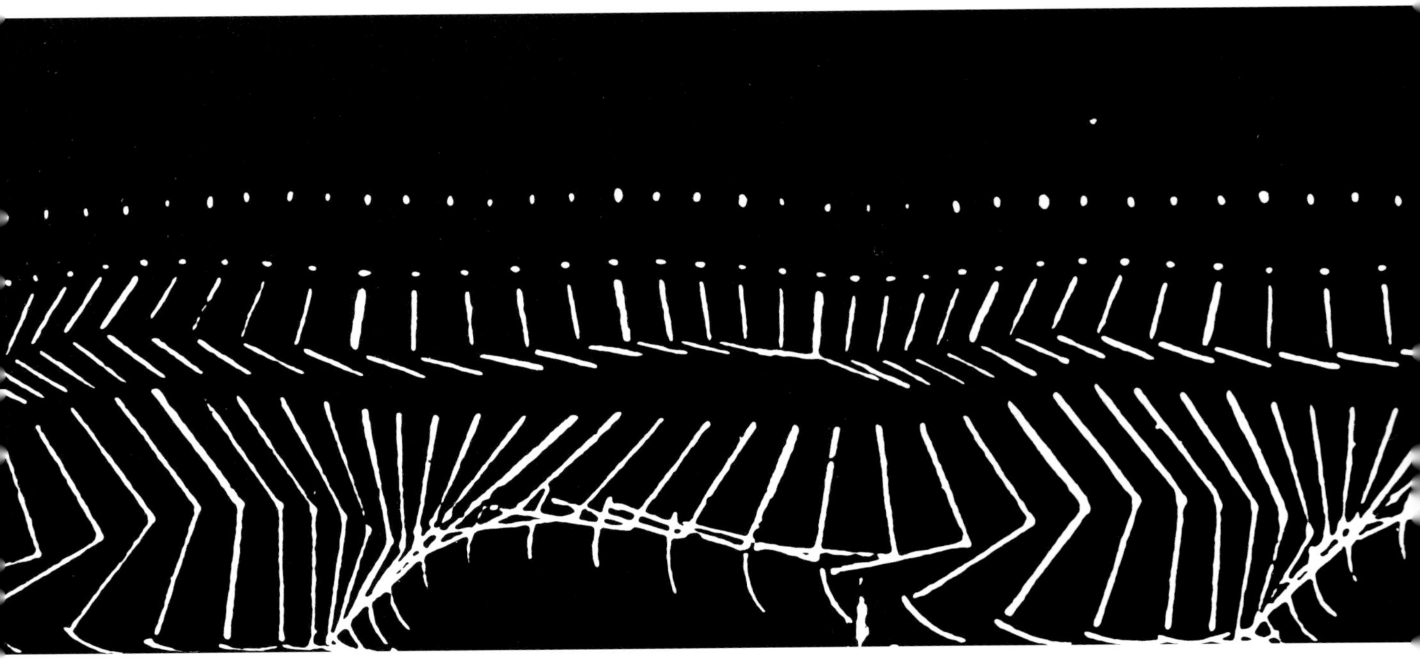

ghosts and machines

(*facing page*) 'Chronophotographic Images of a Runner' (detail of plate 9).

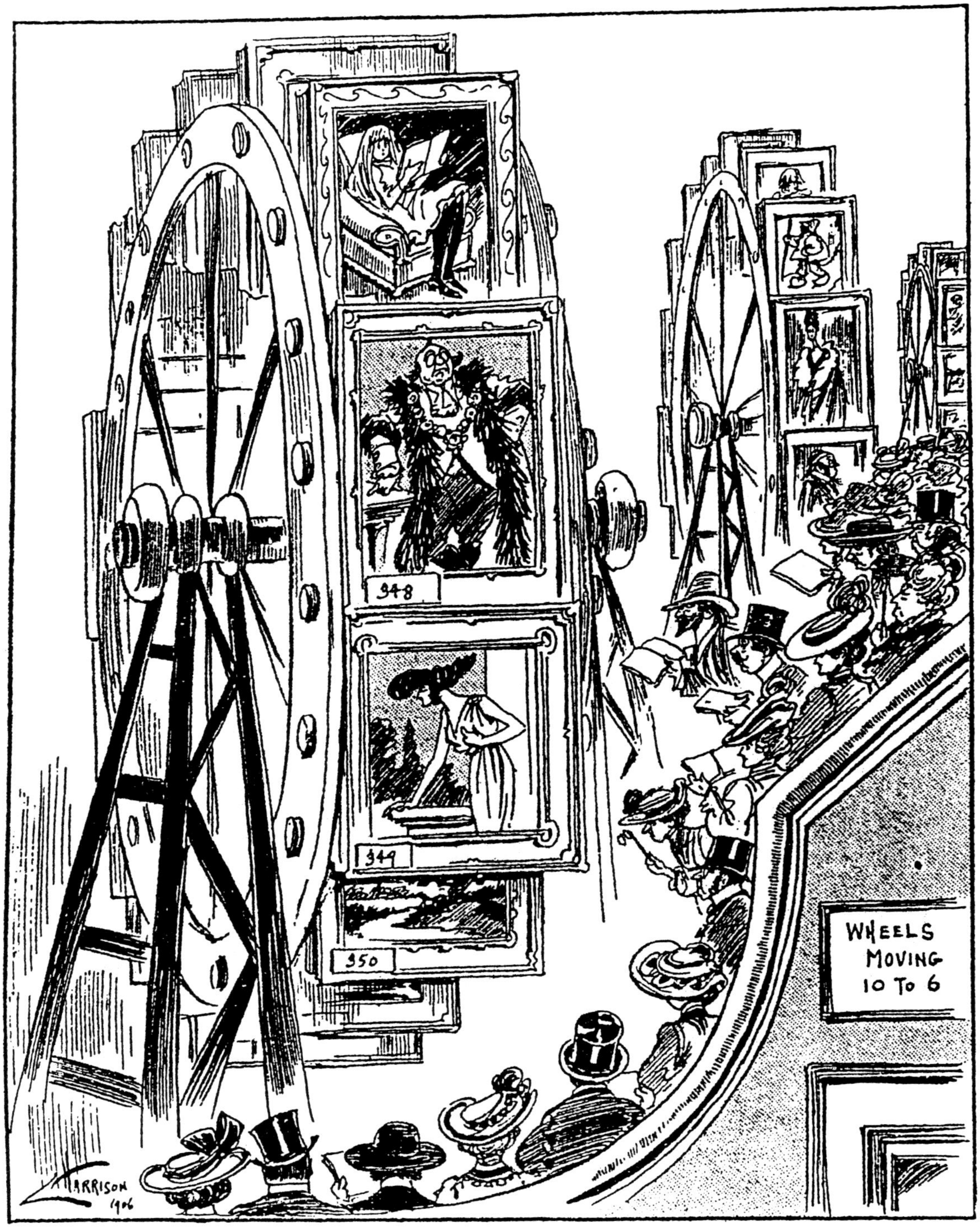

THE AGE OF THE WHEEL.

A SUGGESTION FOR THE ROYAL ACADEMY.

1 'The Age of the Wheel: A Suggestion for the Royal Academy', *Punch, Or the London Charivari*, 16 May 1906, p. 359.

1 velocities of the image *c.*1900

> Many of the pleasures of Muscular Movement . . . may be experienced in the *spectacle* of moving objects. The Massive languid feeling of slow movement, the excitement of a rapid pace, the still higher pleasure of a waxing or waning speed, can all be realised through the muscles of the eye and the head.
>
> Alexander Bain, *The Senses and the Intellect* (1894)[1]

the work of art in the age of the wheel

In May 1906 *Punch* magazine published a cartoon which it called 'The Age of the Wheel: A Suggestion for the Royal Academy' (plate 1). Loosely based on Thomas Rowlandson's 'The Exhibition Stare-Case' (*c.*1800; plate 2), the cartoon proposed a novel solution to the perennial problem of the poor visibility of exhibits at the annual Royal Academy summer show in London.[2] Rather than being hung in tiers from floor to ceiling on the gallery walls, the paintings are mounted on a series of giant wheels and, although the exact nature of the mechanism is unclear, it is evident that the wheels are set in motion between the hours of 10 am and 6 pm. As the wheels move, the pictures are rotated and occupy a position of optimum visibility at least once every revolution as they come into full view of the exhibition audience. In a close quote from Rowlandson, the audience in 'The Age of the Wheel' is crowded along a steeply inclined handrail, clasping their catalogues and peering at the framed pictures being rotated in and out of vision by the great mechanical wheels.

The 1906 cartoon is, in part, the summation of a long-running campaign in *Punch* ridiculing the automation of society. Earlier articles and illustrations had poked fun at 'drop in' amputation centres, teeth extraction machines and automated banking services.[3] Now machines have entered the art gallery and even the viewing of art has become a mechanical process. Both the Rowlandson image and the *Punch* cartoon offer sharp, hard-hitting commentaries on the nature of modern cultural consumption. However, whereas the 'butt' of Rowlandson's comedy is the gross corporeality of the Academy audience who trip, bump and tumble down the length of the famous staircase at Somerset House, the point of *Punch*'s humour is the way in which the cultural spectacle of the Academy exhibition has been wrenched from the corpulent, venal philistines of Rowlandson's world and taken over by machines. In 'The Age of the Wheel', exhibits are no longer 'skied', or subjected to the vagaries and prejudices of the Academy Hanging Committee; instead, they have become part of a standardised, mechanical display. Each picture is now equally visible for the same period of time as they are flipped round on the giant wheels. Moreover, mechanisation has imposed its logic on artistic production; differences in size have been eliminated and all the canvases conform to uniform dimensions to fit the framed slots on the wheels. From 10 till 6 every day the wheels rotate on their giant axes, presenting to the viewers a continuous, alternating rhythm of image and interval.

The experience of the viewer is also radically changed. No longer whimsical, self-determining individuals who can choose how long to look at a picture, whether to linger in a state of extended contemplation, or to pass straight by, the audience's time is now machine time and they are subjected to automated periods of viewing, controlled by the speed of the wheels. Both the Rowlandson image and the *Punch* cartoon are about the kinetic possibilities of staring but, whereas in the earlier context all the motion is invested in the bodies of the dissolute audience, in the cartoon movement is a condition of the image as well as of its consumption.

Like the best *Punch* cartoons and in the highest tradition of graphic satire, 'The Age of the Wheel' draws to itself and re-articulates key social, political and cultural debates of the period. Here every element of the image – the giant wheels, the standardised exhibits and the attentive audience – contributes to this deft account of the nature of modern perception in an age of mechanical image-making and display. Decades of developments in visual technology, psychology, physiology and mechanical engineering are evoked in the brilliant conception of an automated art exhibition and its terse notice 'Wheels Moving 10 to 6'. 'The Age of the Wheel' provides the starting-point for the following account of the emergence of a new regime of mechanised visual media around 1900. I want to tease out the histories that lie behind those brief words of information on the Academy notice and to unravel the social and cultural transformations that must have occurred in the second half of the nineteenth century to make possible this fantasy of mechanical picture wheels. I also want to explore what I believe is the unresolved core of the image, that is, the role of the audience in this new cultural milieu and the impact of movement on the nature of visual perception and aesthetic pleasure.

The kinetic possibilities of viewing high art draw one beyond the common binary structures that have dominated historical readings of visual culture in the twentieth century. High art and mass culture have been differentiated in terms of their distinctive modes of viewing. In his often perplexing but frequently quoted essay 'The Work of Art in the Age of Mechanical Reproduction', Walter Benjamin contrasted the viewer's relationship to the oil painting and the cinema screen: 'The painting invites the spectator to contemplation; before it the spectator can abandon himself to his associations. Before the movie he cannot do so. No sooner has his eye grasped a scene than it is already changed. It cannot be arrested.'[4] Benjamin draws upon and reformulates the historical definition of art as the site of pure,

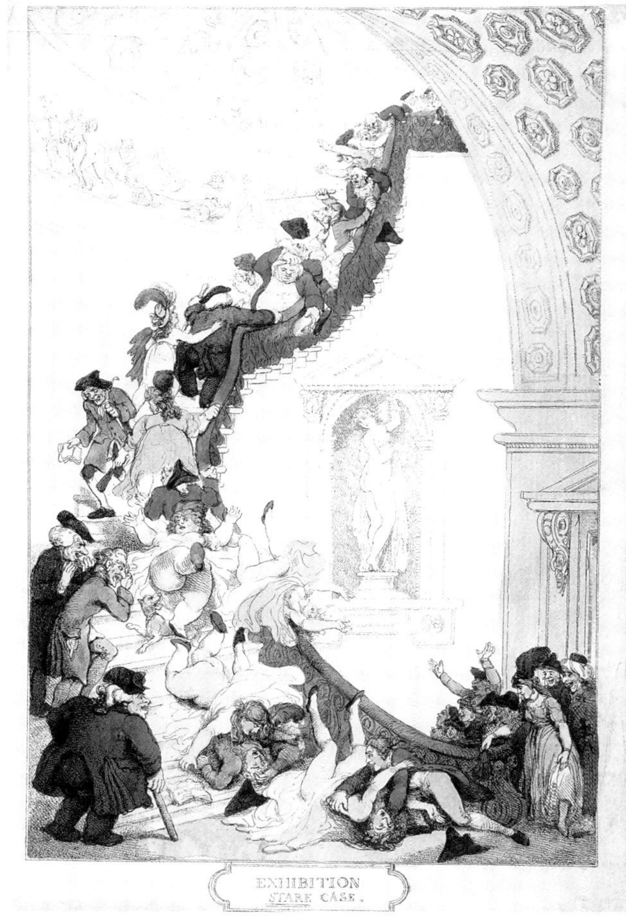

2 Thomas Rowlandson, 'The Exhibition Stare-Case', 1811. Engraving on paper, 45.1 × 30.5 cm. The British Museum.

extended contemplation; a domain that demands a contained concentration from the viewer. Film, on the other hand, is the medium of mass-produced modernity for the masses. It expresses the shock and stimulus of contemporary life and satisfies the desire for distraction and arousal. Art is the medium of stillness; film is the art of movement.

'The Age of the Wheel' prompts a re-examination of this cultural construction. The introduction by *Punch* of movement machines into the space of the Royal Academy fatally compromises the association of art with prolonged stillness. The spectator can only concentrate for as long as the motion of the wheel allows. Like the viewer of the film, therefore, the spectator in the cartoon is confronted by one picture after another, one frame replacing another through the continuous forward movement of mechanised wheels and cranks. Whereas the speed of the film projector moves the strip of film at a rate that produces an illusion of continuous movement, however, the velocity of the great art wheels permits the viewer to perceive each individual picture for a period of time. At least, one imagines it does.

It would also be possible to read the cartoon as a suggestion for a Royal Academy film show, with canvases flickering and jerking in a manner of animated motion.

The point is this: developments in visual technology at the end of the nineteenth century had made the idea of a still image a conceptual impossibility. In the realm of science also, the state of absolute rest was regarded as empirically unprovable; all bodies were in a condition of relative rest and motion. By 1900 it would have been easy to conclude that all images and the act of viewing itself involved some form of motion. Moreover, movement in the modern world was not necessarily fast (as in the shock-inducing speed of city life in the writings of Simmel or Benjamin) or uniform. The motion considered here was diverse and varied, characterised by changes in speed and direction and by acceleration, arrest and reversal. It prompts an examination of velocities of the image across the spectrum of visual media in the period.

This subject cannot be undertaken in relation to a single medium in isolation. It has to be pursued in terms of formal and cultural relations across media at this historical moment. From the second half of the nineteenth century there was an increasing proliferation of image-making machines, alongside changing conceptions of physical movement and the nature of perception. Together, these transformations had a huge impact on the cultural landscape of the industrial West. Old and emergent visual forms did not function independently but were in a constant process of realignment – of cultural and technological adjustment. In their analysis of recent digital media, Jay David Bolter and Richard Grusin proposed a methodology that is equally relevant to the media world of 1900:

> No medium today . . . seems to do its cultural work in isolation from other media, any more than it works in isolation from other social and economic forces. What is new about new media comes from the particular ways in which they refashion older media and the ways in which older media refashion themselves to answer the challenges of new media.[5]

'The Age of the Wheel' can be seen as one version of high art's accommodation of film and moving-image technology in the first decade of cinema. It conveys a fascination with the mechanisation of culture and its implications for the conditions and experiences of modern viewing. It traces the move from an older formulation of an extended, self-determined aesthetic gaze, to a newly mechanised, kinetic experience of the art work. The viewer is at the centre of this cultural reconfiguration but is no longer in control; viewing is managed now by the great art wheels.

movement machines

The contraptions on which the Academy exhibits are mounted are utterly fantastic but also reminiscent of a number of existing mechanical devices. The arrangement of individual images around a central axle recalls the organisation of series

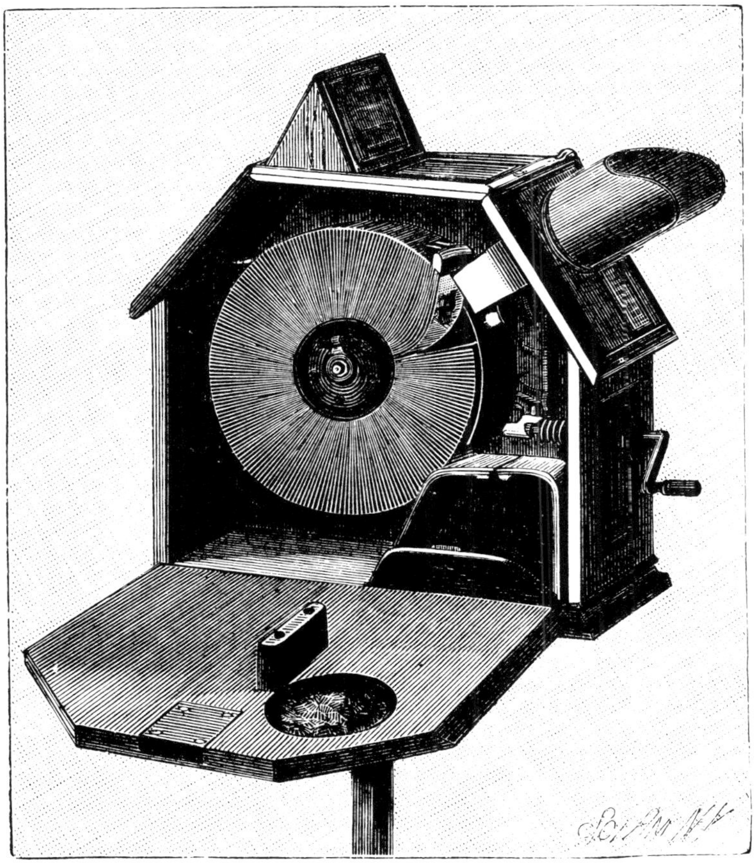

3 'Interior of the "Mutoscope"', from Albert Hopkins, *Magic: Stage illusions and Scientific Diversions including Trick Photography*. London: Sampson Low, Martin and Co. Ltd, 1897, p. 506.

of photographs in the mutoscopes of the 1890s (plate 3). In this simple mechanism, prints are mounted in consecutive order round a cylinder, like the leaves of a book. When the cylinder is revolved by a crank operated by the viewer, each picture card is held under the lens for an instant and then replaced by the next. Operated at the optimum speed, the succession of photographs produces the impression of continuous movement. The *Punch* wheels are clearly not giant mutoscopes, however. For a start, the images are not mounted radially round the axle and, further, from the look of the central wheel, they appear to be not so much flicked into place as trundled round in a fixed position.

There is something both archaic and modern about the look of the art wheels. The axle supports are of the most rudimentary construction and the pictures appear to be held in place by huge bolts projecting along the outer rim of the wheel. Perhaps, then, they are most like ancient water wheels, and their modern, theme-park derivative, Ferris wheels.[6] The Ferris wheel is probably one of the oldest amusement rides and its history is closely tied to the history of the fairground. The modern amusement wheel came into its own in the era of international exhibitions and World Fairs. The transition from exhibition to fair, from education to attraction, provided the perfect cultural context for the triumph of the great wheel.[7] From the Great Exhibition of 1851 to the Paris World Fair of 1900, the scale and ambition of international expositions became increasingly hubristic. By the late nineteenth century, they had grown far beyond the containment of a single building and had begun to occupy tracts of land and a miscellany of pavilions, forming temporary, self-contained cities or worlds for the amazement of their millions of visitors. This changing ethos was symbolised most forcefully by the increasing presence of various kinds of spectacular attractions and amusements. Whereas at the beginning of the period these had been a relatively minor or incidental supplement to the primary display of global commodities, by the time of the Chicago World's Columbian Exposition in 1893, an entire strip of land, the 'Midway Plaisance', had been set aside for privately operated amusements. Amusement in the context of World Fairs took the form of thrilling machine rides such as roller coasters, scenic railways and water chutes which offered new kinds of exhilarating physical experiences. Scale and movement were the prevailing values of the entertainment machines of the modern expositions and theme parks. Thrills were provided by vertiginous heights, fast speeds and rapid acceleration; technology had been harnessed to the production of sensational and kinetic commercial entertainment.

Of the many visual images of the late nineteenth-century World Fair, the form of the giant wheel, often towering over the exhibition landscape, symbolises its diverse and extreme attractions. The first great wheel was designed by George Washington Gale Ferris Jr. for the Chicago Columbian Exposition in 1893. The 250-foot-tall wheel was supported by a huge steel axle and two steel towers; it carried thirty-six cars, each capable of holding sixty people. Statistics like this mattered because the spectacle of the Ferris wheel lay in the principle of gigantism; its commodity value lay in its hugeness and in the panoramic views it offered of the surrounding urban landscape. Unlike the other entertainment machines of the Midway Plaisance, however, speed was not a feature of a Ferris wheel ride; in fact, powered by a steam engine, the great wheel moved slowly and even stopped periodically to load and unload passengers. At the close of the Exposition, the Ferris wheel had carried more than one and a half million visitors and had made a financial profit. Scale, in this case, had proved to be a sound economic principle as well as a sensation.

Following the success of Chicago, an even bigger wheel was built by Walter B. Basset for an exhibition at Earl's Court in London in 1895 (plate 4). This wheel was driven by an electric engine and at night not only the cars themselves but also the entire circumference of the wheel was illuminated by electricity. It was thus a highly visible part of the metropolitan landscape until it was demolished in 1906, the year of the *Punch* cartoon. Perhaps, then, the specific suggestion for the Royal Academy is that the great Earl's Court wheel should be re-assembled in Piccadilly and even the bulbous bolts might then be seen as gaudy electric lights. The contraption which is moving high art is nothing more than a giant fairground attraction; high and low culture are united in their status as entertainment machines.

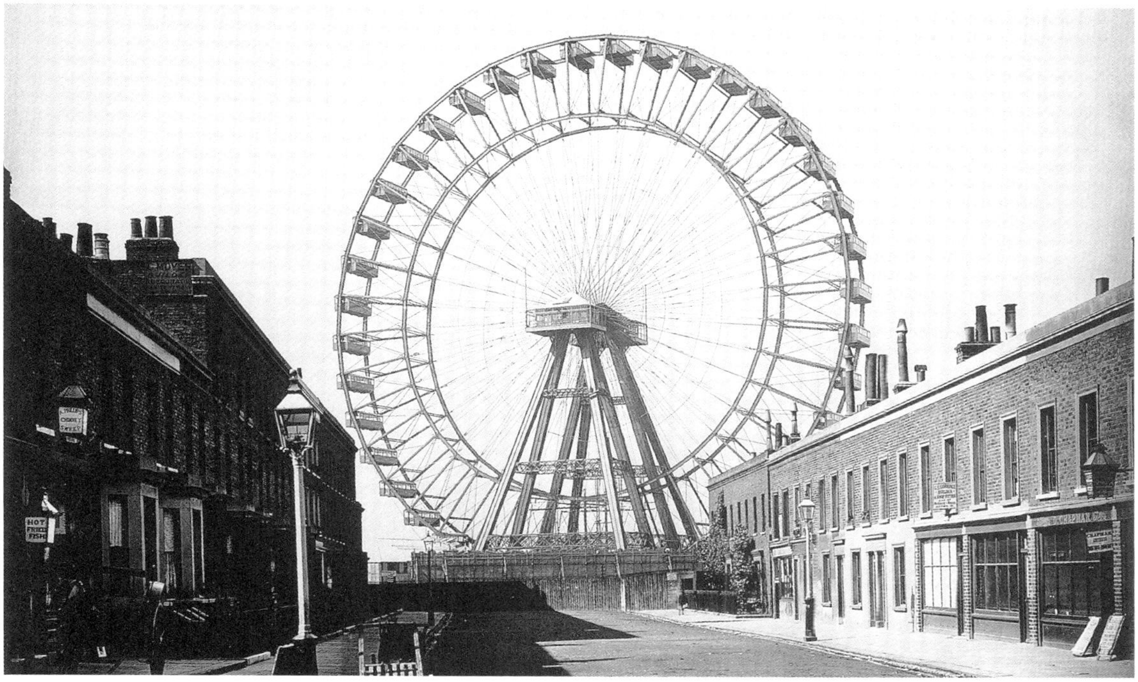

4 'The Great Wheel, Earl's Court Exhibition', *c.*1905. The Museum of London.

The greatest significance of the new theme-park technology lay in its impact on the experience of the user. Audience and activity were no longer separate elements of the entertainment but were merged in a variety of kinaesthetic amusements. The spectator had been redefined as participant, a change which was not confined to mass culture but which also permeated high culture.[8] There is something odd about the audience in the *Punch* cartoon. Whereas in the Rowlandson image the human avalanche is caused by the movement of bodies, tripping and bumping down the staircase, the figures in 'The Age of the Wheel' seem to be being transported along the incline of the stair rail. They look like travellers on an escalator as much as visitors to an art exhibition. Perhaps not only the images but also the audience are being moved by machines at the *Punch* Royal Academy show.

The Paris 1900 Exposition Universelle not only boasted the biggest great wheel ever built but also unveiled the first escalator and a moving pavement. In fact it specialised in novel forms of technology for the slow transportation of large numbers of pedestrians. The *trottoir roulant* was one of the big hits of the Paris Fair (plate 5).[9] It consisted of an elevated platform with two bands moving at different speeds. The first band moved at a speed of about one and a half to two miles per hour; the second, adjacent band, moved at about five miles per hour and was also provided with seats. This moving pavement covered a course of about two miles, connecting key sections of the Exposition grounds. Passengers paid a fare of ten cents and could move from band to band, covering the entire route in about

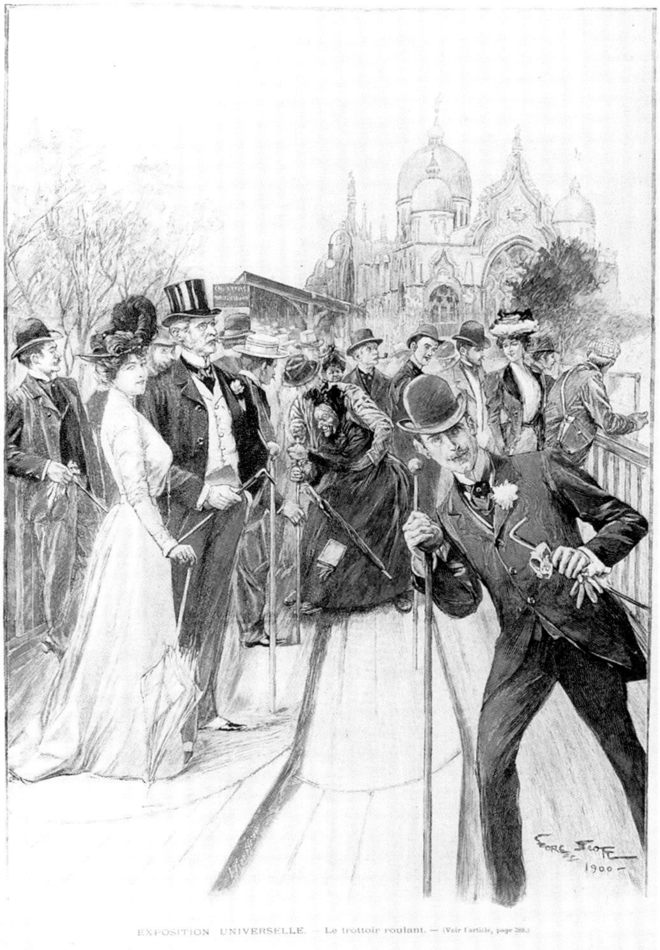

5 'Exposition Universelle – Le trottoir roulant', *L'Illustration*, CXV, 16 June 1900, p. 377.

twenty-five minutes. A contemporary described the structure as 'crowded with passengers, some gliding by, standing still, others walking, running and stepping from one platform to the other'.[10] The device offered visitors a reasonably sedate form of mechanically enhanced movement. It was designed to offer a good view of the Exposition as well as to be a practical way of shifting large numbers of visitors. Travelling at speeds around walking pace, the moving pavement offered a kind of mechanised strolling that conformed to prevailing pedestrian velocities rather than subjecting individuals to the shock of extreme speed.

The escalator also made its debut as a private speculation at the Paris World's Fair and was another example of a movement machine that aped the speeds of human motion (plate 6). A moving stairway had made its first appearance in 1897 as a novelty ride at the amusement park at Coney Island on Long Island, New York State; within a couple of years it had been redesigned and marketed as an 'escalator' by the Otis Elevator Company, for use in elevated and underground

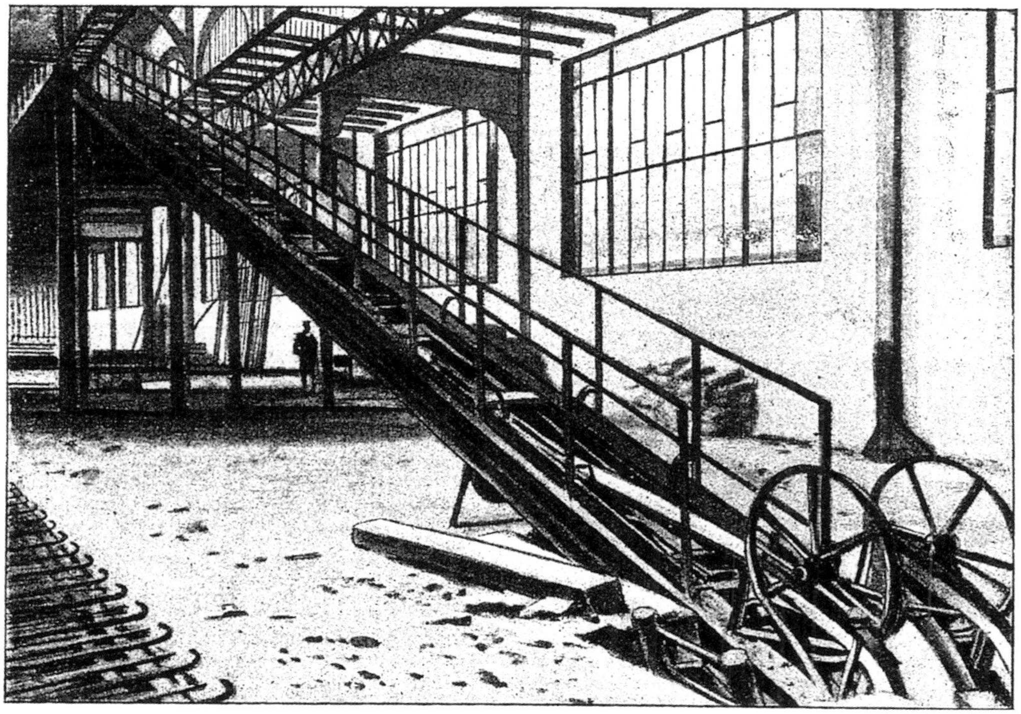

6 'Les élévateurs inclinés de l'exposition', *L'Exposition de Paris (1900) publiée avec la collaboration d'écrivains spéciaux et des meilleurs artistes*, II. Paris: Libraire Illustré, 1900, p. 294.

railway stations and department stores.[11] The escalator works on the principle of a track system that guides a step chain round a hollow core, pulling the steps through an endless loop. Its motion is smooth and steady and, to borrow the words of Rowlandson's title, it offers a moving 'exhibition stare-case'. Like the *trottoir roulant*, it is a mechanical substitute for human propulsion that also provides the user with time to look. And so one arrives at the condition of the work of art in the age of movement machines. The wheels and engines that operate from 10 to 6 in the *Punch* cartoon not only mobilise the pictures, they also transport the audience. By 1900 art was part of a highly developed commercial entertainment world, organised around the logic of motion. The movement machines that often originated as amusements and spectacles within mass culture could also move across into the art gallery, transforming what looking at art meant and the concept of an aesthetic experience. Indeed, to be transported by art in this context had both a literal as well as a metaphorical interpretation.

Movement in 1900 was broadly understood. Speed was not the exclusive goal of mechanised movement within modernity, but diverse velocities were explored in response to different needs and markets. The history of visual media in this period can be properly described as the history of velocities of the image.

* * *

kinematics: the art of motion

Kinematics, the science of pure motion as it occurs in machines, emerged as a specialist branch of mechanical engineering towards the end of the 1870s. It had developed alongside industrialisation in France at the beginning of the nineteenth century within the vocational tradition of the French polytechnic system. There, physicists and engineers moved from the consideration of the machine as a physical and mechanical whole to the study of individual parts of machines called mechanisms. Treating each mechanism as a discrete system, the polytechnic devised a classificatory system, organised according to fundamental types of motion, and by the 1870s a new discipline, kinematics, had been defined.

The history of kinematics is an essential component of the cultural history of movement in the nineteenth century. First, it was specifically devised as the science of motion. Second, one of its primary concerns was the development of a visual syntax for the representation of mechanical movement. Third, it shares more than an etymological root (motion: *κινεμα*) with the history of cinema. Early cinema and kinematics were both concerned with the question of how visual images could convey the idea of movement to an audience and how single units (whether the film frame or individual mechanism) could be combined to express greater significant wholes (the film or machine). It is therefore worth considering the development of this now forgotten science and its contribution to the history and representation of motion in the period.

Within late nineteenth-century kinematics there was a clear distinction between motion and velocity.[12] In its most basic formulation, motion simply described a change of position; time was not a factor, since motion was concerned only with the measurement of the space traversed by an object. Velocity, in contrast, was a measurement of the speed of a motion along its path and, as such, both time and space were involved in its calculation. Moreover, because change of position could only be estimated in relation to some other body, motion was understood to be essentially relative; and since speed and time within this discourse were defined as absolute magnitudes, velocity itself was described as absolute. As a mechanical science, kinematics adhered to these basic principles well into the second decade of the twentieth century. So although it shared the historical moment of Einstein's theory of relativity, the implications of Einstein's work made little or no impact on its perception of time and speed.[13] While Einstein demonstrated that distances and durations were not absolute properties but variable relations, kinematics continued to analyse mechanical movement in terms of the absolute and singular uniformity of the passage of time.

As a science of movement, kinematics was also concerned with rest. Like motion, rest was understood to be a relative property of an object or body, calculable only in relation to the motion of other bodies in space. As one American writer on the subject put it, '*Motion* and *Rest* are essentially relative terms, within the limits of our knowledge. We can conceive a body to remain in a fixed position in space, but we cannot know that there is one which does.'[14] The empirical impossibility of absolute rest, of the complete stillness of an object, was endorsed by most authors in this field. The picture which begins to emerge from kinematics, of a world composed of constant, differentiated motion, is one which can also be traced in this period in widely different discursive fields. Psychologists of perception were also working with a paradigm of the eye and the nervous system as being in a state of constant muscular activity. Stillness was being refuted as a property of the image, the object and the beholder.

Kinematics stripped the machine down to its essential forms – elements, chains and mechanisms. In this sense, all machines could be reduced to a limited vocabulary of forms that connected them to the earliest 'primitive machines' of the Egyptians, Babylonians, Greeks and so on.[15] The revolution of a wheel, the turn of a driving belt and the movement of a lever or crank, united the water wheels of the ancient world and the motion cameras of the late 1890s. Little wonder, then, that *Punch*'s art wheels have something of the elementary and of the modern about them. If, as the pioneering French author, François Reuleaux, argued, the purpose of a machine was to impose law and order on nature and to prevent 'disturbing motions by latent forces',[16] then the art wheels can also be seen as subjecting the chaotic activity of Rowlandson's crowd to the predictable, mechanical forces of modernity.

The purpose of kinematic analysis was to further 'the progressive development of the machine',[17] through a methodology based on graphic representation. It was broadly agreed that graphic and geometric visualisations offered the viewer a stronger and more immediate apprehension of a motion than algebraic calculations. John Barr commended graphic imaging for 'appealing to the mind through the eye much more effectively than do numerical quantities';[18] and C. W. MacCord confirmed that 'a graphic representation is the best if not indeed the only means of conveying to the mind a distinct and comprehensive idea of the law according to which the motion varies in velocity and direction . . . it gives in an instant all the information'.[19] The most basic form of velocity diagram is the simple curve in which the points on the line MN represent units of time and the coordinates 11′, 22′ and so on represent the velocities of the moving object (plate 7). Points above the line indicate motion in one direction; negative points below the line represent motion in the opposite direction. To 'read' this diagram, is to comprehend, to 'see' the motion described in an instant. More complex time–velocity diagrams convey the movements of more complicated mechanisms (plate 8). The trained reader of these images immediately registers variations in velocity – acceleration and retardation – as well as changes in direction and line of travel. This is a new kind of technical image that condenses time and space, the narrative of movement, into a deceptively simple graphic form.

Etienne-Jules Marey was also an advocate of the graphic method of representing motion.[20] The points and curves of the late nineteenth-century velocity diagrams recall the various methods developed by Marey in the 1870s and 1880s to record the locomotion of animals and humans. Within art history, Marey's historical significance has been reduced to the influence of some of his photographic motion studies on later modernist artists such as Marcel Duchamp, but he belongs

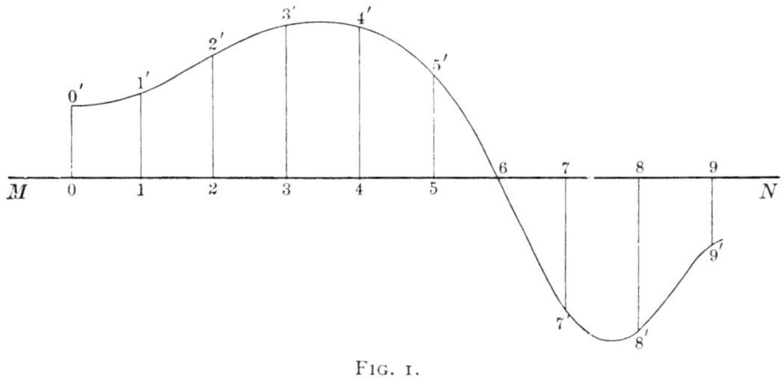

7 Velocity diagram from Charles William MacCord, *Velocity Diagrams: Their Construction and their Uses. Intended for All who are interested in Mechanical Movements*, New York: John Wiley and Sons; London: Chapman and Hall Ltd, 1901, p. 2.

more properly to the historical moment of kinematics and its contribution to the contemporary art of motion. Marey was a designer of machines for simulating and recording movement. Like other figures in this period concerned with the visual transcription of motion, he was engaged in an ongoing process of modifying existing mechanisms and inventing new ones capable of securing the most complete and accurate representation of the phases of movement. Around 1870 Marey designed an apparatus to register the elliptical trajectory of a bird's wing onto a glass plate. Among the many images that were produced to record the experiment and its results were a number of graphic designs that can be described as velocity diagrams of the changing plane, direction and speed of each beat of the wing.[21] Inspired by Eadweard Muybridge's serial photography of a horse in motion, Marey went on to explore the possibilities of photography, in combination with his graphic

8 Velocity diagrams from MacCord, *Velocity Diagrams*, p. 92.

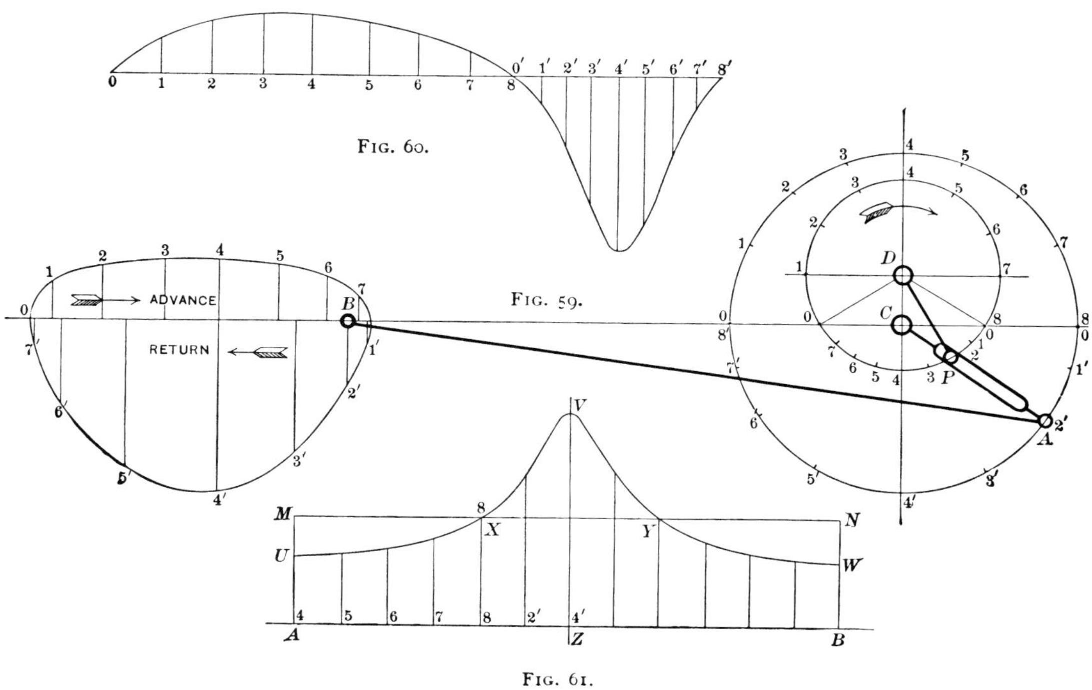

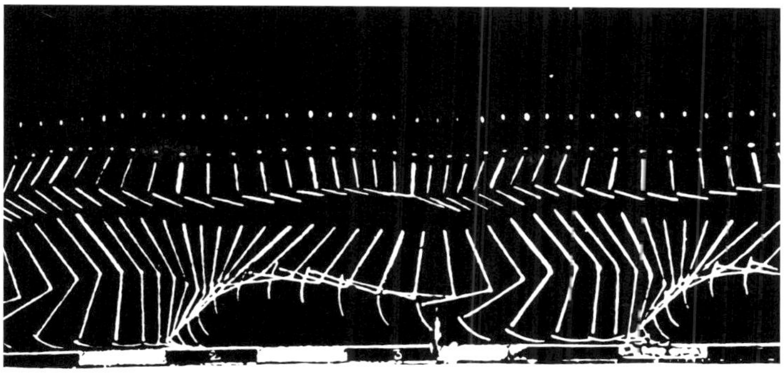

9 'Fig. 12 – Chronophotographic Images of a Runner', from Albert A. Hopkins, *Magic: Stage Illusions and Scientific Diversions including Trick Photography*, 1897. London: Sampson Low, Marston and Co. Ltd, p. 472.

method. By the 1880s he had developed a 'photographic gun', a single camera capable of taking multiple exposures on a single plate, in order to record the successive stages of human movement (plate 10). In one memorable series he dressed his subject in a black costume with silvered strips of tape sewn down the limbs and at key points such as major joints and the head. Against a dark background, Marey photographed the figure running, jumping and walking. The plates capture the consecutive phases of each movement through the shifting positions of the taped lines and points (plate 9). These graphic traces render the velocities of human movement in the same way that kinematic diagrams render the velocities of mechanical movement. Both forms belong to the visual regime of the art of motion and address a viewer who can see time and space and the narrative of movement in a single image.

10 'Fig. 18 – Mechanism of the Photographic Gun', from Hopkins, *Magic*, p. 477.

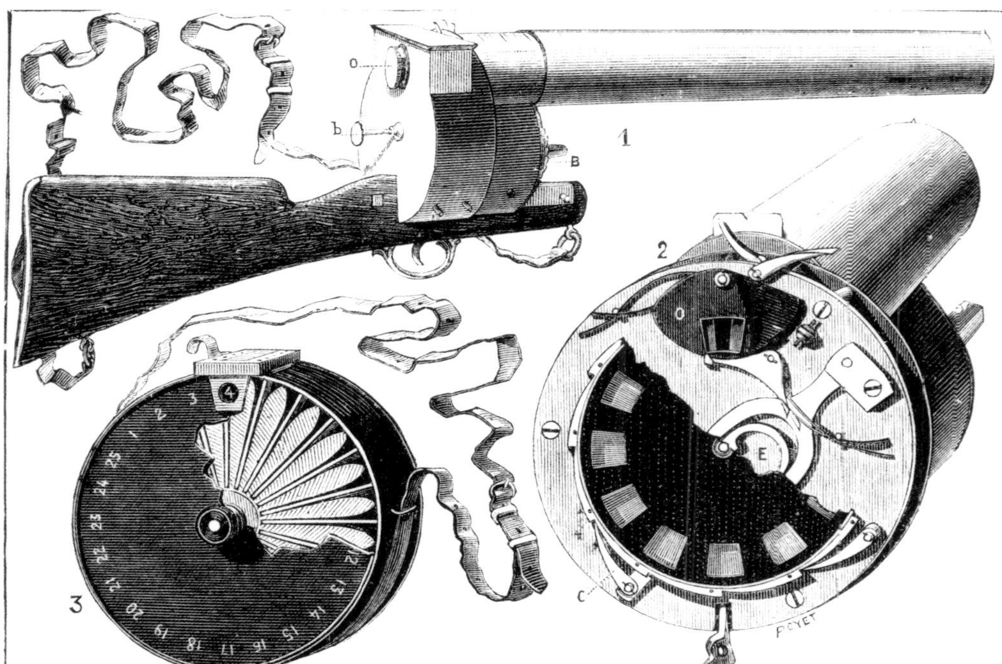

the camera as movement machine

In kinematic terms, the early movie camera was a simple, if somewhat temperamental, movement machine. In an advertisement of 1901 for the latest Bioscope camera, the side of the camera case is shown cut away to display the mechanisms and demonstrate its easy use (plate 11). Indeed, the inside of the camera is remarkably empty; there is not much inside this box. Wheels, rollers and a crank, the fundamental syntax of mechanical design, drive the movie camera on in its pursuit of the reproduction of lifelike motion. The advertisement acknowledges that the camera can only take a strip of film 150 feet in length (approximately three minutes in duration) but points out that this 'is long enough for the majority of scenes or events to be photographed'. This assumed synergy of the technical capabilities of the camera, the duration of filmed time and the demands of pro-filmic events is endorsed by the note at the end which observes that the 'Model B' has been used by staff to record the conflicts in South Africa and China. From its first years, the movie camera generated images and information in segments, regulated by the possibilities of the technology and assumptions concerning audience needs and expectations.

The desire to capture lifelike representations of continuous movement did not develop suddenly at the end of the nineteenth century. For centuries, optical instruments had been devised which sought to create for their viewers the illusion of movement, alongside other types of visual effect.[22] Photography clearly accelerated this ongoing historical process. Instruments such as the mutoscope exploited the rapid succession of multiple photographic prints to create the impression of a continuous flow of movement and narrative, and many attempts were made at the end of the nineteenth century to adapt the camera to project these images for large audiences. The question of who got there first, of who invented the 'movies', therefore, is less relevant now than the fact that in 1895–6 a number of pioneers in Europe and America (among them the Lumières, Robert Paul and Thomas Edison) were drawing on their own and others' experience to produce different versions of a movie camera. In an attempt to break from a dominant teleology of film, which moves progressively through the stages of pre-cinema, primitive cinema and classic cinema, recent film historiography has been concerned to present Victorian cinema as part of a continuum with earlier optical experiments and particularly the photographic devices of the second half of the nineteenth century. While I do not wish to abandon this model altogether, it is also important to acknowledge the generic shift that film presented within this longer history. Dissolving lantern slides, dioramas and panoramas certainly moved the image and the first films undoubtedly drew some of their subjects from already existing media, but they also significantly transformed the conception of moving images and the experience of the viewer.

The central paradox of film is that there is no movement on the screen, only a succession of stationary images. The most common explanation of how the illusion of motion is perceived is in terms of the 'persistence of vision'.[23] According

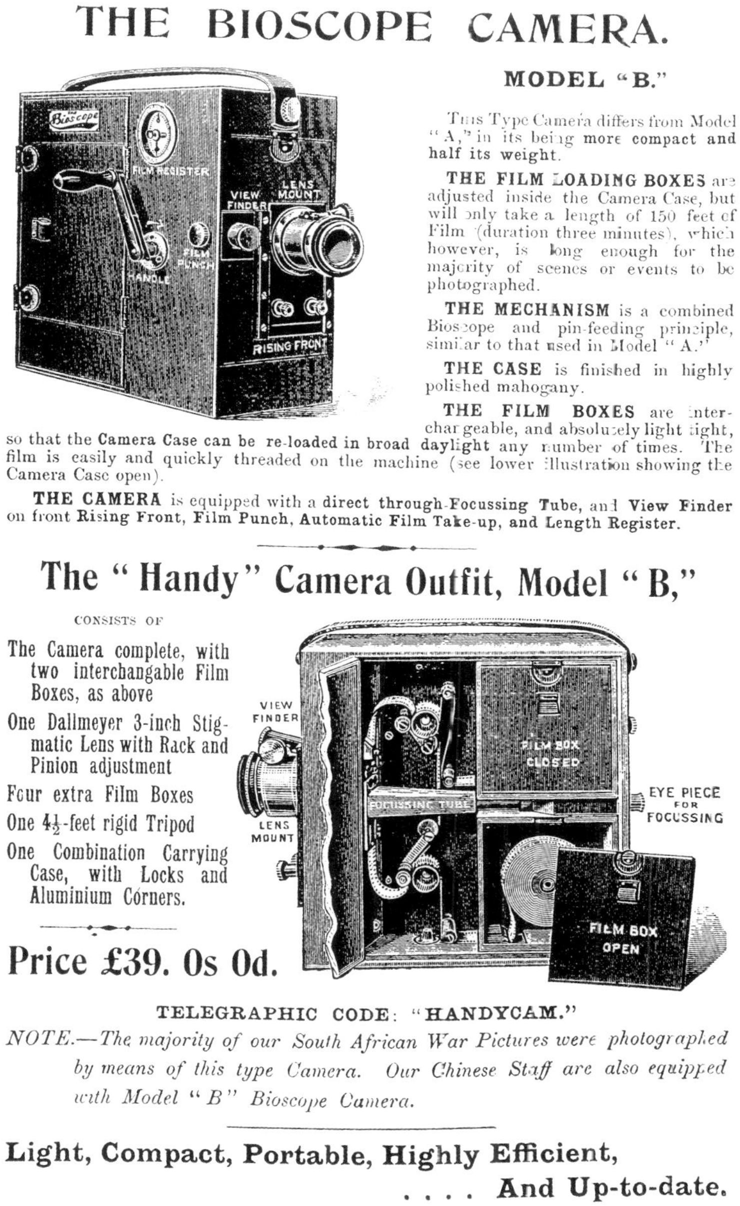

11 Advertisement for the Bioscope Model 'B' Camera, from the *Warwick Trading Co. Ltd. Catalogue*. London, 1901, p. 16.

to this account, when the separate frames of a film are shown in succession at an optimum speed, they are fused or blended in the observer's brain so that the individual pictures can no longer be perceived and an illusion of continuous movement is created. This concept had been around since the first half of the nineteenth century and appeared alongside the first films in barely reconfigured forms.[24] While it was not the only explanation for motion perception in film and other theorists drew on different aspects of the psychology of visual perception, such as the fusion of after-images and the effect of eye movement, the 'persistence of vision' remained the conventional account of the optical illusion of movement in film.

Whichever explication of the filmic illusion was preferred, much depended on the speed at which the film was photographed as well as the speed at which it was projected. Early viewers complained about the technical qualities of the first film exhibitions, about how the pictures flickered or how the frames jerked round the screen, making them difficult to watch and shattering any illusion of natural movement.[25] Furthermore, while film companies in these first years advertised the improved smoothness and steadiness of their products, lifelike movement and uniform motion were not the only aims of film-makers in this period. It was precisely the playful approach to motion and the variable velocities of early film that made it a rich and extraordinary source of entertainment for its first audiences.

The first point to be made about the velocities of film in these years is that there was no absolute cut-off between new and old technologies, between stationary and moving images in the first displays. Some machines were specially designed to project both films and lantern slides as a pragmatic way of covering the frequent change of films, creating a sense of anticipation and offering a varied programme of entertainment.[26] Yet the strip of celluloid itself offered diverse possibilities for the play of speed. The first set of variables was introduced at the point when the picture was shot. The Warwick Trading Company gave the following instructions to novices on how to operate the hand-cranked Bioscope camera:

> Turn the handle evenly at the rate of two complete revolutions per second, which is equivalent to sixteen separate exposures or pictures, the minimum speed allowable to procure even movement of the objects photographed. A less speed than this would result in dislocated or jerky movements of the objects on the film when projected on the screen.
>
> **IMPORTANT: – A funeral procession should be taken at precisely the same speed as a race or an express train in order to assure natural motion.**[27]

The hand-operated film camera was a sensitive and versatile movement machine. It appears that there was a tendency among new users to film sombre subjects slowly; to fit the speed of cranking to a perception of the symbolic meaning of the pro-filmic event. However, speed could also be interfered with at the point of projection. In 1898 the American inventor C. Francis Jenkins observed:

> The lanternist as he watches the picture on the canvas has the exhibition entirely under his control and can turn the crank quickly or slowly . . . A piece of machinery can be photographed slowly and afterwards reproduced rapidly, thus falsifying the record. A train may be photographed while running over a known course, at a rate of, say sixty miles per hour. If this film is put through the projecting machine at twice the speed the train will appear to run at the rate of 120 miles per hour . . . The converse is also true. Photographs made, say thirty-five per second . . . when reproduced in projecting machines feeding the film half as fast, produce a result startlingly comical. For instance, in a fisticuff

> encounter, when the knockdown blow is struck the vanquished fighter falls in the most leisurely manner imaginable.[28]

Cameramen and projectionists meddled with the velocity of the image: they speeded it up and slowed it down; they stopped it; and even reversed it for comic effect.[29] They played with motion in order to play with the audience and developed a nuanced lexicon of movement which was honed at every point of production and exhibition. The film camera was a deceptively simple movement machine, capable of exploiting the physical and psychological experiences of the viewer far in excess of the roller coasters and Ferris wheels whose cultural world of motion it shared.

moving pictures: moving viewers

Imagine a short film, no more than a minute or two in length, made in the late 1890s, in which, for its entire duration, the frame is filled with the waves and watery foam made in the wake of a moving steamship.[30] Still photography had struggled throughout the nineteenth century to find photographic plates fast enough to capture the ever-changing qualities of the sea[31] but here was a photographic method that showed each unique and unrepeatable shift in the water's surface and that caught the sea's mass, effervescence and liquid mutability. Films of turbulent water demonstrated the new medium's fascination with the rendering of movement and its unassailable claim to be the art of pure motion.

Short 'actualities' like this were part of a world of film before cinemas. They were included in programmes offered to a range of social classes at existing places of commercial entertainment. From 1896 they were shown in the more opulent theatres and music halls of London's West End, in the shabbier halls of the suburbs, in shop-fronts, fairgrounds and travelling peepshows. Films were distributed and exhibited by companies and individuals who were acutely aware of the complexity of commercial entertainment at the end of the nineteenth century, of the importance of attracting and keeping audiences and the vicissitudes of profit and loss. Audiences and films grew up alongside each other. As technology changed and film-makers developed their own formal language of shots, editing and narration, so audiences gradually learned to curb the excesses of their music-hall and sideshow behaviour. In the new auditoria that began to appear from about 1907 onwards, audiences were encouraged to sit in rows in relative silence and to regulate their responses and interactions.[32] However, this was not the context of film in its first, early years. Film entered a vibrant and polymorphous world of mass entertainment. In the music halls a selection of half a dozen or so short films might be wedged between a juggling act and a dance troupe; and in the fairground, audiences could be expected to move from a cinematograph display to a freak show or the latest modern amusement ride. The moving images of film added another dimension to the kinetic possibilities of public entertainment in this period more generally. They were part of a world of movement machines in which audiences were attracted to the display of the latest gadgetry or technology as much as to the content of the images.

Until 1903 short 'factuals', or non-fiction films, dominated film exhibition, although narrative fiction films gradually increased in number and came to control the market. Yet categories such as fiction and non-fiction, narrative and actuality, can prove slippery when applied to early film. In a formulation that has proved highly suggestive and influential, the films from this period have been described instead as a 'cinema of attractions'.[33] The term was introduced as a way of refuting the assumption in film history that film necessarily evolved towards the exclusive goal of classic narrative, along with the consequent dismissal of Victorian films as a 'primitive' detour on the way to the medium's true destiny. 'Cinema of attractions' also placed early film firmly within its historical context of spectacular mass entertainment, less concerned with the telling of stories than with competing with the other forms of visual attraction to be found in fairgrounds and urban centres. Early film was thus reconceptualised in terms of its desire to show rather than to tell; as an exhibitionist form, rather than a voyeuristic one, which played on the willingness of its audiences to be amazed and shocked. More recently, the opposition of attraction and narrative has itself been subjected to revision and, rather than early film being categorised simply as a 'cinema of attractions', its engagement with both the aesthetic of narrative and the aesthetic of attraction has been acknowledged.[34]

The experience and sensation of motion that could be conveyed by the medium of moving pictures quickly became the mainstay of its attraction. Furthermore, the concept of attraction denotes the condition and character of the audience, as well as the film. There is a fascinating complementarity between the viewer and the image in contemporary accounts of early film presentations. If the films themselves were a display of the spectacle of movement, then they appeared also to elicit highly motivated physical responses from their audiences, who themselves became a part of the spectacle. In its most extreme form the figure of the over-excited viewer became the subject of film comedies such as Robert Paul's *The Countryman and the Cinematograph* (1901; plate 12). A country bumpkin stands on a platform by the side of a screen. He is shown watching three films: the first, a female dancer; the second, a train coming towards the viewer; and the third, a courting couple. The bumpkin's responses to each film enact a progressive collapse of the physical and perceptual distance between him and the scenes on the screen. During the first film he mimics the dancer's moves; in the second, he gestures wildly that he is about to be hit by the train; and during the third film, his identification is so strong that he indicates to the audience that he is the man in the courting country couple. Paul's film does not assume that the countryman displays the kind of behaviour that would be expected of the film's audience in 1901; indeed, he could be read as an outmoded figure of ridicule for urban audiences who were beginning to learn and understand the ways of film.[35] Nevertheless, the film documents the transposition of moving pictures and moving viewers in these years. In *The Countryman*

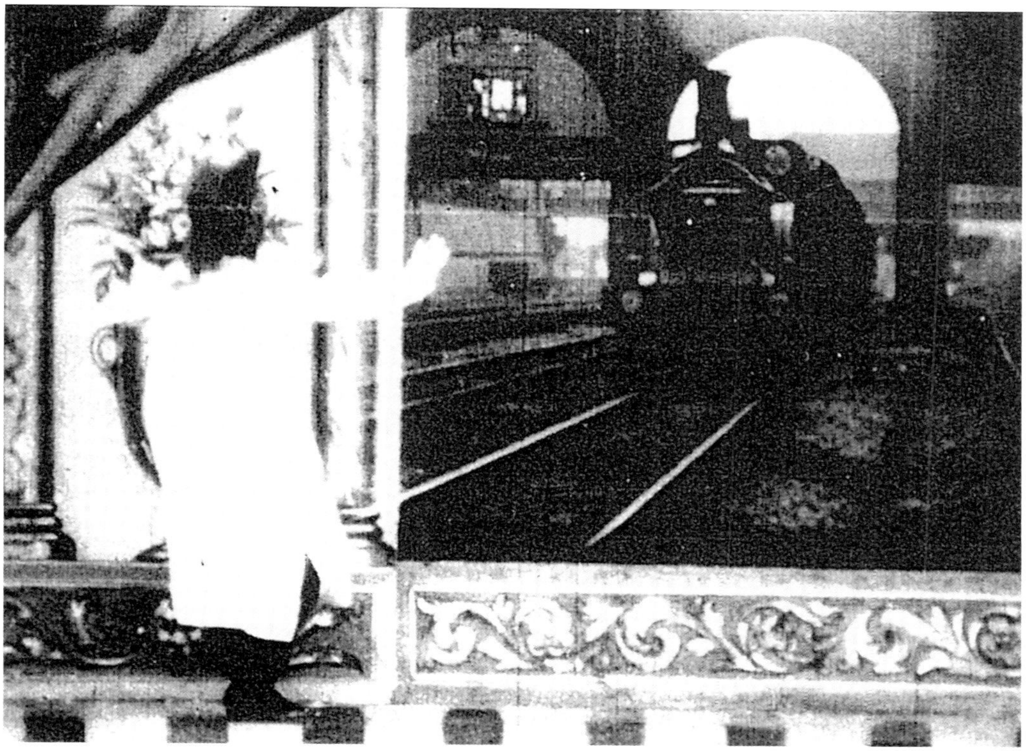

12 Frame still, Robert Paul, *The Countryman and the Cinematograph*, 1901.

and the Cinematograph, the physical motivation of the viewer is explicitly and visibly manifested through the body; but film could be a far more subtle movement machine and could offer even more intense and psychological experiences of speed and motion.

The train that scares the countryman is filmed as though heading straight towards him but film-makers found other, more inventive, ways of exploiting the technology of the film camera and the velocity of the express train.[36] Within months of the first public film exhibitions, a new kind of actuality appeared, the 'phantom ride', in which the film was shot from a speeding locomotive by a camera mounted on the front of the engine.[37] The important development here was that rather than a still camera filming a moving object (as in films of 'the arrival of a train at the station' kind), the camera and the viewpoint of the observer were now, themselves, in motion (plate 13). With this shift, film had made a significant breakthrough in its manipulation of the audience's point of view and its experience of the velocity of the image. In the phantom ride the means of propulsion, the train, is not visible. The viewer only sees on the screen what is ahead of the speeding train, the rush of constantly changing landscape produced by its forward movement. Objects appear from the distance and advance towards the camera and viewer, until they disappear beyond the screen, to be replaced, inexorably, by the next set of expand-

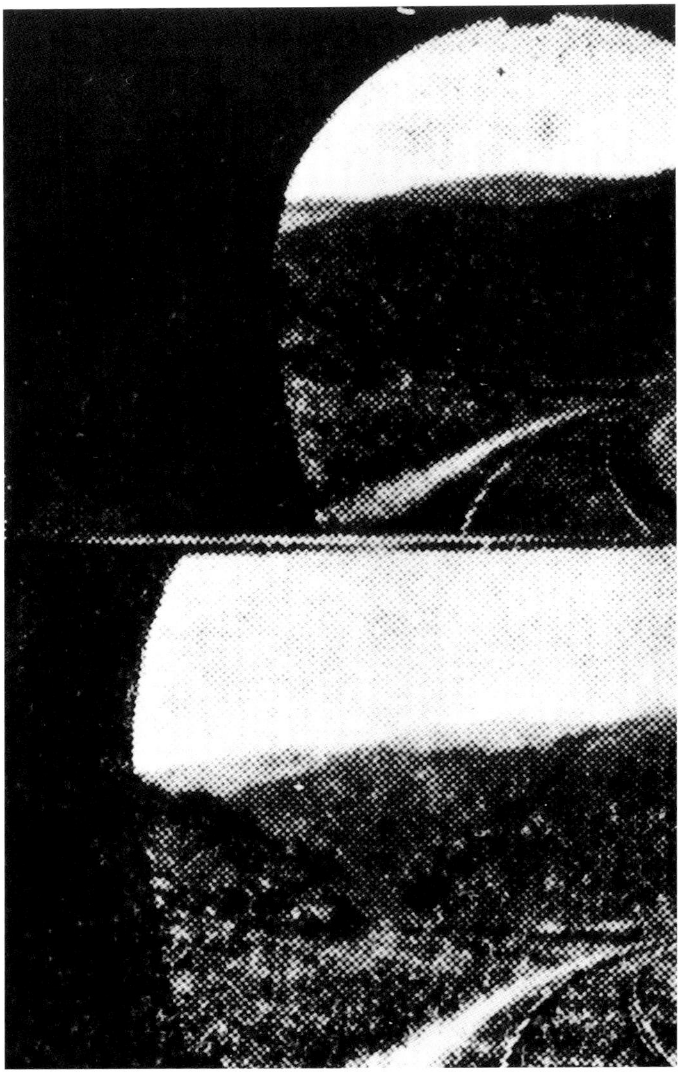

13 Frame stills of phantom rides through Devonshire made by the Warwick Trading Company Ltd, illustrated in *Photogram*, 5 : 60, December 1898, p. 394.

ing and receding objects. This was not just a question of a more mobile point of view; it was undoubtedly the most kinetic experience of speed to have been felt by audiences thus far. It was as though moving images could not get fast enough and so the camera had to be strapped to the embodiment of mechanical speed in order to reach out and beyond its own kinetic possibilities. This was as close as a visual medium had got to the rendering of pure motion; in its pursuit of speed, the phantom ride turned the spectator's body and the train into spectres.

Contemporaries realised that they were witnessing a new kind of film entertainment and distributors and critics scrabbled to find a language to convey the force of the impression of watching a phantom ride. Reviewers wrote of being hurled and flung through space, of a loss of stability and physical grounding. As one account described it in 1897, 'The spectator was not an outsider watching from safety the rush of the cars. He was a passenger on a phantom train ride that whirled him through space at nearly a mile a minute.'[38] The experience of watching phantom rides in the Biograph programmes shown at the Palace Theatre in central London was evidently particularly overwhelming. Biograph films used extra large film that could be projected onto an unusually big screen, filling the theatre's proscenium.[39] The reviewer for the *Era* – the specialist paper for theatre and entertainment news – described how the spectator had become 'part and parcel of the picture'[40] but *Punch*, predictably enough, went much further. Moving from an account of the performance of a well known music-hall singer, the reviewer continued:

> Then comes the 'American Biograph.' Wonderful!! But, my eyes! my head! And the whizzling and whirling and twittering of nerves, and blinkings and winkings that it causes in not a few among the spectators . . . the train having vanished, all the country round takes it into its head to follow as hard as ever it can, rocks, mountains, trees, towns, gateways, castles, rivers, landscapes, bridges, platforms, telegraph-poles all whirling and squirling and racing against one another, as if to see which will get to the audience first, and then, suddenly . . . all disappear into space!![41]

The experience of seeing the images of phantom train-ride films was of a profound physical and spatial disorientation. At times, it was described as if the spectator had been wrenched into the space of the film and was hurtling with the train and the camera through the landscape; elsewhere critics described objects breaking out of the screen space and rushing into the auditorium. To a great extent, these images could only have had this effect on an audience that was relatively new to moving images and unused to its spectacular effects. This also meant, however, that the novelty could and did wear off and film-makers and exhibitors had to find new ways of enhancing the phantom ride and keeping the public interested.

The most direct option was to develop the sensory dimensions of the putative train ride. This took the form of a stationary carriage, with an open front and seating for the passengers/viewers.[42] A screen was set up at the front of the car onto which was projected a phantom ride film, covering the audience's entire field of vision. The illusion of the train journey was then enhanced by swaying and rocking the carriage, introducing a variety of clanking sound effects and even creating the sensation of wind. The Hale's Tour (named after its creator, a Kentucky engineer and fireman, George C. Hale) made its first commercial appearance at the St Louis World Fair of 1904 and the concept was soon developed and exported round the world. Hale's Tours drew on the precedent of the phantom ride and earlier kinetic attractions that were introduced at the 1900 Paris World's Fair, alongside the great wheel, the escalator and the moving pavement. The Mareorama offered visitors the dubious pleasure of being on the pitching deck of a ship at sea, while the Cinéorama used multiple film projection and a polygonal screen to simulate the bird's-eye view of a balloon ascent.

What the phantom train ride and all these spectacular uses of film had in common was a physiological model of the perception and experience of motion, in which the movement of the image is transposed more or less directly to the body of the viewer. The body was an expression of the velocity and intensity of the objects on the screen. Reactions to the first films were physical and if audiences did not actually jump up in fright or feel as though they were being transported through space, then, at the very least, this was how the experience of watching these images was described in the criticism of the period. However, from the second half of the nineteenth century another model of the perception of motion was being developed that shifted attention away from the external actions and gestures of the body to the dynamism of the nervous system. Audiences did not have to fall down stairs as in Rowlandson's drawing or jump around like the bumpkin in Robert Paul's film and the viewers of the phantom rides. They could be physically composed and still engaged in dynamic, muscular forms of looking. They could, in fact, be more like the audience in 'The Age of the Wheel'.

muscular looking

A diagram reproduced in B. Joy Jeffries's *The Eye in Health and Disease* (1871) exemplifies the new approaches to the physiology of the eye and visual perception that emerged from the 1850s (plate 14). Jeffries was a leading figure in the American medical establishment and a lecturer at Harvard University on optical phenomena. His book is a clear and straightforward guide to modern ophthalmic diagnosis and treatment. The diagram is a horizontal section just above the eyeballs, looking down at the cavity of the nose and the optic nerves passing from the eyeballs to inside the skull where they meet and intermingle. What is striking about this image of the eyes is how meaty and muscular they are, not unlike the bodily organs of the reproductive or digestive systems. This is a far cry from earlier conceptions of the eye in which the organ is represented as a hollow ball that receives images of visible objects transmitted by rays of light.[43] This new eye is muscular and mobile. The dominant features of the diagram are the sets of straight and oblique muscles that are attached round the globe of the eye and that move it round its principal axes of vision. These substantial muscles make the eye a precise and highly modulated movement machine; as Jeffries reminded his readers, 'the eyeball hardly ceases motion for an instant.'[44] The implications of this new physiological conception of the eye were far-reaching. First, sight was no longer understood as a purely optical phenomenon but as part of a complex of motor and nervous functions. Second, the nervous system, which had been rigidly divided according to the functions of the cerebral hemisphere (the mind) and the spinal cord (the body), began to be seen as a single system or continuum, uniting voluntary and reflex actions.[45] Third, a new kind of viewer was made possible, one whose body might seem still but who was never at rest and was engaged in constant muscular activity.

Research on visual perception played an important role in the emergence of psychology during the second half of the nineteenth century as a science about

Fig. 1. FROM RUETE.

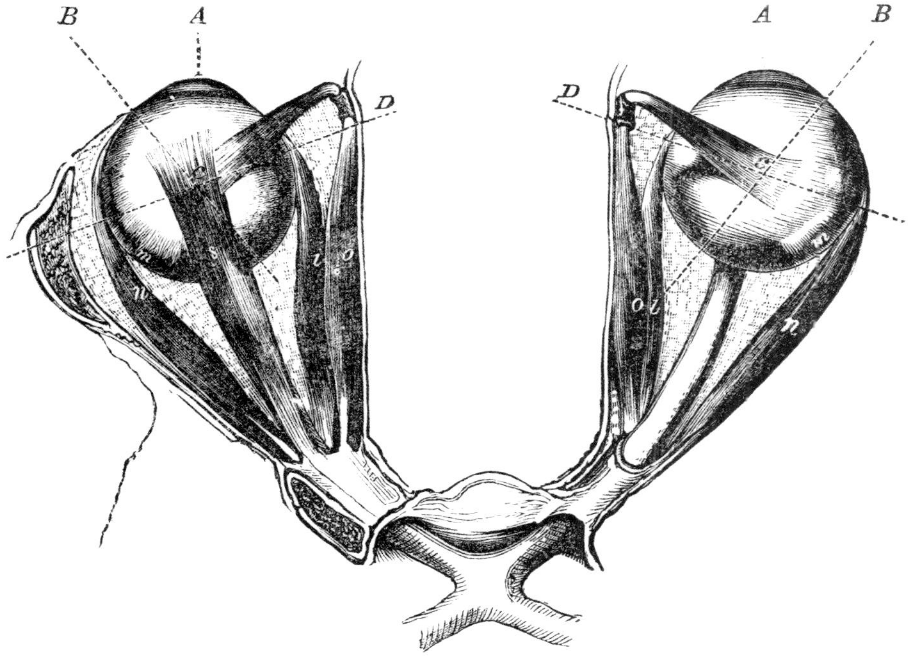

A A, the parallel optic axes. *C C*, the centres of motion of the globes. *B B*, axes of rotation of the oblique muscles. *D D*, axes of rotation of the superior and inferior muscles. *n n*, external straight muscles. *i i*, internal straight muscles. *o o*, superior oblique muscles, running through pulleys at *D D*. *s*, superior straight muscle of one eye. This muscle is removed in the other eye to show the optic nerve. *m m*, attachments of the inferior oblique muscles, which cannot be seen in this view from above. The space between *D D* is the cavity of the nose.

14 Diagram from B. Joy Jeffries, *The Eye in Health and Disease. Being a Series of Articles on the Anatomy and Physiology of the Human Eye, and Its Surgical and Medical Treatment*. Boston: Alexander Moore, 1871, opp. p. 14.

the mind. Modern psychology was formed from the disciplinary interstices of physiology and philosophy.[46] Drawing on the observational and experimental methods of German scientists working on sensory physiology, psychology began to move from its older alliances with philosophy or phrenology and to adapt the techniques of experimental science. It was, however, a long, ongoing process and psychology did not become a really autonomous discipline until the twentieth century.

Optics had been an established field of scientific research from at least the early eighteenth century and the publication of Sir Isaac Newton's *Opticks* in 1704. In the early nineteenth century medicine expanded the subject by working on the anatomy and mechanism of the eye in relation to questions such as binocular vision and the perception of colour and scale. The key figure, however, in the development of experimental optics was Hermann von Helmholtz, a German scientist working in Königsberg, Heidelberg and Berlin, who invented the ophthalmoscope and a range of other instruments, in order to develop his laboratory research into physiological optics. The results of Helmholtz's work on visual perception were brought together in his *Treatise on Physiological Optics*, which was published in three separate volumes between 1856 and 1866 and then in a single volume in 1867.[47] The study dealt in detail with the physiology of vision and the sensory system and used a range of specially designed laboratory experiments to investigate the mechanisms of visual perception. In conjunction with other German scientists such as Gustav Fechner and Wilhelm Wundt, Helmholtz provided a critical bridge between psychology and physiology. He showed how experimental and quantitative methods could be used to construct a science rather than a metaphysics of visual perception and established vision as a function equally of body and of mind.

Advances from Germany in the physiological understanding of the nervous system influenced the direction of Anglo-American psychology from the 1850s onwards. Research on the anatomy and physiology of the eye and nervous system continued to endorse the conception of sight as muscular and embodied. Furthermore, laboratory experiments and self-observation suggested that visual impressions constantly changed from moment to moment and that what had, in the past, been regarded as single impressions were, in fact, multiple and mobile.[48] Given that all visual perception involved muscular movement, the question of the perception of movement itself became particularly compelling. What was the relationship for the beholder between the sensation of ocular movement, other types of muscular stimulation and the perception of motion in an external object? How did the perception of objects in space relate to past experiences of those sensations? The perception of motion – its velocity and direction – seemed fraught with error. No aspect of sight seemed so subject to optical illusions as the perception of movement. It was the psychological study of these aspects of visual perception that brought kinetic viewers back into contact with movement machines and the illusion of motion.

Alexander Bain's *The Senses and the Intellect* (1855) was one of the earliest psychological publications to present a scientific account of the brain and the nervous system as a necessary foundation for the subsequent study of human behaviour. One of a number of transitional figures in this period who drew both on the British philosophical tradition of psychology and the newly emerging scientific discipline, Bain was appointed to a Chair of Logic at the University of Aberdeen in 1860 and in 1876 he founded the journal *Mind*, which became a highly important publication for psychological papers until the beginning of the twentieth century. Based on his study of the physiology of the eye, Bain argued that the eye discriminated direction, duration and velocity of movement through the activation of distinct ocular muscles. Moreover, he suggested that these muscular movements excited feelings of pleasure or displeasure. 'A quick movement excites a different feeling from one that is slow; and we thence acquire graduated sensations, corresponding to degrees of speed up to a certain limit of nicety.'[49] Bain was able to distinguish the degrees of pleasure that were derived from the muscular movement stimulated by different kinds of moving objects. The question he left unanswered and which subsequent psychologists continued to grapple with throughout the century was how much muscular activity took place. Was movement in the beholder restricted to the eye or did it extend to the head, and through the body generally?

In his many psychological publications from the 1870s onwards, James Sully continued the investigation initiated by Bain of the forms of visual pleasure arising from the activity of the eye. Sully had studied under Helmholtz in Berlin and specialised in children's behaviour and the nature of perceptual illusions. In 1892 he was appointed to the Grote Chair of Logic and Philosophy of Mind at University College London, where he later established a laboratory for psychological research. For Sully, ocular movement created the same kind of muscular sensation in the beholder as any kind of manual movement. Sight was thus never an isolated process in any practical or physical sense, for the perception of the eye was always modified and complicated by movement and touch.[50] Through the research of figures such as Bain and Sully, psychology proposed a new scientific account of visual perception that was bound to a kinetic, tactile body. The eye was capable of a vast range of muscular activity and was never absolutely still. Like the image of the physical world proposed by kinematics, psychology's world of perception was full of movement, both within the beholder and beyond; absolute rest was an empirical impossibility.

Perhaps the most influential figure in the formation of experimental psychology at the end of the nineteenth century was William James. In terms of the history of visual media, James provided a crucial link between the cosmopolitan cultural world of Europe in the period and the scientific domain of the new psychology. James came from an affluent, intellectual New York family; his brother Henry became the famous writer and he spent his childhood and youth moving between Europe and America, visiting every major art museum and attending schools in England, France, Switzerland and Germany. He began training as an art student but abandoned this to attend medical school at Harvard. During this time he continued to visit Europe and, like Sully, studied for a while under Helmholtz in Germany. His first academic appointment was as an instructor in anatomy and physiology at Harvard but in 1875 he set up a laboratory at the university to teach experimental psychology, which became one of the most important centres of the new discipline. The publication in 1890 of his two-volume *Principles of Psychology* was the summation of his psychological research thus far and included chapters on habit, memory, association, emotion, imagination and perception. Movement was the basis for his understanding of the perceptual system. In his discussion of the visual imagination, he not only argued that all direct perception involved the movement of the eyes and limbs but that the same must also be an essential factor when the object was seen in the imagination.[51]

In experimental terms, some of James's most significant conclusions regarding sight concerned the errors arising in the perception of movement. Referring to confusions on the part of the beholder between their own bodily movement and the movement of external objects, James observed 'this discrimination cannot be perfectly made. The sensation of the motion spreads over all that we see and infects it.'[52] This rich metaphorical language was criticised by some of James's first reviewers but it was also the feature of his brand of psychology that allowed it to circulate beyond a specialist scientific audience.

Like other researchers on visual perception in this period, James was fascinated by the 'curious illusions of movement' created by the constant movement of the eyeballs and found the railway a prolific source of these sensory tricks and deceptions. However, it was not the sights drawn from a moving train which most interested these scientists but the effects produced when the train had come to a halt in the station. Seated in a stationary carriage, the beholder was in a state of perceptual confusion, unable to discriminate objects in motion and at rest. As James described it:

> when another train comes alongside of ours in a station and fills the entire window, and, after standing still awhile, begins to glide away, we judge that it is *our* train which is moving, and that the other train is still. If, however, we catch a glimpse of any part of the station through the windows, or between the cars, of the other train, the illusion of our own movement instantly disappears, and we perceive the other train to be the one in motion.[53]

For James this effect could be accounted for through a combination of the continuous oscillations of the eyeballs and the influence of habit in the perception of movement. Other psychologists pushed this analysis further in different directions. Illusions were the subject of an entire study by Sully. The most familiar errors concerned the perception of movement; he described it clearly:

> When we are looking at objects, our ocular muscles are apt to execute very slight movements which escape our notice. Hence, we tend, under certain circumstances, to carry over the retinal result of the movement, that is to say, the impression produced by a shifting of the parts of the retinal image to new nervous elements, to the object itself, and so to transform a 'subjective' into an 'objective' motion.[54]

These three factors – muscular slippage, image retention and subject/object projection – were proposed, with certain modifications, by most writers on perception in this period. Writing in 1880 in the specialist journal *Brain*, Silvanus Thompson, Professor of Experimental Physics at University College Bristol, published a series of optical experiments to demonstrate that the illusions associated with the perception of movement were more to do with a compound of retinal after-effects than the muscular oscillation of the eyes.[55] The highly kinetic diagram which he used to illustrate his argument (plate 15), with its concentric circles and cogged wheels, its gentle quivering motion and subtle forward and reverse rotations, recalls the spools and reels of the film camera and the optically confused audiences of the phantom ride.

The physiological and psychological accounts of visual perception and its attendant illusions provide an historical background for understanding the photographic and mechanical experiments that led to the successful production of the film camera and projector in the late 1890s. After-images and the movements of the eye

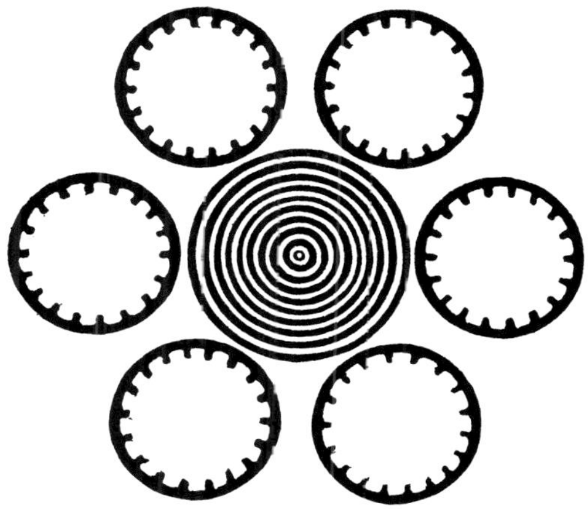

15 Diagram of optical illusion from Silvanus P. Thompson, 'Optical Illusions of Movement', *Brain*, 3, October 1880, p. 293.

were what concerned camera and film manufacturers as well as academic psychologists; to understand the illusions of perception was to understand how to make films. The new model of the kinetic, embodied viewer is also a fruitful context in which to examine the subjects of and responses to the first films. Contemporary scientific literature never clearly differentiated the range of muscular movement involved in visual perception and viewers were prone to confuse eye movements with body movements and to project their own movement onto the movement of an object. Little wonder, then, that the country bumpkin in Robert Paul's film conflates the apparent movement on the screen with his own real movement in front of it; or that the viewers of the phantom ride could not tell whether the images had broken out of the frame or if they had been torn from their seats and dragged into filmic space. Then there are the visitors to the Royal Academy exhibition in 'The Age of the Wheel' (see plate 1), who are more kinetic than one might possibly have first imagined. Not only are the pictures and the staircase moving but also the viewers themselves are not still. Their eyes are constantly moving, following each picture through their field of vision and rapidly jerking back again to catch the next frame and track it through its trajectory. Furthermore, because all visual perception involves muscular movement, looking might also be articulated through their bodies and tactile sensation. There is nothing still in 'The Age of the Wheel'; like the geometric forms in the optical diagram, everything is in a state of motion, moving to the velocities of the image and the viewer.

psychological aesthetics

The investigation of visual pleasure was a specialist field within the new experimental psychology. Drawing on the kinetic models of looking that were being developed in the discipline more generally, psychologists examined which kinds of ocular movement yielded the greatest aesthetic pleasure. In his 1855 *Principles of Psy-*

chology, Herbert Spencer defined this area of research as 'Aestho-Physiology' and came up with the predictable formulation that we derive pleasure from flowing, smooth outlines rather than angular ones because of the unstrained, moderate action of the ocular muscles involved in their perception.[56] Pleasure was to be found in harmony, proportion and moderate variety.

The classification and analysis of visual pleasure was developed more fully by Sully. His professional career spanned essays in the literary periodical press as well as work on psychological subjects and his interest in art undoubtedly fuelled his concern to develop 'a science of aesthetics'.[57] Sully defined the gratification of art as the release of tensions built up within the body and from the external environment; as such, it was an aspect, albeit a distinctive one, of the play instinct. He argued that ocular movement was experienced as a general organic stimulation and that in order to derive pleasure from such muscular activity it should not be excessive in terms of its rapidity, duration and physical demands: 'Hence it may be said that the quieter forms of motor enjoyment are preferred by the eye . . . rapid visible movements are stimulating, while slow ones are more voluptuous and allied to the richer varieties of passive sensation . . . the eye has . . . a choice out of an indefinite number of velocities of movement.'[58] Beauty of form and the laws of agreeable ocular movement conveniently reinforced each other. The eye preferred smoothness of transition and moderate change, completeness of form and a central focal point. Aesthetic preferences such as these, Sully suggested, were the result of the evolution of the sensory organs and occurred at the level of racial disposition and individual inclination. Other writers in this period, such as the novelist and popular science writer, Grant Allen, also drew on Social Darwinism and natural selection to account for the development of aesthetic feelings, which were conceived, in these terms, as the intermediate link between 'the bodily senses and the higher emotions'.[59]

Psychology, particularly in its most experimental forms at the end of the nineteenth century, was not just a simple reiteration, in more or less scientific terms, of existing aesthetic values. Its most interesting and challenging ideas are related to its conception of the bodily nature of aesthetic pleasure and the dynamic condition of the spectator of art. Hugo Münsterberg is one of the most stimulating writers in this vein of psychological research. Brought by William James from Germany in 1892 to run the laboratory at Harvard University, Münsterberg conducted experiments on a wide range of psychological topics but had a particular interest in the visual arts and in the aesthetic and psychological possibilities of film.[60] For Münsterberg every sensation produced a motor response that was expressed through physiological changes; his work, therefore, necessarily concentrated on the effects on the spectator, rather than on the qualities of the object or image viewed. He put it bluntly:

> the work of art itself is never an object of psychology, and the description of it lies outside of the psychologist's province . . . The physical object is in contact with the human mind at two points: at its start and at its goal. Every work of

> art springs from the mind of the artist, and reaches the mind of the public; its origin and its effect are both psychical processes, and both are material for the description and explanation of the psychologist.[61]

In order to carry out this investigation Münsterberg advocated self-observational analysis and experimental methods conducted under laboratory conditions. He set up a black-framed screen in a totally darkened room and introduced on it a sequence of bright lines, points, letters and pictures in a range of positions. During this process the subject of the experiment was asked to select the most pleasing arrangements. Using this apparatus Münsterberg claimed to be able to investigate the influence on aesthetic feelings of the impression of depth, apparent movement, ideational associations and other variables, and suggested that the experiment should be carried out with the subject in different bodily positions and mental conditions. The significance for Münsterberg of this experimental study of the psychological effect of art was in terms of its immediate impact on art education and pedagogy; art was not just a question of individual perception but was a network of social meanings and values, of public responsibilities and duties.

Of all the writers engaged in reconfiguring aesthetics in the light of new psychological methods, none had a greater sense of personal will and duty than Violet Paget or, as she is better known through her assumed name, Vernon Lee.[62] Lee was a formidable woman, intellectually prodigious and erudite and socially tenacious and uncompromising. She was born in 1856 and spent her earliest years travelling round Europe, settling with her family in Italy in her mid-teens. In her later years she divided her time between Italy and England and became part of an advanced literary and cultural circle that included Walter Pater, William and Henry James and Ethel Smyth. George Bernard Shaw neatly captured her social identity when he described her as 'the old guard of Victorian cosmopolitan intellectualism'.[63]

She published vast numbers of essays, short stories and literary works but from the 1890s she became increasingly preoccupied with psychological aesthetics and specifically with the question of the effects on the observer of looking at works of art. Drawing on German psychology and the work of writers such as Herbert Spencer and William James, Lee embarked on a long and intensive study of the physio-psychology of aesthetics. Much of this work was carried out in collaboration with her close friend Clementina Anstruther-Thomson, who had studied painting at the Slade School of Art in London and in Paris. Lee frequently described her as the more visual of the two, possessing a more heightened aesthetic sense. Together they spent much of the 1890s visiting major European museums and galleries and scrutinising their psychological and physical responses to works of art. The writing that came out of this ecstasy of self-observation remains some of the most extraordinary art criticism of the period; it is criticism that answers to the velocities of looking.

It was while Lee was visiting galleries in Florence and Rome that she met Bernhard Berenson, who was in the process of taking over the critical mantle of

Giovanni Morelli and was establishing himself as a major art critic and dealer. In 1896 Berenson published *The Florentine Painters of the Renaissance* in which he drew on the language of psychology in order to develop his theory of the tactile sense: 'every time our eyes recognise reality, we are, as a matter of fact, giving tactile values to retinal impressions'.[64] The painter's task was to rouse in the spectator this tactile sense. Masterpieces such as Giotto's *Madonna Enthroned and Angels* embodied a tactile sense so vivid that the spectator 'sees' the image through the palms and fingers, as well as the eyes. Berenson proposed other ways in which great art was experienced through the body of the viewer. In an extended discussion of looking at two men wrestling, he described how 'my retinal impressions are immediately translated into images of strain and pressure in my muscles, or resistance to my weight, of touch all over my body'.[65] It was through this physical comprehension of the visual image that art achieved its goal of enhancing the vitality of life.

Lee reviewed *Florentine Painters* in *Mind*, where she described it as an innovative synergy of connoisseurship and psychology.[66] However, she identified inconsistencies in the ways in which Berenson described the bodily sensations derived from vivid visual perception. Lee's review exacerbated what was evidently already a difficult relationship with Berenson but it also set out the problem to which she returned throughout her career: to what extent was bodily sensation expressed in bodily movement? Did the body of the enthralled viewer actually move?

At the same time as she was publishing her review, Lee was working with Anstruther-Thomson on a major study of kinaesthetic sensation which was published in two parts, in the *Contemporary Review*, in October and November 1897.[67] The essay, 'Beauty and Ugliness', drew on a number of psychological theories concerning the projection of dynamic experience into external objects, to examine the processes of perceiving form. Lee saw this approach as a way of rejecting 'supernatural explanations' of the aesthetic and of replacing it within 'a continuum of psycho-physiological phenomena' (p. 156). In order to analyse perception, the subject had to isolate, slow down and observe his or her responses to form over and over again. In this way, the phenomenon of looking at a chair, for example, was systematically described in terms of ocular movement, respiratory changes and alterations in posture and balance (p. 163). Every modulation of form, it was concluded, corresponded to an adjustment of motor activity, creating a dynamic interface between viewer and image: 'we follow lines by muscular adjustments more considerable than those of the eye, and . . . these muscular adjustments result in a sense of direction and velocity in ourselves and a consequent attribution of direction and velocity to the lines thus perceived' (p. 228).

A picture could thus be understood as a compound of trajectories – fast and slow – created by the outlines of the forms and the passage of the viewer's eyes. The 'various velocities of the lines of a picture' (p. 229) could then be analysed. A diagram of Titian's *Sacred and Profane Love* was used to demonstrate the path of the eye round the composition (plate 16), while the text described how 'our eye is caught by the two rabbits at the back, and after this pause we are swung again across to the right' (p. 234).[68] Looking, in 'Beauty and Ugliness', is a physical expe-

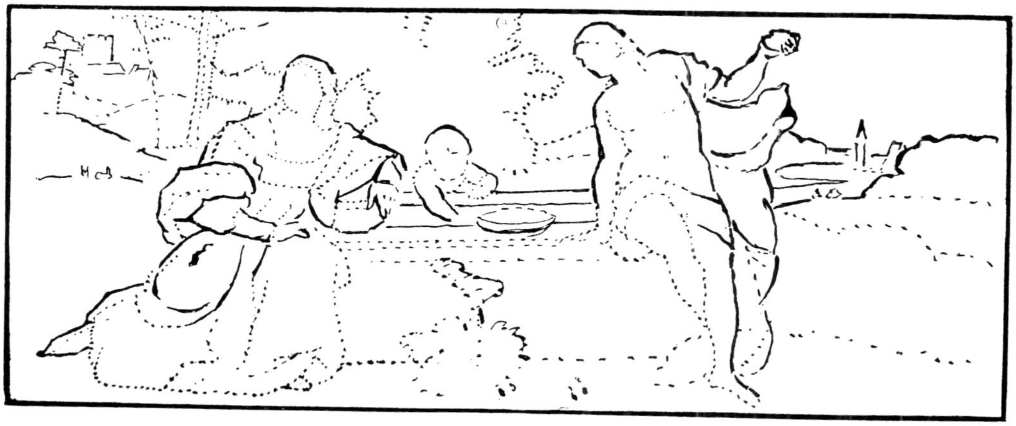

SKELETON DIAGRAM OF TITIAN'S "SACRED AND PROFANE LOVE." THE CONTINUOUS LINE SHOWS THE DIRECTION THAT IS TAKEN BY THE EYE

16 'Skeleton Diagram of Titian's "Sacred and Profane Love". The Continuous Motion Shows the Direction That is Taken by the Eye.' From Vernon Lee and C. Anstruther Thomson, *Beauty and Ugliness and Other Studies in Psychological Aesthetics*. London: John Lane, Bodley Head, 1912, opp. p. 234.

rience. Reference is made to being 'enclosed' by a painting, 'forbidden to escape or lapse, and forced to move through every detail' (p. 235). This may be high art rather than a phantom ride but there is a clear continuum between the kinetic responses generated by the two media.

'Beauty and Ugliness' was reasonably well received by the scientific community and Lee and Anstruther-Thomson continued to use self-observation and other psychological methods such as questionnaires and statistical analysis to pursue their psycho-aesthetic project.[69] Between 1901 and 1904 Lee kept diaries recording her responses on visits to the Uffizi, the Vatican and other major Italian collections, extracts from which were published in 1912.[70] The entries are vivid and revealing, deliberately introspective and almost embarrassing in their obsessive self-examination, were it not for the occasional flash of Lee's self-deprecating sense of irony. In the diaries, Lee used self-observation to revise some of the conclusions reached in 'Beauty and Ugliness'. Earlier, Lee had expressed doubts about the quality of her visual sense and identified many of the richer passages of self-observation in their collaborative work as having been written by Anstruther-Thomson. The diaries are similarly punctuated by doubts concerning the introspective method and the value of her own responses. History interferes most with the reflections of the timeless, introspective viewer. When Lee asks herself how the original audiences would have looked at the works, she admits 'Certainly not going round en touriste, nor like me at present, half killing themselves in trying to fix, process, understand' (17 February 1902, p. 274). Questions such as what the picture represents and why it was made shift the analysis away from the viewer and back onto the image as an historical object and she acknowledges that 'it is reversing the whole process to go and look fixedly at a work of art, and then never see it again' (28 February 1902, p. 278).

At other times, however, her kinaesthetic response to the work of art is so intense that it is practically hallucinatory. On one occasion in 1903 she became intensely stimulated by looking at a Simone Martini in the Uffizi: 'I am bound to say I have such a feeling of excitement that the arabesques of the ceiling, when I *take my eyes* off the picture, seem in movement. A man walks by very fast with creaking boots, his movement is *slow* comparatively; other people pass *quickly*, but slow compared to that picture' (19 January 1903, pp. 294–5). The exhilarating velocity of the painting produces in Lee a state of hyperaesthesia, causing her to become highly sensitive to her surroundings. As she moves her gaze from the picture, other forms and images are mobilised by the ongoing movement of her eyes and the passage of other people in her environment seems retarded in comparison with the maelstrom of motion in the painting.

This extreme sensitivity to movement and the drift between art object and external reality re-occurs in Lee's records. At the Capitoline Museum in spring 1903, she glances out of a window at a statue of Marcus Aurelius:

> Out of the window Marcus Aurelius even seems to be going unpleasantly fast . . . I have very marked palpitations, and I suspect that the over-perception of movement is a summation. Oddly the vague, shifting, gravityless movements . . . of the crowd do not worry me; they are like ghosts compared with the statues and me. (10 April 1903, pp. 300–1)

Lee continued to understand these extraordinary responses as physical in nature. In the 'Central Problem of Aesthetics', first published in 1910, she acknowledged the contribution of psychic life and previous locomotor experience to the formation of aesthetic responses yet maintained that it was not purely a mental process but involved actual muscular and bodily movement. What was needed, she suggested, was some graphic apparatus to measure bodily alterations during aesthetic experiences.[71] For Lee, apparently motionless forms were the source of intensely dynamic visual experiences, which moved the viewer and mobilised their entire surroundings. Lee drew on the latest psychological research and methodologies to investigate the nature of aesthetic response. What she found was something powerful and kinetic, capable of moving and transporting the spectator as effectively as any fairground movement machine. Contemplation, she discovered, was a provocative and dynamic thing.

* * *

velocities of the image

What does it mean to speak of velocities of the image in the years around 1900? To begin with, it means reconceptualising relationships between the viewer and the image in this period. In his 1916 psychological study of film, Münsterberg made the following simple but important observation: '[Depth and movement] are present and yet they are not in the things. We invest the impressions with them.'[72] In this sense, velocity is not in the image, it is a condition of the image; it was generated in the multitude of ways in which viewers interacted with visual media and visual technologies in this period. Increasingly, then, the viewer was drawn to the centre of the meaning of visual representation. The image for itself lost significance and its effect on the viewer and audiences gained interpretative value.

The great art wheels in the *Punch* cartoon (see plate 1), moving the paintings in a continuous loop, echo the mechanism of the film camera, projecting photographic images at a rate of sixteen to twenty-four frames per second. In its first years, film and its audiences were fascinated by the medium's kinetic possibilities. Film took motion as its subject matter and exploited the technology itself to play with velocities – forward and reverse projection, repetition, acceleration and retardation.

Movement is in the eye of the beholder, however, and psychological aesthetics proposed a new scientific model of looking which was embodied and kinetic. Incessant ocular movement and associated muscular adjustments in the body created an effect of motion of images and objects even when there was none. The eyes deceived and the illusions that were the subject of psychological research also constituted the founding principles of motion pictures. Movements of the eye round the image created lines of velocity that extended beyond the frame and blurred distinctions between image and environment. Viewers were transported. Phantom ride films seemed to draw their astonished audiences into the landscape and Italian Renaissance paintings seemed more alive than the public in the street. The experience of visual media at the end of the nineteenth century and the beginning of the twentieth century was kinaesthetic.

Movement was everywhere and stillness nowhere. Kinematics demonstrated that absolute rest was a physical impossibility and so there could be no sensible binary of still and moving images. Apparently motionless paintings and statues were in a state of agitated motion and the illusion of continuous movement in film was created by a sequence of stationary pictures. If art and film were close partners in this world of velocity, then how to distinguish between experiences of the two media? Historically, the extended contemplation of a work of art has been contrasted with the distracted stimulation of film but modern technology and psychology made these two forms of cultural consumption more like each other than has previously been recognised. The temporality of looking at art was not unrestricted; it was part of the mechanical organisation of modern life, fitted in during opening hours, when the cranks and wheels were moving. Optical machines had infiltrated the contemplative and humanistic domain of the art gallery. The 'Pic-

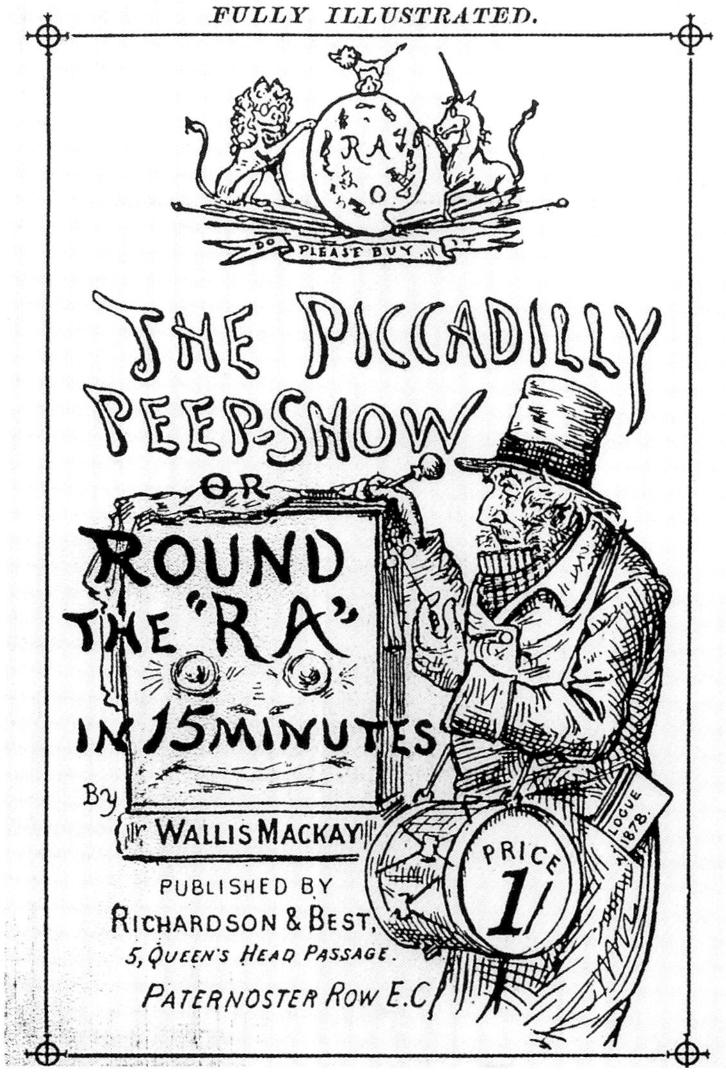

17 Anon., *The Piccadilly Peep-show or Round the RA in 15 Minutes*. London: Richardson and Best, 1878.

cadilly Peepshow' now offered a complete tour of the Royal Academy exhibition in fifteen minutes flat (plate 17) and in 1899 a *Punch* cartoon unveiled the mutoscope that could 'do' the show in five minutes, providing a moving version of the exhibits for 'visitors in a hurry', with end-of-the-pier tastes (plate 18). Under these conditions, the spectator of art could be as agitated and embodied as the mythic country bumpkin in the first years of film. The audience at the *Punch* Royal Academy exhibition could get off the moving stare-case; the pictures could be put back on the walls – the viewers themselves were already part of the velocity of the image.

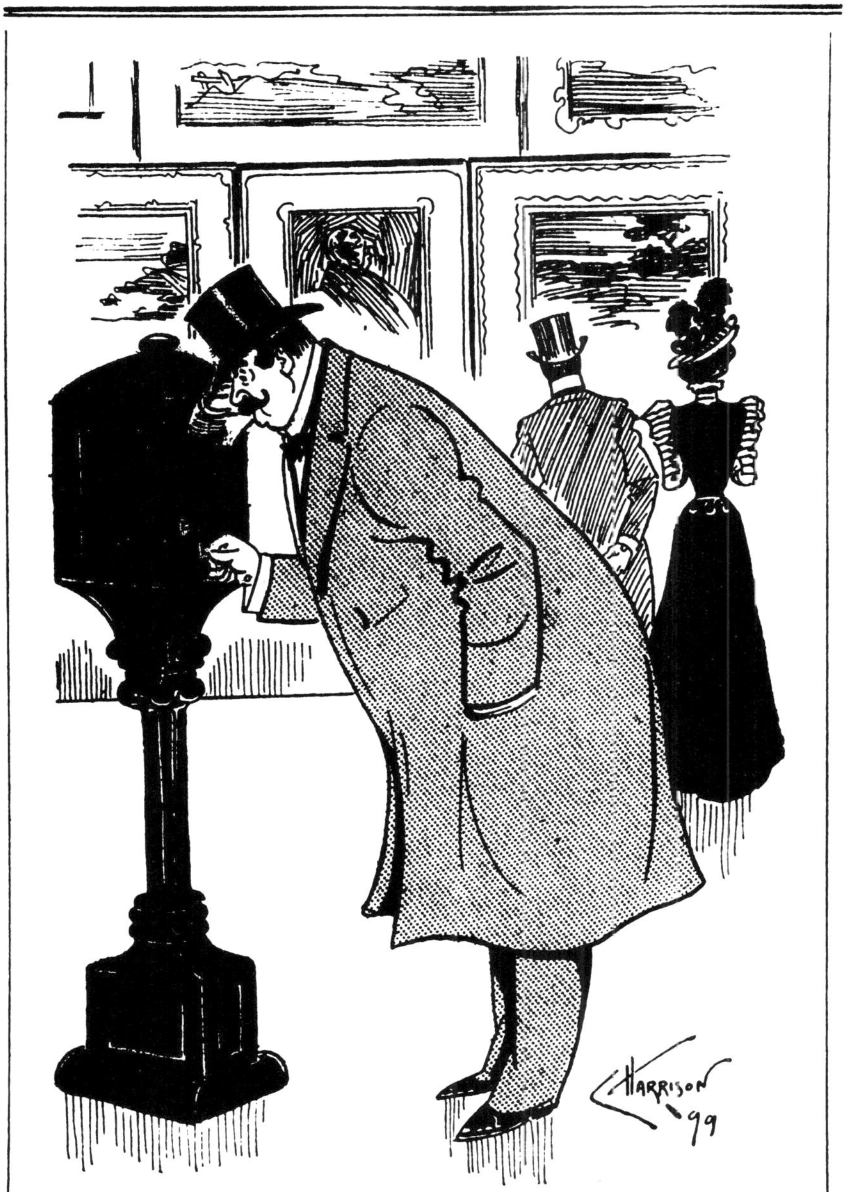

SUGGESTION FOR THE R.A.

A Mutoscope of the Pictures, for the use of visitors in a hurry. The Royal Academy "done" in five minutes.

18 'A Mutoscope of the Pictures, for the use of visitors in a hurry. The Royal Academy "done" in five minutes', *Punch*, 10 May 1899, p. 255.

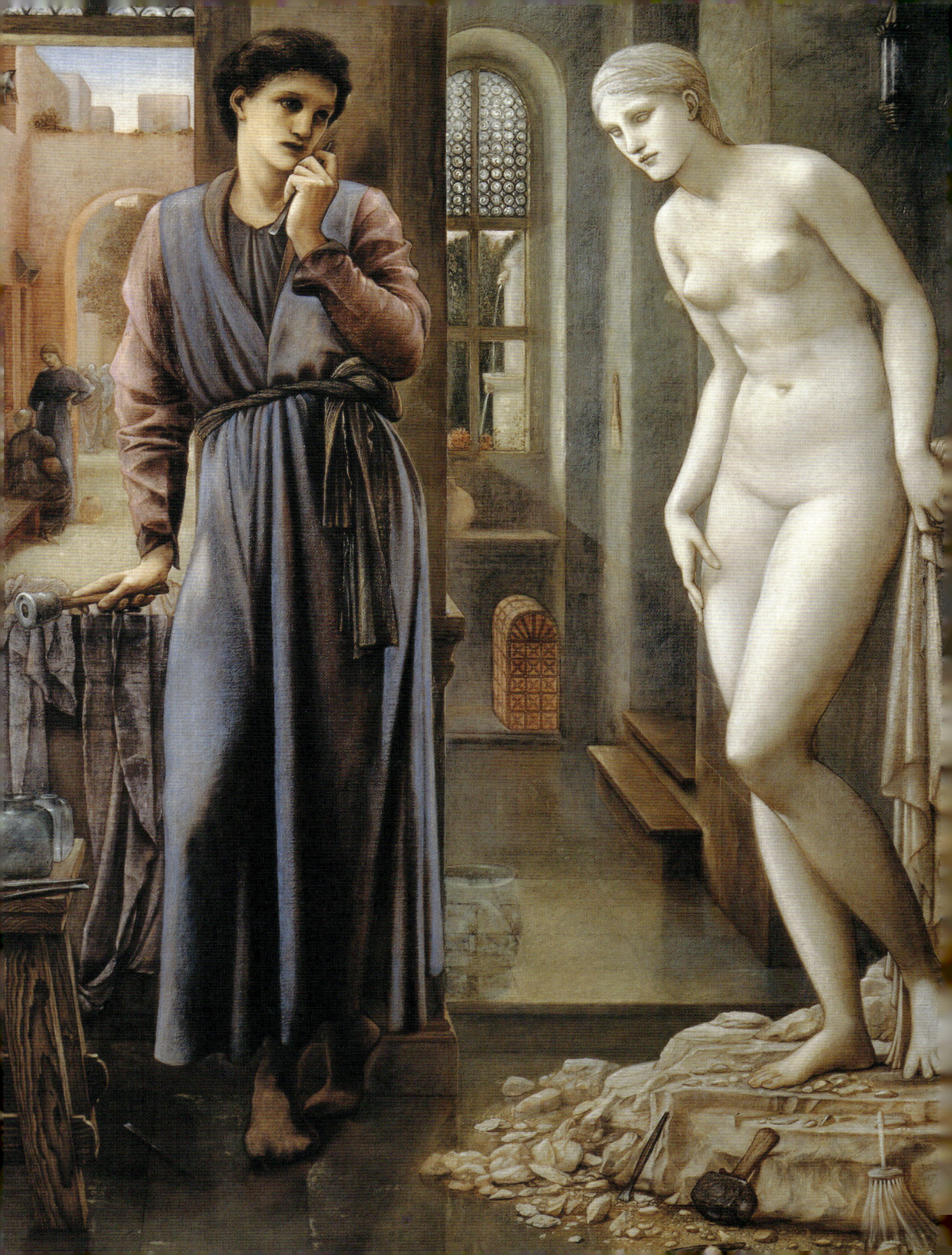

2 the haunted gallery

Long time thy shadow hath been thrall to me,
For in my gallery thy Picture hangs
Shakespeare, *I Henry VI*, II, iii, 37

hauntings

The dream of motion haunts the visual arts from the classical period to the present day. Myths of enchanted images and moving statues can be traced through the history of Western art. Galatea steps down from her pedestal, portrait figures break free of their frames; the gallery is haunted by the possibilities of life and imminent movement. Moving statues and haunted portraits convey a sense of the art object as the trace of a once-living body that has been stilled and transformed: turned to stone or bronze, caught between layers of canvas and pigment.[1] Life is suspended rather than terminated by these representations. The decay and putrefaction of the body in everyday life is deferred until the life that is arrested within the image can be re-animated by some magical power. Until such time, the painted or stone body transcends physical change and lived experience; it becomes detached from the space and time of the observer and is turned instead into an unresisting object of desire and fascination. Stasis, the absence of movement and change, provides the ground for the creation of this aesthetic and erotic ideal, in which the body is forever the same and always available to the unwavering gaze of the viewer. There is always more, though, for the haunted image hovers on the brink of life, seems to be not simply petrified but rather hesitating before breaking into movement, breathing, seeing and responding to the viewer's attentions and fantasies.

It is this promise of animation that haunts the gallery. The word 'animate' is derived from Latin *animatus*, meaning both to be filled with life and also to be disposed or inclined towards an object or idea. Its etymological roots are also drawn from Latin *anima*, which can be translated as air, breath, life or soul. To be animate, therefore, is not simply to be living but to possess the desire for life, as well as its very essence and spirit. As a verb, to animate is to breathe life into inert matter, to

19 (*facing page*) Edward Burne-Jones, *Pygmalion and the Image: II The Hand Refrains* (detail of plate 23).

make it alive or active. Life and movement are thus entirely synonymous in the notion of animation.[2] Life is expressed as motion, which in turn is the sign that the object concerned is living. However, to animate can also mean only to give the impression or appearance of life, rather than life itself. The example that the *Oxford English Dictionary* provides for this definition is from Reynolds's *Seventh Discourse*: 'That Promethean fire, which animates the canvas and vivifies the marble.' Artistic genius imparts a vividness and lifelike intensity to the art object, creating the illusion rather than the actuality of life. To animate is thus to impart either the appearance or the reality of motion or life in a previously lifeless or dormant figure. In this context, it may be most accurate to describe the portrait or statue as being in a state of suspended animation, a condition in which the vital functions have temporarily ceased but in which there is no death.

The transition from an inanimate to an animate state, the first sign or moment of movement is thus a process of immense cultural and psychological potency. A figure comes back to life. It is the moment when the spatial and temporal separation of the viewer from the image breaks down and the secret life of the image is revealed once more. An animated figure never fully casts off its previous, deathly existence, however. There remain traces of its former petrified state and doubts concerning its hold on life. The transformation might be reversed and the living portrait or statue be stilled once more. Thus the animated figure troubles the boundaries between life and death, nature and representation, movement and stasis, sensibility and lack of feeling. Its apparent ability to move between these states is the source of its uncanny and disturbing power over the viewer.

The worrying and uncomfortable ambiguities of the boundaries between the animate and the inanimate were explored, briefly, by Freud, in the context of his 1919 essay 'The Uncanny'.[3] There Freud situated his investigation of the uncanny within the subject of aesthetics, that is, the study of forms of feeling. Freud defined the uncanny as a sub-category in the wider field of that which is frightening and arouses dread and horror. What distinguishes the uncanny, however, from other types of fearful experience is its tendency to lead back to what is 'known of old and long familiar' (p. 220). In this sense, then, there is a linguistic and a psychic association between the sensations of the uncanny and of the familiar. This relationship is traced by Freud through etymology, which confirms that the uncanny, the *unheimlich*, is rooted in and comes out of the German word for the familiar, the *heimlich*. Definitions of the *heimlich* associate the term with the domestic environment, with familiarity and ease; but they also include the meanings of concealment and of secretive or deceitful actions. It is at this point, when its meaning shifts toward mischievous or magical trickery that the *heimlich* becomes identical with its opposite term, the *unheimlich*. For Freud the uncanny is much more than a sense of unfamiliarity, or intellectual ambiguity; it is the tendency of the familiar to become defamiliarised, as in a dream or in the confusion of imagination and reality. The sense of the uncanny describes the return of something familiar and long-established that has been repressed; it is 'something which ought to have remained hidden but has come to light' (p. 241). The uncanny is a condition of disturbing ambiguity that cannot be surmounted; it is the moment of slippage between the real and the unreal, the familiar and the strange, the living and the ghostly. It is the condition of the viewer in the haunted gallery when the eyes in the portrait appear to move, when the religious icon bleeds and the marble seems soft and warm to the touch.

Freud's discussion weaves in and out of the themes and images that constitute the world of the haunted gallery as it is represented in literature and the visual arts in the eighteenth and nineteenth centuries. Among the most common sources of the uncanny are ghosts and spirits, childhood phantoms and the bodies of the dead that return to haunt the living. Indeed, the association is so strong that Freud points out that in some languages *unheimlich* is translated as haunted. Freud identifies the anxiety aroused by these spectral forms as the resurfacing of an old but powerful fear of the dead; a pre-modern, irrational belief that the dead return to claim the living, that the past reaches out to the present and draws it back.

The basis, for Freud, of nearly all uncanny effects is when the distinctions between reality and imagination are erased and the viewer can no longer differentiate the fantasy from the actual physical form. Included in this class of experiences is an inanimate object coming to life or an apparently animate figure turning out to be a waxwork or mechanical doll.[4] He retells the story, published in an issue of the *Strand Magazine*, of a couple who move into a house in which there is a wooden table carved with crocodiles. Towards evening they begin to notice a terrible smell and they see vague, ghostly forms gliding through the house. The carved crocodiles have become animated, haunting and disturbing the comfort of the domestic sphere and rendering it uncanny. Freud identifies experiences of this kind as a form of neurotic attachment to magical practices. He sees the subject's belief in the omnipotence of their own thoughts and their power to give life to inanimate forms as the residual trace of an early stage of individual and human development based on a magical, animistic conception of the universe. Within this framework, animation is defined as the atavistic preservation of the belief that inanimate objects have a living soul. The retention of this belief and its expression, early in the twentieth century, in the uncanny confusion of living and inanimate forms is, for Freud, a kind of modern magical thinking. Like the form of the ancestral ghost, animation disturbs chronology, drawing the past into the present and reintroducing pre-modern beliefs to modernity. This is the folded time of the haunted gallery, where living pictures and moving statues confuse past, present and future and in which new technologies express archaic, magical thinking.

One final point needs to be made about Freud's discussion of the uncanny, as it bears on the conception of the haunted gallery. As a source of uncanny feelings, animation may not necessarily be derived from repressed childhood fears or even excite fear in the beholder. For evidence of this claim Freud points to the way that in play children treat their dolls like living people. He also refers to a woman patient who recalled in her childhood longing to be able to animate her dolls with her gaze. From this Freud concludes that the confusion of inanimate and animate objects and the dream of animation may arouse strong desire, rather than fear. Elsewhere in the essay he questions whether certain uncanny themes can really be defined as such:

> We have heard that it is in the highest degree uncanny when an inanimate object – a picture or a doll – comes to life; nevertheless in Hans Andersen's stories the household utensils, furniture and tin soldiers are alive, yet nothing could well be more remote from the uncanny. And we should hardly call it uncanny when Pygmalion's beautiful statue comes to life. (p. 246)

What seems to rob these examples of their uncanny effect is their cultural familiarity and explicit fictionality. For Freud, literature must retain a strong hold on reality to arouse in the reader feelings of the uncanny. Where artifice takes over uncanny motifs can prompt laughter rather than anxiety. Desire and comedy also have their place in the haunted gallery. By the middle of the nineteenth century it was used as the setting and alibi for the display of nudity in artistic poses and, by the end of the century, the haunted gallery was the theme for early cinema's parody of artistic creativity and its irreverent dismissal of the traditional arts of painting, sculpture and even still photography.

Freud's discussion of the uncanny suggests a range of readings for the transformations that take place in the metaphorical space of the haunted gallery. Below the inert surfaces of paint, canvas, stone and metal there lie the spectres of the dead, the spirits of our ancestors, who return to haunt the living. They are relics of earlier stages of psychic development in which animistic conceptions of the world endowed people and images with magic powers. Living pictures and moving statues disturb the boundaries between imagination and reality; they reintroduce the fears and fantasies of the past into the present and the time of the beholder. The frame and the pedestal are the key elements within this configuration, marking the borders between the living and the dead and the conceptual possibilities of animation. Confined within its frame or anchored to its pedestal, the art object remains inert, lifeless; the moment the object is brought to life it breaks free of the world of representation and enters the reality of the viewer. This is also a narrative of intense desire, in which the viewer is omnipotent and the power and intensity of the gaze becomes the instrument for generating life. However, the space of the haunted gallery also marks the suspension of these higher discourses and, in the hands of late nineteenth-century magicians, film-makers and advertisers it became a place of artifice and parodic comedy in which 'spirits' might appear in the shape of a whisky bottle, rather than as the return of the repressed.

The 'golden age' of the haunted gallery, of fantasies of animated paintings and moving statues, lasts from the beginning of the eighteenth century, for nearly two hundred years, reaching a peak at the end of the nineteenth century and in the early years of the twentieth century. This cultural history coincides in Britain with the history of industrial modernisation and, to a significant degree, the haunted gallery provided a subversive, counter-space to that of the factory. The gallery's meaning and potency lies in its age and the traces of the past that are suspended within its walls. It is an aristocratic, ancestral space, open only to the few who have access to its high cultural forms and fantasies. There is no labour in the haunted gallery and its only products are those of the imagination. Visitors communicate with the spirits of past culture and indulge in ancestor worship. It is a place of ambiguous sights and visions, as opposed to the assault of mechanical sound in the industrial factory. The haunted gallery is essentially the setting for optical illusions and special effects. People go there to suspend their disbelief and to revel in the exquisite terrors of animation.

The histories of industrialisation and of the haunted gallery converge in the eighteenth-century novel. The public for the haunted gallery was increased immeasurably by the printing revolution and the emergence of the novel in the first half of the eighteenth century. Haunted portraits and moving statues became accessible to a literate, fiction-reading public who could experience the sensations of the gallery vicariously through the printed pages of a gothic novel. One of the earliest and best-known examples of a walking portrait in the literature of this period is Horace Walpole's *The Castle of Otranto* (1764). Set in an old castle, the novel teems with medieval motifs and supernatural manifestations. In one scene the villain, Manfred, forces himself on the princess, Isabella. At that moment, the portrait of his grandfather, which hangs in the room where they are sitting, comes to life and utters a deep sigh:

> Manfred, distracted between the flight of Isabella, who had now reached the stairs, and his inability to keep his eyes from the picture, which began to move, had however advanced some steps after her, still looking backwards on the portrait, when he saw it quit its panel, and descend on the floor with a grave and melancholy air. 'Do I dream?' cried Manfred, returning, 'or are the devils themselves in league against me?' . . . Ere he could finish the sentence the vision sighed again, and made a sign to Manfred to follow him.[5]

This scene, with the walking picture as a form of ancestral hubris for an errant living relative, was illustrated, dramatised, quoted and reworked well into the twentieth century.[6] As interesting as the scene itself, however, is the explanation that Walpole gave of its inspiration:

> When you read of the picture quitting its panel, did not you recollect the portrait of Lord Falkland, all in white, in my gallery? Shall I even confess to you, what was the origin of this romance! I waked one morning, in the beginning of last June, from a dream, of which all I could recover was, that I had thought myself in an ancient castle (a very natural dream for a head filled like mine with Gothic story), and that on the uppermost banister of a great staircase I saw a gigantic hand in armour.[7]

Walpole's half-waking state, his suspension between dream and reality, mirrors the perceptual uncertainty that characterises the haunted gallery. The animation of the image (the portrait, the suit of armour) depends on a suspension of consciousness and physical vivacity in the viewer. The intense pleasure and thrill of this condition and the magical images that it generated were highly sought by both elite and middle-class audiences in the second half of the eighteenth century. Where readers could simulate the experience through the novel and its various cultural spin-offs, European travellers and connoisseurs arranged to visit Italian art galleries at night, when the special effects created by torchlight produced the illusion, in a willing audience, that the statues had come to life.[8] By the last decades of the eighteenth century, audiences were seeking hallucinatory and sensational effects from literature, theatre and the visual arts and magical images were an effective source for these intense, moving cultural experiences. They drew on the familiar forms of high culture and made them strange, invested with the miraculous powers of religious icons to breathe, weep, bleed and move. The haunted gallery broke down the barriers between viewer and object and evolved an increasingly prevalent fantasy on the theme of animation. Rather than making the states of motion and stillness absolute and distinct, industrialisation and machine production generated a discourse in which they were fluid and subject to thrilling visual uncertainties and transformations.

The development of the haunted gallery as a space of cultural fantasy and the history of machines for creating optical illusions continuously traverse each other during the eighteenth and nineteenth centuries. As far as the spectral effects of animated paintings and statues were concerned, projected images created particularly compelling and terrifying effects that blended magic and science, the sacred and the secular, enchantment and technology. The separation of the image from its point of production, its luminosity, scale, transparency and mutability made the projected image the perfect medium for the creation of apparently supernatural effects. This was the art of the magic lantern, an instrument dating back at least to the seventeenth century.[9] In its earliest form, it consisted of a lantern containing a candle and a concave mirror and a tube fitted with a lens and a groove to hold the glass slide. The scientific and entertainment possibilities of the apparatus were quickly understood and by the second half of the seventeenth century the sensational and novel effects of the lantern were being demonstrated across Europe. The magic lantern was an adaptable and effective form of modern entertainment. It was portable and could be easily set up by individual showmen in a range of different venues from small country fairs to large urban theatres (plate 20). Showmen at the end of the eighteenth century created extravagant theatrical performances, in which supernatural forms were projected onto a range of surfaces by machines hidden from the view of the audience. These phantasmagoria reached their height of popular success in the performances created by Etienne Gaspard Robertson, a physicist and showman from Liège, who took his particular version of the ghostly spectacle round European capitals at the end of the eighteenth century, finding a permanent home in a ruined convent in Paris which he transformed into a theatre of the macabre. His nightmarish performances, with their animated, shimmering, spectral forms, terrified and delighted the viewing public. The visual effects of the slides were enhanced by smoke, lighting, glass and mirrors, creating a total environment devoted to the representation and experience of haunting.

Images created by the magic lantern were highly animated. Robertson built a track for his large magic lantern so that it could slide back and forth, producing

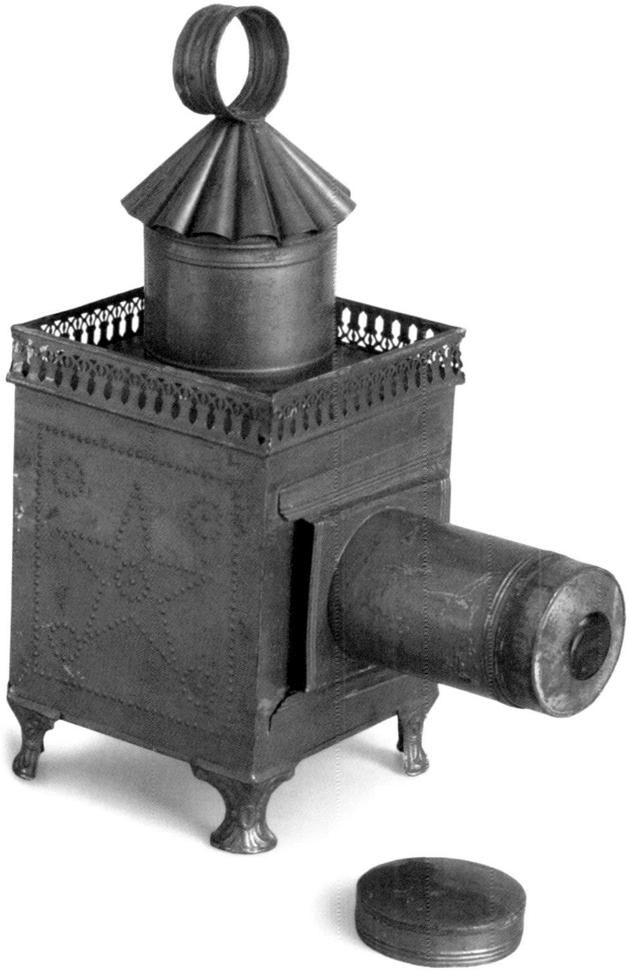

20 Lapierre magic lantern, 1860s. Courtesy of University of Exeter Library (Bill Douglas Centre).

rapid changes of scale. The lanterns themselves were also developed and modified to enable smooth dissolves between slides and multiple projection. Metamorphosis and the animation of dead or inert figures were among the greatest triumphs of the lanternists in this period. The fear that was generated by watching the first magic lantern shows was exploited by the lanternists and continued to characterise the reactions of their audiences even into the twentieth century.[10] At the end of the nineteenth century, the excitement and anticipation of setting up a magic lantern show in a farmhouse kitchen is clearly conveyed in the memoirs of Alison Uttley, the author of children's fiction and books on country life. She describes saving her money and ordering a magic lantern from London, and the imaginative world that is opened up by the intensely dynamic projected images:

> We set it up in the kitchen, on the servant boy's stool, placed on a table. A sheet was hung from the clothes-line, across the room, to take the pictures . . . and the lamp was extinguished so that the place was in darkness . . . My brother stood on the chair and manipulated the slides: the tiny lantern sent a stream of smoke

> to the low ceiling, and there was a delicious odour of hot japanned metal. The brightly coloured pictures filled us with joy, and we looked at them over and over again, inventing tales about them, swept into a world of romance . . . The wind then blew through an open door, and the little lantern flame flared up; the sheet flew out like a sail, and the circular picture of a ship in a storm rocked violently as it was flung on the billowing field. It was worth everything to see such a wonder, we thought, as we steadied the lantern and gazed at the projection.[11]

These pleasures are experienced through the apparatus itself and through the images projected on the makeshift screen. Details of the kitchen and domestic equipment as they are converted into a space for projection are carefully delineated and then erased, as the bright, coloured images take form on the white surface of the sheet. The condition of the magic lantern show is a state of wonder, as fantasy and imagination take hold of even the simplest images and give them a story, a life. It is a restless, agitated environment, in which even with the most rudimentary projector, a novice operator and individual slides shown singly, a sudden movement of the sheet screen animates the picture and endows the image with spirit and violent motion.

The magic lantern projects pictures of distant scenes on the white screen in a darkened room. Experiencing them is remarkable and seems inexplicable; for a time, even the well-to-do farmhouse kitchen becomes a haunted gallery, filled with shadows, ghostly images and phantom illusions. Furthermore, the memory of childish excitement inevitably bears a melancholy aspect, as one recalls that the child is as ephemeral and phantasmatic as the projected image or the smoke from the lantern. All are gone. Image and child inevitably age and decay and are equally ghost forms in the present.

From here, it is merely the slightest move to the projected images of film and the haunted gallery of cinema. The theme of the animated painting or sculpture took on a renewed significance at the end of the nineteenth century, with the development of new forms of photographic technology for the creation of lifelike moving images. For the first public film show, staged by the Lumière brothers at the Grand Café in Paris in December 1895, the programme announced: 'For only one franc you'll see life-size figures move and come to life before your very eyes.'[12] This was the gothic nightmare in celluloid form, a photographic enactment of the living portrait. Some of the first film shows began with a still frame that the projectionist then cranked into action. Life-size figures walked from the distance, towards the audience, like an ancestral portrait stepping out of its frame and laying its hand on the shoulders of the living. Is it surprising that early film-makers turned frequently to the subject of the animated painting, to the image or statue that is magically endowed with a mischievous life? The theme was a metaphor for the new medium and its representational powers. It surpassed the illusionistic capacities of the traditional arts. Inanimate forms could be endowed with life but they were only shadows and illusions of absent originals. The monochrome of early film and the absence of synchronised sound were constant reminders of the deceptive nature of film and the inevitable, dreadful failure of its claims to capture life.

At the end of the nineteenth century the search for the spirit or life within the inert art object was evident across all forms of visual media. The exquisite passage from stasis to movement, the hesitation and moment of delay prior to motion, became the fool's gold of representational practices in the period. In an age when lovelorn sculptors could no longer pray to benign goddesses to animate their creations, the power to endow the image with life was handed over to magicians, lanternists and film-makers.

This still left the matter of the life within the art object itself – the spirit of the masterpiece that could animate apparently inert pigment, as opposed to the smoke and mirrors special effects of popular culture. As seen in chapter 1, psychological aesthetics drew on developments in the physiognomy of the eye to evolve a theory of dynamic viewing. A train of constant ocular movements, at a range of velocities, over points, lines and surfaces of a picture, created the illusion of dynamic movement in inert images. This explanation was focused almost entirely on the vivacity of the viewer; it still did not account for the *anima* of the art object. It became the function of a particular style of writing about art to draw out the life of the painting; to give it an extension in time, an historical being.

For Walter Pater all great art was a kind of haunting; a spiritual and sensory presence that had been caught in the image, but which was nevertheless a thing in time and subject to the flow of past, present and future. Through intense contemplation of the work of art and subjective observation, the critic was able to recognise the 'genius' of the work, the spirit or life of the period that haunted it and that defined the most significant and beautiful examples of painting and sculpture. Although Pater's criticism was firmly centred on the temperament and sensibility of the individual critic, it was also dependent on an aesthetic communion between the responsive viewer and the beautiful object. As he famously asked in the preface to his first book, *Studies in the History of the Renaissance* (1873): 'What effect does [this song or picture] really produce on me? Does it give me pleasure? And if so, what sort or degree of pleasure? How is my nature modified by its presence and under its influence?'[13] The consequence of this reflection was a form of writing about art in which life appears to break out of the image; in which figures and forms become animated and possessed of a history and a temporality beyond the moment of the making of the image.

Life stories dominate Pater's thinking – those of the critic, the artist and the painted or sculpted figure – and biography provides the structure for *Studies in the History of the Renaissance*, which is divided into four essays on Renaissance artists: Leonardo, Michelangelo, Botticelli, Luca della Robbia. The essay on Leonardo exemplifies Pater's criticism and his interpretation of the impression or affect of the work of art. For Pater, Leonardo was an alchemist, seeking to discover the secret of making art immortal. Pater describes him as a sorcerer and, more significantly, as 'a clairvoyant' (p. 100), one possessed of a supernatural vision or perception. The theme of spectral embodiment recurs frequently in Pater's writing on Leonardo.

Of his portraits, he writes: 'faces of a modelling more skilful than has been seen before or since, embodied with a reality which almost amounts to illusion on dark air' (p. 104). This image of an uncanny likeness formed on smoke or air immediately recalls the ghostly projections and manifestations of the phantasmagoria. Both portraits and lantern images have a spectral quality that transcends their material production; they are images that are conjured by the artist or lanternist to create wonder in their audiences.

The uncanny temporality of the work of art, the way in which the patina of age renders the image strange and unreal, is made even more explicit in Pater's discussion of the fresco of *The Last Supper*. Decaying on the wall of the Dominican refectory, the figures appear like 'ghosts through which you see the wall, faint as the shadow of the leaves upon the wall on autumn afternoons, [the central figure of Christ] is but the faintest, most spectral of them all . . . transparent shadows, spirits which have not flesh and bones' (p. 114). For the sensitive viewer, the aesthetic experience of *The Last Supper* is, in the keenest sense, a haunting; a séance in which the critic medium summons the spirits of the picture into the present, transforming wherever the image is seen into a haunted gallery.

Pater's model of aesthetic contemplation rests on a direct involvement with the art work of such intensity that the distinctions between looking and experiencing, between art and life, are entirely eroded. Aesthetic pleasure is thus found in the conjoining of the worlds of the image and the critic. The painted lives haunt the present of the connoisseur, who is able in turn to enter the time and space of the image. Nowhere is this mutual possession more vividly expressed than in Pater's *Imaginary Portraits*, four short stories, each based on the fictional life of a young man, which were first published in *Macmillan's Magazine* between 1885 and 1887.[14] All the stories are set in the past and take as their narrative cue a visual image or, more precisely, a fragment or detail of an image, that sets the 'life story' in train. The tale of 'Sebastian van Storck' opens with an astonishingly vivid description of a winter skating scene by a seventeenth-century Dutch genre painter such as Adrian van de Velde or Isaac van Ostade.[15] Almost immediately, the narrator is drawn from the surface into the illusory space of the picture. The image, as a framed and discrete unit, is abandoned, as the gaze is drawn round and into the composition, from figure to figure. Everything is animated, from the mobile gaze of the fictional observer to the gliding bodies of the painted skaters, cutting through the icy space of the winter landscape. At last, the viewer's eyes rest on one figure among the crowd; this is Sebastian van Storck, whose life haunts the painting and provides the narrative for the subsequent story.

The initial image – the genre painting – represents both a moment, an instant of frozen time, and the flow of life before and after. Through his intense observation and description of the image, Pater animates the instant. It is as though the individual picture has been switched into life, as Pater's cinematic gaze pans across the painted canvas and finally closes in on the figure of the protagonist. In the move from image to narrative, Pater's critical practice recalls Henri Bergson's conviction that images immobilise the continuous flux of time. In *Matter and Memory*

(1896), and elsewhere in his writing, he describes pure duration as a constant flow of becoming.[16] Individual instants or moments are thus, in reality, an impossibility and exist only as a pragmatic, social imposition to meet the exigencies of daily life. Pater's method releases the image, returning the painted instant to the Bergsonian moving continuity of time.

In *Imaginary Portraits* the image discovered in the present becomes a point of entry into and a means of opening out the past. In 'Denys L'Auxerrois', Pater tells the story of the rebirth of Dionysus in the countryside around Auxerre and its impact on the artistic production of the city and the French revival of classicism. The tale is triggered by the narrator's visit to an Auxerre bric-a-brac shop and the discovery there of a fragment of stained glass, depicting an unidentified male figure. In his attempt to solve the mystery of the identity of the stained-glass figure, the narrator is shown a set of tapestries portraying an animated procession of dancing figures and leaping animals that includes the beautiful young man represented on the glass shard. The woven images finally lead the narrator to the tragic story of Denys and the building of the cathedral at Auxerre. In establishing the narrative, Pater moves the reader swiftly through successive stages of representation, from the fragment of glass to the series of tapestries with their fuller narrative to the life story of Denys in Auxerre – a pagan divinity who is initially worshipped and then finally spurned and savagely murdered by the population of the city. The nature of the mediating image becomes increasingly animated until the language itself becomes a living picture – a narrative portrait – of the Dionysian myth.

Pater's method of sweeping the static fragment into a flow of narrative is a common feature of the use of ekphrasis in critical writing. Ekphrasis is a rhetorical term that describes a particularly vivid descriptive passage. Later, this meaning became more specialised, referring specifically to poetical or literary descriptions of works of art.[17] Ekphrasis is a written evocation of a pictorial representation of such intensity that it presumes to simulate in the reader the visual effect of the art object on the eye of the beholder. To this extent, ekphrasis is a form of rhetorical trickery, 'an art of make believe . . . [and] illusion'.[18] In Pater's *Imaginary Portraits* the visual fragment – the marginal figure in the genre painting or the portion of stained glass – is transformed into a living history. The reader is drawn by the written narrative into the life that lies within the image and that is resurrected by the critic's language. There is, moreover, one final stage in Pater's ekphratic evocation of life and death – haunting. The lives that are summoned from the painted figures are so powerful and vivid that they are able to haunt the present reality of the narrator and, by extension, of the reader. At the end of 'Denys L'Auxerrois', Pater observes: 'To me, Denys seemed to have been a real resident at Auxerre. On days of a certain atmosphere, when the trace of the Middle Age comes out, like old marks in the stones in rainy weather, I seemed actually to have seen the tortured figure there – to have met Denys l'Auxerrois in the streets.'[19]

The idea of the art object as a kind of ghostly apparition unites Pater's writing, across his studies of the Renaissance and his short stories. It also provides a cultural link between the new art criticism arising from aestheticism at the end of the nineteenth century and the gothic fictions of Walpole, or the uncanny effects of the magic lantern. All share a deep-seated belief in the dormant life within the art object and in the power of the critic, or of technology or indeed magic, to awaken and mobilise that life.

Pater's themes of the haunted life of the painting and the seductive and destructive power of male beauty are also at the heart of Oscar Wilde's novel *The Picture of Dorian Gray*, first published in 1891. Wilde gives the subject a new twist through his story of a man and his portrait: the latter changes and decays, while the former, in spite of a life of corruption, apparently remains physically unaltered. In Pater's review of the novel, he identified both the conventional and the innovatory aspects of the narrative; its use of the traditional Doppelgänger theme and the stories of Edgar Allen Poe, and its departure from these sources.[20] Indeed, there are passages in *Dorian Gray* that seem straight out of Walpole, such as when Gray describes his experience of walking through the picture gallery of his country house and looking at the portraits of his ancestors: '[The eyes] seemed to follow him wherever he went.'[21] However, Wilde's description of the gradual corruption of Gray's portrait offers a new interpretation of the living picture. The portrait is a corpse but it is also alive and haunted by the immorality of Gray's soul: 'What the worm was to the corpse, his sins would be to the painted image on the canvas. They would mar its beauty, and eat away its grace. They would defile it, and make it shameful. And yet the thing would still live on. It would always be alive.'[22] The portrait steals the life and morals of the living Gray and finally claims his life when Dorian stabs the picture but is himself found dead. It is the portrait that regains its original beautiful appearance and Dorian who is transformed into an old and loathsome corpse. The story is an extended commentary on the relationship between beauty and morality or the intellect, and between physical stasis and change. Thus the trope of the haunted portrait provides Wilde with the perfect means to register the transformation from suspended life to animation.

Connoisseurship and a life devoted to intense looking and scrutiny of aesthetic pleasure created a hallucinatory impression of the vivacity of the painted image among writers on art at the end of the nineteenth century. Following a particularly hectic account of the physical experience of looking at the wrestling figures in Pollaiuolo's *Battle of the Nudes*, Berenson admitted to having been under the 'spell' of the painting and to having received from the image a transfusion of 'the elixir of life'.[23]

This notion that the painted image is more intensely alive than the rapt viewer is also to be found in Vernon Lee's gallery diaries. Through periods of prolonged gazing at the works of art in Italian museums, she reaches the conclusion that 'real movements of people and carriages [seem] dull and dead compared with the intensity of movement attributed to painted or carved shapes'.[24] In this sense, the gallery is haunted not by the animated materialisations of painted figures but by the shades of visitors and passers-by, who become spectral in comparison with the mobilised images created by the responsive viewer. For Lee, and for Pater and Berenson, the aesthetic experience is also powerfully erotic, as she finds herself taken over, possessed, by certain figures in Renaissance art. In the Uffizi Gallery she recalls how 'Titian's *Flora* takes me. Her glance, gesture, drapery, all drags one in. I have no desire to stroke, touch, or kiss, but there is a delight of life, of clean, warm life.'[25] Whatever the nature of this pleasure, its source lies in the overwhelming life that the critic discovers in the image. In an act of mutual aesthetic vampirism, the painted figure is given life by the critic's absorbed response and, in turn, the critic feeds on the vivacity of the living picture.

Lee explored art's seductive and occasionally malevolent power over the enchanted viewer in a number of short stories, published in the 1890s and early 1900s. In the preface to *Hauntings*, a collection of four fantasy and supernatural tales, she explained that the ghostly subjects of these stories dwell in the vague and liminal states that lie between image and reality. Two of the stories are based on the ghostly after-life of painted portraits: one, a sixteenth-century painting of an Italian noblewoman, discovered centuries later by a young historian; the second, a miniature of a cavalier poet, with whose ghost a young woman becomes obsessed.[26] In both narratives there is a repeated play on the themes of image, time and mortality. The painted likeness is the device that draws together the past and the present, as the ghostly spirit of the portrait figure arouses a desire of such power that it erodes the passage of time and is ultimately fatal to the living subject. At the most intense and dangerous stage of these supernatural love stories, the time of the portrait and that of the present become entirely conflated. In 'Amour Dure: Passages from the Diary of Spiridion Trepka', the young scholar researches the life of Medea da Carpi, with whose image he becomes obsessed: he sees her figure in the streets, receives letters from her and follows her to a church, where he leaves behind his own world and enters a ghostly parallel space, suspended in the sixteenth century of Medea.

For the slightly later collection, *Pope Jacynth and Other Fantastic Tales*, Lee continued with the theme of the enchanted and enchanting image. In 'Prince Alberic and the Snake Lady', the stimulus for the supernatural manipulation of time and desire is a detail on a faded gothic tapestry. The young isolated nobleman discovers a hidden portion of the image that reveals that the lower portion of a beautiful woman depicted in the scene takes the form of a snake. The very threads from which the Snake Lady is woven seem alive: the gold patterns on her bodice appear to writhe and twist about each other and when the snake tail is disclosed, the colours of the scales are not faded, like the rest of the tapestry, but are vivid and fresh. Alberic scrutinises every part of the scene, which becomes for him a physical space, rather than woven fabric. 'Thus Alberic rambled on, from discovery to discovery, with the growing sense that he was in the tapestry, but that the tapestry had become the whole world.'[27]

In the aesthetic world of Vernon Lee, images are haunted with the traces of life – paint that does not fix, threads that twist and cannot fade, stone that breathes or blushes. It is the protagonist's obsession with the image, in these stories, that leads to the subsequent elision of representation and reality. The frame and surfaces of the living picture become permeable under the unwavering gaze of the enchanted beholder, creating inhabited pictures and haunted worlds. For Lee, the power to play with time and space in this way came from the 'historical imagination', a fusion of history and memory, which she described as 'a sort of second-sight'.[28] In her short stories, as in the fiction and criticism of Walter Pater, figures are faded traces and fragments of lives that haunt the art object with their narratives of desire and fantasy. It is the viewer, however, who holds the key to life. Animation is a consequence of the long, lingering and penetrating gaze into the image. Looking becomes an aesthetic and erotic reverie, a kind of enchanted rapture that creates life.

pygmalionism and the image

The prototype of the nineteenth-century narrative of life-giving erotic rapture can be found in Ovid's story of the sculptor Pygmalion and his obsessive love for his ivory statue. The story is one of those told by Orpheus in Book x of the *Metamorphoses*. It comes immediately after the contrasting story of the Propoetides, the first prostitutes, who denied Venus's divinity and who, as a punishment, were turned to stone. The stories are linked by Pygmalion's disgust at the immorality of these women and his subsequent decision to live a life of celibacy. At the same time, he carves an astonishingly realistic statue of a beautiful woman, from the purest ivory. From Ovid's first description of the figure, it is evident that it bears within itself a secret, suspended life:

> It had the face of a real maiden who, you would have thought,
> was living
> and, if self-respect were not stopping her, wanted to move.[29]

These are significant lines in Ovid's text, suggesting that the subsequent transformation of the stone statue into living flesh is not simply a divine creation of life but a realisation and animation of an immanence already in the work of art.

Pygmalion falls in love with the beautiful statue. He caresses it and begins to imagine that the figure's form is soft and responsive and that it returns his kisses. The sculptor woos his creation; he brings it gifts of jewellery, dresses it and finally lays it in his bed where it becomes his bedfellow. It is in this state of intense, erotic delusion that he attends the festival of Venus where he prays to the goddess. At first he asks for the ivory maiden to be his wife but then he stops himself and prays instead for a wife like the statue. Venus, however, understands and responds to his original appeal. Pygmalion returns to the statue and resumes his love-making but this time the figure begins to change its nature; it grows warm and soft, it yields to his touch like warm wax. The carver of stone moulds and palpates the metamorphosing figure and is convinced of her reality when he sees the blood flowing through her body and infusing it with colour. She blushes at his kisses; she opens her eyes and gazes at her lover maker. Ovid's description of the animation of the stone statue is the climax of the narrative. Critically, the actual transformation has to be differentiated from Pygmalion's earlier delusional belief in the life of the statue. Through the intervention of the goddess, the figure becomes not simply a moving statue but a woman; she feels embarrassment, manifests signs of modesty and responds with desire to the life-giving desire of Pygmalion.

The transgressive nature of Pygmalion's obsession with his ivory statue and his behaviour towards it was explicitly acknowledged in subsequent versions of the fetishistic desire for statues and images, and pervades late nineteenth-century representations of the myth. During the Renaissance, a number of stories circulated of beautiful nude statues of Venus arousing the lust of male viewers and, centuries later, the fantasy was still being reworked in accounts such as that given by the bibliophile Henry George Quinn in 1785, who described breaking into the Tribuna of the Uffizi in Florence and making love to the Medici Venus.[30] Such was the cultural resonance of this narrative of the power of male sexual desire that it was able to make the move in the late nineteenth century from versions of classical mythology and erotic writing to the developing science of sexology and its classification of erotic mania and sexual perversion. For Benjamin Tarnowsky the desire for and adoration of pictures and statues were symptomatic of those suffering from particularly pronounced forms of erotic delirium. Tarnowsky was a Russian sexologist whose study *The Sexual Instinct and its Morbid Manifestations* was published in English in 1898 and cited alongside other European writers in the field such as Bloch and Krafft-Ebing and by Havelock Ellis in his exhaustive *Studies in the Psychology of Sex*. Tarnowsky identified ancient Greece as being especially rich in cases of erotomaniacs attempting sexual congress with a statue. In particular, he referred to the story of Clysophus who became infatuated with a marble statue in the Temple of Samos. When his attempt to make love to the statue failed as a result of the coldness of the stone, he apparently placed a slab of raw meat over the genital area of the figure and, in this way, was able to satisfy his desire.[31] If the story of Clysophus reduced the piety and sexual longing of Pygmalion to the humiliating image of sex with a piece of meat, then such crude realisations of the ancient myth were also to be found in recent cases. Tarnowsky cited the example from France in 1877 of a gardener who fell in love with a statue representing Venus de Milo in a park. Even more recently, in St Petersburg a man had been arrested for paying nightly visits to the statue of a nymph, located on a terrace in a private country estate.

Havelock Ellis drew on these and similar cases in order to define the specific form of sexual perversion which he called 'Pygmalionism' – the love of statues.[32] Pygmalionism was included in the broader class of perversions founded on vision and erotic symbolism. In all these forms, the lover's sexual attention is displaced from the central object of desire to some other object on the margins of, or merely associated with, that primary focus. Statues were thus only one instance of a wide range of objects that might accidentally acquire the power to arouse sexual feelings in the auto-erotic. Pygmalionism was thus enshrined within sexology as an abnormal form of arousal through vision. The statue, however, does not function like other inanimate objects within erotic symbolism, for in this case the focus of desire is not simply on the lifeless thing but is also produced through the power of process and the fantasy that the statue might come to life. In his account of the sexual appeal to vision, Ellis argued that it was intensified by the secondary appeal to movement. Although the statue could never be said to dance, Pygmalionism offered the dual appeals of vision and animation. Ellis cited 'cases in which a man requires of a prostitute that she shall assume the part of a statue which gradually comes to life, and finds sexual gratification in this performance alone'.[33] Furthermore, Ellis disagreed that necrophily – a sexual attraction for corpses – was a related form of erotomania. Pygmalionism was founded on the imagined gratification of transformation and movement; of the beautiful, motionless statue awakened by the caresses of her adoring lover.

The profusion of anecdotes, from classical antiquity to the early twentieth century, of sexual encounters with statues is predicated on the exquisite balancing act between the absolute stillness and unresponsiveness of the stone nude and the fantasy of animation; of the unblemished perfection of the figure aroused by the will and desire of the male viewer and lover. It is hard to say at times, in these accounts, which state appears more desirable – hard motionlessness or yielding corporeality. The optimum condition, therefore, is that of becoming, of transforming, metamorphosing, when the figure possesses the properties of both marble and flesh. For Ovid's Pygmalion, this would be the moment when he returns to his statue after praying to Venus, resumes his love-making and notices the physical changes in his creation. Ecstasy for Pygmalion must surely be experienced at the moment he recognises the differences between his earlier illusions of metamorphosis and their present reality and fulfilment.

In the second part of the nineteenth century the resilient myth of Pygmalion and the animated statue can be said to have undergone a further reinvention through the impetus of the new interpretations of sexology and the wider cultural fascination with the representation of states of motion. Not surprisingly, the moment of transformation, with its first, miraculous signs of life, continued to be the point in the narrative that most fascinated artists, writers and audiences. The particular challenge for visual artists was how to capture the erotic charge of process and to render visible the duration of metamorphosis. An obvious solution to this artistic problem could be found in Ovid's reference to the statue's first blush and Pygmalion's realisation that blood was circulating through the figure. Colour, then, was the medium for the visual depiction of the state of becoming animated. In nearly every case of paintings from this period, however, it is the lingering signs of the figure's lapidarian, inanimate existence that most forcefully signify the imminent realisation of motionful, sexual life. Without these, the living statue was simply a nude.

In Jean-Léon Gérôme's version of *Pygmalion and Galatea* of about 1890 (plate 21), the liminal state of the figure is conveyed by the contrast between the upper and lower parts of the body. From the waist upwards, the form takes on the pink carnation of living flesh; below the arm of the sculptor, it remains a pale ivory, with the feet apparently less modelled and still part of the stone plinth. As in other

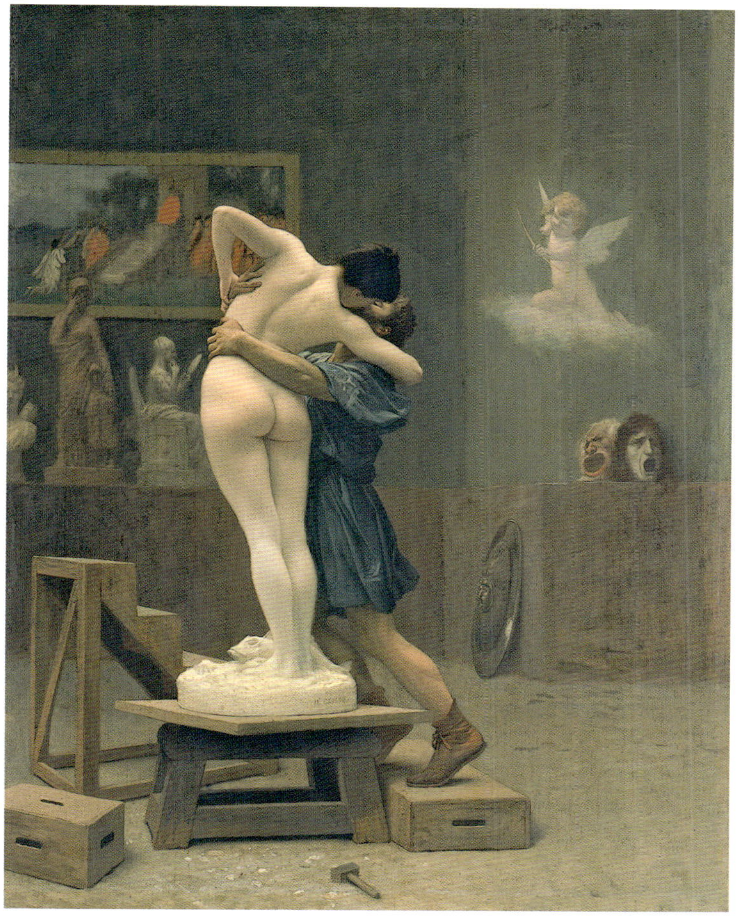

21 Jean-Léon Gérôme, *Pygmalion and Galatea*, c.1890. Oil on canvas, 88.9 × 68.6 cm. New York, The Metropolitan Museum of Art, Gift of Louis C. Raegner, 1927 (27.200).

depictions of the subject, it appears as though the sculptor was still working on the figure when the goddess intervened; the wooden hammer lies abandoned on the floor and the statue stands on a raised wooden platform, allowing the artist to work on all the surfaces of the free-standing figure. The metamorphosing figure thus leans down to embrace Pygmalion but does so awkwardly, as though the stony condition of her lower body prevented completely lifelike movement. She is caught between the states of posed sculpture and natural living body. Moreover, in common with nineteenth-century reworkings of Ovid's tale in which the animated figure returns to stone, there is a disturbing ambiguity in the image:[34] is the statue in the process of becoming human or is this a real woman who is being turned to stone? Is Pygmalion's embrace one of greeting or of valediction? In many ways the image is a *tour-de-force*; Gérôme's ostentatious display of his technical abilities and his skill at painting the female nude. It is a demonstration of painting's powers of illusion, displayed in the artist's name carved on the marble pedestal. Flesh and stone succumb to the artist's magic but true metamorphosis and the dream of animation remained an aesthetic chimera.

From the 1860s artists and sculptors turned repeatedly to the subject of Pygmalion and his animated statue, as though drawn by its explicit and unavoidable evocation of the enduring aesthetic problem of how the still image or object might represent the beginnings of life and movement. Subjects derived from Ovid's narrative, however, presented a different challenge from that of realism or verisimilitude in general. They required that the artist made visible incipient life and the commencement of motion; the simultaneous presence, within the single female figure, of inert matter and living flesh. In England, Edward Burne-Jones adopted a different solution to the question of how to depict the temporality of this metamorphosis from statue to woman. There are four paintings in his series *Pygmalion and the Image* (1868–78). The project was originally developed as a set of illustrations to William Morris's reworking of Ovid in *The Earthly Paradise* (1868–70). Burne-Jones made a first set of small oil paintings that was completed in 1870 and then worked on a larger series that was exhibited at the Grosvenor Gallery, London, in 1879.[35] In the first picture of the series, *The Heart Desires*, Pygmalion is represented, deep in thought, before an unfinished marble group of the Three Graces (plate 22). Set within its original gilt frame, the canvas may be seen as a meditation on pictorial containment and the power of aesthetic desire. The carved frame is extremely architectural, with a moulded base and sides and heavy classical entablature. This motif is repeated several times within the image, in painted picture frames, arches, doorways and windows. Figures are framed and isolated by these devices, which also emphasise the visual exchanges between living and sculptural forms. Thus, the two girls framed by the arched doorway on the left create a living mirror image of the pose of the two marble figures on the right. The third female statue is detached from this group and seems to gaze back at the contemplative sculptor and in the echoing of their postures becomes the visual source of Pygamlion's desire to create life in a stone figure. Perhaps the most extraordinary passage in the image is the bottom right-hand section which appears as a geometric pattern created by the polished marble floor, bearing reflections of parts of the sculptural group. It is a jigsaw made of reflected fragments of stone bodies: feet, ankles, calves, knees, thighs and buttocks – broken up, dismantled and unreal, needing to be reconfigured in the transformation from representation to palpable flesh.

This reconfiguration begins in the second picture, sub-titled *The Hand Refrains* (plate 23). In this scene Pygmalion has sculpted a new marble figure. The scale of the statue has changed and is now life size, a viable fantasy lover for the longing sculptor. Whereas in the earlier version of this picture, the plinth on which the figure stands was neatly finished, in this version it is a roughly hewn rock, surrounded by loose chippings. This reminder of the stony origins of the figure is significant because it is already showing signs of corporeality, such as the fleshy tones on the legs and torso and the disposition of fingers and toes. The general pose is reminiscent of the celebrated *Venus de Medici*, itself a Roman marble copy based on Praxiteles's *Aphrodite of Cnidus*. Both the *Aphrodite* and the *Venus de Medici* had been the subjects of centuries of erotic myth and speculation and, for this reason alone, they make suitable prototypes for the ideal woman created by Burne-Jones's

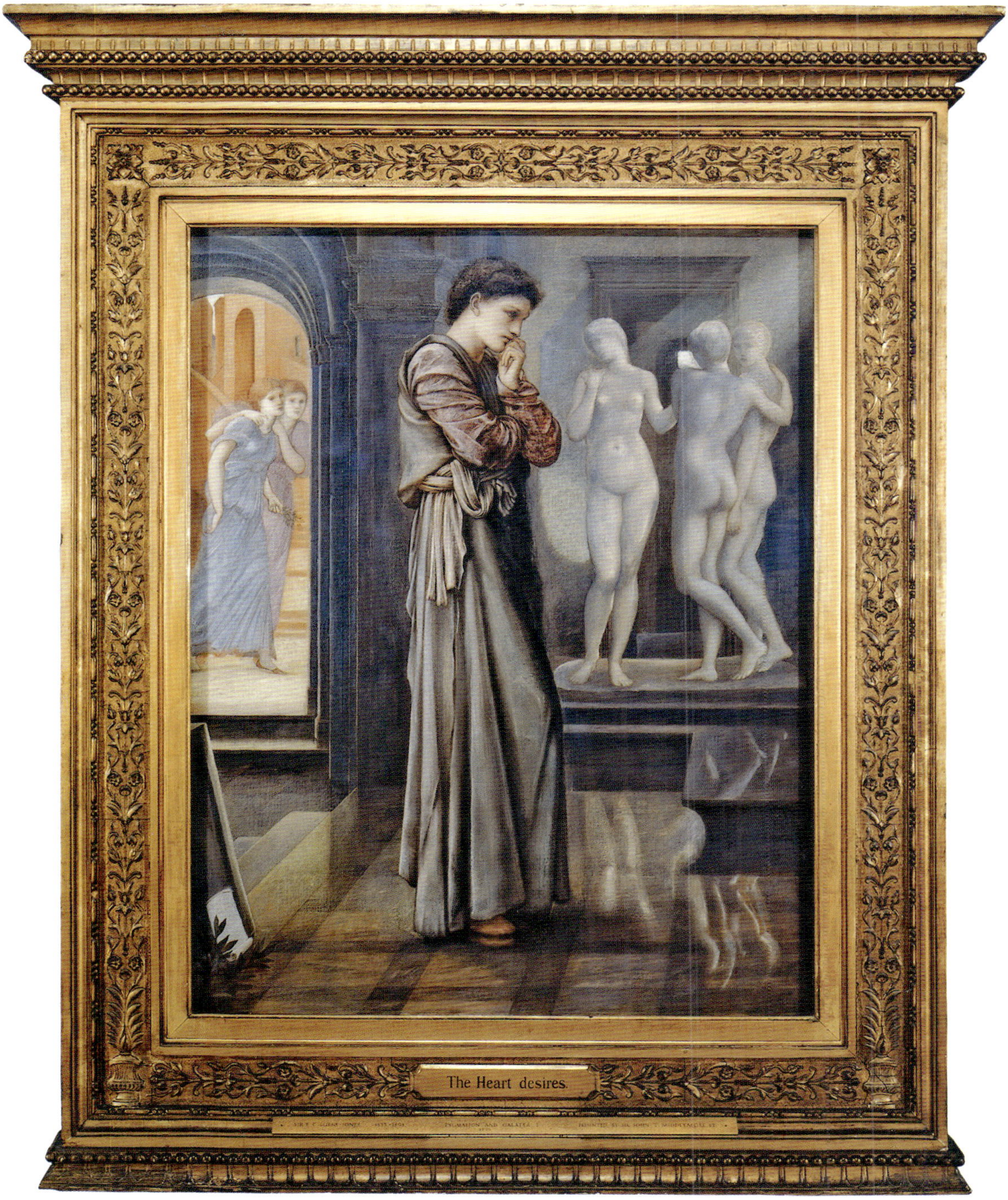

22 Edward Burne-Jones, *Pygmalion and the Image: I The Heart Desires*, 1875–8 (in gilt frame). Oil on canvas, 99 × 76.3 cm. Birmingham Museums and Art Gallery.

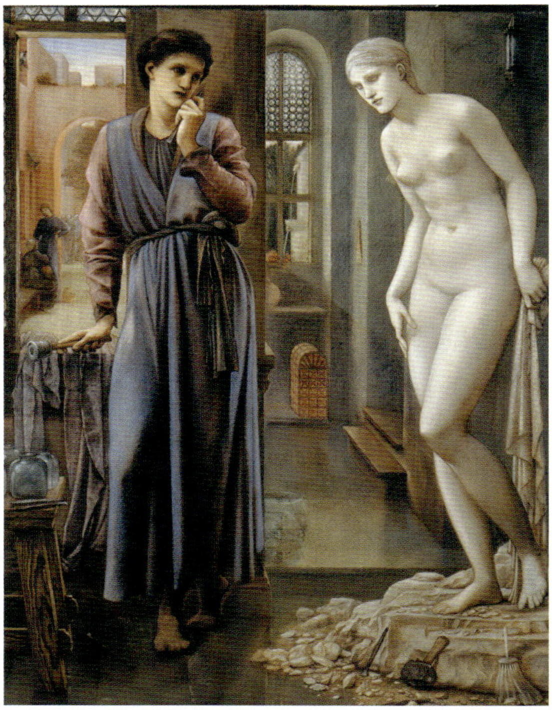

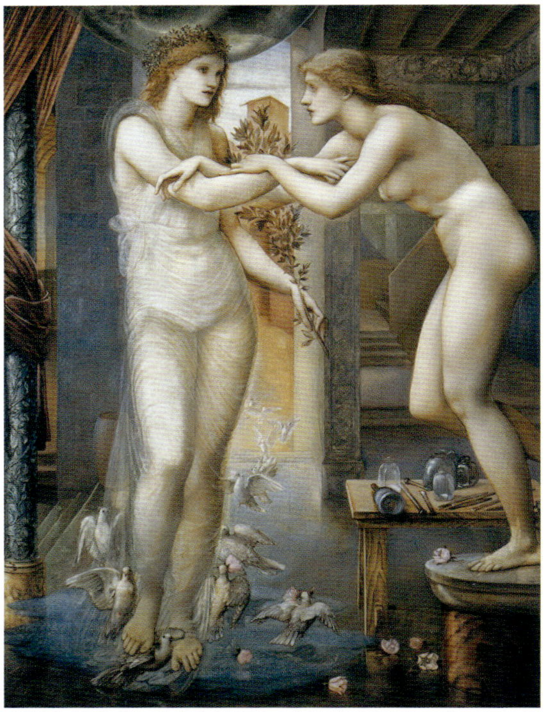

sculptor.[36] In the eyes of Pygmalion and, doubtless, those of the sexual fantasists defined by Havelock Ellis, the statue in this second painting is the perfect love object – a stone woman, on the brink of animated desire.

The third painting depicts the goddess's intercession and the moment that the statue is brought to life and helped down from the marble plinth (plate 24). Neither female figure displays any significant degree of animation, however. Both have expressionless, glazed eyes and their physical contact is concentrated in the elegant knot of arms and hands at the centre of the canvas. In the final picture, *The Soul Attains*, Pygmalion is united with his living statue (plate 25). Curiously, though, life seems to have drained from the figure, which now appears more statue-like and impassive than in the previous painting. Desire, for Burne-Jones's Pygmalion, is precarious, destined to remain fixated on the figure in a liminal state between stone and flesh.

Although the pictorial device of narration through a series of paintings suggests a morphological sequence in which the statue is progressively transformed into a living woman, this is not the case in *Pygmalion and the Image*. Rather, it appears as though the woman is reverting to her former, lapidary state. In fact, the most resonant sign of the figure's latent life and metamorphosis is the roughly chiselled stone plinth, the statue's base in the second picture. She may be made from the same lifeless block of marble but there is a corporeality and sentience within the stone figure and it is at this point alone in the series that the potential interior life

23 (*facing page left*) Edward Burne-Jones, *Pygmalion and the Image: II The Hand Refrains*, 1875–8. Oil on canvas, 99 × 76.3 cm. Birmingham Museums and Art Gallery.

24 (*facing page right*) Edward Burne-Jones, *Pygmalion and the Image: III The Godhead Fires*, 1875–8. Oil on canvas, 99 × 76.3 cm. Birmingham Museums and Art Gallery.

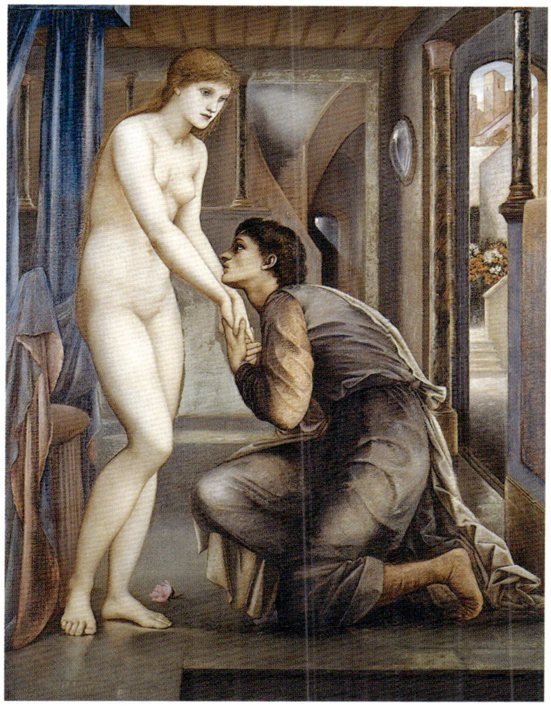

25 (*right*) Edward Burne-Jones, *Pygmalion and the Image: IV The Soul Attains*, 1875–8. Oil on canvas, 99 × 76.3 cm. Birmingham Museums and Art Gallery.

and animation of the figure is made visible. It is not the completed figure, then, or the blush of circulating blood that express life and movement but the traces of incompletion and shapeless mass.

In his description of Michelangelo's sculpture, Walter Pater emphasised that it was the lack of finish that gave the impression 'that some spirit in the thing seems always on the point of breaking out of it'. The emergence of pure form out of roughly hewn stone endowed the figure with a greater sense of life than any technical realism could achieve. He continued:

> In this way [Michelangelo] combines the utmost amount of passion and intensity with the expression of a yielding and flexible life: he gets not vitality merely, but a wonderful force of expression . . . [The] creation of life, life coming always as relief or recovery, and always in strong contrast with the rough-hewn mass in which it is kindled.[37]

Pater's recognition of the creative tension in Michelangelo's work between the unmodelled block of stone and the form that emerges from it provides a way of interpreting late nineteenth-century representations of the Pygmalion myth. For the 'coming to life' to be made visual, the figure must always have about it some traces of its former, lifeless state. It must retain visible links to its origins as statue for the significance of metamorphosis to be effectively represented. Rodin clearly understood the importance of the unfinished stone as a sign of the living body in

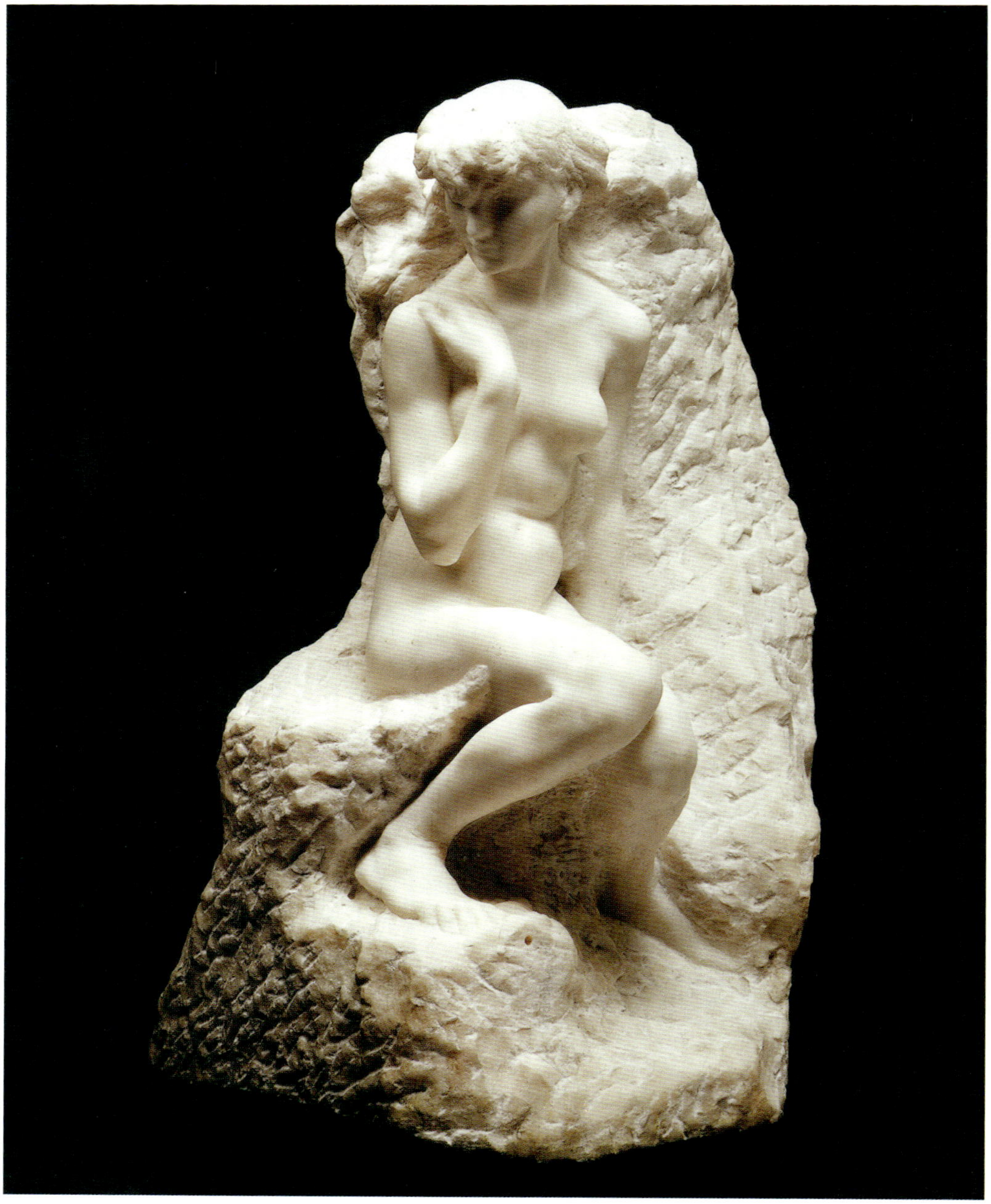

26 Auguste Rodin, *Galatée*, 1889. Marble, 60.8 × 40.6 × 39 cm. Musée Rodin, Paris.

the creation of his marble *Galatée* of 1889, in which the female figure seems to twist its way out of the slab of stone (plate 26). This unfinished process also suggests the duration of metamorphosis as something that happens over time, rather than a sudden and abrupt transformation. How would it be otherwise? If all signs of the unworked stone and its fashioning are eliminated, the object is reduced to the absurd image of the highly finished marble sculpture of *Pygmalion and Galatea* (plate 27), advertised on an internet sculpture gallery, in which either the female figure is, indeed, merely an unremarkable statue, in which case the myth is redundant, or her kiss has turned Pygmalion to stone and we are left with the marble embrace of statues. Sculptural finish, completion, eliminates life and turns both figures in the narrative to stone.

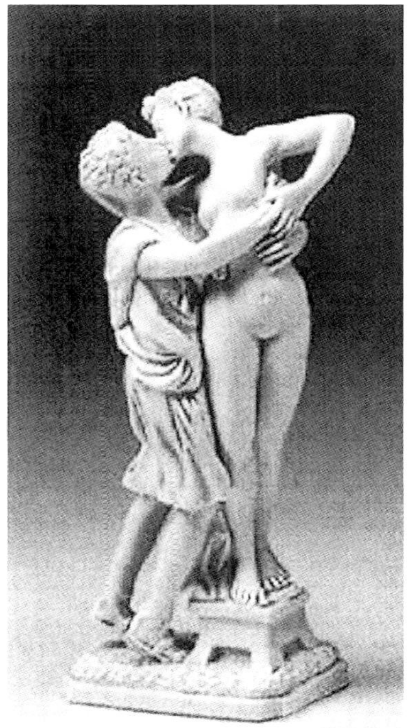

27 Anon., *Pygmalion and Galatea*, n.d. Marble, h. 27.9 cm.

In painting also there are usually signs that the artists have understood the fatal effects of eradicating the stony existence of the animated statue. Gérôme's signature on the painted marble plinth emphasises the object's stoniness and, by association, the origins of the figure that is coming to life in the arms of Pygmalion. Even in the most formulaic treatments of the subject, such as Ernest Normand's 1886 painting of *Pygmalion and Galatea* (plate 28), the colour and modelling of the sculptural lower half of the body are clearly differentiated from the tinted flesh of the upper half. Yet Normand comes close to losing the critical ambiguity of Galatea's body. Even though the stony folds of drapery try to suggest the appearance of a classical column, the figure is too complete.[38] Pygmalion's living statue-bride is reduced to the genre of academic nude.

It is historically consistent that the story of Pygmalion enjoyed a renewed popularity in the visual arts late in the nineteenth century, just when attempts to design machines to create living pictures and moving images were escalating and had assumed a pressing momentum. The shift from inert matter to living, breathing flesh, which was embodied in Pygmalion's story, must have seemed especially compelling to image-makers who were testing the limits of existing visual media and seeking new ways of representing life and movement. This fascination with the shifts between inanimate and animate states can be traced across a range of popular and high art forms in the period. Not only did statues and pictures come to life but also the living seemed constantly on the brink of turning to stone and being transformed into a frozen image. In the late 1890s the 'statuette portrait' became a fashionable photographic amusement that involved turning the subject into a marble bust (plate 29).[39] The simplest method of achieving this effect was to place the model behind a pedestal of painted wood and to whiten the hair and skin. Classical props and drapery could be added as necessary and the whole artistic arrangement set against a black velvet background. After the negative was developed the desired figure was cut out and any details that were not required for the

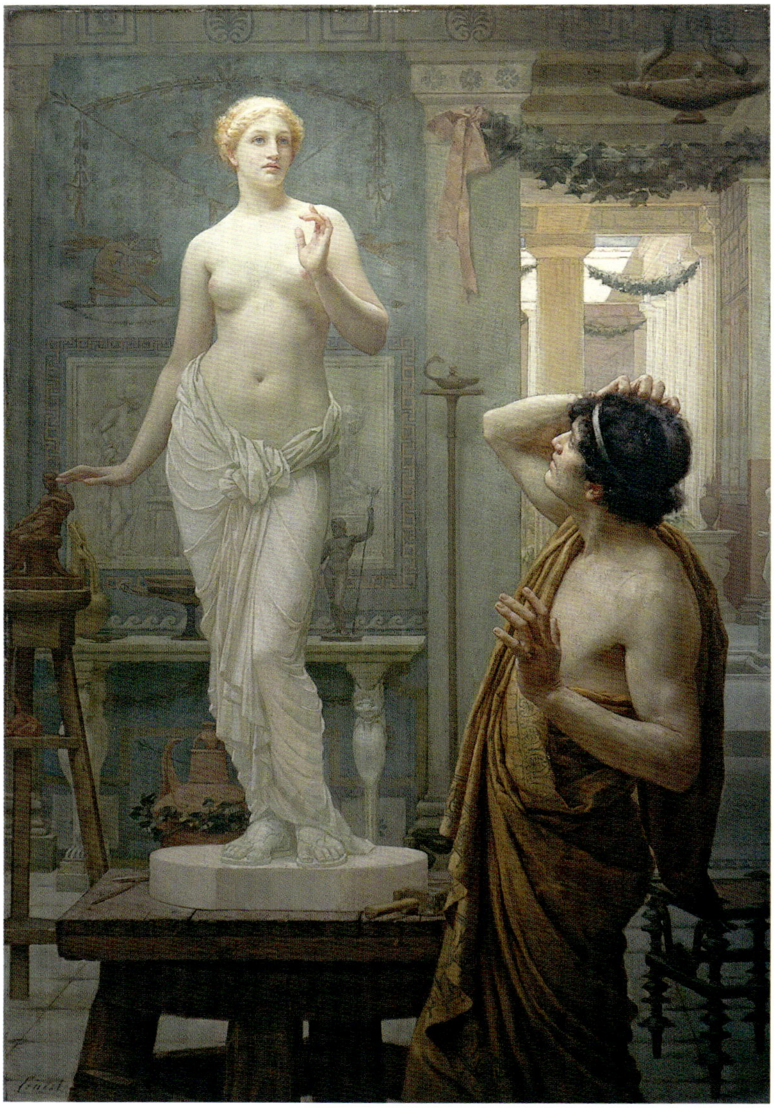

28 Ernest Normand, *Pygmalion and Galatea*, 1886. Oil on canvas, 152.5 × 121 cm. Atkinson Art Gallery, Southport.

statuette effect, such as arms, were scratched out. In the print, the bust stands out from the background and the individual takes on the appearance of a marble statue (plate 30). This desire to turn oneself to stone must be understood in relation to the cluster of narratives of metamorphosis and animation in the period. If art could claim the power to create life, then it could also obliterate the body and turn living flesh to stone. Trick photography allowed its subjects to become their own living statues and to freeze mortality through the illusions created by rice flour and carefully doctored negatives.

* * *

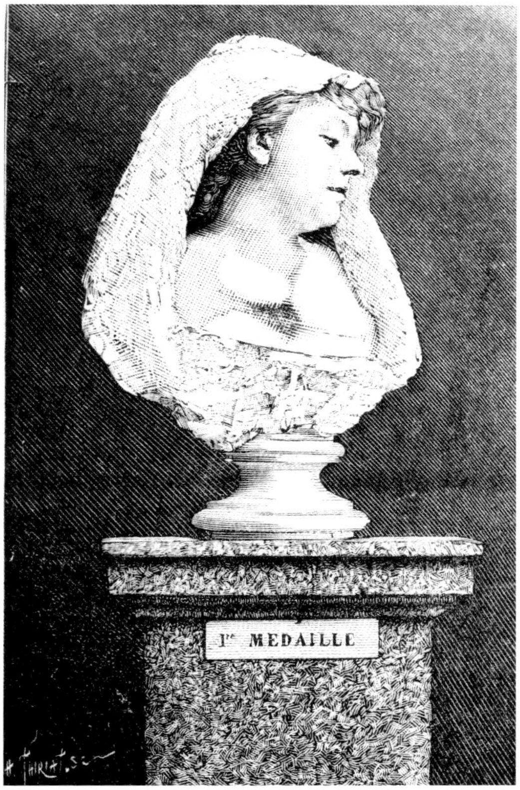

29 'New Type of Photographic Portrait', from Albert A. Hopkins, *Magic: Stage Illusions and Scientific Diversions including Trick Photography*, London: Sampson, Low, Marston and Co. Ltd, 1897, p. 449.

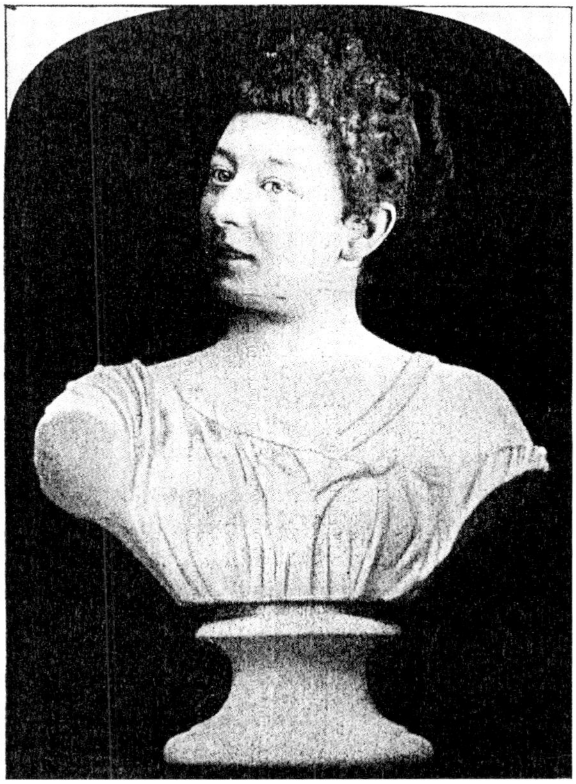

30 'The Statuette Portrait', from Walter E. Woodbury, *Photographic Amusements: Including a Description of a Number of Novel Effects obtainable with the Camera*, New York: Scovill and Adams, 1898, p. 18.

tableaux vivants

There is a continuous interplay in the nineteenth century between the fantasy of the inanimate object that comes to life and the dream of the living body that turns to stone. This cultural oscillation across states of animation and petrification, movement and stillness, softness and hardness, can be traced to early Christian beliefs in miraculous images and relics but it was endowed with a new magical power through the visual illusions created by the technologies of nineteenth-century mass entertainment.[40]

It is a common device in Victorian reworkings of the Pygmalion narrative for the animated statue to return to its marble state, as noted earlier. In many ways, however, there was little to distinguish in these versions between the vivacity of the sculpted figure and that of the living woman, since both effectively embodied conservative feminine values of modesty and reticence. Since Galatea was 'born with a blush into silence',[41] there was little to stop nineteenth-century dramatists and poets from simply allowing the process of metamorphosis to continue and turning her back to stone. The body of stone and, more especially, the female figure of pure, white marble or ivory, was an ideal body. Becoming a statue not only arrested life, it also staved off the physical manifestations of death. The statue is freed from the corporeality of the living, ageing body and is suspended forever in an ideal, unchanging state. As Kenneth Clark argued in *The Nude: A Study in Ideal Art* (1956), in order to depict the body in motion it is necessary to introduce a degree of physical distortion that inevitably subverts the harmonious proportions and balance of the classical ideal.[42] According to this account, the ideal female body within the Western tradition is built on an aesthetic of stillness and the related conviction that physical perfection is unchanging and transcendent.

The desire for an inviolate physical perfection and the simultaneous recognition of its absolute impossibility are at the heart of one of the nineteenth century's most enduring and popular forms of live entertainment. Histories of the *tableau vivant* usually trace its beginnings to the performances given by Emma Hamilton at the end of the eighteenth century and in the early years of the nineteenth century, to audiences of friends and acquaintances at her home in Naples. At the same time as her husband, Sir William Hamilton, was creating his outstanding collection of antique sculpture and artefacts, made fashionable by the rediscovery of the sites at Pompeii and Herculaneum, his wife was freezing her body in expressive and artistic poses and turning herself into living statuary.[43] As well as these social and domestic origins, *tableaux vivants* also developed in the context of the public theatre. Groups of performers, suspended in *tableau* arrangements, were incorporated into dramatic performances in English theatres from the first decades of the nineteenth century and had become self-contained presentations by the late 1830s.[44] The *tableaux* continued this bipartite development, as amateur pastime and as commercial entertainment, throughout the nineteenth century and even into the first decades of the twentieth century in the contexts of Edwardian music halls and domestic leisure.

A *tableau vivant* was, simply, a performance in which live models reproduced a well-known painting or sculpture and held the pose for a set period of time. The resulting picture was thus living but devoid of movement. As the genre developed, the arrangements became increasingly elaborate, using props, costumes, lighting and specially designed theatrical machinery to make the resulting *tableau* as much like the original as possible. This style of performance became popular under a number of different names such as *tableaux vivants*, living statuary and living pictures (plate 31). *Poses plastiques* developed as a more specialist form of presentation in which models assumed the positions of nude figures in well-known works of art or generic mythological and classical subjects (plate 32). The performers themselves were not naked but were generally covered by close-fitting body stockings or gauze curtains; nevertheless, there was much scope for 'sexing up' these presentations, depending on the nature of the venue and the expectations of the audience. So, although *tableaux vivants* and their off-shoot, the *poses plastiques*, were nearly always publicised in terms of their 'artistic' qualities, they were also a significant feature of the sex-

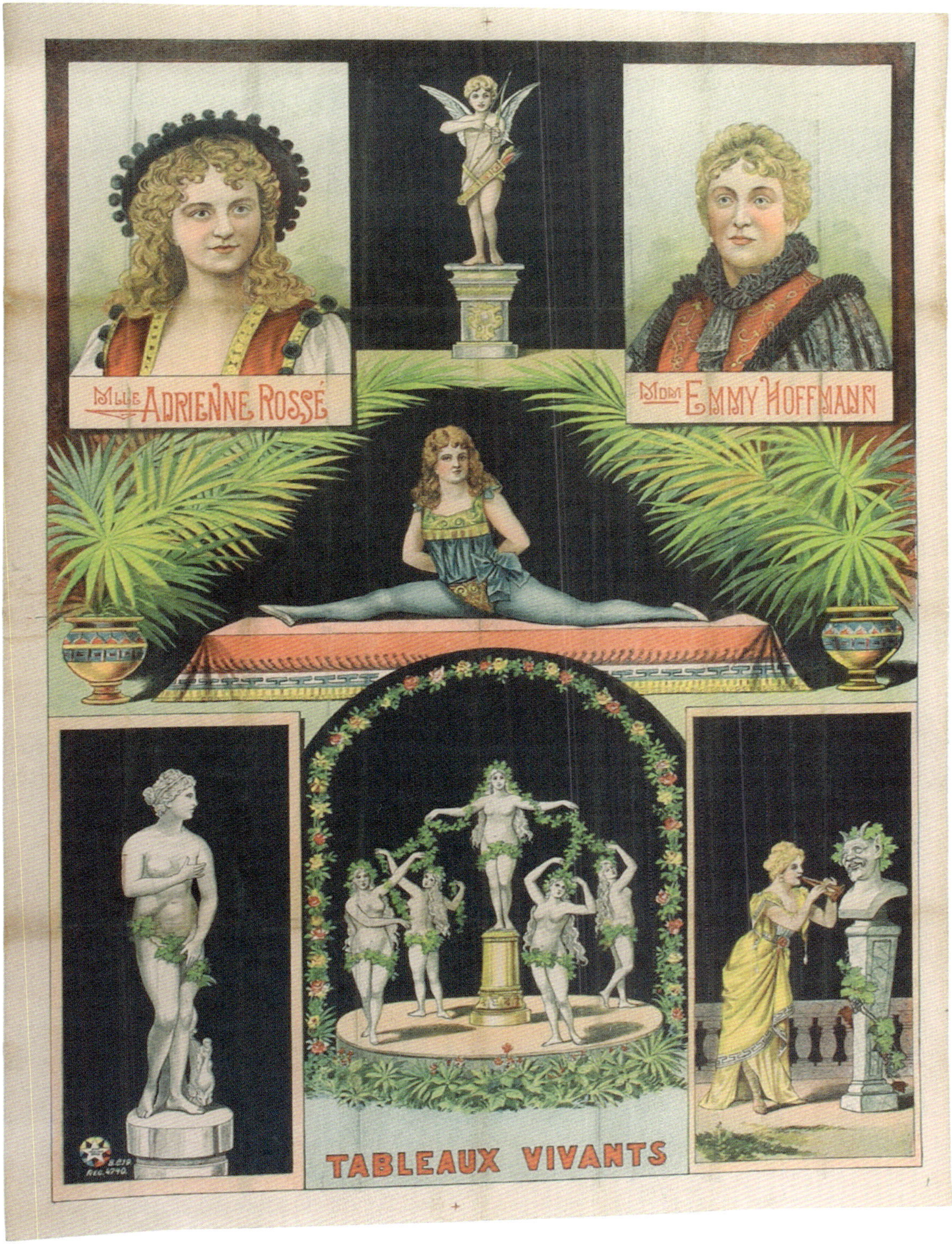

31 'Pose plastique', from advertising poster, 1880s. The National Fairground Archive, University of Sheffield.

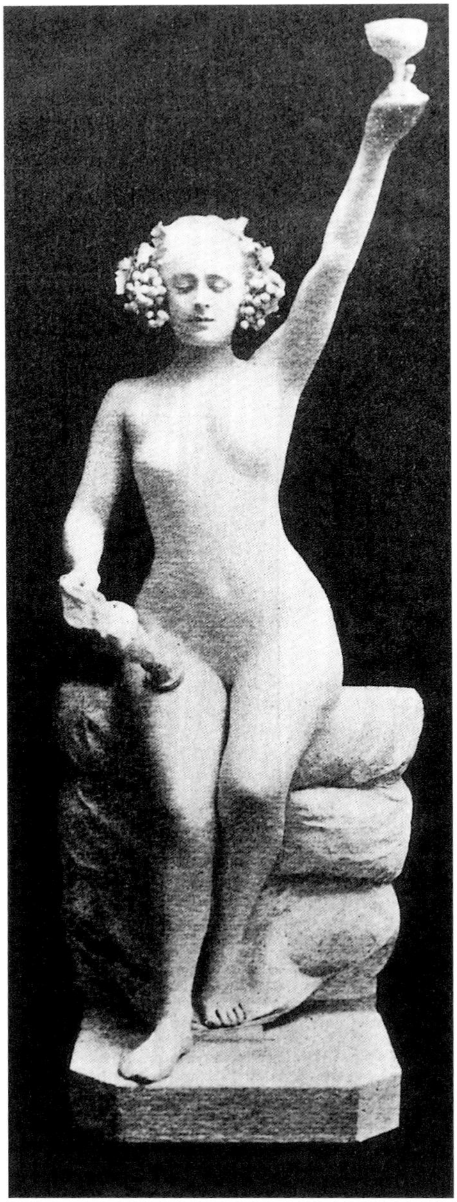

32 'La Milo as Bacchante', 1906. The Ray-mond Mander and Joe Mitchenson Theatre Collection.

ualised side of nineteenth-century mass entertainment and were regularly attacked by individual and government regulators for their obscenity and depravity.[45]

Tableaux vivants thus enjoyed a range of cultural identities from sleazy, vaudeville nudity at one end of the scale to the artistic and edifying reproduction of the finest examples of Western art at the other. In either case, the essential nature and attraction of the *tableau vivant* performance was the constant and provocative oscillation between stasis and movement. Although the holding of the *tableau* arrangement was obviously a triumph of the performers' capacity to keep still, this protracted stillness was always an inevitable assertion of the desire for and possibility of movement.[46] Moreover, a critical element of the performance was the transition between *tableaux* and the range of human and mechanical means deployed to change the performers from one arrangement to another. Part of the exquisite fascination for audiences must surely have been watching for signs of life and movement throughout the duration of a pose and observing the performers release one pose and settle into another. Given that the costumes were often made to simulate the colours and textures of painted canvas and sculpted marble, this rhythmic alternation between suspended *tableau* and mobile re-arrangement must also have appeared as a continuous metamorphosis between the soft flesh of the actor and the hard surface of the simulated image. In truth, then, the *tableau vivant* was as much an art of animation, of coming into movement, as it was an art of de-animation and stasis. Pygmalion's statue came to life and reverted to stone several times a night in the creation of living pictures.

Movement was a central part of the *tableau vivant* performance in a variety of ways. To begin with, arrangements were frequently chosen that exaggerated the perception of arrested movement and increased the danger of performers dropping the pose. Thus the author of a guide to historical *tableaux* for domestic production recommended a scene with '*the boy just rising to his feet*' and a finale of a '*rough and tumble fight with four boys*'.[47] In the professional theatre, motionless, posed performers were moved around by stage machinery in order to enhance the view of the audience. By the middle of the

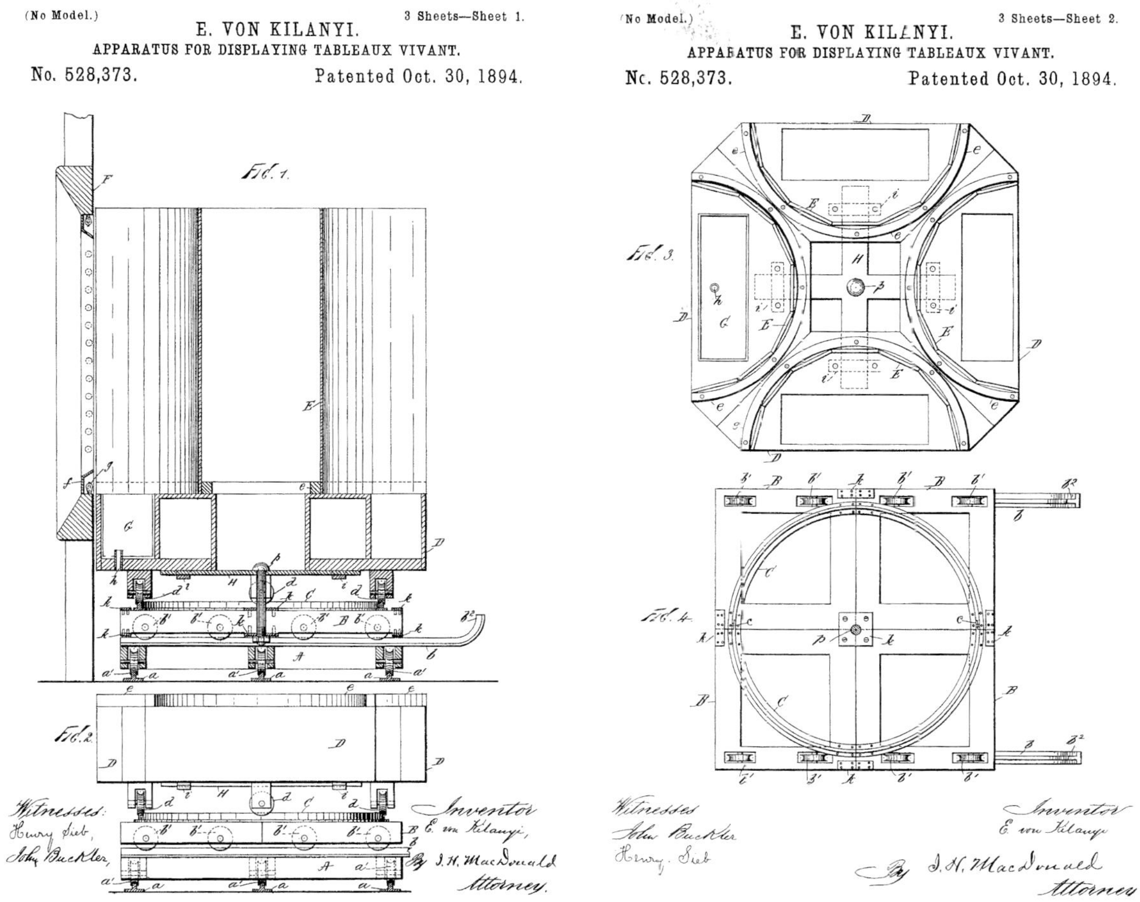

33 'Apparatus for Displaying Tableaux Vivants', 1894. United States Patent and Trademark Office.

century, a circular revolving pedestal was being used to rotate statuary groups such as the Three Graces, enabling theatre audiences to simulate the spatial experience of walking round sculpture in a gallery, as well as offering the optimum visibility of the bodies on display.[48] By the end of the century far more complicated machines were being introduced to transport motionless groups or to organise the transitional intervals between *tableaux*. The Glyptorama was invented in 1894 by Edward von Kilanyi, a major entrepreneur of living pictures. Advertised as 'a moving reproduction of the principal paintings of the great masters of the world', the mechanism was essentially a giant slide-holder or carriage on wheels (plate 33). Divided into four sections in which the *tableaux* were arranged, the scenes could either be positioned in a cube and moved on a circular track or in a straight line and rolled back and forth. The beauty of the Glyptorama was that it removed the need for curtains to disguise the change of poses. As a promotional announcement put it, the Glyptorama 'will show in frames 14 feet high and 22 feet wide living reproductions of some of the largest pictures ever painted . . . As in changes of slide in a stereopticon, one picture will dissolve into another.'[49] Enhanced by the use of electrical lighting and a gilt frame into which each section was carried, the Glyptorama put the magic back into the magic lantern show. It shared the temporal rhythm of the lantern slide show – the alternation of luminous views and dissolves – but it added a further layer of illusion. It used rollers and cranks, painted panoramas, orchestral music, electric lighting and the mechanism of the slide carriage to recreate great art for vaudeville audiences.

Most *tableaux* performances, however, did not benefit from the vast resources invested in the Glyptorama. Amateur displays and cheaper theatrical shows in the first half of the nineteenth century tended to use curtains to disguise the changing *tableaux*.[50] Yet even this apparently simple device left scope for variation and much attention was paid to the mechanism and motion of the curtains, how smoothly or dramatically they could be drawn to reveal the posed figures. Other performers seem to have made the visible transition from one attitude to another part of the virtuosity of the display. Andrew Ducrow was a leading artiste in the early nineteenth-century circus.[51] He was primarily an equestrian performer but also took part in and directed a range of spectacular entertainments, including *tableaux vivants*. For these he invented equestrian *poses plastiques*, in which he rode round the circus ring while striking attitudes of various well-known classical and mythological subjects. After more than a decade of these horse-powered living statues, Ducrow evidently decided to focus exclusively on the poses and to emphasise the artistic values of the performance. The circling horse was abandoned and a new act was publicised in which Ducrow struck his poses on a pedestal in the ring. Without the continuous motion of the horse, the nuances of physical movement in Ducrow's performance of 'animated statues' were made more visible. An account of his act from 1828 vividly conveys the rhythm of animation and stillness in his performance:

> When the curtain draws up, you see a motionless statue on a lofty pedestal in the centre of the stage. This is Ducrow . . . He appeared first as the Hercules Farnese. With the greatest skill and precision he then gradually quitted his attitude from one gradation to another, of display of strength; but at the moment in which he presented a perfect copy of the most celebrated statues of antiquity, he suddenly became fixed as if changed to marble . . . his form is faultless, and he can throw himself into any attitude with the utmost ease and grace. It struck me how greatly our unmeaning dancing might be ennobled; if something like what I have described were introduced; instead of the absurd and vulgar hopping and jumping with which we are now entertained.[52]

As well as the spectacle of physical immobility, *tableaux vivants* introduced a different kind of motion to popular entertainment. Smooth, flowing passages of movement linked the sudden freezing of the body into a living picture or statue, creating a distinctive temporality and rhythm in the performance. Early nineteenth-century *tableaux* were, in essence, reflections on the nature of movement, its diversity, suspension and anticipation, and in this way they looked forward to the playful and spectacular display of movement in the first years of film. These popular early Victorian motion performances used living, breathing bodies to create icons of inert stillness that would suddenly break into movement. The pleasure for audiences lay in their willing participation in the ensuing paradoxes of animation and de-animation. Performers like Ducrow, clothed in white body stockings to simulate the purest marble, suspended their bodies in the silent poses and gestures of high art. They momentarily trapped movement within the contours of a pose and then gradually dissolved back into soft, smooth motion. Statues started into life and living bodies became hard stone. *Tableaux vivants* created a magical, haunted gallery that played across the borders between art and life.

The stillness of the body and its presentation in the recognisable forms of art contributed to the social acceptability of the *tableaux vivants* and set them apart from more kinetic and provocative displays of the body in live entertainment during this period. *Tableaux* producers introduced a range of devices to enhance the pictorial qualities of the posed figures and to reinforce the transcendent, aesthetic values conveyed by the performances. Staging and lighting emphasised the two-dimensionality of the arrangement, which was frequently set within an elaborate, gilt 'picture frame'. This double framing of the *tableau vivant* – contained within a frame, set on the restricted space of the stage – enhanced its status as representation rather than life; it was isolated from the temporality and meanings of the everyday and occupied its own dream world of art and fantasy. The *tableau*, defined by Roland Barthes as 'a pure cut-out segment with clearly defined edges, irreversible and incorruptible', defined the field of vision.[53] The succession of *tableaux* created a fantasy gallery of images that bore a secret life, on the brink of animation. Ducrow's pedestal and Kilanyi's mechanical frames separated the bodies in the living pictures from the bodies in the audience. Frames and pedestals turned people into images and defined the relationship between performer and audience as that of passive object and discerning viewer.

When the figure steps out of the frame, or down from the pedestal, the distinctions between the worlds of the living and of the lifeless are broken down. This is the uncanny moment of haunting. It is not surprising, therefore, that many Victorian and Edwardian supernatural stories on this theme focus on the magical power of the frame, rather than of the painted canvas. In Edith Nesbit's short story 'The Ebony Frame', the narrator, a young journalist, discovers a strange ebony frame in a house that he has recently inherited. Later, he comes across two old portraits in the attic. He becomes infatuated with one of these images, the likeness of a beautiful woman, and discovers that the picture originally belonged in the ebony frame but had been removed. Replacing the portrait in its true frame animates the image. The young man hangs the painting over his mantelpiece and prays, Pygmalion-style, for the figure to 'come down'. As he watches the picture he thinks he sees the face and hands move and when he later returns to it, he discovers that the frame is empty and that the woman from the picture is in the room with him: 'I hardly know how to express it, but at once it seemed not awful, not even unusual, for portraits to become flesh – only most natural, most right.'[54] She then tells him the highly unusual story of her tragic love and of her death, burnt as a witch. Before she died, she gave her soul to the devil in exchange for immortality, within the portrait in its ebony frame. Just as the narrator prepares to surrender his own soul, the house is burnt down, destroying the picture in its frame.

One of the best-known comic examples from this period of the animated portrait leaving its frame and entering the world of the living is the scene of the 'walking ancestors' in Gilbert and Sullivan's *Ruddigore* of 1887. W. S. Gilbert had already drawn on the subject of living pictures in his drama *Pygmalion and Galatea*, which was first performed at the Haymarket Theatre in December 1871.[55] There the transformation was achieved through basic means: a statue was modelled to resemble the actress playing the part of the living Galatea; statue and woman were placed behind curtains, back to back on a turntable and a simple switch was made at the appropriate moment. Compared with the sophisticated *tableaux vivants* being staged in London theatres at this time, the staging of Gilbert's play must have appeared comically makeshift.

By comparison, the scene of the haunted portrait gallery in *Ruddigore* was far more developed and provided the centrepiece of the libretto and its staging.[56] Briefly, the story concerns a young aristocrat who seeks to escape a family curse that each generation of baronets must commit a terrible crime every day. In the scene in the Picture Gallery at Ruddigore Castle, a chorus of ancestral ghosts remind the young baronet of the curse, while he pleads with them for mercy. The scene opens in an ancient picture gallery, whose walls are covered with full-length portraits of the Baronets of Ruddigore from the time of James I. Stage directions show that the lights were darkened and then brought up again to reveal that the figures in the portraits have come to life. It is not entirely clear from the stage directions how this effect was achieved but it seems likely that it involved hinged costume portraits that could be swung aside and replaced by performers (plate 34). 'The pictures step from their frames and march round the stage.'[57] As in 'The Ebony Frame', the key motif is the empty frame and the dramatic gesture of the figures stepping across its protective boundary into the world of the hapless living. The vulnerability of the haunted is comically enacted in *Ruddigore* in the savage assaults made by the ancestral ghosts, which leave their victim writhing in agony. After forcing the young baronet to concede to the terms of the curse, the ghosts step back into their frames and revert to pictures. Although this scene has to be considered in the broader cultural context of a comic opera by Gilbert and Sullivan, its savagery exposes the underlying unease that the haunted gallery continued to suggest. The animated portraits are menacing. The libretto plays on the anticipation of the audience and its familiarity with the trope of living, silent pictures; out of their frames, however, these spectres are unexpectedly violent and dangerous. There remains in this scene and in the supernatural fiction of the period a trace of that animistic fear of the past disturbing the comfortable space of the present, described by Freud in his discussion of the uncanny.

Developments in nineteenth-century stage practices were driven by commercial imperatives. As entertainments became increasingly spectacular, audiences came to

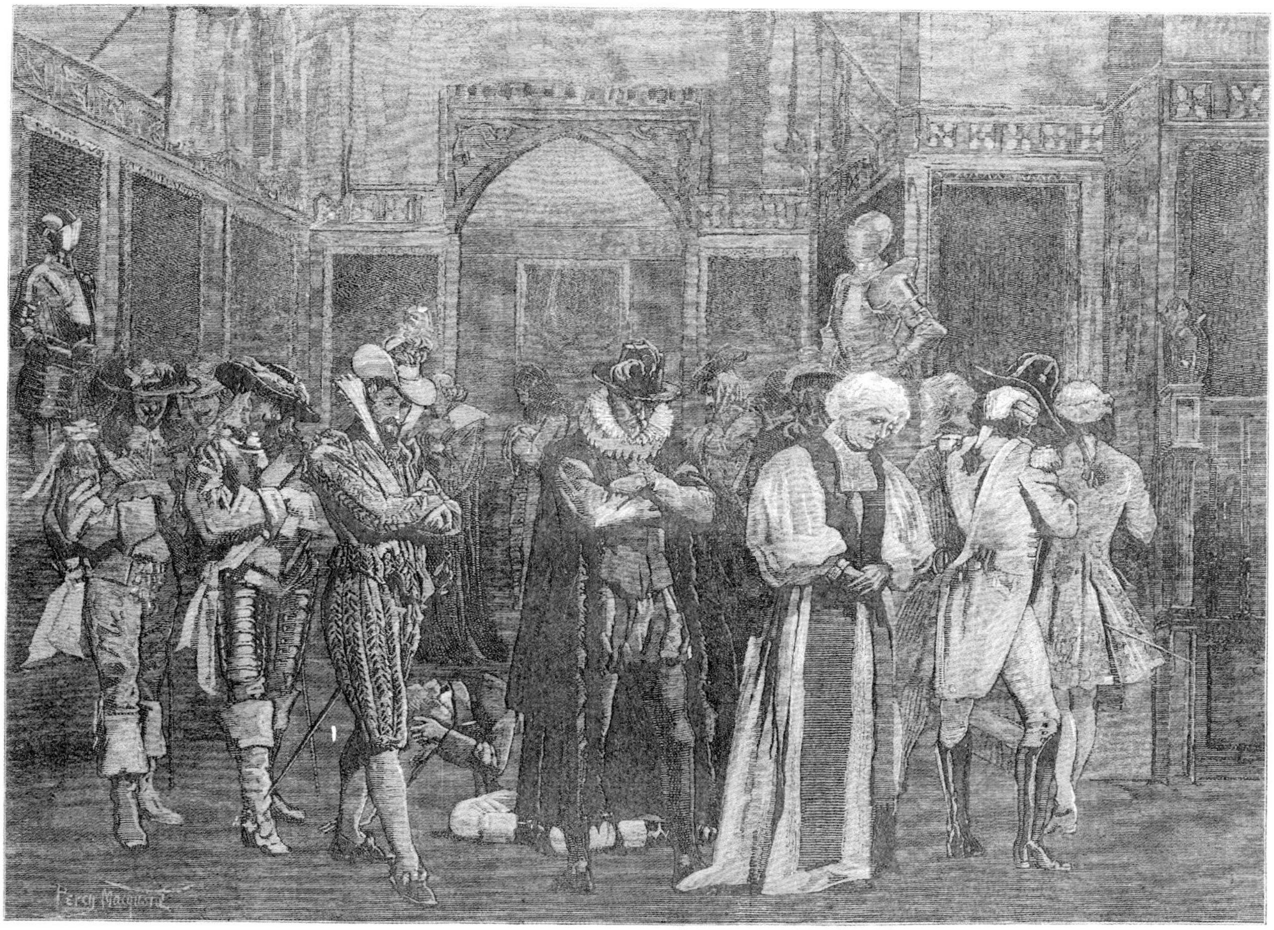

34 'Scene from Gilbert and Sullivan's New Opera, "Ruddygore", at the Savoy Theatre', *Graphic*, 29 January 1887, p. 101.

expect novelty and would quickly tire of familiar routines and effects. Given this economic environment, the continued popularity of *tableaux vivants* throughout the nineteenth century is even more striking. While it is true that producers of 'living pictures' embraced a range of theatrical technologies to upgrade the performances, the basic fascination of *tableaux vivants*, the display of arrested motion and the animation of apparently lifeless forms, essentially remained the same. It is clear that the miscellany of entrepreneurs – the lanternists, fairground showmen and optical instrument-makers – who constituted the first film-makers, understood the power of these metaphors and the long history of media and performance practices that had engaged with the paradoxes of 'living pictures'. Moreover, film-makers seem to have consciously entered into a form of dialogue with these existing media, in which the moving pictures of film were positioned as 'the new kid on the block', surpassing all previous pictorial attempts at creating and suspending life.[58]

The mutoscope series 'The Birth of the Pearl', made by the American Mutoscope and Biograph Company in 1903, is an elaboration of the play on life, art and motion created in the *tableaux vivants* (plate 35).[59] The series was advertised as 'Moving Pictures Taken from Life', and the viewer is invited to turn the crank rapidly to the right in order to witness this modern Venus arise from her oyster shell. The series is presented in the form of a theatrical *tableau vivant*, complete with stage set and costumed assistants who pull aside the curtains to reveal the mythological picture. As the viewer turns the handle, the picture comes to life and the woman rises, thus breaking the pose and turning the motionless image into a moving picture that is itself a mechanical simulation of life. The initial movement of the handle, released by dropping a coin in a slot, begins the temporal sequence of the mutoscope *tableau*. In this case, however, the beginning is repeated, as the first cards in the series reveal a curtained stage. The frame of the eyepiece shields and isolates the gaze of the viewer as he or she watches the animated figure framed firstly by her shell and then by the arch of the stage. Furthermore, the lifelikeness of the movement depends on the speed at which the crank is turned. Too slow and the artifice of the individual photographic cards will be exposed; too fast and the already brief performance will be over even sooner. It is a display guaranteed to leave the viewer wanting more of this hybrid, interactive version of the *tableau vivant*.

The cheapness of the mutoscope and its location in urban kiosks and on seaside piers compromised the artistic pretensions of the *tableau vivant*. If it was difficult to convince critics of the idealised, aesthetic nature of the representations created in theatrical *tableaux*, it was even harder to make this case for mutoscope and film versions of 'living pictures'. Indeed, filmed *tableaux* seemed designed to expose the fallacy of such claims.[60] With the camera usually positioned as if in the audience of a theatrical performance, 'Living Picture' films (in itself something of a tautological concept) seemed to strip the arrangements of any resemblance to artistic prototypes and showed them for what they were – chorus girls in clinging leotards in more or less provocative attitudes.

The original theatrical *tableaux vivants* used human agents to create motionless pictures; film used sequences of photographs to create moving images that simulated life. Both were essentially concerned with the construction and dismantling of lifelike effects and both were equally capable of producing a manner of anxiety about the confusion of the real and the representational, the living and the dead. It is perhaps not surprising, then, that film-makers were drawn to subjects that highlighted these themes and relationships. Charles Urban's *A Modern Galatea* (1904–5) was explicitly marketed in relation to 'the present rage, at the variety theatres, for Living Pictures of statuary and other works of art'.[61] Urban updates the narrative, however, to suit his medium and has the *poseur* constantly changing attitudes, rather than assuming the singular form of the beloved statue. In a similar way, the Warwick Film Company was quick to distribute a film *Pygmalion and Galatea* that twisted the familiar tale, in order to show off the spectacular trick effects of the new medium. As the catalogue described it:

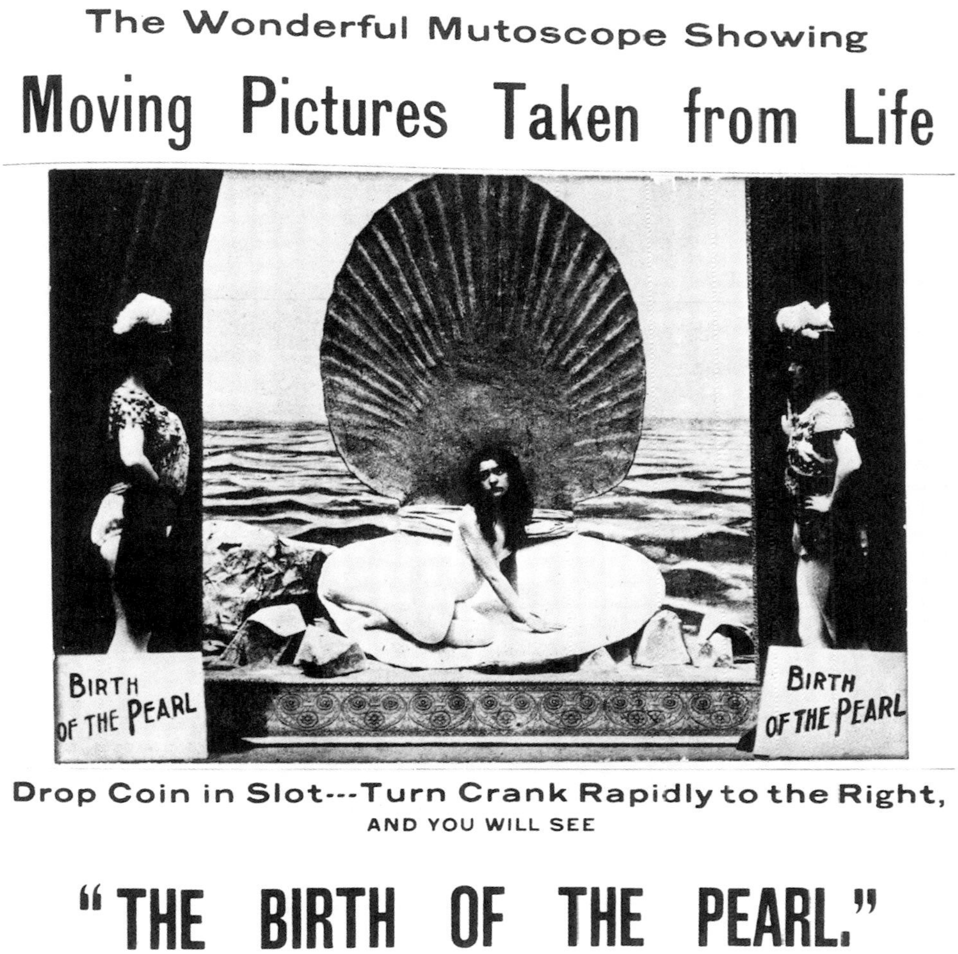

35 'The Wonderful Mutoscope Showing Moving Pictures Taken from Life: "The Birth of the Pearl"', 1903, from Kemp R. Niver, *Biograph Bulletins 1896–1908*, Los Angeles: Locare Research Group, 1971, p. 57.

> Scene – in the studio of Pygmalion, who is noted at work upon the statue of Galatea, who suddenly comes to life as per the old story. Pygmalion is amazed, and in endeavouring to clasp Galatea round the waist he finds that he has in his arms only the lower portion of the lady, while the live bust and head appear on the pedestal. Further startling illusions are enacted in rapid succession. A most interesting subject and full of animation.[62]

It was not enough for film merely to bring the statue to life, it had to be 'full of animation', including the violent dismembering of the woman's body.[63] Film's powers of animation drew on and conspicuously exceeded the effects of existing

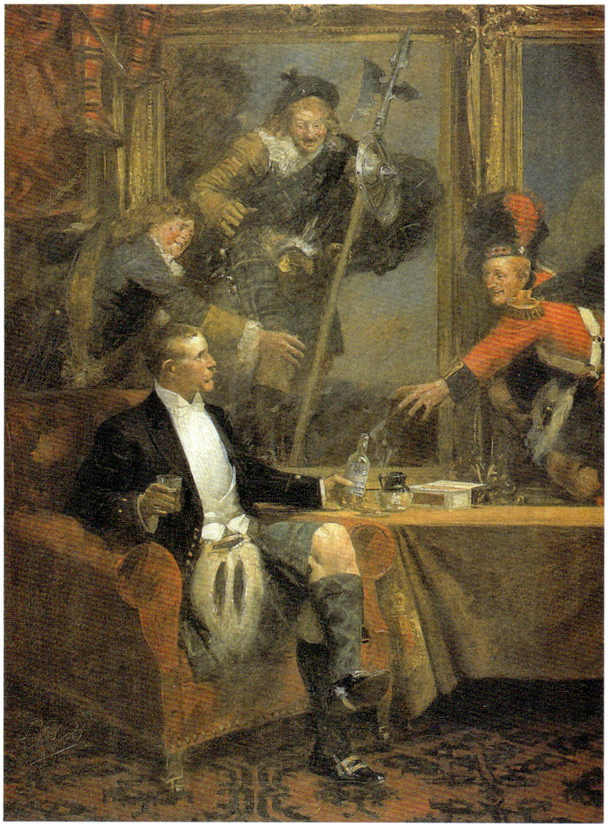

36 Matthew B. Hewerdine, *The Whisky of his Forefathers*, 1894. Oil on canvas, dimensions unknown. John Dewar & Sons Ltd, Glasgow.

visual media and the magic theatre. In 1899, George Albert Smith, a lanternist, astronomer, mesmerist and film-maker based in Hove, on the south coast of England, made the ultimate nineteenth-century version of *The Haunted Picture Gallery*, for the Warwick Trading Company. Where Rupert d'Oyly Carte had used stage props and lighting to produce the ancestral ghosts in *Ruddigore*, Smith's trick film made use of double exposure and all the illusionistic capacities of celluloid and the camera, to create the transparent figures of 'Two pictures (Duchess of Gainsborough and Cavalier) [which] leave their frames and execute a ghastly minuet in the moonlight.'[64]

The picture that comes to life was a theme that, by the end of the nineteenth century, was both thoroughly familiar and still capable of producing arresting and disturbing effects. Living statues and haunted portraits might have been domesticated in the comic operas of Gilbert and Sullivan but they still belonged to the unsettling world of dreams, illusions and even drunken hallucinations. The cultural resonance of the haunted gallery was harnessed to commercial interests in a highly adventurous advertising campaign of the period. In 1894, Dewar's, the Scottish whisky company, commissioned Matthew B. Hewerdine to make a painting that would provide the basis for a major, international advertising campaign.[65] The painting, *The Whisky of his Forefathers* (plate 36), shows a laird, drinking whisky in his ancestral home while his 'forefathers' climb out of their portraits in their longing to try the drink. This image works because of the familiarity of the haunted picture theme. Ruddy-faced, corporeal spirits lean across the gilt frames of their portraits and reach out for the bottle of whisky; in the top left corner, a pair of tartan-clad legs suggests that a second tier of ghostly figures is making its way down to the bottle. Up to this point, the campaign remains firmly within the conventions of late Victorian advertising inspired by fine art. With the appearance of film, however, an advertisement like this was no longer innovative and Dewar's went on to use the concept for one of the earliest film advertisements. There are two versions of the advertising film, the first made by Edison in 1898 and a later version made by the British Mutoscope and Biograph Company in

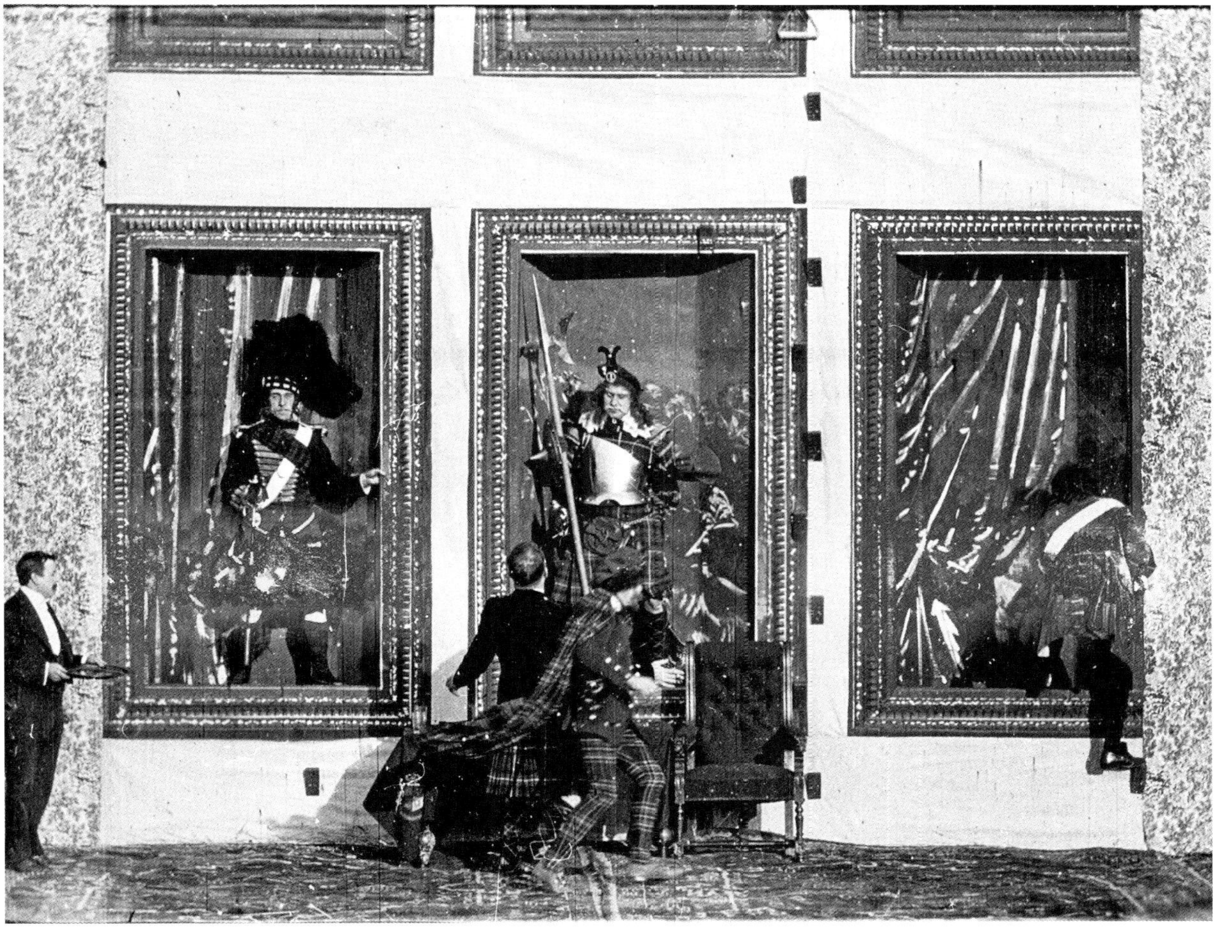

37 *The Spirit of his Forefathers*, *c.*1900. British Mutoscope and Biograph Company. Frame enlargement, Nederlands Filmmuseum.

1900.[66] In the film the advertisement sticks closely to the treatment in the still image but adds a crucial temporal dimension to the narrative. The laird is first shown being served a drink and it is only after this that the figures in the portraits begin to come alive (plate 37). Two side portraits climb across their frames to the centre, then a figure climbs down from an upper tier of portraits. Against a background of empty frames, the man shakes hands with his ancestors and they share a drink together. The figures then climb back into their frames and resume their poses. The extension of the animated portrait theme from a single, painted image, into the duration of the moving images of film, gives it a greater impact and humour. Moreover, the projected image was big and Edison's version was projected onto the side of the Pepper Building in New York's Times Square. Film, advertising and ghostly, animated paintings come together in perfect synergy in the service of late Victorian commodification.

The enduring fascination of the trope of the haunted picture gallery lies, in part, in its mutability and adaptation to new forms of visual media. Successive technologies demonstrated their magical properties through their power to animate the dead image. To this extent, it is an ongoing history, as the digital effects of haunted portraits in films of *Harry Potter* (2001–4) and *The Haunted Mansion* (2003) demonstrate.[67]

magic, art, technology

Magic theatre was a laboratory for many of the themes of animation and transformation that were played out in the visual culture of Victorian and Edwardian Britain. Performances of magic produced the supreme modern acts of metamorphosis, exploiting audience expectation and confounding perception in their displays of appearance and disappearance and of animation and annihilation. The major illusions of the Victorian theatre often exploited the oscillation between extreme physical states – levitating heavy objects, fragmenting ideal bodies, bringing inert matter to life and discovering death in apparently living forms. The magicians themselves were scientific and objective about their art and embraced any form of modern technology that would enhance their acts or create new illusions. In nineteenth-century magic, art and technology were brought together in contemporary performances that continued to provide the subjects for visual media well into the twentieth century.

By the end of the nineteenth century spiritualism, which had first appeared in Europe and America in the 1840s, had become a pervasive and potent force at all levels of society and culture.[68] Operating across a wide range of activities and motives, from the shabbiest hoax mediums and table-rappers, to serious scientific investigations of psychic phenomena, spiritualism was a significant material presence in the late Victorian and Edwardian periods. The Spiritualist movement – including mesmerism, spirit images, séances and levitation – was the bizarre progeny of Victorian modernity and materialism and the hubristic conviction that nothing was beyond the reach and control of the great imperial nations of the west. While many were willing to believe that death was no longer final and that the barrier between the living and the dead could be manipulated at will, others were happy to draw on the novel effects of photography, electricity and engineering to produce supernatural visions to satisfy this longing to animate the dead.

The central tenet of spiritualism, to put the living in touch with the dead, along with its reliance on visual manifestations of spirit activity, made the movement a key participant in the cultural expression of animation and visibility that generated much pictorial, literary and theatrical production in this period. In the same way that statues came to life and portraits were haunted by ancestral spectres in novels and plays, so spiritualism played with motion and stillness, life and death, in its séance performances and spirit photographs. Mediums would commonly move through a sequence of physical collapse and animated spirit possession; the presence of ghostly loved ones was often demonstrated by shadowy faces and figures in portrait photography or through ectoplasmic emanations from the bodies of spiritualist mediums.

By the end of the nineteenth century Victorian society could be divided into the believers and the non-believers; those who supported and those who wished to expose the Spiritualist movement. Among the groups of detractors were the illusionists and professional theatrical magicians, who sought to distance their own brand of mechanical skills and technical effects from the fraudulent claims and swindles of bogus mediums and spiritualists. This desire to put as much ground as possible between honest 'illusion' and spiritual trickery resulted in magicians of this period aligning themselves with science, with the new psychology and electrical engineering, as opposed to the supernatural forces associated with spiritualism. Magic might be an art of illusion but most of its great nineteenth-century practitioners were keen to differentiate the physical and material sources of their performances from the psychic origins of the spirit manifestations and séances.[69]

It was in the light of this conception of modern magic that a number of books were published in the last years of the century, explaining and illustrating the mechanics of some of the most famous theatrical illusions.[70] In most cases, the spectacular effects of appearance and disappearance and other forms of physical transformation were the result of the skilful manipulation of optical illusions that exploited the physiology of the eye to create magic entertainment. For Albert Hopkins, author of an 1897 compendium of stage magic, significantly sub-titled 'Stage Illusions and Scientific Diversions', modern magic was produced through the union of 'optics, mechanics, sound and electricity'.[71] This exposure of stage illusion was not simply a matter of demystification, it was an attempt to enhance the status and authority of the modern magician and to distance them from what was seen by many in the profession as the mumbo-jumbo of spiritualism.

The gulf between stage magic and spiritualism was asserted even more emphatically by the historian of magic Arprey Vere, in his 1879 study of the illusions of the world-renowned magicians Maskelyne and Cooke. Vere used the phrase 'mechanical magic' to describe the modern 'art of deceiving on the stage in a legitimate manner'; this he contrasted to the spiritualists 'who pander to the credulity, bigotry and fanaticism of the imbecile'.[72] Modern magic was the world of honest legerdemain. It was also kinematic, in the sense that its effects were achieved primarily through the laws of mechanical motion. The dexterity and imagination of 'the modern wizard' produced wonder and amazement but made no claims to supernatural origins.[73] Stage illusions might play with the states of life and death but, as another author writing in 1896 confirmed, these were created solely through the artful management of 'electricity, acoustics and hydraulics'.[74]

If magic was, at one level, merely a form of technology, yet it could also aspire to greatness. At its most basic, stage magic might simply be a matter of concealed mechanisms and sleight of hand; in its most advanced forms, it was an art. One of the great exponents of the 'art in magic' was the legendary British magician John Nevil Maskelyne.[75] He had first attracted public attention in the 1860s when he

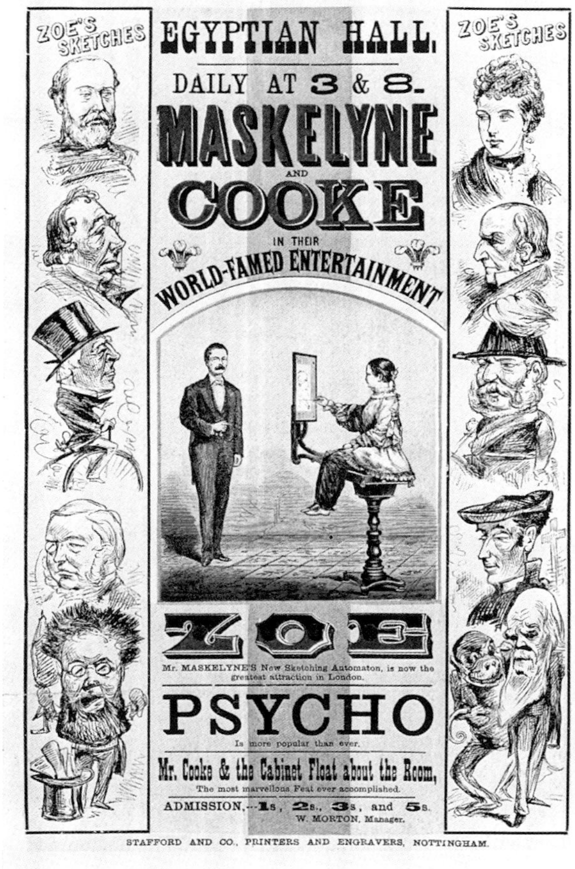

38 'Zoe Showcard', from George A. Jenness, *Maskelyne and Cooke: Egyptian Hall, London, 1873–1904*, Enfield: George A. Jenness, 1967, p. 44.

had exposed as frauds the popular American spiritualist mediums the Davenport Brothers. With his partner, George A. Cooke, he opened his own magic theatre at the Egyptian Hall in London in 1873, where he developed a number of highly influential stage illusions. When Cooke died in 1904, Maskelyne began a new partnership with David Devant, an outstanding magician who had established his reputation with Maskelyne and Cooke at the Egyptian Hall. In 1911, Maskelyne and Devant published *Our Magic*, a textbook of their cumulative experience of the theory and practice of magic. It is also the definitive statement of the artistic claims of great magic. Through an extended comparison of painting and magic, they identify three phases or levels of practice: False Art/Magic – which is simply an imitation of the mediocre work of others; Normal Art/Magic – which imitates things that exist in Nature but which creates nothing original; and High Art/Magic – which is an original conception and the highest expression of the imagination. 'As in painting so also in magic. To produce a magical effect . . . is a work of high art.'[76]

The language and values embedded in the concept of 'High Art in Magic' are straight out of Reynolds's *Discourses* and subsequent nineteenth-century academic art theory. To imitate in painting and in magic is to be relegated to the position of an inferior mechanical craft, performed by a tradesperson. The artist magician is one who 'originates and executes truly artistic conceptions' and who has the power to create timeless works of art.[77] True masterpieces of magic display artistic originality and technical perfection. Maskelyne and Devant draw on the analogy between magic and painting throughout the book; it is central to their definition of the status of the best magic creations and it also provides the terms for their conception of the magic stage. Describing the optimum composition of the stage for an illusion, they advise: '*Let every accessory and incidental detail be kept well "within the picture" and in harmony with the general impression which is intended to be conveyed*.'[78] This basic rule of magic illusion imagines the stage as a framed picture in which, according to prevailing academic conventions, all details are subordinated to the

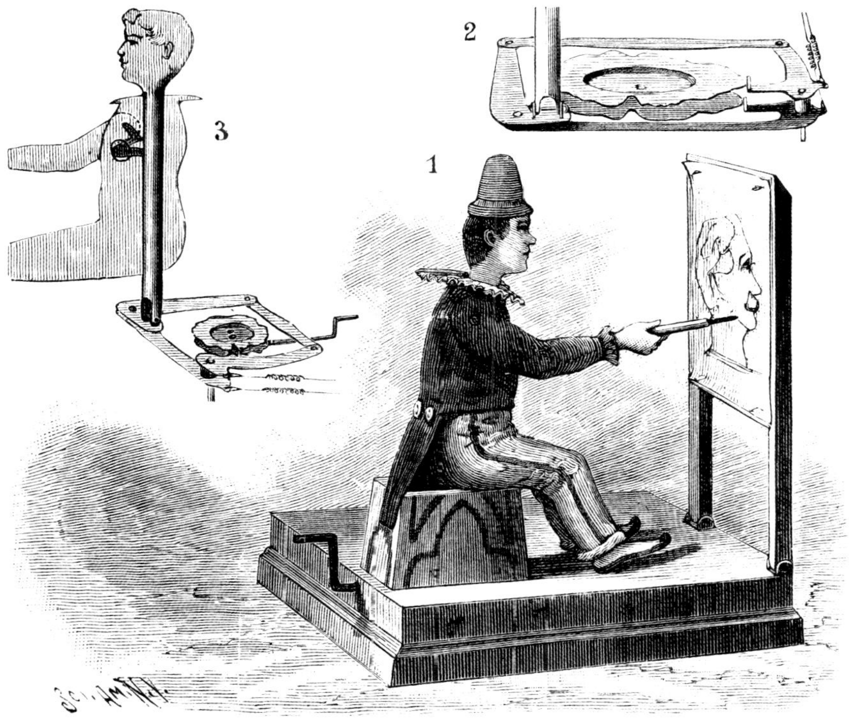

39 'The Toy Artist', from Albert A. Hopkins, *Magic: Stage Illusions and Scientific Diversions including Trick Photography*, London: Sampson, Low, Marston and Co. Ltd, 1897, p. 376.

creation of a general harmonious whole. Magic and art are utterly imbricated at this point, as pictorial values determine the visual arrangement of the magic stage.

Art, magic and technology overlapped continuously in this period. The shadow of the artist and the spectre of artistic creativity haunted the world of modern magic and illusion, as they went on to haunt the conceptions of early cinema. Magic drew on all its technological resources both to fashion itself in the likeness of art and to demonstrate its illusionistic powers.

The ambiguous relations of magic to art were most clearly revealed in the creation of automata, mechanical figures that assumed the persona of an artist and were able to sketch portraits of famous people in front of theatre audiences. Zoe, a life-size 'sketching automaton' first appeared at Maskelyne and Cooke's Egyptian Hall in 1877 (plate 38).[79] Seated on a stool, in front of a frame, she would produce sketch after sketch of contemporary political figures and celebrities, while 'visitors from all parts of the Globe'[80] marvelled at the technological ingenuity that had transformed artistic creativity into mechanical motion. After the performance, the audience could buy Zoe's sketches in the foyer, along with souvenir photographs of Zoe herself. Through its liberal embrace of scientific invention, magic reduced art to a series of wheels, shafts and levers (plate 39). Writing in 1897, Albert Hopkins described the 'Toy Artist' as 'one of the most original and ingenious things of its kind'.[81] In the accompanying illustration, the mechanical toy is shown in a kind of clown's outfit, seated at an easel, while details reveal the workings of the mechanism that moves the artist's pencil across the paper. The foremost magicians of the late nineteenth century, such as Maskelyne and Cooke, envied art and sought its cultural and creative status; but they also mocked its pretensions and used their skills to reduce artistic creativity to a theatrical trick and magical illusion. For popular media, such as magic theatre and early film, art was the gold standard of official culture and represented the apogee of individualised creativity; so they returned to art again and again as the subject for their own productions, where they played with its values and transformed its images. If the artist was a creative genius, then magic would turn the artist into a mechanical toy; if the work of art was just so many pencil or brushmarks on paper and canvas, then magicians and film-makers would bring those inanimate images to life. They would create their own haunted galleries on the stages and screens of the popular theatres and music halls.

Magic pictures proliferated in the late Victorian theatre. Optical tricks such as the 'Tavern of the Dead', which was exhibited in Paris and New York, used the picture gallery as the setting for ghost illusions.[82] The visitor entered a chamber hung with black and with a number of figure paintings on the walls. Seen by the reflected light of the room, the pictures appeared perfectly normal but when lit from behind, the figures were transformed into ghostly skeletons. The picture frame enclosed a fantasy space of transformation in magic theatre. Illusions, or magical effects, could be concentrated within the frame. It marked the threshold between the ordinary, mortal world and its magical, ghostly counterpart. It directed the rapt spectator's gaze and was the focus for dramatic narrative and theatrical spectacle.

In September 1893 programmes for the Egyptian Hall advertised a spectacular new magical illusion, devised by David Devant and called 'The Artist's Dream' (plate 40).[83] Like many of the major illusions of this period, the performance was not simply a matter of the execution of the trick itself but included a fairly extended narrative that provided the dramatic setting for the magic act.[84] The central effect was that of a picture that comes to life. An artist is working on a life-size portrait of his dead wife. Overcome with tiredness, he covers the picture with a cloth and falls asleep on a nearby chair. At this point the female figure of the Spirit of Mercy mysteriously appears at the back of the stage. She approaches the picture and removes the cloth to reveal that the painted figure is alive. That figure then steps out of the frame and embraces her husband, before returning to the frame, disappearing behind the curtain and reverting to an image. Her husband rushes to the picture, tears it down from the easel and then moves towards the Spirit of Mercy who also disappears. The secret of the illusion was in the frame. Although the easel looked ordinary enough, it had a hidden platform where the living woman remained until her appearance. Through a complicated sequence of pulleys, a rotating drum and rollers, the painted portrait could be substituted for an empty painted background. Then the woman could swing herself into position, in front of the backdrop, ready to make her entrance as the living picture.[85] The appearance of the Spirit of Mercy was managed more simply through the removal of a series of gauze screens that gave the impression of the figure's gradual materialisation.

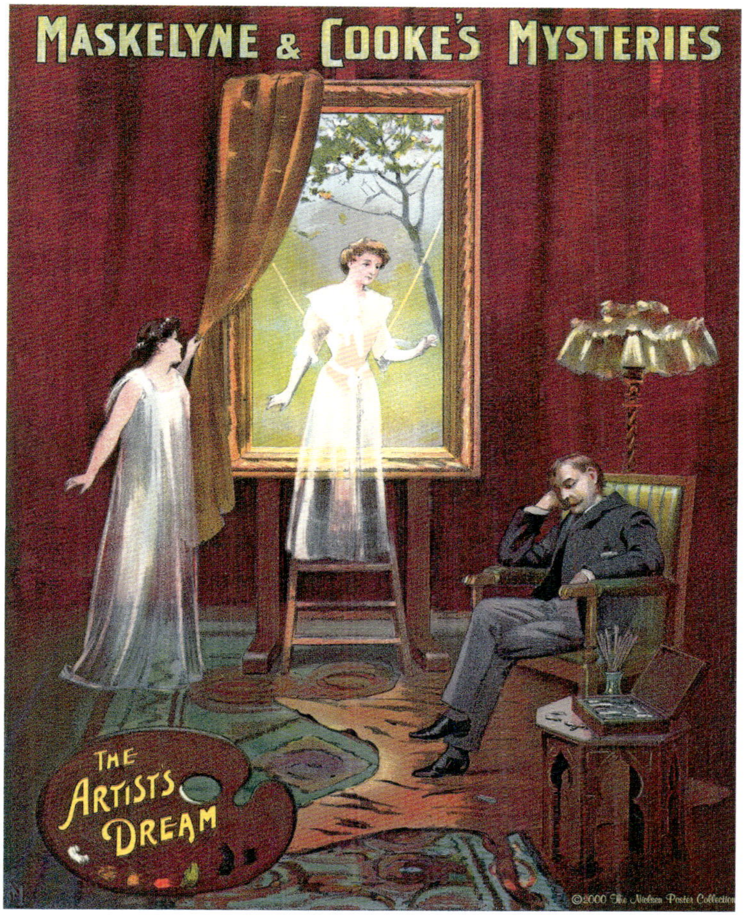

40 'Maskelyne and Cooke's Mysteries: The Artist's Dream', n.d. The Nielsen Poster Collection.

Devant 'sold' the idea of 'The Artist's Dream' to Maskelyne and Cooke with the slogan 'The Picture Comes to Life' and it became one of his most successful and enduring illusions, with an initial run of well over two years and regular revivals, right up to his final tour in 1919. With the renewed interest in spiritualism generated by the First World War, it is possible that audiences for those last performances saw in 'The Artist's Dream' a new message of hope embodied in the idea of the picture of the dead relative that is brought to life. In the 1890s, however, theatre audiences were not attracted by supernatural explanations of magic; they wanted to be impressed and entertained but not terrified.[86] They were happy to surrender themselves to the thrills of stage technology and deceptive sleights of hand that made 'The Artist's Dream' an effective piece of magical drama. It is not surprising, therefore, that an early advertising poster shows both the transparent, ghostly figure of the dead wife and the robust wires that lowered the performer's body into place.

The poster exemplifies the hybridity of magic theatre in the late nineteenth century. It was a period of promiscuous cross-fertilisation between popular forms and media; programmes at Georges Méliès's Théâtre Robert-Houdin in Paris, or at the Egyptian Hall in London, were a daily *mêlée* of conjuring tricks, fantasy illusions, automata and, by the late 1890s, film projections. In April 1896 Méliès started showing moving pictures at his theatre and they were introduced by David Devant to the Egyptian Hall the following year. There is a strong sense of historical and cultural continuity, then, between the ideas originated in the Victorian magic theatre and the conceptions of the early film-makers.[87] In some cases, such as that of Méliès, magician and film-maker were the same person; more generally, however, there was a powerful synergy of magic, art and technology in this period. Art had a significant presence in the lives and work of many of these pioneers: David Devant claimed that his father had been an artist and was the inspiration for 'The Artist's Dream' and Méliès drew incessantly, throughout his career, sketching the settings, figures and costumes that would appear in his films. Art was the base matter of this cultural discourse, the stuff that could be changed by technology into the precious forms of life. The conceptual bond that brought these elements together was the theme of metamorphosis – the possibility of visual transformation, of the transmutation of inanimate objects into living flesh. To a degree, this had always been the ambition of representational art, but each new medium took up the challenge and tried to surpass its rivals in the power to create the illusion of life.

the enchanted painting

The number of early films that take as their subject the enchanted painting is striking indeed. Makers of trick or transformation films in the late 1890s and early 1900s used all the available techniques of filmed illusion, such as stop-motion effects, multiple exposure and dissolves, to create spectacular visions of pictures that come to life and figures that metamorphose, appear and disappear, in the blink of an eye. More often than not in these films, the animated figure is a source of pandemonium who wrecks the world of the bemused artist and ridicules their attempts at artistic creativity. In the end, the demonic magician is usually triumphant and the artist is abandoned to his unrequited desire and inadequate creative powers.

Thomas Edison's *An Artist's Dream* (1900; plate 41) opens in an artist's studio, with the artist asleep in a chair. There is a framed picture on the wall behind him and a painting on an easel to the left. However, most of the studio space is taken up by two nearly full-length female figures in elaborately decorated frames. A Mephisto figure appears and gestures to the pictures to come to life; they step out of their frames and begin to inspect their bodies admiringly. At this point, Mephisto wakes the artist and disappears. The dopey artist sees the living picture on his right-hand side and goes over to her, kissing her hand and lifting her off the floor, but as he releases her from his embrace, she disappears. As he grasps the thin air, he

41 *(facing page top)* Thomas A. Edison, *An Artist's Dream*, 1900. Frame stills, courtesy of Library of Congress, Motion Picture, Broadcasting and Recorded Sound Division.

42 *(facing page bottom)* Thomas A. Edison, *The Artist's Dilemma*, 1901. Frame stills, courtesy Library of Congress, Motion Picture, Broadcasting and Recorded Sound Division.

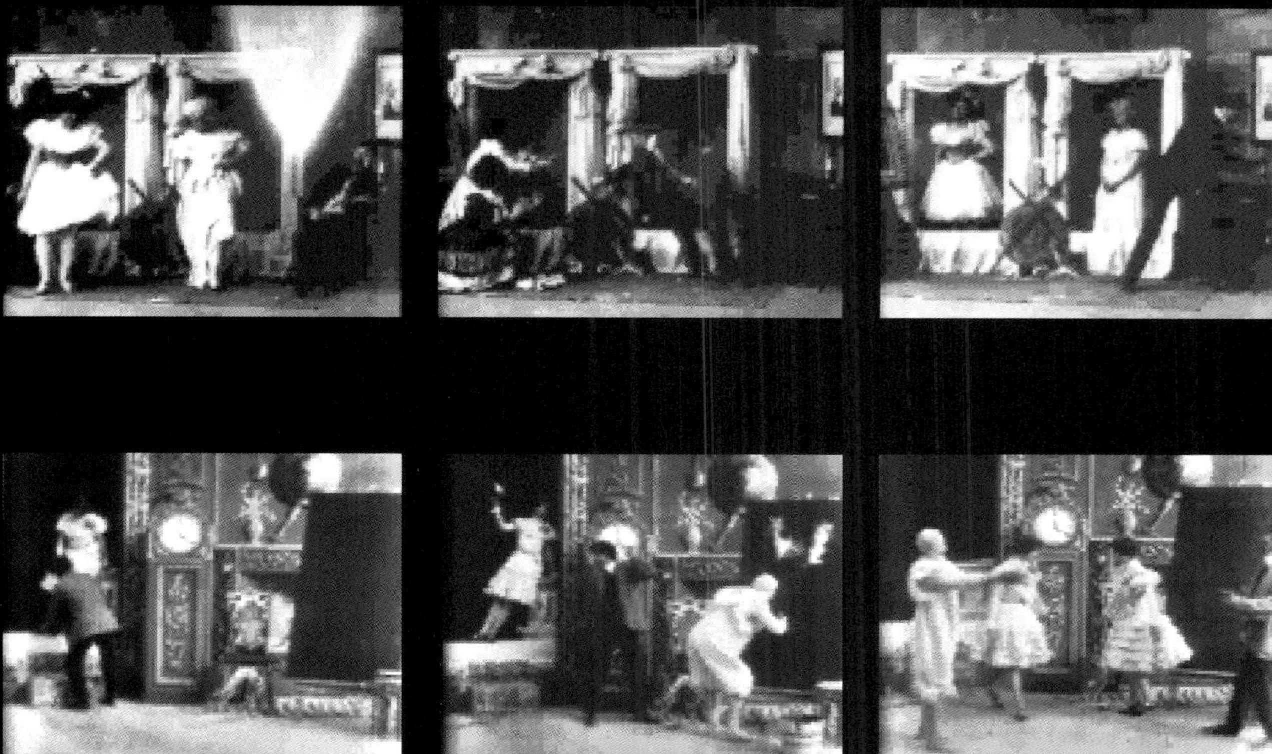

turns and notices the second animated painting; moving over to her, he goes through the same courtship ritual until she also disappears from his clumsy grasp. Meanwhile, two more women, dressed in elaborate peasant costumes, appear in the studio; they fling themselves at the artist who, on this occasion, pushes them off and is about to attack them with a sword when they disappear, to be replaced by the original figure of Mephisto. The artist falls to his knees, begging for forgiveness. Mephisto makes a sweeping gesture and the artist is suddenly back, sleeping in his chair. Another magical sign and the empty frames are filled once again with the two, still, female figures. Mephisto awakens the artist, leaps into the air and disappears. The film ends with the puzzled artist, looking at the framed pictures and having a stiff drink.

This is a short but action-packed film. Rough comedy and physical transformations take place at a fast pace and the viewer's attention is drawn rapidly from one filmic trick to another. It has an entirely different rhythm and feel from the romantic mystery of David Devant's 'The Artist's Dream'. Although film continued the themes and drew on the trap-door special effects of magic theatre, the world of the haunted studio that it created was altogether more unruly and dangerous than its live counterpart.

The fascination with the female body and the aggressive sexuality of the animated figures are also made explicit. As the two female figures step out from their frames in Edison's film, they scrutinise their bodies before embarking on their bizarre love-making with the hapless artist. In many transformation films of this period, the sexualised female body provides the matter through which the power of the film magic is displayed. Women's bodies are fragmented and annihilated and their flesh turned to bone. In the American Mutoscope and Biograph Company's *The Artist's Dream* (1899; plate 43), a beautiful, fleshy life model in a leotard is transformed into a skeleton, while an artist dozes at his easel.

In her account of magic films produced by Méliès, Pathé, Edison and others, between 1896 and 1912, Lucy Fischer identifies a particular cinematic vision of women. She traces the relationship of the male magician and his female subject back to performers in the magic theatre and describes it as a form of sexual role-playing that articulates a specific, patriarchal discourse. The female subjects in the films are, she argues, often the product of dreamlike fantasies and have no existence independent of the male magician. All the women are decorative and strangely de-corporealised, as they are made repeatedly to materialise and dematerialise through the duration of the film.[88] Fischer sees this regime of images as expressive of both male power and male anxieties. She likens the perversity of female action in magic films to a kind of treacherous enchantment associated with witchcraft and to a superstitious fear of female magic and carnality. Fischer's influential essay introduces an invaluable gender dimension to the understanding of early transformation films; there is evidence to suggest, however, that the production of gender and sexual identities is more polyvalent than her argument might at first imply. The male body is also frequently the object of a variety of corporeal metamorphoses and the conjured women often exert a powerful, disruptive force in the worlds

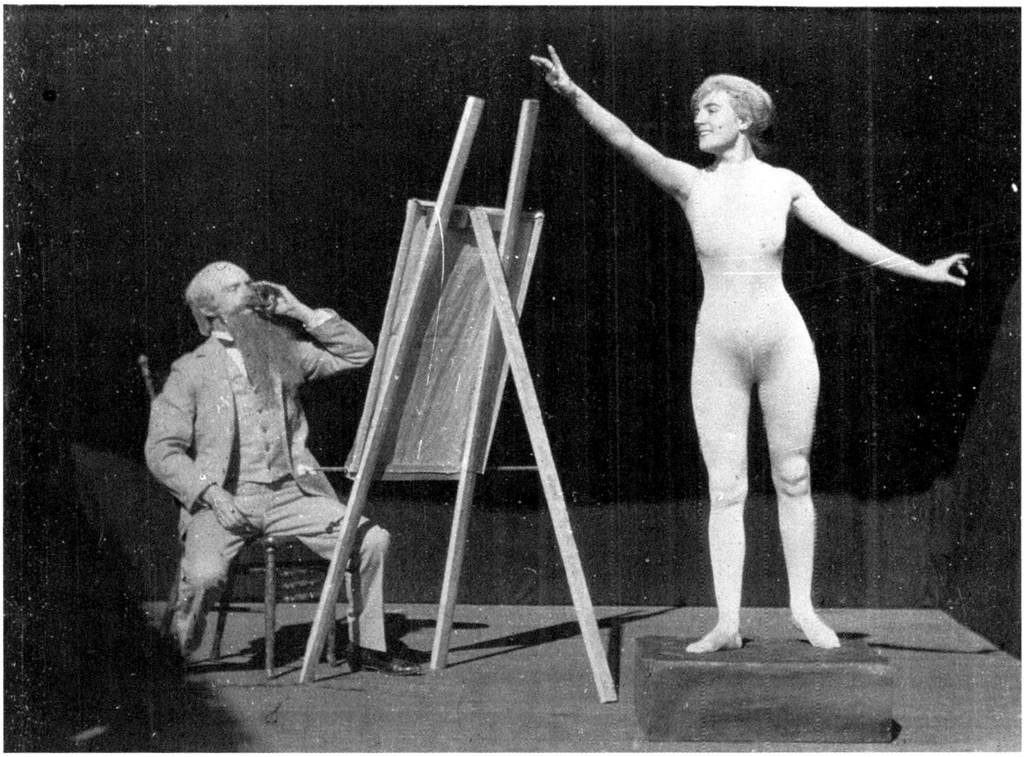

43 *The Artist's Dream*, 1899. Frame enlargement, Nederlands Filmmuseum.

to which they are introduced. Compared with the docile, blushing being created from Pygmalion's statue, the animated women in trick films are often unpredictable, physically assertive and threaten to break free of the magical charms that have produced them.

Artists in these films are a pretty sorry bunch. Either sleeping or in a state of waking amazement, they are rarely at work and are always outdone by the film's magic effects or their demonic personification. It can often seem, in enchanted painting films, that their central purpose is to undermine the long-established mythology of artistic creativity. Trick effects are used to flaunt the ease with which film can simulate the making and unmaking of art and impart life to the lifeless image. In the face of this technical ease, the artists in these films are often reduced to a state of helpless rage, or resigned sleep. Robert Paul's *The Devil in the Studio* has the artist subjected to a series of humiliating transformations when Mephisto materialises in his studio from a tube of paint. Paul's catalogue of 1900–01 describes the ensuing play with visual images:

> The painter is astonished to see work done without effort, and shakes his head dubiously at his own portrait filling the canvas, when Mephisto makes a second pass from model to easel and vanishes. The canvas is once more blank, and, as

> the artist stands between the two, he perceives, to his great amazement, that the model is slowly fading from her platform, and at the same time is gradually appearing on the canvas like a developing photograph. When the model is clearly defined, the artist, in a transport of delight at the production of a painting in a few minutes, rushes from the studio and quickly returns with a dealer . . . Just as they turn to look at the picture, it immediately changes to a comic caricature making fun of them.[89]

Driven wild with frustration at the demon's tricks, the artist finally wrecks his own canvas and smashes up the studio. The hundred feet of Paul's film are a catalogue of pictorial media that dissolve and mutate into each other. It begins with the artist, accompanied by a model, preparing his palette for the creation of a 'masterpiece'. The idea of the painting is then substituted by a sequence of more automatic and instantaneous forms of picture-making, such as photography and rapid caricature. In the face of each of these transformations the artist is a helpless victim and even the art dealer turns out to be Mephisto. As his creative powers are progressively stripped away, the artist can do nothing but destroy his own means of picture making.

Film played with the time of painting. If masterpieces took a long time to create, then magic films could make them in an instant; and when the painting was finally complete, film would transform the still image into a living human being.[90] Edison's 1901 film *The Artist's Dilemma* is a fascinating summation of these themes (plate 42). The film begins with the familiar scene of the artist asleep in his studio. As he sleeps, the door of a carved grandfather clock opens and out steps a female figure in a theatrical dancer's costume. She wakes the artist who takes her to a raised platform and indicates that he wishes to paint her portrait. Placing her in a conventional pose, reclining against a pedestal and holding a bouquet of flowers (indeed, the very conventionality of the pose signifies the painterly status of the proposed image), he takes up his palette, brushes and mahlstick. As he begins work on his canvas another figure emerges from the clock; half-clown, half-demon, this mysterious figure is the *genius machinae*, or the spirit of film, who will unravel all the artist's attempts to paint a likeness of the model. The clown shows his admiration for the model and begins to disrupt the artist's work, suggesting that he can do better. Rejecting the painter's palette and brushes, he reaches into the clock and grabs a large bucket of 'paint' and a huge paintbrush. With a few strokes he covers the canvas and, to the distress and amazement of the artist, a perfect likeness of the model is produced. As film historian Mary Ann Doane has shown, this section of the film was created by reverse motion, so that a sequence in which the demon actually painted a rough coat of black paint over a finished portrait of the model was run backwards to look as though a few strokes had produced the finished picture.[91] The demon clown then goes over to the canvas, holds out his hand and the image comes to life and steps out of the picture. She is joined by the model and together they dance a cancan, before kicking the artist and the demon to the floor. The men pick themselves up, the two women merge into one and the demon disappears into the remaining female figure. Delighted to be left with his beautiful model, the artist embraces her and she turns back into the demon. The demon strikes the artist, jumps into the air and disappears; the artist is left alone again, with his blank canvas.

This exhilarating film is like a short discourse on the nature of visual representation in the age of film. It is significant for this reading that both the model and the demon emerge from a clock, introducing the theme of time and representation that runs throughout the piece. Through the figure of the demon clown, film usurps all the illusionistic functions of art. It can make and unmake painting in a moment and it can animate the lifeless image. The artist is the dupe, turned upon by both his model and his living image. There can be no doting Galatea in this world, just the agonising blankness of the empty canvas.

When pictures come to life they do not become part of the ordinary, everyday world but enter a kind of dream time, haunted by visions and mischief-makers. This is the space created by magic films, with their relentless mockery of still images and traditional media. In order to demonstrate its own mastery, however, film had to keep returning to the still image – the basic component of its own modern life – and show its power to transform stasis into motion. That this could, at times, be a self-conscious process, is suggested in a 1905 Pathé film, *A Wonderful Album*. The film opens with a man in eighteenth-century costume, seated at a table in a formal garden. A visitor enters, carrying an album that he props up against a bench and 'magics' larger and larger, until it has become life size. The man opens the giant book to the first page, which bears the words 'Album Pathé Frères'. He tears out a page, crumples it up and the ball of paper turns into a 'page boy'. On the next page, there is an image of an odalisque; the album-bearer tears it out, crumples it up and it is transformed into a real woman. The following pages depict a series of generic portrait types: a seventeenth-century courtier, a Spanish dancer, an eighteenth-century aristocrat. Each in turn is torn from the album and turned into a living, moving person. At last, the living pictures begin to surround the visitor but he corrals them together and they disappear, leaving only their costumes. The repeated gesture of tearing the page from the album and discarding it becomes a metaphor for film's dismissive, but anxious, relationship to art. In fact, the entire filmic trope of the enchanted painting must be seen as a founding myth of the new medium and a potent visual expression of its own existence through the animation of still images to create living pictures.

The importance of early film's visible display of its own means of image production and its simultaneous dependence on and transcendence of older forms of still media is demonstrated by a sub-group within the genre of animated painting films, depicting the figure of the artist, or the artist's hand, in the act of creating a picture.[92] In nearly every case, trick effects are used to transform the nature and condition of the resulting image. For example, the process of drawing is accelerated by deliberately changing the speed at which the camera is cranked. Drawings are transformed into people by using stop-motion substitution. Cartoon portraits become animated and interact with a series of drawn and real objects. The origins of this type of trick film can be traced, in part, to the music-hall entertainment called 'lightning sketches', in which a cartoonist displayed their technical dexterity by rapidly executing a series of drawings and changing their subject matter with a few deft lines and alterations. Trick films went far beyond the illusions of the lightning sketcher, however. They took off from where the music-hall performance necessarily concluded, giving the artist the magical power of animation. In *The Enchanted Drawing*, an Edison film made in 1900, a cartoonist – the artist-conjurer J. Stuart Blackton – is shown in front of a large, blank sheet of paper on an easel.[93] He rapidly sketches the comic portrait of a man. Then he draws a bottle of wine and a glass; he reaches towards them and as he removes them from the sheet of paper they become real in his hands (plate 44). The artist pours himself a drink and the expression on the watching cartoon face changes to a frown. When the artist pours another drink and offers it to the cartoon, the face smiles happily. The rest of the short film continues with this play on reality and representation, as the cartoon face reacts to the addition of hats and a cigar. This is much more than a filmic record of a vaudeville act or a celebration of the art of the caricaturist; it is a display of film's ability to move between documentary and magic, between the real world and the world of images.

Comedy cartoons 'By the Hand of the Artist' were among the most successful trick films in Charles Urban's lists and became an ongoing series in the early 1900s. Advertising his latest addition to the series in 1904, the catalogue described the film as the most 'amazing and amusing' magic film ever made. It continued:

> Illusion follows illusion, mystery succeeds mystery in this most attractive subject, until the spectators are lost in amazement and delight.
>
> The 'Hand of the Artist' draws outline faces in chalk upon a blackboard. The outlines fill and assume living form and muscular movement. They eat, drink, smoke, express pleasure and satisfaction, without leaving the blackboard, after which the images are removed by an ordinary duster, or mysteriously disappear, feature by feature.[94]

The film offers a cornucopia of film illusions, above and beyond simple animated cartoons. A cut-out paper clown becomes a real figure and performs tricks in a circus ring drawn on the blackboard; smoke issues from the mouth of a Pierrot and a seemingly endless length of tape is drawn from the mouth of a cartoon head. Urban's catalogues also advertised other trick films that offered variations on the 'enchanted drawing' type. *The Sorcerer's Scissors* showed figures cut out from paper and coming to life. *Paper Tearing* depicted figures in costume, made from torn paper, creating in their turn further figures from 'shreds, rolls, sheets and strips of paper'.[95] Whatever the medium used to create inanimate images, film demonstrated its capacity to bring life. Frequently, at the end of these sequences, there would be a knowing, comic gesture to the audience. A hand crumples the paper from which the figures have been formed and turns it into confetti. An eye, the last remaining feature of an erased cartoon head, winks out at the audience from the screen. Who was the butt of this ongoing joke? Neither the audience nor the film-makers but

44 Thomas A. Edison, *The Enchanted Drawing*, 1900. Frame stills, courtesy Library of Congress, Motion Picture, Broadcasting and Recorded Sound Division.

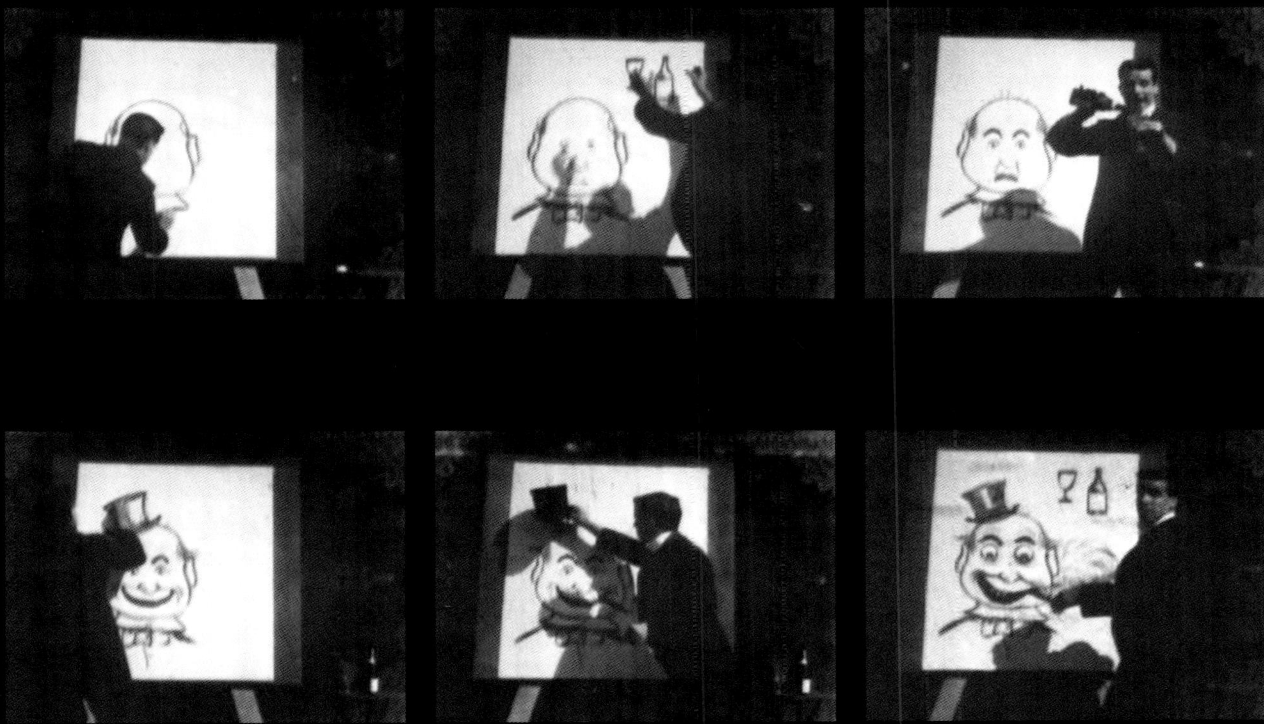

the artists, whose medium was being conjured with and mocked through the trickery of film.

Urban added one further twist to the 'Hand of the Artist' illusion: he got rid of the hand. *The Lightning Post Card Artist* enhanced the mystery of the magic film by eliminating the signs of human agency.[96] A pencil is sharpened and comic pictures are drawn on postcards in the absence of any controlling hand. Although this trick film can be interpreted as the medium's supreme triumph over the artist, it can also be seen as a reformulation of the mysterious power of artistic creativity, in which art remains strange, unknowable and beyond everyday comprehension.[97] However, these are grand claims for a film whose genre was comedy and whose outstanding feature was the production of new and original trick effects. Perhaps what it really represents is the triumph of the visual image in the age of mechanical animation and its ongoing power to seduce and amaze.

No discussion of enchanted pictures in early film would be complete without special reference to the oeuvre of Georges Méliès. In many of his films there is a shifting between the states of lifeless image and living form. Almost every type of visual representation is animated in Méliès films. Statues, paintings, advertising posters and playing cards are all magically brought to life, only to overturn or confound the human world in which they find themselves. The number and inventiveness of Méliès's films on this theme suggest that it held a special fascination for him and that he was drawn to its symbolic significance as a metaphor for the animating power of film and to its focus on the relation between still and moving images. Enchanted pictures were narrative condensations of the history of image-making that confirmed the magic and mystery of watching pictures move into life.

More than any other individual in this period, Méliès embodied in his life and in his work the interface of magic, art and technology. He was born in Paris in 1861 to a wealthy manufacturing family who made footwear.[98] As a boy, Méliès soon demonstrated his skills as a draughtsman and his passion for art; later, after completing a period of military service, he wanted to attend the Ecole des Beaux-Arts but was refused by his parents. It is likely, then, that his love of art contributed in a significant way to his resistance to following his father in the family boot business. In 1884 Méliès was sent to live and work in London and it was during this stay that he came into contact with the spectacular stage effects that characterised London pantomime and magic theatre in the 1880s. As well as visits to the Alhambra and the other major West End theatres, he also diligently attended Maskelyne and Cooke's magic theatre at the Egyptian Hall. There he watched the extraordinary variety of dramatic illusions that distinguished the venue's programmes in this period – the Vanishing Lady, Zoe, the sketching automaton, animated skeletons, ghostly apparitions, the entire repertoire of magic effects that subsequently featured and were reworked in Méliès's trick films. Méliès became hooked on magic; he studied the great illusionists and practised and honed his own skills of prestidigitation. On his return to Paris he continued his magic apprenticeship with trips to the great 'Theatre of Illusions' established by Robert-Houdin and began giving performances at other popular venues in the city. From this period, art and magic, drawing and illusion, were the driving forces in Méliès's life. He became, briefly, a political cartoonist, an occupation that allowed him to develop the graphic skills that continued to feed his cinematic imagination throughout his career. When his father retired in 1888, Méliès made the inevitable decision to sell his share of the family business in order to buy the Théâtre Robert-Houdin. He took over the management of the theatre and also created and performed magic illusions. It was a success; the theatre offered a varied and spectacular programme, similar to that at the Egyptian Hall, often ending with an elaborate series of magic lantern projections.

The Théâtre Robert-Houdin was located on the Boulevard des Italiens, a few minutes' walk from the Grand Café, where the Lumière Cinématographe was given its first public performance.[99] It is inconceivable that Méliès did not attend this show, especially given the fact that, shortly before, Antoine Lumière had rented space above Méliès's theatre for use as a photographic studio. Méliès clearly realised the commercial potential of the projector and tried, unsuccessfully, to buy a machine from the Lumières. Eventually he bought one from Robert Paul in London; he bought films from Edison and Paul and introduced them to the programmes at the Théâtre Robert-Houdin. He quickly moved into his own film production, developing his own camera, purchasing film stock and erecting a 'studio' in his back garden.

Méliès's extraordinary creative energy propelled the expansion of his film making from its makeshift beginnings to the growth of his production company and the exploitation of major visual effects made possible by the film camera. The magic in Méliès's films changed from the straightforward filming of tricks, as performed by a magician on the stage, to the creation of major special effects, involving multiple exposure, stop-motion and other devices, which were difficult or impossible to achieve in the theatre in front of a live audience.[100]

The question remains why so many of Méliès's special effects were performed on the still image. Méliès occupied an interstitial space created by the cultural blending of art, magic and film at the end of the nineteenth century. He might have attended the Ecole des Beaux-Arts and become a fine artist and it is clear that his pictorial imagination continued to work in terms of still images throughout his film-making career. Art was the foundation of his creative life and it is as though he continually returned to this medium as he developed the range of his filmic language. In a number of Méliès trick films, the art image and the film image can be said to be in an aesthetic dialogue, jockeying for position and influence in the new world of modern visual media.

These issues are explored in Méliès's trick film *The Mysterious Portrait*, made in 1899 (plate 45). The film opens in a well appointed interior. In the centre is a large, ornately carved, but empty, picture frame. Behind the frame there is a backdrop depicting a panelled wooden door with conventional portraits, of a man and a woman, on either side. On the right, by the man's portrait, there are shelves of books and papers and a framed mirror. On the left, below the woman's portrait, there are posters advertising the Robert-Houdin theatre, one with the full-length

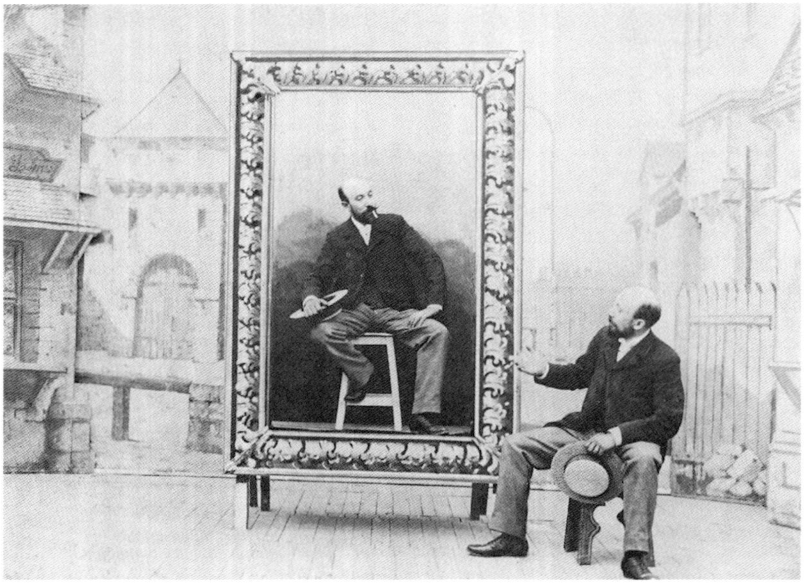

45 Georges Méliès, *The Mysterious Portrait*, 1899. Frame still.

figure of a showgirl and another including the words '*Passez Muscades*' ('Hey Presto'). This setting establishes the cultural parameters of the ensuing transformations: magic and art, wonder and knowledge, illusion and reality, animation and stillness. Méliès enters and walks round the frame. He mimes its rectangular form and steps carefully through it from behind, drawing on devices from the magic theatre to demonstrate to the film's audience that the frame is indeed empty and that the apparatus is not 'rigged'. Then the backdrop rolls up to reveal a second backdrop of a medieval townscape. Méliès then takes a canvas, depicting a rural landscape, and places it inside the gilt frame and puts a stool on its bottom edge. He gestures to his own face, makes a magical sweep of the canvas with his hand and sits down to wait. The canvas darkens and gradually the blurred photographic image of Méliès, dressed identically to the figure by the side of the frame, begins to appear on the canvas. When the transformation is complete, Méliès's double sits inside the frame in a formal, 'seated portrait' pose, with his head inclined at an angle and a thoughtful expression on his face. The Doppelgänger remains in this position while the delighted magician gestures at himself and to the audience. Slowly, the portrait Méliès turns to his double; they size each other up and greet each other and seem, initially, to be delighted by the magical phenomenon.

Méliès continues gesturing to his own bald head, clothes and beard and his animated portrait watches and laughs. The living picture repeats the gestures and the relationship between the two figures begins to alter. Méliès makes an expansive motion with his hand and at this point it is unclear whether he is inviting the living portrait to step out of the frame or to return to its former, lifeless state. The figure in the frame tries to resist; he puts his hands in front of his head and turns away, but his form gradually disappears until only a dark rectangle remains inside the frame. Méliès walks behind the frame again, demonstrates that the equipment has not been tampered with and the illusion/film is complete.

This illusion was achieved by using a matte shot. The part of the camera lens where the portrait would be was masked and the rest of the scene was shot; the film was then rewound and the living portrait was filmed while everything else was blocked out. Film historians have described *The Mysterious Portrait* as knowing and self-referential.[101] The allusions to the Robert-Houdin theatre at the beginning and the later progression within the frame from painted landscape to photograph to animated figure indicate both a recognition of film's pictorial ancestry and of the roles of Méliès and magic within that teleology. It is also knowing in the way that it extends the trope of the enchanted painting. An animated portrait enters a dialogue with its living, film counterpart and, just at the point at which it seems it must break free of the frame, the magician Méliès magics it away. The picture lives and moves but only within the confine of the gilded frame. Its animation is not self-generated but is created and then removed by the magician film-maker Méliès.

Film triumphs once more but the doubling of Méliès as living and painted figure complicates the conventional use of the theme in films during this period. Méliès controls the artistic aspect of his persona but he cannot avoid mocking his film identity in the process. Magic provides the medial form for this gentle, but insistent, aesthetic tussle.

Méliès reappears as a magician and creator of living pictures in *The Living Playing Cards* of 1904 (plate 46). Here the backdrop is a pastoral landscape, complete with classical temple and an ornate, rococo-style platform in the foreground. Méliès enters, dressed as the elegant stage magician in an evening suit. He sweeps below and round the platform to show that there is nothing hidden and then places a

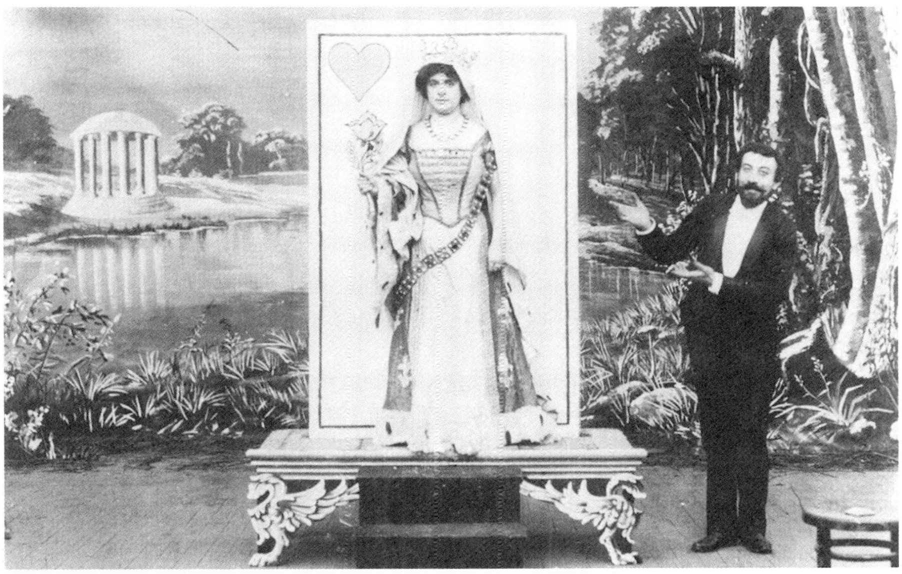

46 Georges Méliès, *The Living Playing Cards*, 1904. Frame still.

large white panel on top of it. Next, in a playful exchange with the film audience, Méliès takes a playing card from a deck and shows it to the camera. Apparently realising that it is too small and that his audience cannot read the number and suit, he comes closer to the camera and then magically 'grows' the card into a giant nine of spades. He throws the card at the blank 'canvas', which becomes the playing card. Méliès takes another card from the deck, this time a queen; he tears it into small pieces, which he places in a burner at the foot of the bench. Lighting a magic flame, the giant nine of spades dissolves and is transformed into a queen of hearts, with the name 'Judith' written in the top right-hand corner. Méliès gestures to his audience that the figure in the playing card might come to life and step down from the rectangular panel on its bench support. The picture card gradually dissolves into a real woman; Méliès helps her down, kisses her hand and then returns her to the panel where she is turned back into a playing card. He selects another card, enlarges it and the queen of hearts turns into 'Alexandre', the king of clubs. Suddenly, the 'real' king bursts through the white panel and Méliès leaves the stage. The king laughs and then pulls off his costume to reveal that he is, in fact, Méliès. The magician jumps at the now empty panel and disappears, only to reappear behind it and make his final exit.

In *The Living Playing Cards*, the power of the hand of the artist to create life is superseded by the hand of the magician and the special effects of film, which create a bravura sequence of animation and petrifaction. The rate of transformations and substitutions escalates towards the end of the film, as queen turns to king, king becomes Méliès and Méliès disappears into the blank panel, until the routine is terminated by the return of the magician and his conventional exit from the stage, waving to the camera. The magician's sleight of hand is replaced by dissolves and stop-substitution, creating a new kind of spectacular illusion that renders Méliès king of magic and 'king of cinema'.[102]

Although there are many films by Méliès and other companies in this period that play on the theme of the enchanted image, one more 'Star' film represents an additional stage in its development. In *The Hilarious Posters* of 1906 (plate 47), a wall of advertising posters comes to life by itself, without the magical intervention of either artist or magician.[103] The animated poster figures flirt with and mock each other. The humour is ribald and physical, as the figures shift from images to animated figures and *tableaux vivants*. The living posters assault a passer-by and attack the police when they come to investigate. Following a wild slapstick routine in which the wall of posters collapses onto the heads of the policemen, the rowdy animated figures link arms and dance out of the film frame.

As the wall, divided into its eight posters, comes to life, the film frame becomes increasingly vivid and animated, until the entire surface of the image is alive with changes of scale and dynamic physical movement. The 'life' of these poster figures is so vigorous that even the police cannot control them or manage to corral them back to their places on the wall. Dancing out of the frame, at the end of the film, it seems that the lunatics have, finally, taken over the asylum; or, to put it more precisely, the animated figures have taken control of the film and the magician has been relegated to his place behind the camera.

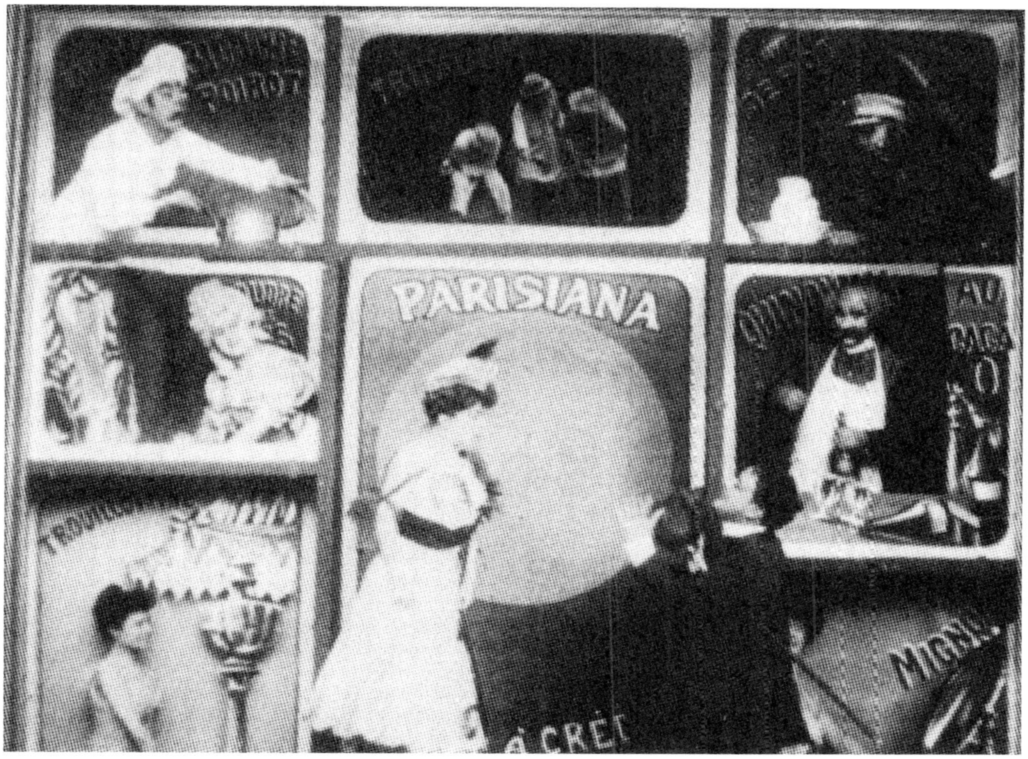

47 Georges Méliès, *The Hilarious Posters*, 1906. Frame still.

There is an archaeological history of picture-making to be found in Méliès's transformation films. Nearest the surface is the pictorialism of film; at the deepest level are the arts of painting and drawing. The theme of the enchanted image allowed Méliès to draw on the full range of magic theatre and film trickery to create a visual conversation between the pictorial arts. An animated portrait has a dialogue with its filmic Doppelgänger, picture cards grow and become living people and advertising posters auto-animate, see-sawing between motion and stasis and resisting all attempts at regulation from the living world.

The sources of Méliès's visual imagination were magic and art which, along with film, were forms concerned with the creation of illusions. Within the first decade of the twentieth century there were profound changes in the business of film-making. The medium had become a success and the issues of organisation and profits, standardisation and control provided the most pressing debates at the first Congrès International des Editeurs du Film, which took place in Paris in 1909. Méliès was elected President of the association but nevertheless found himself accused by Pathé of being only 'an artist' and of not understanding business. He replied: 'I am only an artist, so be it . . . I say that cinema is an art, for it is the product of all the arts.'[104]

It should come as no surprise that Méliès was the spokesperson for the artistic values of cinema. The young man who was denied the chance to attend the Ecole

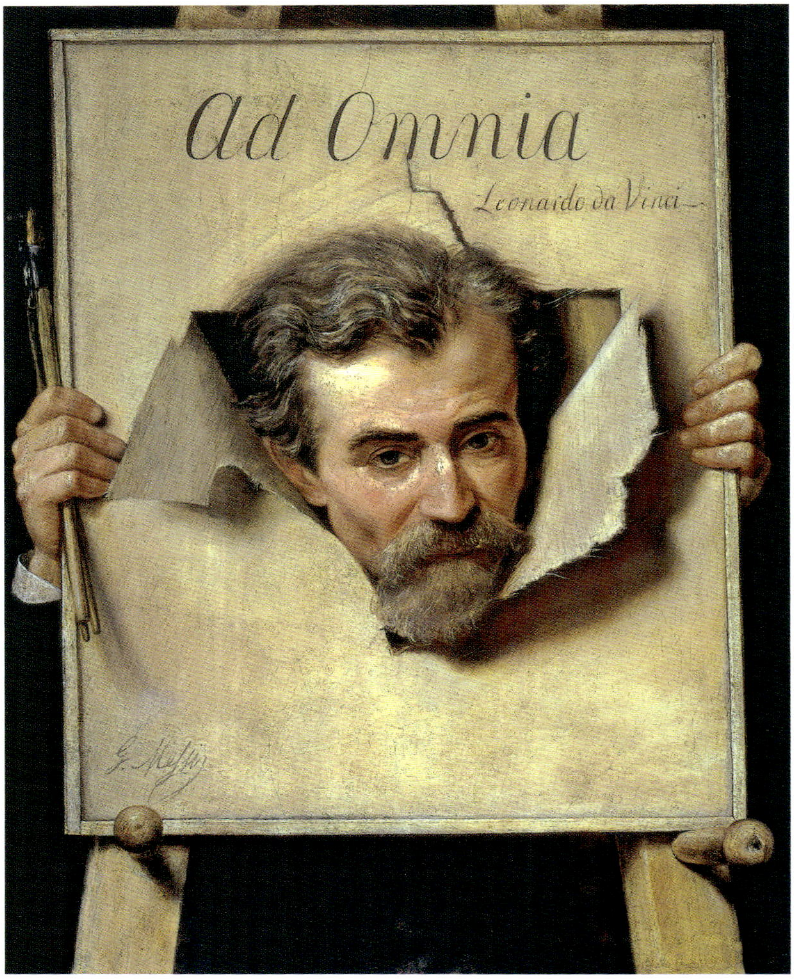

48 Georges Méliès, *Self-Portrait of the Artist*, n.d. Oil on canvas, 63.5 × 52 cm. Private collection.

des Beaux-Arts, who drew and sketched throughout his life and who dedicated much of his film-making to bringing pictures to life, was an artist and a magician who remained drawn to the still image, even as his films secured the domination of moving images. It was precisely this ambivalent relationship to the painted image that Méliès explored in his *Self-Portrait* (plate 48).[105] In this *trompe l'oeil* picture, Méliès depicts himself behind a canvas on an easel, his hands gripped to the sides while his head bursts through and tears the canvas. An image representing the end of painting? Possibly, but the painted inscription on the canvas reads '*Ad Omnia Leonardo da Vinci*', 'To Everything Leonardo da Vinci' – suggesting that, for the visual artist, everything is derived from the work of Leonardo. It is a perplexing image, full of ambiguities, but it testifies to Méliès's lifelong commitment both to art and to film.

* * *

the haunted gallery

The Haunted Gallery at Hampton Court, on the Thames above London, was opened to the public in March 1918, in the last months of the First World War (plate 49).[106] Hampton Court, the largest royal palace in England, was founded by Cardinal Wolsey in 1515 and, notoriously, taken into possession by Henry VIII who spent time there with his six wives. The Haunted Gallery belongs to this Tudor period. A hundred and sixty feet in length, fifteen feet in width and punctuated by six large Gothic windows, it is said to be haunted by the ghost of Henry's fifth

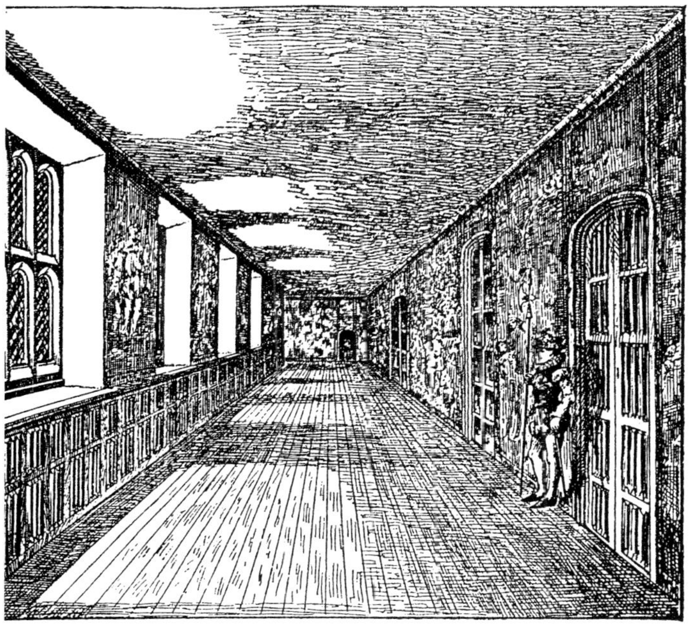

49 'The Haunted Gallery', from Ernest Law, *A Short History of Hampton Court*, London: George Bell and Sons, 1897, p. 109.

wife, Catherine Howard. By 1918 it had become an emblem of English history, picturesque and romantic. Opening the site to civilians and the armed forces was a gesture that symbolised the values of ancient monarchy and popular freedom for which Britain was fighting. Furthermore, in a world in which the spirits of the dead were an almost palpable dimension of everyday experience, the Haunted Gallery held an especially powerful fascination for its visitors.

A space for pictures and for ghosts, the gallery is also for endless pacing, watched by portraits of generations of the dead. It is a place of presences but not life, of likenesses which seem real but which are merely representations or figments of the imagination. The picture gallery is also a place of alternating light and darkness; it is a narrow apartment illuminated by shafts of light created by a series of apertures and of shadows cast by unseen objects, obliterating the light. An 1897 *History of Hampton Court* illustrated 'The Haunted Gallery'. How apt that the shadows cast on the ceiling by the windows and tapestried walls look like a strip of film, with intermittent, spaced-out picture frames, separated by short intervals of blank darkness. Set this sequence in motion and the enchantment begins; the pictures come to life and the ghosts haunt the gallery.

The haunted gallery is a powerful metaphor for the uncanny magic of early film. Every still frame is haunted by the photographic likenesses of those who are no longer there; each time the projector is set in motion the figures step out of their frames and come to life. There is, however, an instant of hesitation and doubt – does the image move, can it live? – but the moment cannot be held for long. Early film animates; it must create hauntings and motion. 'For only one franc see lifesize figures . . . come to life before your very eyes.' Come to life but not live. The Lumière boast carries an acknowledgement of the nature and limits of the medium, of its ability to simulate life and to create ghosts. This is what Maxim Gorky experienced when he watched a Lumière programme in Russia in 1896. Looking at a film of a street scene in Paris, Gorky saw absence not presence, lack of sound and lack of colour. It was a scene full of movement but without life that was terrifying to behold: 'Curses and ghosts, the evil spirits that have cast entire cities into eternal sleep, come to mind and you feel as though Merlin's vicious trick is being enacted before you.' Gorky recognised the primitive within the modern, the magical antecedents of modern technology. A short comedy provoked anxiety: 'It seems as though it carries a warning, fraught with a vague but sinister meaning that makes your heart grow faint . . . Strange imaginings invade your mind and your consciousness begins to wane and grow dim.'[107] Here was the experience of the haunted gallery stripped of its romanticism and pleasant familiarity and filled with the dark spectres of the symbolist imagination, a setting for Freud's *unheimlich*.

cameras and cars

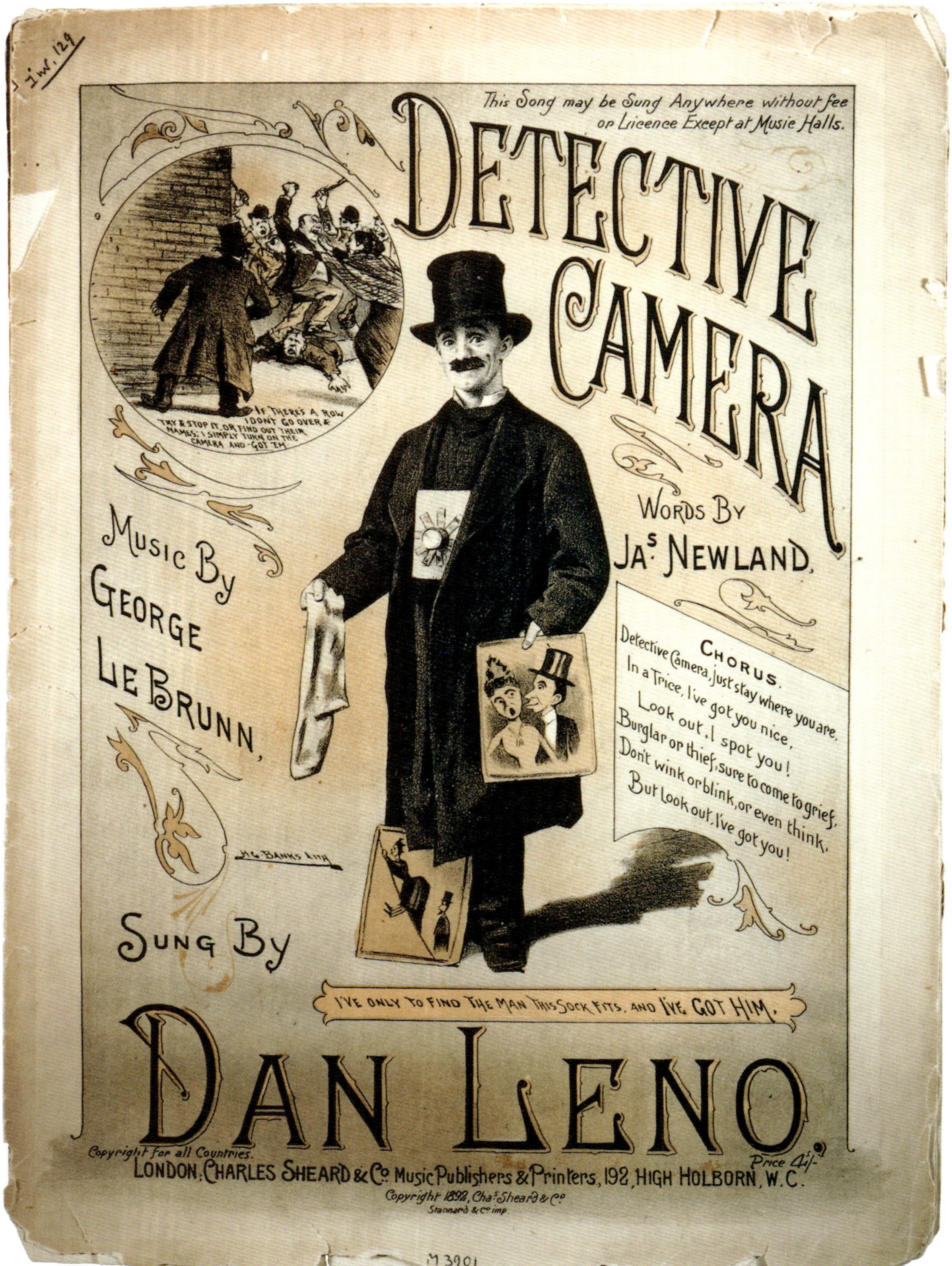

50 Music cover sheet for Dan Leno, 'Detective Camera', n.d. National Museum of Photography, Film and Television, Bradford.

3 animating the everyday

Through the mediation of rhythms . . . an animated space comes into being which is an extension of the space of bodies.

Henri Lefebvre, *The Production of Space* (1974)

The image becomes authentically cinematic when (amongst other things) not only does it live within time, but time also lives within it, even within each separate frame.

Andrey Tarkovsky, *Sculpting in Time* (1989)[1]

london's modernity

To walk and travel around major cities such as London in the early years of the twenty-first century is to be acutely aware of the ubiquity of the camera in contemporary urban life and of its powers of surveillance. Photographic technologies such as closed-circuit television have become part of the fabric of the city and the consciousness of being constantly on camera is now a familiar part of urban experience. In the area of King's Cross, in central London, police notices on street lamps at the height of the upper deck of a bus ask: 'Are you on camera now?' We know that we are being photographed but we cannot be certain exactly when. We cannot refuse and we cannot fully prepare ourselves for being turned into an image. During the last few years, it has become clear that the history of the city is also the history of those photographic technologies that record its populations. For those living through this history, it might be helpful to understand how this started: how it came about that the camera would record all the ephemera of the urban crowd – its law-abiding citizens and its criminals, its licit and most illicit acts; how it would throw prevailing notions of privacy and public life into disarray and force new civil and legal definitions of the individual subject and citizen. This chapter is a political and a cultural history. It recounts the appearance of new photographic technologies in London at the end of the nineteenth century and the new representations and perceptions of the city that were thereby released, or unleashed. It is the pre-history of the urban environment in which many of us now conduct our everyday lives.

The 1880s and 1890s were years of extraordinary innovation within photographic and camera technologies. New photographic plates were developed that were easier and faster to handle; exposure times were shorter and cameras became smaller and lighter and could be held in the hands rather than needing to be supported on a tripod. Camera designs appeared with incredible rapidity and photography changed from being a medium of the professional to being a popular amateur pastime. These innovations in instantaneous photography provided the precedent for film. Advances in the manufacture of roll film and projector technology enabled strips of film to be drawn through the machine and across a lens at a steady rate and, projected at a rate of approximately twenty-four frames per second, gave the illusion of continuous, uninterrupted movement. By the middle of the 1890s, ongoing attempts to film and project moving photographic images were successfully realised and the first short films were shown to paying public audiences in Europe and North America. It is no exaggeration, therefore, to say that by 1896 modern visual culture had been transformed and that individuals and societies had become the subject of representational practices that were without precedent in their nature and scope.

What follows is an account of those changes and their impact on the perception and representation of contemporary urban life in the metropolis around 1900. The images and debates that were generated by these technologies constitute a unique archive of the history of the metropolis in this period, which possesses a richness and complexity that sets it apart from other metropolitan archives. As seen in chapter 1, the particular wonder of cinema was recognised at the time by its first audiences.[2] Films of street life revealed people and objects moving through time and space in a way that was both strikingly lifelike and strangely unfamiliar. These were ambiguous and unsettling images that insisted at once on the presence of the figures represented and their physical absence, as mere photographic images. The temporal complexity of early film still strikes viewers now, more than a century after their first exhibition. Again people are brought to life, animated, as the film unfolds and yet viewing late Victorian actuality films today can seem like an uncanny encounter with the dead, as the time of the past intrudes within the time of the present in a particularly poignant and vivid manner. It is this temporal relationship, created by the moving image, between the figures on the screen and the audience that makes film a dynamic and compelling historical archive.

Yet this regime of images and image debates has been curiously under-exploited by urban historians. Wrenched from its original contexts and structures of meaning, it has been reduced to little more than supporting illustration for written documentation. Still photography and film in the 1890s gave the metropolis a visual form and presence; they actively constructed the image of the modern imperial city and mediated its meaning for viewers and audiences. Once treated as dynamic representations as opposed to passive illustrations, this body of images allows an account of the nature of urban modernity that challenges some of the tropes that have come to dominate cultural history and to constitute an intellectual orthodoxy of the period.

Many accounts of modernity have, to varying degrees, conformed to a model of historical break and cultural rupture, suggesting that major Western cities such as London underwent an overwhelming transformation at the end of the nineteenth century. According to these accounts, London, Paris and Berlin experienced extraordinary changes in the last years of the nineteenth century. These changes were expressed most vividly in terms of a transformation in the pace of life. It became faster and more dynamic and urban experience in this environment was one of hyper-stimulation and a constant bombardment of the senses. The cultural historian Leo Charney puts it simply and unambiguously: 'The post-1870 transformations of modernity generated a perceptual climate of overstimulation, distraction, and sensation.'[3] In order to adapt to the conditions of the modern world, a new urban subjectivity developed to manage and protect itself from the psychological effects of sensory overload.

Within this analytical model, one text or, rather, one passage from that text, has played a crucial role. This is the paragraph from Georg Simmel's now well rehearsed essay 'The Metropolis and Mental Life' (first published in 1903), albeit refracted through the subsequent work of his student Siegfried Kracauer and of Walter Benjamin. The passage goes like this:

> The rapid crowding of changing images, the sharp discontinuity of the grasp of a single glance, and the unexpectedness of onrushing impression. These are the psychological conditions which the metropolis creates. With each crossing of the street, with the tempo and multiplicity of economic, occupational and social life, the city sets up a deep contrast with small town and rural life . . .[4]

This textual fragment has taken on a life of its own and has been made to speak for all the moves and diversions in Simmel's powerful evocation of historical modernity. Its circulation and repetition in this partial form has rendered it a canonical, orthodox account of the modern urban experience and it has been taken as an accurate description of the nature and experience of cities around 1900. Certainly, the 'Metropolis' essay offers a compelling account of the formation of metropolitan subjectivity and elsewhere in his work Simmel draws this transformation of individual existence into a wider network of economic and social exchange. The problem arises when Simmel's work is adopted literally as an account of the nature of the city at the turn of the twentieth century and of the spatial and temporal qualities of urban space at that time. Moreover, cinema has been drawn into this narrative as the pre-eminent medium of this age, as the form that most nearly expresses the pace and discontinuities of modern life. For example, in Giuliana Bruno's otherwise exquisite account of early Neapolitan cinema, she states 'Simmel speaks the language of motion pictures.'[5]

The problem here is two-fold, involving an historical and a cultural conflation. Simmel's analysis has been taken out of its original context and been drawn into the world of 1920s cinematic culture. Film can be said to express this reading of modernity when the filmic language concerned is one of formal experimentation, radical editing and montage. However, it does not work when the modernity concerned is that of a city such as London and when the visual forms are those of instantaneous photography and the earliest projected moving film. By drawing on this visual archive it is possible to challenge both this lumpen analysis of modernity and the city, and to offer a different account of the metropolis in that era, with a more varied concept of its temporality and visuality. Streets have a depth of time and social use; not only are they crowded and stressful, they are also places of stillness, amusement and of interactions that, in London's case, seem to belong more to the world of Henry Mayhew than of Simmel. This means understanding the concept of the city in a culturally and topographically more diverse way and appreciating that modernity is a process of historical fits and starts.

Like Janus, London's modernity faced in two opposite directions – towards the nineteenth century and towards the twentieth century. For most of Victoria's reign, the image of the metropolis had been forged and reworked to meet the changing requirements of an imperial nation. It was the largest city in the world; its needs were immense and its scale sublime.[6] It had been improved and it was modern, yet its distinctive character lay in its individual personalities and residual forms. It was in the side streets and on the street corners, as much as in the new roads and thoroughfares, that London's special qualities could be found.

It is this dialectic of change and continuity that characterises nearly all representations of London in the late Victorian and Edwardian years. In 1901, the year of Victoria's death, George R. Sims – a prolific journalist and editor of the period – introduced his new fortnightly series, *Living London*. With its magazine format and uncritical medley of articles on the capital, *Living London* must surely have been an easy and reliable source of income to a professional journalist whose career embraced a breadth of genres including novels and poetry, social reform and investigations of London slum life. The impressive range of articles and images in the pages of each issue gives a strong sense of the particular and ambiguous nature of London's modernity in these years. Although some attention is paid to what might be described as the new or innovatory aspects of the metropolis – to 'Motoring London', or 'Going to Business London', for example – the majority of articles pick up a thematic rhetoric that had been established in this genre for fifty years or more. London is thus defined as a city of contrasts, of social and economic extremes represented, geographically and symbolically, by the poverty of St Giles's and the riches of St James's. A number of the contributors adopt an ethnographic approach to the population of London, focusing on picturesque types such as the kerbsellers, flower girls, street dancers and loafers. Shorn of any social criticism that might have driven Mayhew's earlier studies or, indeed, previous volumes by Sims himself, the metropolitan types depicted in *Living London* are little more than familiar cockney characters, caught in the text and re-animated for the purposes of representing London at the turn of the century.[7]

Topographically, also, the metropolis that emerges from the pages of *Living London* is a place of contrasts. Sims's contributors are drawn to the kerbsides and street corners, to the places of stasis and social theatre in the capital. Although they acknowledge the traffic and rush-hour crowds of the city, their attention is constantly drawn to individual anecdote and character; they search for and find familiar *tableaux* of picturesque urban life. Modernity, in this context, is characterised not so much in terms of an acceleration of the pace of life but of a multiplicity of changing rhythms that require different spatial practices from those who wish to comprehend its diversity.

A highly successful user of this form was Mrs Emily Constance Cook, whose many handbooks to London convey a strong sense of the modern city as a combination of dynamic commercial life side by side with antiquity and conservatism. In *Highways and Byways in London* (1902) the varied nature of London's space and temporality required Cook to adopt different forms of urban practice as she moved her reader round the city. Her preferred mode of travel was 'wandering and leisured perambulation' but for the business thoroughfares of the City of London she recommended 'the top of an omnibus'.[8] It was precisely these changes of space and pace that, for Cook and other writers in the period, distinguished London from other capital cities.

Cook described the archaeological nature of the metropolis, the way in which highways still followed the routes of Roman roads and bore the same names as in earlier centuries. For her, thoroughfare urbanism was always attended by side-street historicism: 'The great charm . . . of London lies in its unsuspected courts and byways. From most of the big thoroughfares you may be transported, with hardly more than a step, into picturesque nooks of sudden and almost startling silence . . . All who know and love London will recall this.'[9]

The figure that still defined London's picturesque modernity in the years around 1900 was Charles Dickens. Since the writer's death in 1870, the idea of 'Dickensian London', drawn from the locations and characters of his novels, had become lodged in the cultural imaginary. Cook and other writers in this period saw London through a filter of Dickens. She compared faces on penny steamers to 'Cruikshank pictures, Dickens sketches' and referred throughout her handbooks to novels such as *The Old Curiosity Shop* and *Our Mutual Friend*. This is a version of modernity that should begin to question some of the prevailing accounts of urban history. Evoking the mysterious beauty of London in its winter months, Henry James admitted: 'Then it is that I am most haunted with the London of Charles Dickens, feel most as if it were still recoverable, still exhaling its queerness in patches perceptible to the appreciative.'[10]

This was the complex and haunted perception of modernity in which photographers and film-makers participated at the end of the nineteenth century. Victorian photographs and films of London do much more than show images of the city, or what places, things and people actually looked like. Individually and collectively, they reveal far more fundamental and structural conceptions of the city. They convey the social topography of the period and the changing patterns of observation and visibility in the urban context. They expose modern subjectivity in its individual forms and in its relation to the crowd. The new photographic practices forced a reassessment of social behaviour in the city streets and of individual rights to a private self within public space. These concepts were a critical dimension of the experience of urban modernity that can only really be accessed through the contemporary debates concerning visuality and representation. For visual representation had never before been so potent and omnipresent. Still and moving images subjected the smallest gestures of everyday life to a new visual scrutiny. The most insignificant details of behaviour were recorded and viewed over and over again, creating a new, common rhetoric within the everyday. Small, hand-held cameras made the streets alive to the possibility of being seen without knowing. Films exposed the complex temporality of those individual actions and social relations and gave contingency and the everyday a new topicality and currency.

the hand camera

By the second half of the 1880s photography was half a century old. It had become a familiar aspect of Victorian culture and had infiltrated both domestic and public relations. Photography was the medium for expressing emotive life and for giving form to civic and social power. It was, by this time, an old and familiar technology yet in the middle of revolutionary innovation. These changes affected both the camera apparatus and its image-making techniques. Most significantly, the older style of wet-glass plates had been replaced by gelatin dry plates. This liberated the photographer from a complex chemical process that required bulky equipment and immediate development of the image. The subsequent advent of roll film simplified the photographic process even further and continued the detachment of the photographer from the technical aspects of image development and production. With simplified processes and shorter exposure times cameras became far more portable; hand cameras appeared at the beginning of the 1880s and photography became 'instantaneous'.[11] The new technology was cheaper, easy to use and remarkably successful. New models and designs were continuously advertised but the market was effectively cornered by the American camera and film manufacturer George Eastman.

Eastman's first Kodak camera appeared in the late 1880s, marketed with the slogan: 'You press the button, we do the rest'. The phrase encapsulated the significant implications of the new technology: photography was no longer a specialist practice, it was easy to use and was popular and accessible. More people than ever before could take photographs and new subjects had been opened up to the photographic apparatus. The revolution in visual representation was thus two-fold. First, it created a new aesthetic and a new way of looking and, second, it expanded the range of possible subjects that could be turned into an image. Both the person behind the camera and his or her relationship to the subjects in front of the lens were involved. This was acknowledged in Eastman's account of his invention in 1888 of the name Kodak: '[It was] terse, abrupt to the point of rudeness, literally bitten off by firm and unyielding consonants at both ends, it snaps like a camera shutter in your face. What more could one ask?'[12] Eastman fully understood the social implications of his new 'in your face' camera. Metaphorically, at least, it seemed that the new hand cameras had broken down the tacit distance and norms of social interaction that had evolved among individuals in social space.[13] Their speed and intrusion into new areas of representation transgressed and subjected to scrutiny an assumed sense of decorum that had come to define the conduct of social relations in the mid-Victorian period; nowhere was this confrontation between modern technology and social behaviour keener than on the city streets.

The technical advantages of the hand camera were believed to be most suited to the demands of street photography. From its inception, photography had sought to record the appearance of modern life as seen in the major cities of the industrial world. However, with the long exposure times and awkward equipment of the medium's first decades, the resulting images were aesthetically limited. The qualities of Victorian street life seemed, to some photographic writers of the period, to demand a distinctive point of view or perspective, one which would allow the viewer to be drawn into the crowd and to be a part of the street. In 1899 the *British Journal of Photography* – arguably the most important periodical at the time for professional photographers – recommended stereoscopic photography for street scenes.[14] Here, two slightly discrepant images of the same subject were taken and, when viewed through a special device (the stereoscope), were superimposed to approximate binocular vision. The illusion was of three-dimensional space and of figures located in that space and almost tangible to the viewer.[15] Whether taken from the top of an omnibus, viewed in a stereoscope or projected as a lantern slide, the pedestrians and vehicles of the city streets required a different kind of image and aesthetic from those offered by traditional pictorial media.

A hand camera provided an unrivalled technique for drawing the photographer and the viewer down onto the streets and capturing the special character of contemporary urban life. Walter D. Welford, the great exponent in the 1880s and 1890s of hand-camera photography and editor of the *Photographic Review*, explained its advantages over other forms of picture-making:

> What wealth of subject lies here [in the streets of London], often touched, but, oh! to what a slight degree. The varying incidents of every-day life, the characters we know by sight . . . and the thousands of things we see and know so well in our daily life. The painter oft depicts them, but he needs much study of surrounding, much help of models and months of labour. The hand-camera worker secures a pictorial note of the scene in a moment. The ordinary camera man can by dint of careful posing, a certain amount of cheek, and several little dips into his pocket, get sometimes a really good street incident. But the hand-camera worker troubles no one, he merely waits his opportunity, and when it comes seizes it, then passes on without anyone being the wiser.[16]

For Welford, the hand camera operates within the boundaries of an already defined rhetoric of picturesque imagery, but the vital new ingredient that creates the distinction between instantaneous photography and other media is that it is unnoticed. It is fast, unseen and its subjects cannot pose or prepare themselves to become pictures. For the first time, in theory at least, the city's inhabitants could be captured pictorially, without prior knowledge or agreement to the process; for if the camera could not be seen, then the subject did not have to give their consent. Instant photography exposed the ethical dimension of image making and disturbed the hitherto neglected question of individual rights to privacy in the public urban sphere.

For the hand-camera photographer the expressed goal was the unstudied or unposed qualities of everyday life. Freed, at last, from the long exposure times and formal conventions of studio photography and previous outdoor work, they sought animation and natural effects, bound together with 'character' and 'variety'.[17] Expertly used, the new technology eliminated the subject's self-awareness and by creating images of individuals prior to their self-fashioning, it could reveal a new and hitherto unrecordable aspect of the modern city.

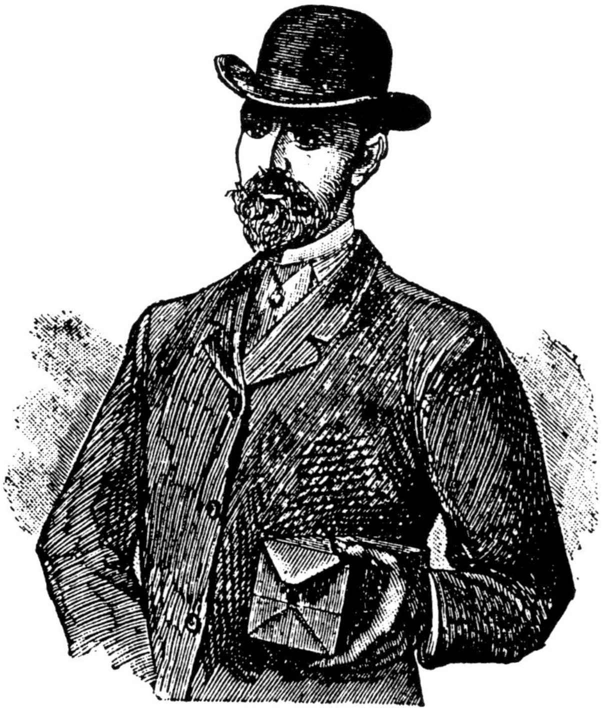

51 'The Parcel Detective', from *The Photographer's Indispensable Handbook: A Complete Cyclopaedia upon the Subject of Photographic Apparatus, Material and Processes*, compiled by Walter D. Welford, London: Iliffe and Son, 1887, p. 63.

The nature of this technology, therefore, was that it should be operated surreptitiously. What made it different, as a commodity, was its secrecy.[18] The concept of the detective camera was thus simply an elaboration of what had always been acknowledged to be the prime attraction of hand cameras in general. Detective cameras exploited the voyeuristic pleasures of hand-camera technology – of small gadgets hidden from the public eye, ennabling observation without the operator being observed. The cameras were disguised about the body of the photographer, in hats and cravats, and in the form of bodily accessories such as parcels, books and walking sticks (plates 50 and 51). The 'Pic-Nic Basket Detective Camera' was advertised as 'Most Deceptive in Ap-pearance' and 'Unobtrusive. Free from Observation' and was specifically recommended for use in 'thronged thoroughfares'.[19] When reading the photographic press and publications from this period it is easy to get the sense of a public world obsessed with photographic technology and perhaps this is not too far from the truth. Within a few years, photography had been transformed into a popular, amateur activity that had opened up new types of demand in the market.[20] Cameras were ubiquitous and at the same time invisible, creating an environment that was always alive to the presence of a camera.

With the first appearance of detective cameras, the focus on concealment inevitably also brought discomfort and voices of disapproval. Among the advocates of instantaneous photography were many who were keen to distance themselves from the sneaky connotations of detective cameras. Welford explained his dislike of the designation, if not the practice:

> It implies a use of the instrument for purposes to which some of the public emphatically object, *viz.*: – the securing of scenes or incidents, pleasant or otherwise (in their minds generally very much otherwise) which could not be obtained by other means . . . a hand-camera by real workers, at all events, is very little utilized for purposes of that sort. True, we may all of us occasionally indulge in surreptitious shooting, but it is not necessary to emphasize the fact by proclaiming ourselves 'Detectives' . . . Tell a man that it is a Detective Camera and he averts his face, turns his head, or bolts down the nearest street.[21]

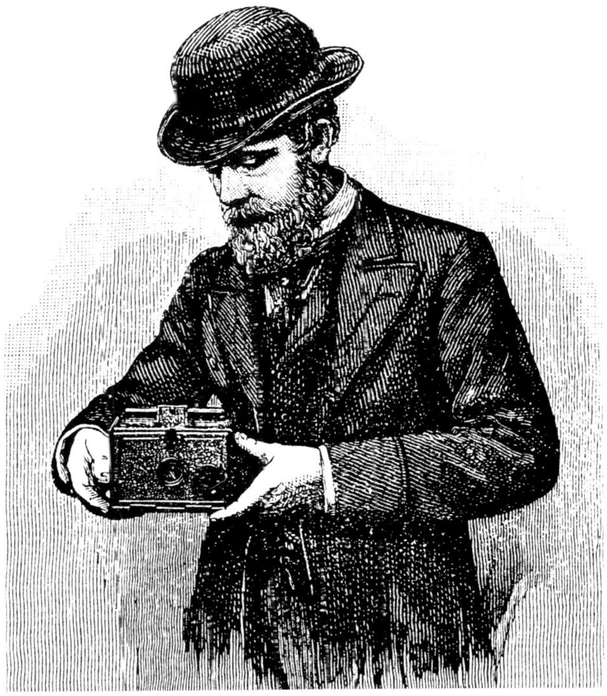

52 From Walter D. Welford, *The Hand Camera Manual: A Beginner's Guide to Photography in its Connection with the Hand Camera*, London: L. Upcott Gill, 1893, p. 72.

Welford's tone of disapproval is compromised by his inability to resist the temptation of 'surreptitious shooting' and his regret that once a subject realises there is a detective camera around they will flee rather than be photographed. His ambivalence is hardly surprising, however. All hand cameras were potential detective cameras, since the designation was primarily a question of intention and use, rather than of distinctions in technology. This was made explicit in Welford's subsequent advice to beginners with the hand camera: 'Every endeavour . . . should be made to prevent the people in the scene knowing that they are "going to be took".' Yet, rather than hiding the camera, he recommends a number of 'wiles and tricks' that can be used to distract subjects from the photographer's true purpose: 'Anything and everything in fact to cheat the public, to deceive them as to purpose.'[22]

If further confirmation of the underhand motives of the hand-camera worker were needed, it could be found in bodily deportment. Welford offered one more, somewhat curious, piece of advice: 'avoid looking at the subject any more than is absolutely necessary. I don't mean on the finder or through the camera, but with the eyes.'[23] Avoidance of eye contact was a bodily enactment of the shifty activities of the hand-camera photographer. The technology required a new bodily practice in which the camera apparatus was taken from the body's symbolically exalted site of reason – the eye and the head – and withdrawn to the debased site of the belly and torso. In order to keep the camera steady and to avoid drawing attention to it, hand cameras were generally held under the arm by the side of the body, or clasped to the stomach (plate 52). Although this made framing the scene difficult, it concealed the fact that a photograph was being taken. Furthermore, as the technology necessitated physical repositioning from high to low, it became part of a cultural and corporeal hierarchy.[24] The photographer, clutching a camera to his or her stomach or side, and wandering the streets of the city waiting to snatch a photograph of an unwitting subject, was the perfect physical embodiment of the debased nature of modern commercial culture.[25] If late Victorian culture imagined technology as a kind of prosthetic enhancement of the body, then the hand camera was an appalling and aberrant prosthesis in which enhanced sight was no longer an extension of the eye but had evolved as a projection of the belly.[26]

The symbolic properties of the hand camera surfaced most explicitly in contemporary debates concerning the obtrusiveness of the photographers and the rights of individuals in the street not to be photographed without their consent. Predictably, the issue mattered most when the subjects belonged to the respectable middle classes, for whom character and reputation were believed to matter most. The working classes were generally regarded as a cast of picturesque types who could not possibly object to being photographed unless they were being deliberately awkward. Reflecting on this issue, the specialist journal *Photography* concluded:

> that although the vast majority of the British public, especially those of the lower orders, are only too pleased to be 'took' in a picture they can never have the pleasure of looking upon, still, all persons are not constituted that way, and many have strong objections, which objections it is the duty of all photographers *and gentlemen* to consider.[27]

Appropriate behaviour was a key issue in this situation because individuals had no other protection from the promiscuous photographic activities of the hand-camera worker. In the course of half a century, the photographic image had been transformed from the formalities of the studio portrait to the apparently unposed informalities of the instantaneous process. The minutiae and incidental aspects of contemporary life were the purpose and driving motive of the new hand-held cameras that were redefining the value of everyday life. Whereas in the 1850s the question of respect for privacy had never really arisen due to the technical limitations of the medium, instantaneous processes had forced apparently shared assumptions concerning social morality and decorum into the open. Quoting an article from an American journal, the *Amateur Photographer* endorsed the view that: 'The rights of private property, personal liberty and personal security . . . are distinctly inconsistent with the unlicensed use of the instantaneous process.'[28] These terms had less resonance in Britain than in the United States. With no written constitution upholding 'personal liberty', respectable British citizens depended instead on 'morality and discretion' to protect their privacy and freedom.[29] Even so, there was little consensus among photographers concerning the nature of individual privacy and subjectivity in the context of Britain's city streets at the end of the nineteenth century. *Photography* attempted to formulate a consistent position for its readers in an article published in 1891:

> We do not consider that any one has a right to steal a photograph of another person, except as an adjunct to an ordinary view; and most certainly we have no right to snatch a photograph of a person in any compromising position or circumstances. Persons walking the streets are objects of public view, and conduct themselves with a knowledge that they are so, but to us it appears the height of impertinence to take surreptitious shots at – for example – ladies bathing, and unaware that they are the victims of such indecent officiousness.[30]

The issue hinged on how much privacy an individual could claim in the public sphere. On the streets, people were aware that they were exposed to public view and might justifiably be expected to present themselves appropriately; exposure to the camera in this context should not require a change of conduct. In contrast to this constant state of readiness and alertness to public visibility, the paper lists other situations in which, although public, people might reasonably expect not to be exposed to photographic scrutiny. Such a compromise was necessary to protect the photographer of 'street life', in which individuals might find themselves an extra in a general *tableau* of modern urban life. The situation was further complicated by the fact that these kinds of photographs were not necessarily intended for private viewing but frequently appeared as lantern slides, projected to an audience at an evening's public entertainment. Hand cameras introduced a new promiscuous visual environment in the city streets. Uncertainties concerning both who was making and who was the subject of the photographic image created an intense awareness of the possibilities of being part of visual representation, which was in turn exploited by commercial culture. In 1899 the photographic press reported a sales gimmick that had been introduced by some 'yellow journals' in New York. A young woman was paid to walk round the city streets; her photograph was published in the *Photographer* and a reward offered to the first person who stopped and identified her.[31] This simple and now familiar newspaper ploy testifies to the ways in which photographic technologies participated in and affected the nature of urban modernity at the end of the nineteenth century. Passers-by could be unknown to each other but they could also be the subject of unprecedented self-awareness and public scrutiny.

Whereas commentators appealed to professional dignity, self-discipline and etiquette to control the situation, others felt that only legislation could address the unruly social relations that had emerged with the new technology.[32] As it stood, the law seemed ill-equipped to deal with the kinds of offence created by the new photographic technology. Although the rights of individuals photographed by hand cameras could be protected by recourse to libel or copyright legislation, this did not address the many, varied disputes that could and did arise in the context of street photography.[33] Libel could be claimed only if it could be proved that a photograph had damaged the reputation of the individual concerned and copyright was more concerned with the image as property and in establishing ownership of the image than with the offence of taking it. The idea of privacy and intrusion into the personal life of individuals was thus exercised on the pages of the photographic and national press but was not taken up by the judiciary. In the 1880s and 1890s instantaneous photography and the detective camera dragged into the foreground the question of rights and consent in relationship to the photographic image and unsettled the stable social relations embodied in the studio dynamic of photographer and sitter. Correspondence in the period's photographic press reads at times like an agony column, as professional and amateur photographers waded through the minutiae of copyright legislation to clarify what they were and were not able to do. On the other side of the lens, individuals expressed helpless outrage when confronted by their photographic image, taken without consent and exhibited in a public context.[34]

The situation was going to get worse. If the law had been slow to respond to the implications of instantaneous photography, then it was completely unprepared for the cinematograph. Here were moving images, made explicitly for public exhibition, that could capture individuals in time and that offered narrative episodes rather than frozen details and gestures. The matter was drawn to the attention of the British press by the case of Madame Dreyfus who, following the commital of her husband in France for treason, had been photographed and filmed during her visits to him in prison. The *British Journal of Photography* declared: 'To be snapshotted against one's will by hand cameras is bad enough, but being cinematographed is infinitely worse. Hand-camera pictures, as a rule, are principally confined to private collections. Not so, however, with cinematographs, they are taken for exhibition at places of public entertainment. Madame Dreyfus has our sympathy.'[35]

In the last years of the nineteenth century, changes in photographic technologies exposed inconsistencies and tensions in the forms of social etiquette relating to urban space. Questions arose as to the extent that an individual in a public thoroughfare could be said to be always already on show and what rights they had to prevent their image being taken and exhibited without their consent. There was power in the act of observation, particularly when it was itself unobserved, but it was questioned whether photographers could be trusted to exercise this power responsibly or whether the law should be forced to intervene.

These issues and questions coalesce in the person of Paul Martin, a photographer whose images of London street life have become a staple of heritage representations of the late Victorian metropolis (plate 53). Martin's career mirrors the growing dominance of photography in the second half of the nineteenth century. Trained as a wood engraver producing images for the illustrated press, he took up photography as a hobby but later set up in business in the 1890s as a freelance photographer.[36] His preferred camera was the Facile, a detective camera that was camouflaged in a brown-paper parcel with a strap round it (plate 51). With holes

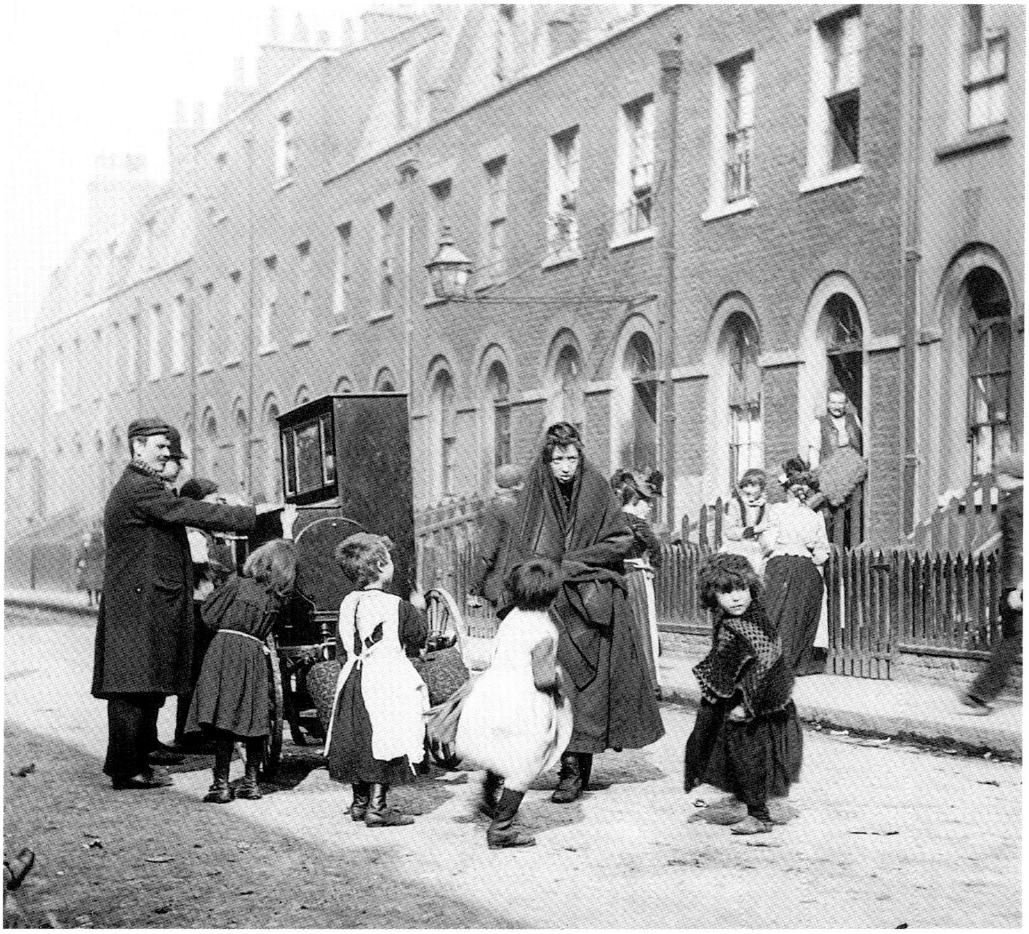

53 Paul Martin, 'Dancing to the Organ', 1893. Harry Ransom Humanities Research Center, University of Texas at Austin.

for the lens and viewfinder, there was little to give away the presence of a camera and Martin was able to move around London without suspicion, with what looked like a parcel of books tucked under his arm. He did everything he could to conceal the camera mechanism and the photographic process; in his brief autobiography he describes holding the camera on its side to prevent the thud as the plates dropped down.[37] His subterfuge was highly successful, yielding both unsuspecting subjects and intense personal pleasure. 'It is impossible to describe the thrill which taking the first snaps without being noticed gave one.'[38]

Martin evolved a pragmatic response to the contingencies of instantaneous street photography in the 1890s. In summary, the difficulties boiled down to what might be defined as the extrinsic or incidental details of the image. As an editorial in the *British Journal of Photography* put it:

> how is it possible for any one to secure instantaneous street scenes, say, in such places as Cheapside, the Strand, Regent-street, &c., without including the pedestrians and vehicles passing at the time, and by the score, too? In a good photograph the persons will be perfectly recognisable. Now, can any one, or all, of these persons so depicted prohibit the pictures being publicly shown?[39]

It was the figures on the margins of the image that were at the centre of the debate. Photography's relentless ability to record everything placed before the lens had produced an excess of detail and a surplus of meaning that had to be reined in or eradicated.

Martin eliminated potential legal challenges by concentrating on London's working classes. The kerbsellers, itinerant musicians and street urchins fitted easily into existing anecdotal genre formats and satisfied the contemporary taste for character, life and variety in metropolitan representation which was also met in the literature of the period. Moreover, these subjects would never see the resulting publications or exhibits, which helpfully ruled out the danger of legal claims. Yet this still left the possibility of rogue background details; unnoticed faces, trade names, passing presences, caught for ever by the lens of Martin's parcel detective camera. His solution was extraordinary. In the middle of the 1890s he developed a novel technique for making images for lantern slides. Given the recent arrival of film on the London entertainment scene, the need for novelty in the more traditional media had become even more pressing. Martin's slides were derived from existing images of statues in which all but the statue and pedestal were painted out of the picture. As Martin explained at the time: 'When I first saw one of these slides the idea struck me . . . that living objects might be substituted for the statues.'[40] Working with his hand camera, he photographed street characters and then painted round the figures and wiped out the background with Indian ink (plate 54). In transforming his subjects into 'imitation statuary', he effectively eradicated the volatile elements of instantaneous photography. Wrenched from all historical context, the figures look like ceramic statuettes, petrified within a late Victorian taxonomy of social investigation. At some level, Martin evidently understood the implications of his method; he reflected on other suitable projects for his technique: 'I would have made a set of slides of animals at the Zoo.'[41]

The search for a means of representing everyday urban life had finally led Martin to a method of pictorial embalming rather than animation. Elsewhere, however, photographers of the metropolis endlessly sought to capture its life and movement. However, movement was precisely the fatal paradox of late Victorian street photography. On the one hand, it was photography's ultimate, chimeric, object but, on the other hand, movement was unpictorial, it dismantled composition and resulted in unwanted formal relationships and obtrusive details. The noted photographer T. C. Hepworth concluded that instantaneous street photography was doomed to failure, 'so rigid is it in arrested motion . . . nature is burlesqued'.[42]

In the light of these debates it is easy to make a teleological move from the failure of still photography to represent the urban everyday to the subsequent success of film. Indeed, the next section will present a highly modified version of

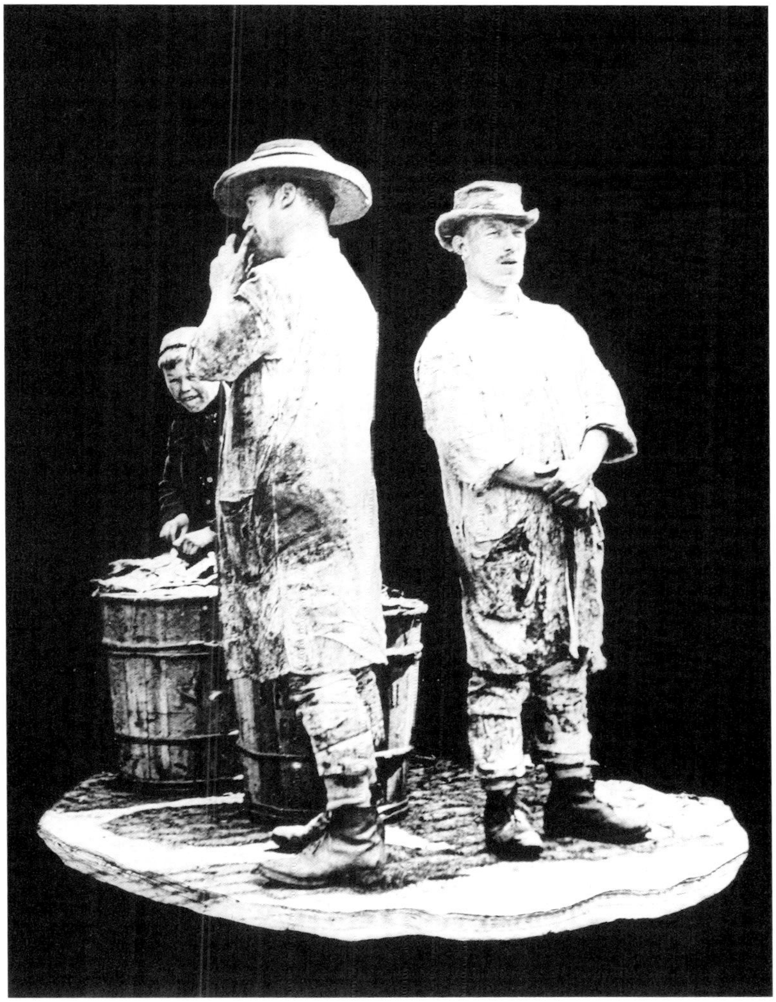

54 Paul Martin, 'Loading Up at Billingsgate Market: Cut-Out Figures', n.d. Harry Ransom Humanities Research Center, University of Texas at Austin.

this argument. Yet in fact these media coexisted in a context of highly developed structures of commercial entertainment. Still photographs were commonly presented as lantern slides, and magic lantern shows in the late 1890s included film projections. Individual careers in these years moved from photographer or lanternist to film-maker. However, as well as being part of this continuum of late Victorian visual culture, film also represented a significant historical break. Like the impact of hand-camera technology, film changed the landscape of representational practice. It offered new ways of seeing the city and of conceiving individual subjectivity in a modern urban context. Films drew the camera-sensitive populations of the metropolis from the streets and into the music halls where they further eroded the distinctions between the experience of urban space and its representation. Film spectators not only had the pleasure of watching scenes of urban life through which they had only just passed on their way to the theatre or hall, but were also enticed by the narcissistic possibilities of seeing themselves, filmed shortly before, projected on the screen.[43]

the cinematograph

The history of the city and the history of the cinema are closely interwoven. Film found its earliest homes in the music halls and other spaces of entertainment that already existed in the major cities of Britain and, in turn, street life (particularly that of the metropolis) and the urban everyday were among the most popular subjects of the first film-makers. Yet the question remains of what these short films, made in the first years of cinema, can say about the nature and experience of the cities that they represent. Films at the turn of the century were short, often well under a minute; and camerawork was fairly minimal, frequently nothing more than a static camera and a single shot filmed without editing and in real time. In spite of, or perhaps because of, this apparent simplicity, however, these first films of the city offer a new and distinctive way of interpreting the experience of the modern metropolis that cannot be found in other forms of visual or textual representation. They give the everyday movement and the passage of time. Films release new kinds of representations of people in space; they make visible the idea of inhabiting and being in the city. The urban everyday has an extensive tradition of visual representation in what might be described as the long history of modernity from the end of the seventeenth century to the middle of the twentieth century. It has been the subject of successive new forms of mass-produced imaging, from prints and engravings, to photography and projected moving images. Each medium responds differently to the potential of the city and contributes, within the parameters of its particular form, to the development of cultural conceptions of the urban.

In 1901, in his first editorial for *Living London*, George R. Sims drew on the metaphor of film to convey the realism of the writing that would be found in its pages: 'we are to find a breathing, pulsing panorama of Living London. Panorama is hardly the word – cinematograph would be a better one, for it is not a London of bricks and mortar that will pass before our eyes, but a London of flesh and blood.'[44] Sims rejected the panorama because it could only provide a backdrop of the built environment. The cinematograph animates the city; it gives depth and a rounded corporeality to the place. So, in the year of Queen Victoria's death, film represented the apogee of lifelike representation. It was novel and part of the fabric of modern urban life but it also bore the traces of the previous century. It came out of at least a hundred years of optical experiments and drew on a Victorian, as much as an Edwardian, tradition of pictorial representation. In this way, its history shares a structure with the history of the metropolis.

In spite of celebrating the centenary of cinema in 1995, film historians now agree that cinema did not suddenly appear on the scene in 1895, when the Lumière brothers projected animated photographs onto a screen in front of an audience at the Grand Café in Paris. Projected images have a long history; cinema came out of a tradition of older, popular forms of entertainment such as the magic lantern show. Yet, while the longer tradition to which cinema belongs may be acknowledged, it is also true that in the mid-1890s certain conditions were in place that facilitated and made possible the success of the new medium. In his *Mass Entertainment: The Origins of a Modern Industry* (1960), Asa Briggs suggested five economic conditions that are necessary for the development of a mass entertainment industry:

1. A large, concentrated urban population that can constitute the new 'great audience'.
2. A sufficient level of income enabling a large section of this public to buy regular, cheap entertainment.
3. An increase in available leisure time open to commercial exploitation.
4. Improved urban transport systems that allow, for example, night travel from city centres to the suburbs.
5. Technological developments that have a commercial impact on the entertainment industry.[45]

All five of these factors were present together in London and other urban centres by 1896. In February of that year the Lumière Cinématographe was shown to the London press at the Polytechnic in Regent Street and opened to the public at the Empire Music Hall in Leicester Square in March. In exactly the same months, the British inventor Robert Paul's Theatrograph was demonstrated at the Egyptian Hall in Piccadilly and became a regular item at the Alhambra Music Hall. This was a world of vibrant, modern mass entertainment, which was driven by the engines of competition and novelty. Film provided exactly the right ingredient to music-hall proprietors wanting to perk up flagging audiences or to maintain healthy takings.[46]

Music-hall programmes in this period were full and varied. They were pacey and drew on a wide range of turns to keep their audiences entertained. Cinema was drawn into this style of programming. Film was treated as one other kind of variety turn within the mixed programme.[47] However, what film offered which the more traditional acts did not was visual topicality, combined with the latest technology – features that were always emphasised in the venue's publicity. Thus, the Alhambra promoted Robert Paul's films of the Derby in terms of 'Constant Change . . . The Prince's Derby, will be run Daily' and 'Scenes of London Life. Selections from 50 Stirring Subjects'.[48] It was even suggested that Paul had set up his camera on the roof of the Alhamabra so that he could maintain the production of new films of the city for audiences hungry for the spectacle of moving images of their own lives or, at least, of lives much like their own. Everyday life was turned into a cultural commodity for fairly immediate consumption. Film-makers used various strategies to cut down the period between production and consumption and to introduce 'local actualities' into the programmes of regional venues.[49]

So, by 1896, the new camera technologies – the hand camera with its instantaneous photographs and the cinematograph and its derivatives with their moving pictures – had created a different visual regime for the representation of the city. It was a regime that drew on decades of development in optical technology but was relentlessly marketed in terms of the new. The urban everyday was a central theme for these technologies but it is in the early films of London that one can find perhaps the richest representation of the specific qualities of modern life around 1900 and where the condition of modernity itself can be reassessed.

In the last years of the 1890s, operatives from the Lumière company made a number of films of London street scenes.[50] These might have been seen as part of a music-hall programme in London but they could also have been shown in cities in Europe, Asia or America. In London their appeal would have been the immediate topicality of life as it goes on outside the doors of the theatre; abroad they would have taken on the different fascination of foreign travel and the spectacular sights of the world's leading imperial metropolis.[51] Success for the Lumière company rested both on the nature of the machine which they developed and their organisation of the business of making and exhibiting films. The special feature of the Cinématographe was that it was a camera, printer and projector in one. It was lightweight and allowed specially trained operatives to travel all over the world, making films on the spot, developing them and showing them to local audiences. In this way, they regulated quality and, as one film historian has put it, '[collapsed] the functions of filmmaker, distributor, exhibitor, and projectionist into a single individual'.[52] As for the hand camera, the public world was the movie camera's habitat and together they gave the city and its inhabitants an unprecedented visibility and turned everyday life into the most characteristic theme of popular leisure.

The Lumière company made a considerable number of films of London.[53] Not surprisingly, perhaps, their subjects conformed to the familiar itineraries of handbooks or tourist guides to London: the Thames, Regent Street, Piccadilly Circus and the City of London, with special attention to ceremonial and royal London.[54] There is a spatial and temporal richness and variety in these films that offer the viewer a more complex representation of modernity than is encompassed in the notion of speed and more diverse social interactions than relations of indifference or marginality. The forms of Victorian social ethnography are combined with the signs of urban modernisation to express a unique view of the contemporary metropolis.

A single-shot film, the *Empire Theatre, Leicester Square* (1896; plate 55), shows street traffic and pedestrians outside the theatre; the camera is still, while figures and objects move in and out of and across the range of the lens. The film is evidently the kind of local actuality that was a feature of many film programmes in this period and is complete with a promotion for the Lumière Cinématograph on the canopy at the entrance to the theatre and the recognisable figure of the manager of the theatre, a detail which was picked up by reviews of the programme.[55] Early film programmes would often open with a film shot at the entrance of the theatre; it was a device that drew the spectators into spatial and temporal proximity to the images projected on the screen and that created a continuity between the physical and imaginary experiences of the city outside and of the theatre within.[56]

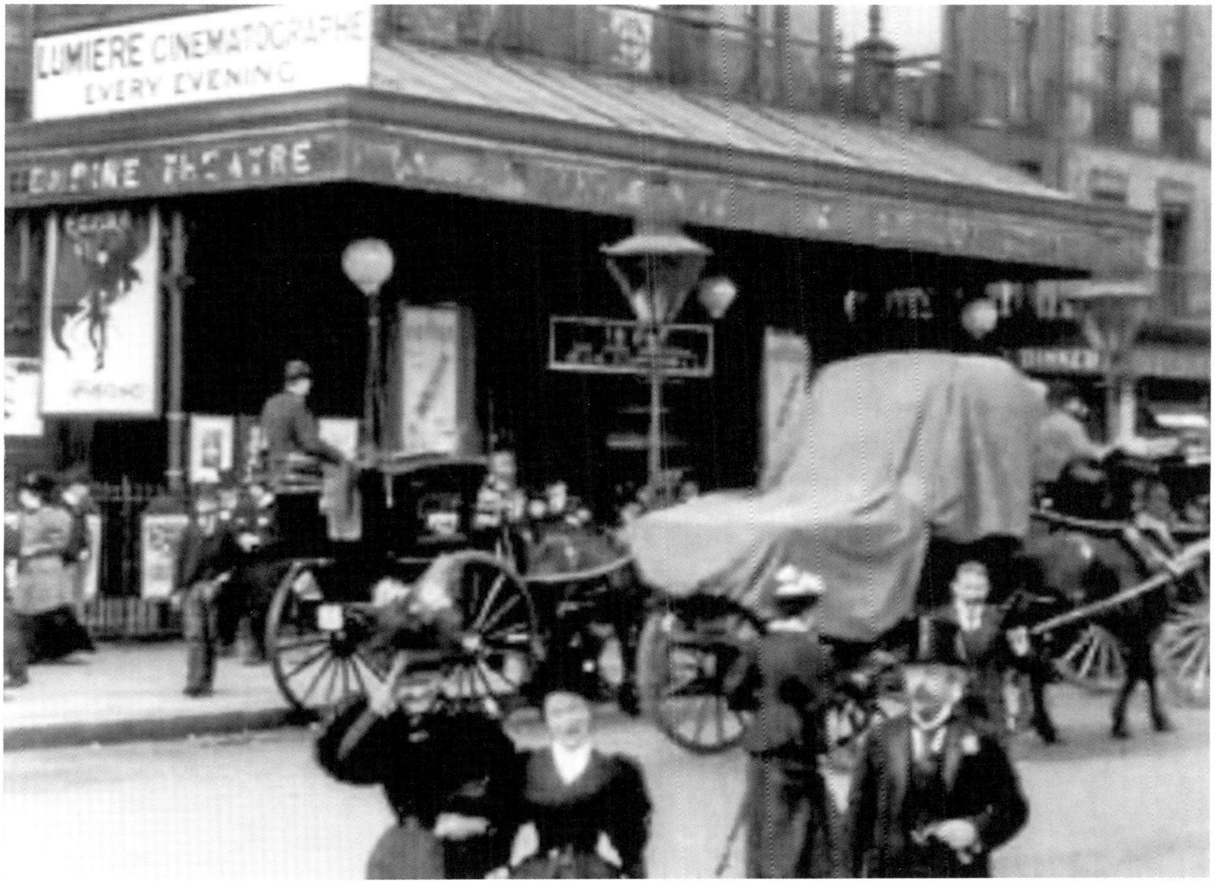

55 Lumière, *The Empire, Leicester Square*, 1896. Frame still.

To look at films of this kind is to witness the historical past drawn into the time of the present. The viewer's gaze is drawn to the details of gesture, expression and appearance that exist momentarily within the space of the screen – the pleasure of two women who cross the road, realise that they are being filmed and salute the cameraman; or the lingering trail of cigar smoke from a gentleman who has passed out of view. Roland Barthes has described the power and affect of this kind of moment in the still photograph as the 'punctum', that is, the individual detail that escapes the conventional language of the image and that addresses the viewer in a direct and physical way – a gut reaction.[57] For Barthes the punctum was an effect of the still image, rather than the moving image; as the film historian Mark-Paul Meyer has suggested, however, there are casual moments in early non-fiction film that possess precisely the qualities of the punctum as defined by Barthes.[58] This might have been part of the delight of contemporary audiences at the Empire. The magic lanternist G. R. Baker was among a number of contemporary commentators who were astonished by the rendering of detail in moving pictures: 'The marvellous detail, even to the puffs of smoke from the cigarette, spoke volumes for the perfection of the apparatus employed.'[59]

Part of the affective power of these films also lies in their reproduction of real time. The time of the film is the time of the actions, movements and gestures caught by the camera as they took place on the street. Although the scene was not necessarily spontaneous and might have been orchestrated by the film-maker, the film itself was not cut or edited; it was not shot fast or slow but purports to be an unmediated moving image of an actual episode of modern urban life. In films such as this, the contingencies and minutiae of everyday life were caught on camera and shown to audiences over and over again, even within a single programme.[60] Audiences could identify with the figures recorded on the film and, in turn, those in the street would catch the eye of the camera and seem to stare out at the audience. In these moments, in which passers-by acknowledge the act of being filmed, the image captures the temporal process of self-conscious awareness; of a give-and-take between camera and pedestrian that testifies to the fact that in the city you are seen as well as see. In this sense the urban subject is differently positioned by film than by hand-camera photography. Although both technologies stage identity in terms of visual observation, in the still image the subject should not know that they have been taken, whereas in the moving image temporality is dramatised by the representation of the individual's realisation that they are in the frame. City films in the 1890s captured the transition from exposure to composure that has come to define the experience of urban subjectivity in the modern period.

Time and space are caught in the film's act of representation. Andrey Tarkovsky captured this quality definitively when he wrote that 'time lives within [the image] . . . The dominant, all powerful factor of the film image is *rhythm*, expressing the course of time within the frame . . . and rhythm is determined not by the length of the edited pieces, but by the pressure of time that runs through them.'[61] It is these concepts of rhythm and time that begin to convey the special qualities of early film representations of the city. There is a spatial and temporal depth to these short films that gives access to a diverse and varied picture of modernity around 1900. Lumière films frequently use a diagonal axis to organise the composition and the movement. Figures move across this depth of field; they approach the camera from a deep space within the image and pass across and beyond the camera's frame. In Lumière street scenes there is a domain of selected and composed images and an aleatory register of unwitting intrusion within the frame, or unplanned engagement between passer-by and camera. Always, the frame of the image or, more accurately perhaps, the aperture of the lens, provides a stable boundary. At no point is the viewer able to forget the act of filming. There is a constant interplay between that which is within the view of the frame and that which lies beyond it. Figures and objects deep within the space of the image move forward and out of the field of vision and, for a moment only, the film retains a trace of their presence after they have moved into the unseen zone beyond the frame. The films are snatches of a historical present that is past, traces of an urban everyday that existed once and that continues to exist in the frames of the film.[62]

The projection of the pressure of time – in all its diversity – in the modern metropolis is unique to film representations of the city. *London Street Dancers* (1896; plate 56) was shot in the vicinity of the Empire Theatre and shows an itinerant musician and dancers on a street corner.[63] The subject was a conventional one, a generic feature of London literature by writers such as George R. Sims and Mrs Cook and in the photographic snapshots of Paul Martin (see plate 53) and others. Yet the film gives the viewer just enough time to notice the man choreographing the dancers and gesturing them back into the frame of the lens; the top-hatted gentleman who crosses from the foreground, momentarily blocking the camera, and stops with patriarchal assurance at the front of the watching crowd; and the glistening surfaces of the pavements, wet from recent rain. Films capture something of the rhythm and changing intensities of life in different parts of the metropolis around 1900. This was not a world of ceaseless traffic and constant speed but of haste and arrest, of street dancing and of lounging.

By the end of Victoria's reign, Piccadilly Circus had become the physical and symbolic heart of commercial London. The Eros monument to Shaftesbury had been erected in 1893 and soon after the island on which it stood became a place of momentary stasis in the midst of the constant bustle of Regent Street, Piccadilly and Shaftesbury Avenue. For Mrs Cook, Piccadilly Circus was the core of London; a site of continuous movement and change: 'a restless activity reigns here all through the long hours of day and night . . . people seem to swarm incessantly, to go and come, in consequent but feverishly active sequence'.[64] For the hand-camera photographer the challenge was precisely how to capture this heterogeneous motion in a still image. The difficulties were clearly conveyed in an article in the *British Journal of Photography* in 1902:

> Let us suppose that with our best hand camera we have taken up a position at some commanding point . . . at Piccadilly Circus, looking East. It is a decidedly pleasant prospect that we have before us; the handsome façade of the Pavilion Music Hall occupying the middle distance, and the bronze fountain with the groups of idlers and flower girls in the foreground. At least, not in the immediate foreground, for we must stand back at a sufficient distance to include the figure of Mercury at the top of the fountain, and we have, therefore, a belt of roadway that must be filled in some way. There are plenty of omnibuses and other vehicles passing and re-passing but we must look upon them as necessary intruders, and wait until chance, or the policeman, stops the stream of traffic to let pedestrians cross the road. Now is our time . . . We wait until these figures occupy the right position, or what we conceive to be the best place for our purpose, press the button . . .[65]

The multiplicity of aesthetic factors, the perception of the final image in terms of foreground, middleground and background, and the necessary dismissal of traffic and pedestrians as intruders clearly suggest the paradoxes of street photography with the hand camera. In the end, the photographer must wait for a cessation of movement. The cinematographer also had to deal with the aesthetics of the crowd and

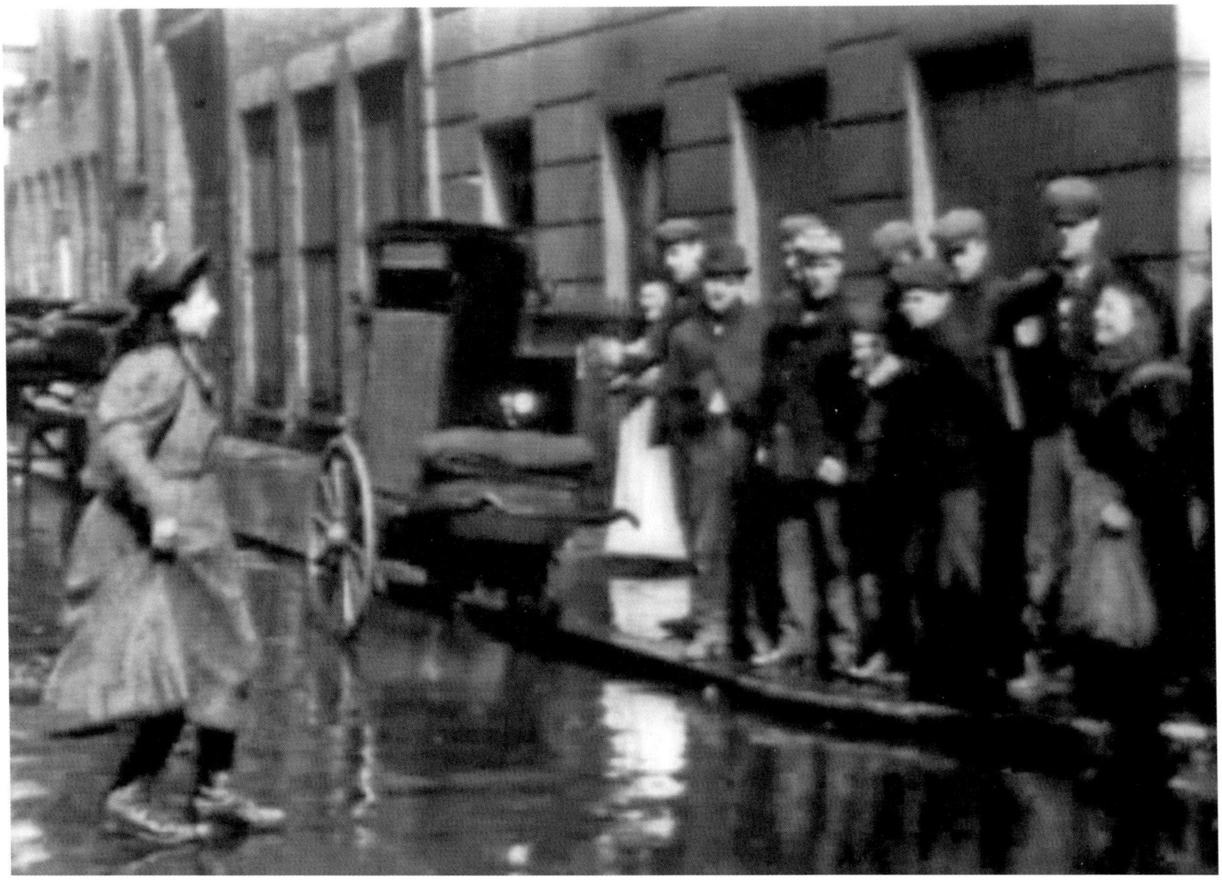

56 Lumière, *London Street Dancers*, 1896. Frame still.

its unpredictability but the duration of the film altered the relationship between subject and image and destroyed the hegemony of the single frame. Cecil Hepworth described the problem for the film-maker: 'precaution should be taken to prevent people passing just in front of the camera and blotting out the whole picture for a time with their huge and ill-defined forms'.[66] In these circumstances, it was advisable to take an assistant to usher people away from the camera and to ensure that they did not block the shot and ruin its focus. Clearly, then, selection and composition remained important considerations for the film-maker; the contingent created the magic of the street film but it had to be controlled.

The Lumière film *Piccadilly Circus* (1896; plate 57), illustrates how film-makers negotiated the dual expectations of animated life and framed composition in these years. The fixed camera position conveys something of the diverse nature of metropolitan life, even at its centre. As a result of an unusually low and tight camera angle, the viewpoint seems literally absorbed into the passage of people and things. Women walk towards the camera and out of view, blocked momentarily by passing

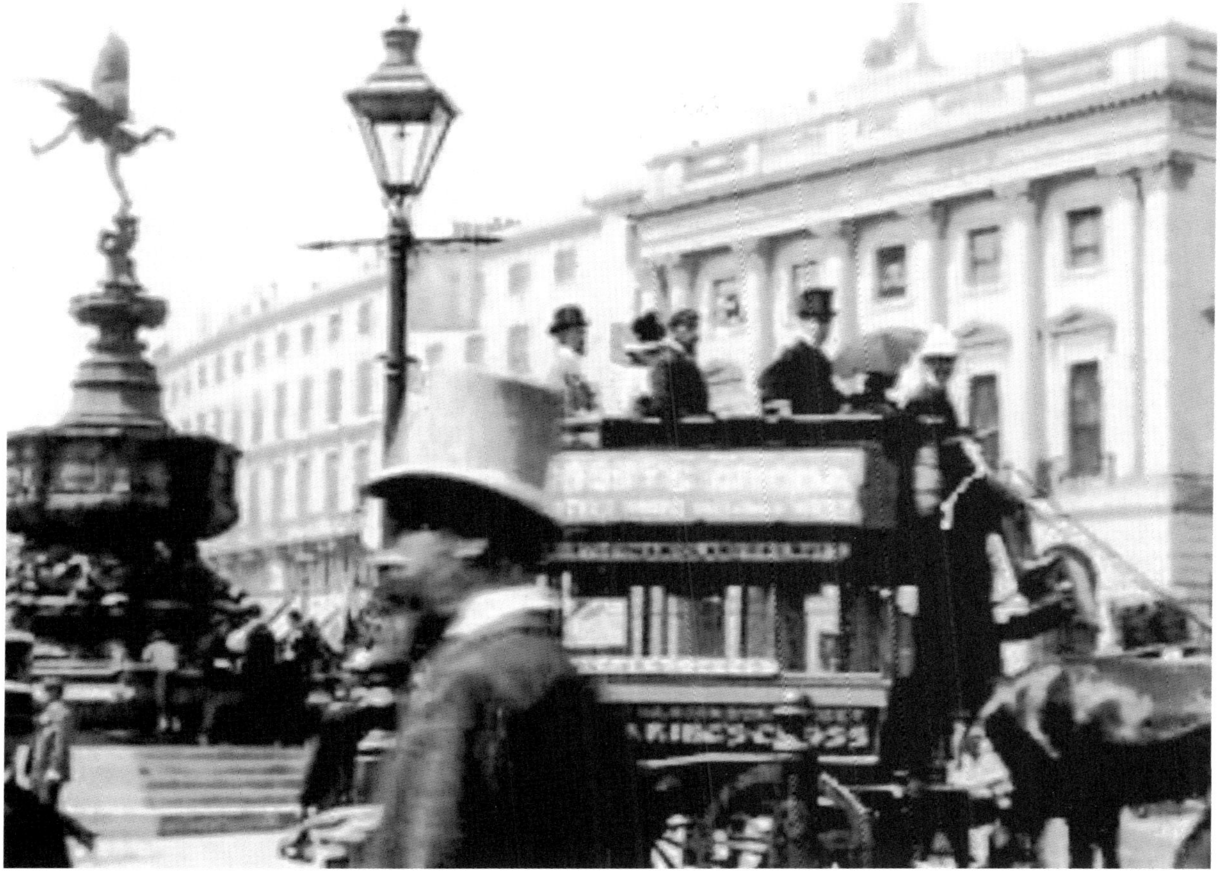

57 Lumière, *Piccadilly Circus*, 1896. Frame still.

traffic. And in the background, figures lounge around the Eros Fountain, taking time out from the circulation of goods and people. While the immediate view of the camera lens is never obscured, there is a ceaseless flow of people and objects across and within the film frame. Composition appears subordinated to movement.

Simmel has limited use as a means of understanding these images. More specifically, his essay 'The Metropolis and Mental Life' flattens possible readings of urban space in this period. What is clear is that these films and the aesthetic with which they are involved do not articulate metropolitan life in simple terms of sensory bombardment or neurasthenia and it is necessary to look elsewhere for a methodological framework for an historical analysis. Gaston Bachelard's *Dialectic of Duration* was first published in France in 1950, as a sustained critique of Henri Bergson's notion of temporal continuity.[67] For Bachelard, all time is polymorphous and comprises 'a duality of events and intervals . . . a precise, concrete duration that [teems] with lacunae'. Time will necessarily comprise a plurality of durations 'that have neither the same rhythm nor the same solidity in their sequence, nor the same power of continuity . . . all true duration is polymorphous'.[68] While there is much in this work that can be dismissed as essentialist or sentimental, Bachelard's chapter on 'Rhythmanalysis' is highly suggestive for revising dominant characterisations of urban modernity. (The theme was taken up by Henri Lefebvre and Michel de Certeau, but is, arguably, most exciting in its 'raw' state in Bachelard's work.) Rhythmanalysis is concerned with the diverse speeds and intensities within any given temporality; time – even modern time – is a question of stasis, repose and intertia as much as speed, productivity and stimulation. Victorian films convey something of the rhythmic diversities of London around 1900. To put it simply, they are evidence of the diversity of urban rhythm; for example, of street corners, close to Piccadilly Circus, where musician and cameraman orchestrate dancers in an urbanised jig, where passers-by stop and smile for the camera.

the animated everyday

The changes in social relations brought about by these shifts in modern urban visuality were acknowledged almost immediately. These were issues concerning privacy, rights and representation in the public sphere that had been raised, but left hopelessly unresolved, in relation to instantaneous photography and that reappeared in different forms in connection with the moving images of film. In the early years in which filmed street scenes were being exhibited to paying audiences, a new type of urban myth appeared based on the theme of accidental encounters or confrontations made possible by the arbitrary presence of individuals within the crowds of the actuality scenes. Short stories, novels and even films themselves repeated the narrative of prodigal children reconciled with their families through being seen on the screen after years of absence. More sensationally, adulterous affairs were exposed by the unfaithful partner being unintentionally caught with his or her lover by the film camera and projected to an audience including the deceived husband or wife.[69] The point of these narratives is that film conveyed a sense of modern urban life as unpredictably interconnected rather than as alienated or indifferent. The contingent was the site of an endless production of significance in which any individual might find themself caught up in urban drama.

Victorian actuality films reversed the conventional values of the banal and the extraordinary within contemporary life. Mundane, everyday life was recorded and monumentalised and the exceptional was subjected to endless repetition. The films subjected the small, unobtrusive gestures of daily life and the minutiae of social interaction on the city streets to unprecedented scrutiny. In another cultural field, too, apparently insignificant everyday forms were being watched as Freud interpreted this repertoire of accidental actions as symptoms that manifested everyday disturbances of thought. If the flow of city crowds provided the subject for spectacular commercial entertainment, then it also exposed the 'field of phenomena' defined by Freud in 1901 as *The Psychopathology of Everyday Life*:

> the irritating and clumsy process of dodging someone in the street, when for several seconds one steps first to one side then to the other, but always to the same side as the other person, till finally one comes to a standstill face to face with him (or her) – this 'getting in someone's way' . . . is once more a repetition of an improper and provocative piece of behaviour from earlier times and behind a mask of clumsiness, pursues sexual aims.[70]

By 1900 the conduct of everyday urban life had become the subject of photographic technologies that exposed the smallest and most contingent gestures to examination and interpretation. Everyday life expressed both modernity's surface appearances and its unconscious origins and drives.

If the cameramen of the 1890s took snapshots and made films in order to capture 'Living London', a city of 'flesh and blood', as Sims described it, there is, however, surely also something spectral and deathly about these figures that returns this chapter to the theme of haunting.[71] As instantaneous photographs and actuality films strove to endow the image with life and animation, they also confirmed that they were only representations, simulacra and never life itself. For all the early accounts that emphasised the realism and lifelike qualities of early film, there was also something deathly in the ephemerality of the lives animated on the screen. In the summer of 1896, when Gorky wrote about the first Lumière programme shown in Russia (referred to in chapter 2), he not only saw magic and curses, he also glimpsed shadows and ghosts:

> Last night I was in the Kingdom of Shadows . . .
>
> When the lights go out in the room in which Lumière's invention is shown, there suddenly appears on the screen a large grey picture . . . As you gaze at it, you see carriages, buildings and people in various poses, all frozen into immobility. But suddenly a strange flicker passes through the screen and the picture stirs to life. Carriages coming from somewhere in the perspective of the picture are moving straight at you, into the darkness in which you sit; somewhere from afar people appear and loom larger as they come closer to you . . . All this moves, teems with life and, upon approaching the edge of the screen, vanishes somewhere beyond it . . .
>
> Before you a life is surging, a life deprived of words and shorn of the spectrum of colours – the grey, the soundless, the bleak and dismal life.
>
> It is terrifying to see, but it is the movement of shadows, only of shadows.[72]

This compelling piece of writing begins to bring one close to the uncanny effect of looking at late Victorian photographs and films of the metropolis, an effect which was expressed both in the late 1890s and which can be experienced now. We viewers in the present know that these people were once there but the closer the images get to simulating life, the more we are reminded of their spectral presence and of death. As Gorky's words and the photographic images of the archive demonstrate, the streets of modern London were not simply living and breathing, they were also the habitat of colourless ghosts.

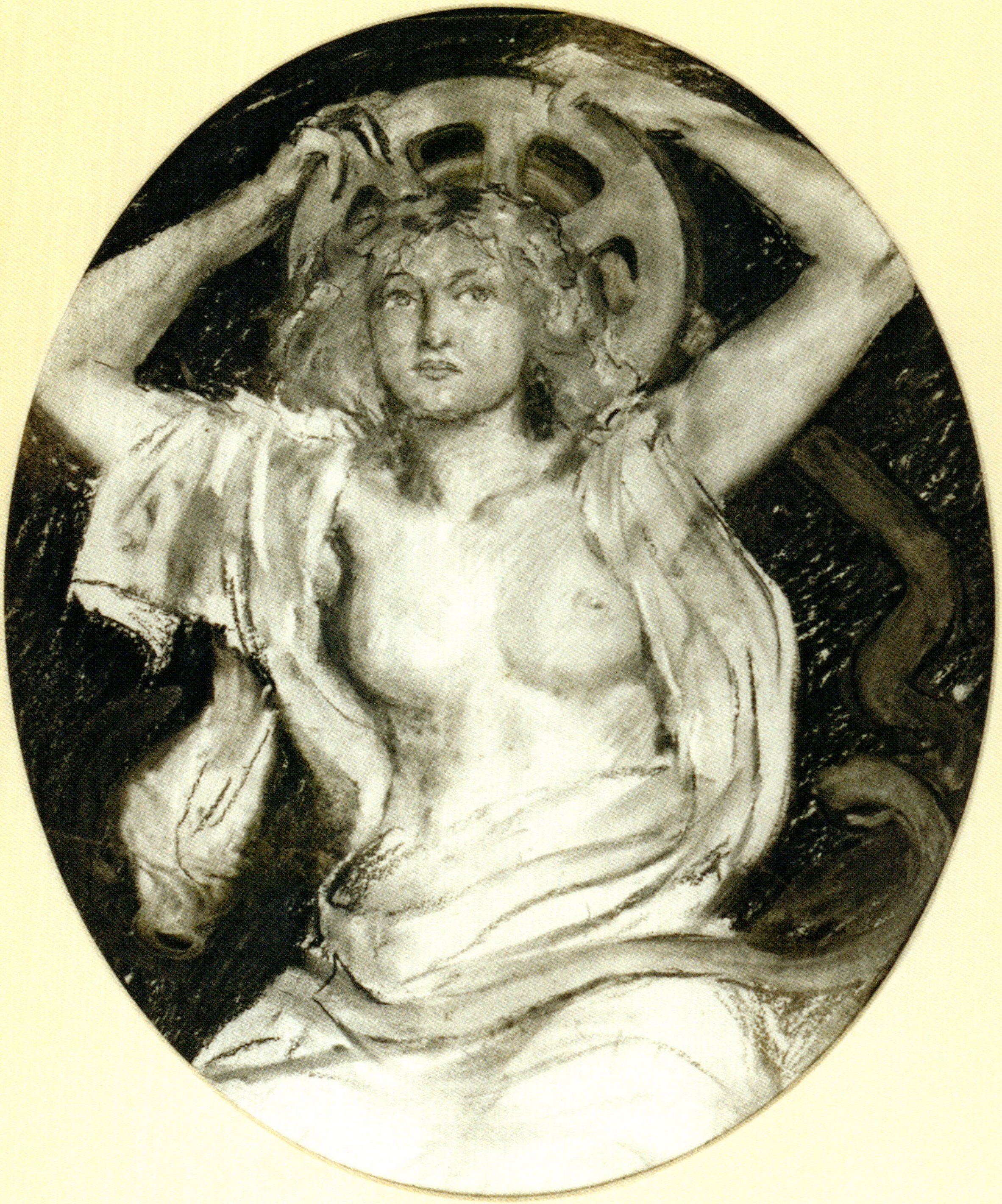

4 paintings, films and fast cars

Hills of the ruggedest,
Vales of the comeliest;
Barrows and cromlechs,
Ancestral ossuaries,
Whence (you may fancy)
The troubled grey ghosts
Of your forefathers peer,
As you swoop down on them,
With a wild, wondering
Pride in their seed . . .

William Ernest Henley, *A Song of Speed* (1903)[1]

the reel and the wheel

In the first watercolour sketch for the logo of the Herkomer Film Company a female nude holds a film reel behind her head while the film snakes, like a living creature, round her body (plate 58). The reel is also a halo, which transforms Herkomer's allegorical figure into a madonna of the cinematograph; emblems of the secular and the sacred, the reel and the halo are both associated with magical light and the generation of miraculous images. There is one further association, however, that completes the triptych of related meanings – reel, halo and wheel. Reel and wheel, film and car, are here drawn into an intimate visual proximity that acts as an historical reminder of the long and tangled relationship between these two technologies of modern motion. The cinema and the motor car seem to share a history: from the moment of their first commercial production to the time of their institutionalisation, rapid expansion and absorption in the everyday life of twentieth-century industrial societies. More than this, both were instrumental in bringing about a shift in what might be described as modern vision and in reconfiguring conceptions of subjectivity in relation to time and space. Films and cars are powerful cultural symbols of industrial modernity but in order to understand

58 Hubert von Herkomer, first watercolour sketch for the logo of the Herkomer Film Company, *c.* 1913.

how they acquired this meaning one needs to go back to those first years, when neither motoring nor film-making was properly institutionalised, when the implications of both technologies were not self-evident and when the changes in vision made possible by motion pictures and motor cars were uncertain and frequently contradictory. The motor car also relocates the history of twentieth-century visual media in the countryside. It took film away from its urban contexts and its examination of everyday street life and drove it out into the lanes and picturesque settings of the rural world, where it established an alternative pictorial aesthetic, representing a different style of modern identity. A nostalgic and conservative image of the national past was effectively created out of types of movement made possible by the latest forms of modern technology.

This historical encounter between older cultural forms and traditions and new and innovative modes of production and comprehension is elaborated in the work of the French philosopher Michel Serres. His books examine the interrelationships between science and magic and science and culture and the ongoing dialectic between the present and the past in modern societies. He sees the motor car as symptomatic of these historical exchanges, its chronology representing an aggregate of technical and cultural solutions that draws together, in a single object, 'the archaic, the modern and the futuristic'. In a published conversation with the sociologist of science Bruno Latour, Serres explains his conception of historical time and periodisation.[2] Rejecting classical theories of linear and geometric time, he presents instead an image of time as multi-layered, almost geological and apparently disordered. At any given moment, he suggests, there can be no pure or singular periodisation, for the present always belongs to several eras at once and is inundated with traces of the past and gestures to the future. At this point, Serres illustrates his position by drawing on the example of a modern car:

> It is a disparate aggregate of scientific and technical solutions dating from different periods. One can date it component by component: this part was invented at the turn of the century, another, ten years ago . . . Not to mention that the wheel dates back to neolithic times. The ensemble is only contemporary by assemblage, by its design, its finish, sometimes only by the slickness of the advertising surrounding it. (p. 45)

For Serres, all objects or circumstances share the historical condition of the car; that is, they are polychronic and multi-temporal, they belong to historical time that is pleated, constantly folded back on itself, or torn asunder, creating an ongoing dialogue with 'the archaic, the modern and the futuristic' (p. 60).

Serres's image of time and historical periodisation – particularly as it is figured in the image of the motor car – is suggestive and useful. It offers a way of writing the history of visual culture and technology that is freed from the ceaseless exertion of a model of progress dictated by novelty. It is sometimes assumed that new media and technologies emerge fully formed, prepared to take their place in and perhaps for ever to transform the social scene. Consider the Model T Ford car, the supreme articulation of the twentieth-century desire for standardised speed; or the

Hollywood film as the pre-eminent expression of commercialised mass culture. Serres's work suggests that one should look for a more uncertain and uneven history of the emergence of such forms and that one should take account of how new forms are used in old ways and how older objects are adapted to new uses.

Cultural forms can thus be understood as multi-temporal. They have no clear or natural historical edges that mark them out as either modern or obsolete and at any given moment they will be part of a social world defined by the 'coexistence of the old and the new'.[3] In this context, it makes no sense to write the history of any single medium – to take some well worn examples, to trace or contest the failure of nineteenth-century British painting or to reconstruct the early years of film. Individually, these forms have limited historical meaning and can deliver only a predetermined set of responses. Taken together, visual media represent the exchange of social meanings through the circulation of images and ideas and the landscape of cultural relations that characterise specific historical moments. I am interested, then, in an integrated history of visual media and for this reason I am drawn to an historical moment when relations between new and old visual forms were at their most tenuous and unformed and when visual culture and technology were meeting head-on in an unprecedented, explosive creativity. I want to go back to the early years of the motor car and moving pictures and uncover the different ways of seeing and of imaging that were emerging with the new experiences of mechanical motor travel. This means recalling names, images or circumstances that previous histories have chosen to forget and placing them in a new set of relationships and concerns. With this broader project in mind, I want to remember Hubert von Herkomer – painter, motorist and film-maker – and see whether a re-examination of his work generates a different picture of British culture at the end of the nineteenth century and the beginning of the twentieth century.

hubert von herkomer: a case study of animated vision

For those who are unfamiliar with the name and work of Herkomer, here is a brief biography.[4] Herkomer was one of the most highly rewarded and officially respected painters in Britain in the nineteenth century. He was made a Royal Academician and succeeded John Ruskin as Slade Professor of Fine Art in Oxford; he was lavished with honours and distinctions, including Officer of the Legion of Honour and Knight of the Prussian Order. If he was never quite regarded as the most outstanding artist of his age, he was, without question, acknowledged to be a major player in all the main arenas of the late Victorian art world.

Herkomer was an immigrant to Britain, a factor that had a significant impact on his participation in and negotiation of British and continental culture. He was born in Bavaria in 1849; his family emigrated to the United States in 1851 but finding little success there they moved again in 1857 to England, settling in Southampton. Herkomer's initial art education was received from his father who was a carver and engraver; this patriarchal figure, symbolising traditional craft values,

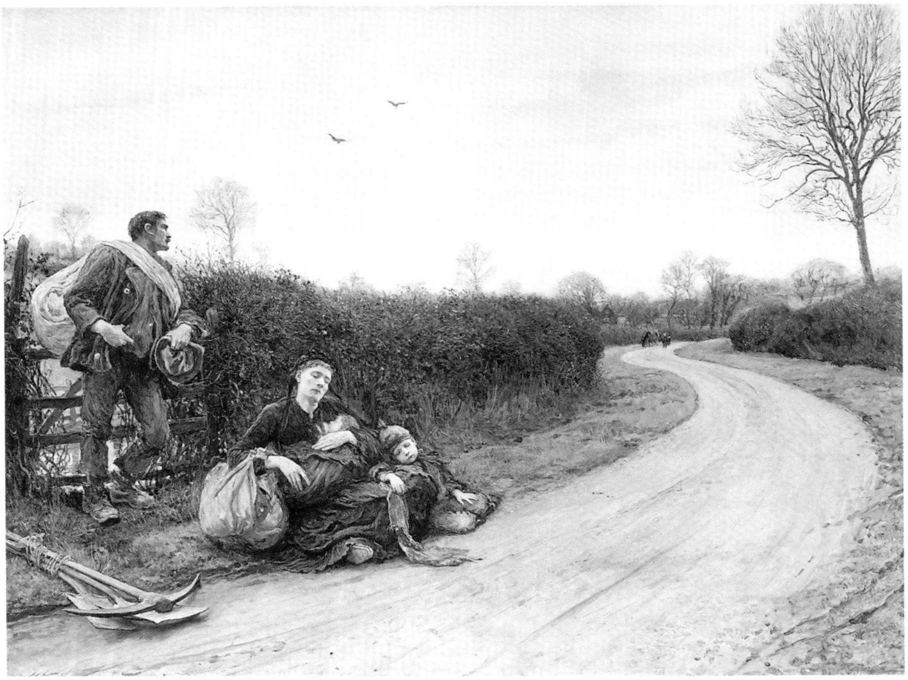

remained central to Herkomer's autobiographical narrative and to the creation of visual narrative throughout his career. In one of his autobiographical publications, Herkomer recalled his childhood and being urged by his father to lie in the fields near their Southampton home and to 'dream' pictures.[5] Pictures, story-telling and cultural identity were closely related in Herkomer's personal beliefs and pictorial practices and can be traced across his work in a range of visual media. Moreover, the association of these themes with a particular vision of rural England was also a founding passion. While this vision might be explained as arising from the particular experiences of immigration in this period, it was also one that was widely shared by cultural producers within the indigenous culture and that came to define an influential and enduring version of national identity from the 1890s to the present. In a lecture on English landscape delivered at the Royal Academy of Arts in 1900, Herkomer exhorted the students:

> I urge you to cherish your England, to cherish its cottage homes, its farmsteads, its village greens, and its shady lanes. Let painter and poet paint and write to keep these treasures warm in our hearts, for the beauties of England are assuredly shrinking under the encroaching newness of all things, with a future of inartistic repair and of citydom everywhere . . . let [the English painter] proclaim the great truth that England is one of the most lovable and paintable countries in the world.[6]

Although the general elements of this landscape and the rhetoric are broadly familiar from the mid-Victorian period and the imagery is derived from the paintings

59 (*facing page*) Hubert von Herkomer, *Hard Times*, 1885. Oil on canvas, 86.5 × 112 cm. Manchester Art Gallery.

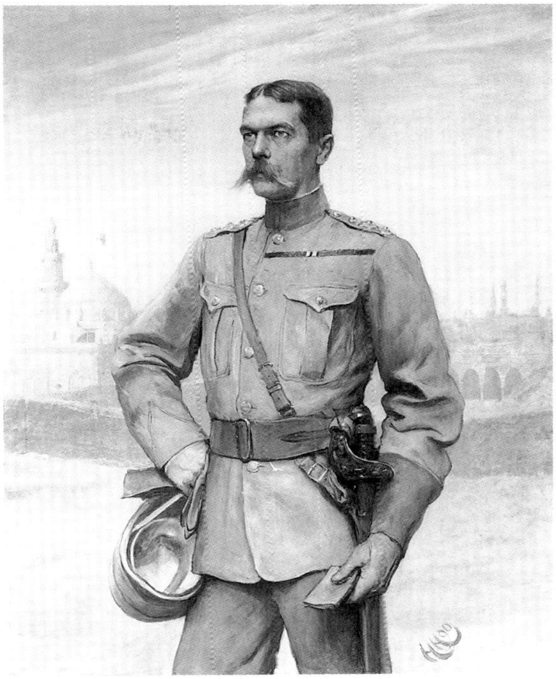

60 (*right*) Hubert von Herkomer (background by Frederick Goodall), *1st Earl Kitchener of Khartoum*, 1890. Oil on canvas, 139.7 × 109.2 cm. National Portrait Gallery, London.

of Constable and Birket Foster, by 1900 they had different inflections and had absorbed the more recent idioms of conservation, urban blight and modernity. Furthermore, the tensions in Herkomer's vision of a rural way of life steadily yielding to the assault of modern life frequently recur in what will be examined later in this chapter in terms of 'motorised vision'. For many early motorists, including Herkomer, the motor car was a means of discovering the beauty and 'paintability' of England; for them motoring, while it remained an elite mode of transport, could be excluded from the 'encroaching newness' that threatened to destroy its picturesque qualities.

Herkomer makes his way into the historiography of nineteenth-century British art through the pages of the illustrated periodical press and the emergence of a group of artists in the 1870s working for the *Graphic* and the *Illustrated London News*.[7] Drawing their subjects from the more disturbing and grimmer aspects of contemporary life, artists such as Frank Holl, Luke Fildes and Herkomer developed a new mode of social realism that took the themes of urban and rural poverty from graphic journalism and turned them into paintings for the walls of art galleries such as the Royal Academy. A number of Victorian social realism's most familiar and powerful images, such as *Hard Times* (plate 59), were painted by Herkomer, and although they played a major part in the creation of his artistic identity and the consolidation of his reputation, he did not remain committed to this genre.

The other string to his artistic bow was portrait painting (plate 60). Herkomer established a highly successful and lucrative practice as a portrait painter that he kept going until the end of his life. His sitters came from the royal families of

Europe and were major figures in late nineteenth-century public life; their status was an index of Herkomer's centrality to the social and artistic establishment of the period. This is where history abandons Herkomer, as a distinctive painter of his age but not for all time – in other words, forgettable. Up to this point, Herkomer's career apparently tells the familiar story of the failure of modern British art; of its lack of direction in the late nineteenth century and its failure to grasp properly the direction of advanced European art in the first years of the twentieth century. However, I want to continue tracking Herkomer through the last years of his life (1900–14) and to propose a different picture of British visual culture in this period. It is in these years that Herkomer's career exemplifies the connectedness of old and new media, traditional and emergent technologies, that was referred to at the beginning of this chapter. Demonstrating a persistent fascination with diverse aspects of motion, Herkomer pursued the idea of animated vision to the end of his life and work. While remaining entrenched within certain academic ideals and procedures, he was one of the most vociferous public supporters of popular film art of his artistic generation and can be described, without misrepresentation, as a key player in the campaign to legitimise and regulate the British film industry in the years immediately preceding the First World War.

Herkomer loved motor cars and made moving pictures. In the last years of his life he embraced the possibilities of motion and attempted to reconcile the pictorial languages of art and film. He recognised a new kind of mobilised perception through the windscreen of his Daimler, which he understood could be recreated and aestheticised in the medium of the moving picture. Yet he was no modernist. He wanted to bring art to the fledgling film industry and to drag film up from its nineteenth-century, music-hall and fairground roots and imbue it with the values and artistic ideals of mainstream narrative painting.

The setting for Herkomer's encounter with the technologies of speed was Bushey in Hertfordshire, north of London. There he built an extraordinary residence called Lululaund, a kind of Xanadu confection of Bavarian stone carving and Gothic space that he dedicated to the memory of his first, dead wife (plates 61 and 62).[8] If the scale and style of the interiors seem to recall the ambitions and aesthetics of historical film-set design, that is correct for Herkomer indeed used both the grounds and the interiors of his home to shoot scenes for his films. However, the house was much more than the monumental folly of a rich and whimsical émigré artist; it was the tangible and visible expression of Herkomer's life story. It was a paean to the crafts and skills of his father that had been inexorably superseded by Herkomer's own lucrative engagement with the high art of painting and the new technologies of mechanical reproduction.

At the end of the nineteenth century Bushey, in common with many English villages close to major cities, was on the brink of transformation into a commuter town. Animals gave way to motor cars and buses and the place became repopulated with city workers, commuting by rail to London. In his art, however, Herkomer continued to propagate a nostalgic image of a sleepy picturesque village – complete with church, elm tree and quaint high street – long after the com-

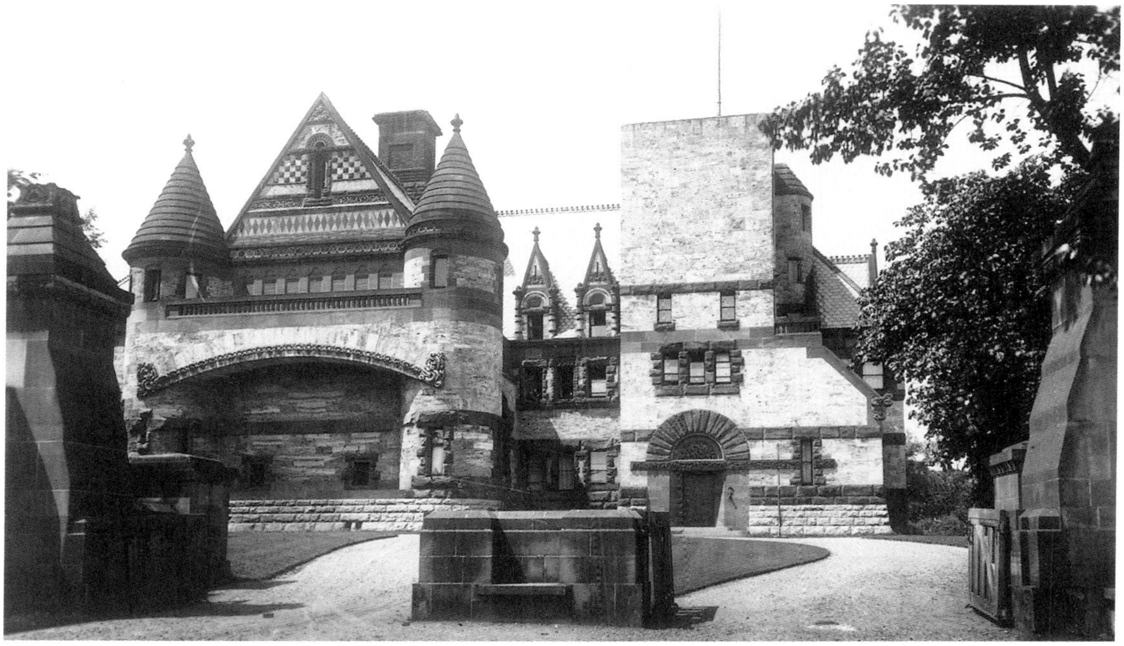

61 The exterior of Lululaund, Bushey, Hertfordshire, *c.*1900.

62 The interior of Lululaund, Bushey, Hertfordshire, *c.*1900.

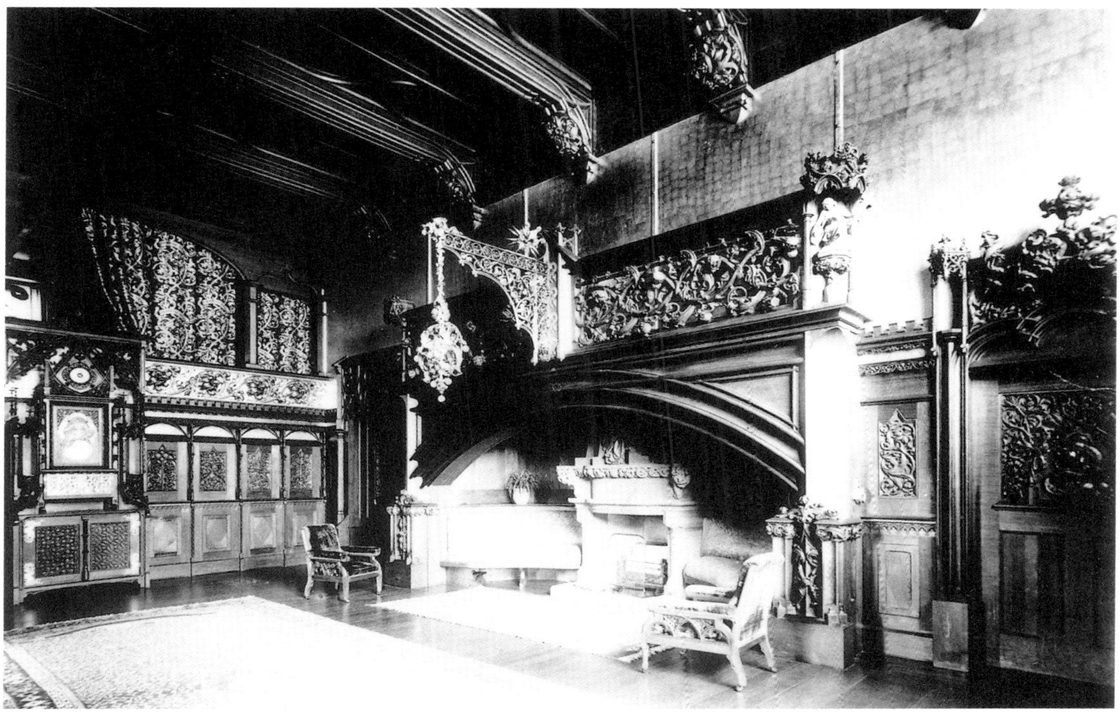

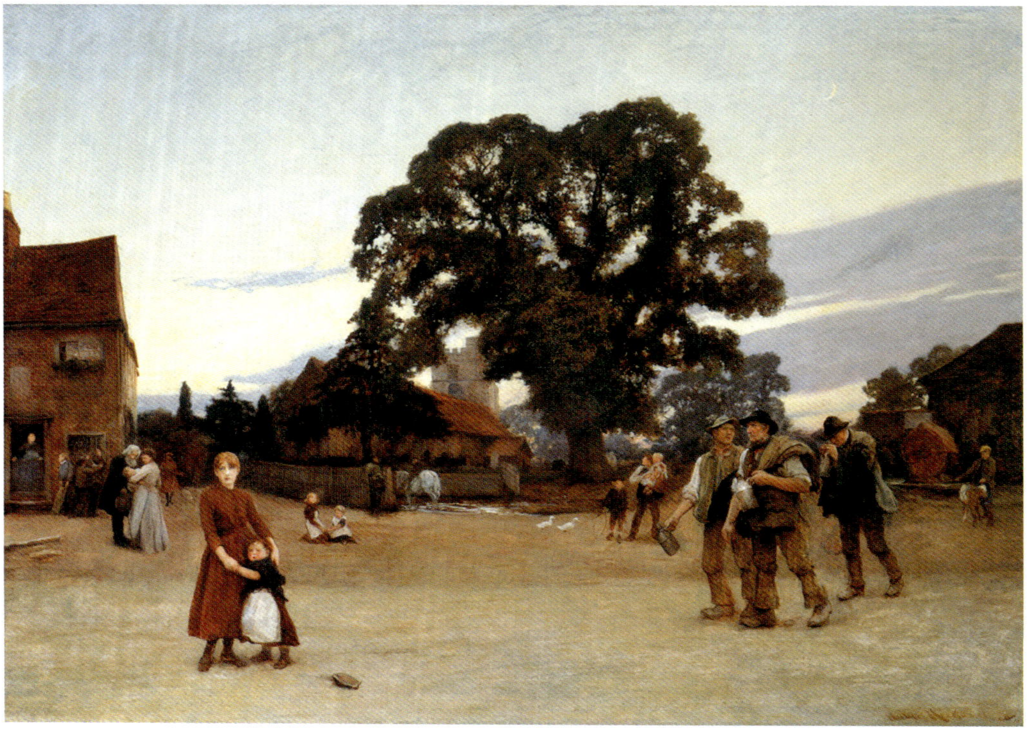

63 Hubert von Herkomer, *Our Village*, 1890. Oil on canvas, 172.7 × 234.9 cm. Aberdeen Art Gallery and Museums Collections.

muters had moved in.[9] Reminiscing at the beginning of the twentieth century about the image of Bushey captured in his painting *Our Village* in 1890 (plate 63), he wrote: 'The full-branched elm still enframed the old church, with its picturesque setting of yews and tombs. There was still the somnolent air about the village . . . There was no hooting of motor horns; there was no blinding dust thrown into [the villagers'] eyes by the rush of passing motor-cars.'[10] He celebrates the values of the good old days, when labour was plentiful and the sons of labourers aspired only to become labourers in their turn, but comes to the somewhat unexpected conclusion that it is better to adapt to new values than forever to lament the loss of old ones. He comforts himself with the thought that 'true it is that I have benefited in a most pronounced way by the advent of one new thing – the motor-car' (p. 61). This passage demonstrates the futility of trying to fit Herkomer into single categories such as conservative or modernist and exposes the limitations of these classifications in the context of a revised history of twentieth-century British culture. Herkomer was a traditionalist who was thrilled and empowered by new technologies and was equally at home regretting the dust thrown in labourers' eyes by the motorist invasion of Bushey and enthusing about the motor car like Toad in Kenneth Grahame's *Wind in the Willows* (1908).

Bushey was also the backdrop for the creation of Herkomer's School of Art. Run according to a strictly defined curriculum of drawing and painting from the life model, the School rejected a number of the mainstays of academic training, including its study of the antique and its system of competitions and prizes. For Herkomer, figure painting was about rooting the subject, the artist and the viewer in a fixed and consistent set of relations. He directed students to situate their subjects a few yards from their feet and to use brushwork and colour to convey recession of planes and perspective. Herkomer had an utterly static perception of the painted image and trained his students precisely according to this system. In spite of the rigidity of its pedagogy, however, the primary goal of the School was expressed in liberal terms: it aimed to 'search for the personality of each student',[11] although it is clear that the prevailing personality in the School belonged to its founder. The students were drawn into a total cultural environment that included musical evenings and dramatic performances and that sought to generate an 'art atmosphere'.

Herkomer applied a number of his principles of picture-making to his staging of theatrical performances. Shortly after the opening of the art school, he and his students created an auditorium, modelled on Wagner's Festspielhaus in Bayreuth, for public performances of plays, written, directed and, indeed, performed by Herkomer.[12] In some ways, the Herkomer Theatre Company was a logical extension, in a different medium, of the aesthetic principles taught in the art school. He claimed that: 'The rehearsals were lessons in picture-making, and the students learnt the art of grouping figures artistically within a given space, and of a fixed character.'[13] For Herkomer, his pictorial-music plays gave life, depth and movement to the formal qualities of the painted image and he described the resulting heightened reality as 'stereoscopic'.[14] More significantly, he also conceived of his theatrical productions as enchanted pictures. Referring to his 1889 play, *An Idyl*, he wrote: 'It was based upon the fantasy of a painter who used as pigment living colours, and a magic canvas, his mind all aflame with the excitement from a new experiment.'[15] In fact, the libretto is a dull romance set in a medieval village; nevertheless, Herkomer imagined the staging as the setting in motion of a sequence of *tableaux*. It was a dream of movement presented in precisely the terms of the cultural fantasy of the haunted gallery, described in chapter 2 of this book.

The stage also offered Herkomer a different space for experimenting with optical effect and narrative action. He wrote passionately about his most successful technical innovations in stage lighting; for example, a moonlight effect in which the moon was seen to rise and pass across a sky that changed from night to dawn (plate 64). In his memoirs, Herkomer compared the inspired decision to turn to theatrical experiments to the thrill of starting the engine of a motor car:

> I can only compare my mental condition at that moment to a motor-car, when the ignition-switch is turned on, making the engine run at a great pace, producing great noise and causing the whole car to vibrate . . . Then the clutch was slipped in, and away we went on a pleasure trip, that had only, up to that moment, been a dream. (p. 147)

This is not a casual reference, but a metaphor that is extended and lovingly explored, till the figure takes on a life of its own. All points of reference at this

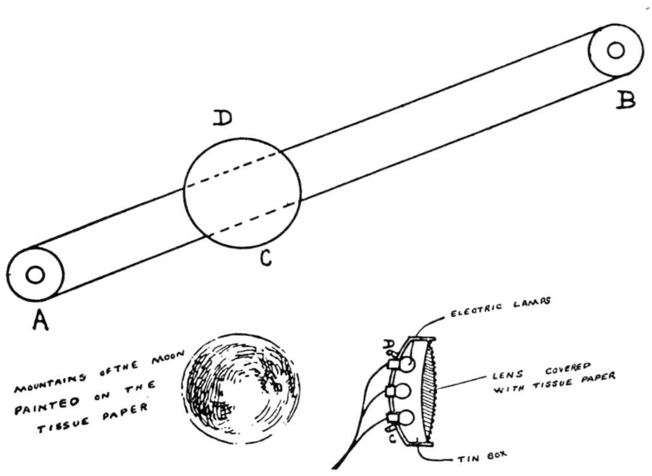

64 Diagram of 'moon-mechanism', from Hubert von Herkomer, *My School and My Gospel*, London: Archibald Constable and Co. Ltd, 1908, p. 209.

moment are energised. The shift from the still, two-dimensional image to the three-dimensional space and extended temporality of the stage is expressed in terms of the preparations for and beginnings of movement, and a fantasy journey that sets painting in motion and intensifies its powers of illusion.

Herkomer's fascination with animated vision continued unabated into the early years of the twentieth century as he sought different ways of bringing images to life. In 1912 he wrote the preface to A. Wallace Rimington's *Colour-Music: The Art of Mobile Colour*.[16] Rimington, a watercolourist and professor of fine arts in London, had invented a musical keyboard in which each note had a corresponding colour that was projected onto a screen when a note or chord was struck (plate 65). The 'screening' took place in a darkened room with a large screen of white drapery in folds, framed with black (plate 66). Rimington described the gradual appearance and fading of hues, colours that changed in tempo and intensity, with periodic returns to darkness. For Rimington, his colour music necessarily went far beyond any previous attempts by artists to suggest analogies between pictures and music; his was an art of pure colour that had broken through the fixed boundaries of the still image and had been set into fluid motion. According to Herkomer, Rimington's instrument was an invaluable stimulant for the visual artist but he could not abandon narrative and questioned whether the contemplation of formless colour could ever be as pleasurable as colour attached to form. What Herkomer was searching for was a medium that could mobilise form without neglecting content, a technology for animating narrative pictures.

The step from this set of interests to the making of films is a small and rational one. In 1892 Herkomer had invited Eadweard Muybridge to his School of Art in order to demonstrate the photographic sequences of animal locomotion that Herkomer later described as 'the beginning of the picture film of today'.[17] Given his passion for animated vision, it is perhaps surprising that it was not until some time in 1912 that Herkomer and his son Siegfried began making films and in 1913 the Herkomer Film Company was formally launched (plate 67).[18] Siegfried had

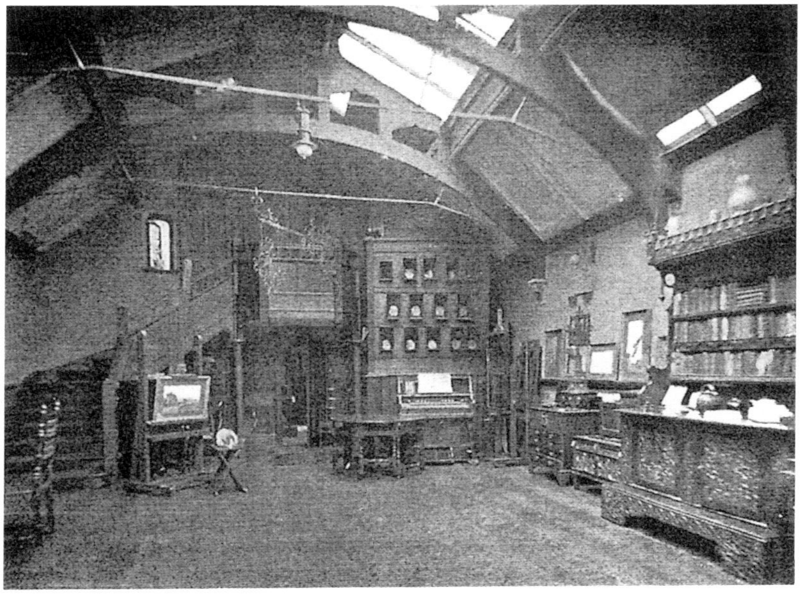

65 'Keyboard colour-organ as used in the author's studio', from A. Wallace Rimington, *Colour-Music: The Art of Mobile Colour*, London: Hutchinson and Co., 1912, opp. p. 107.

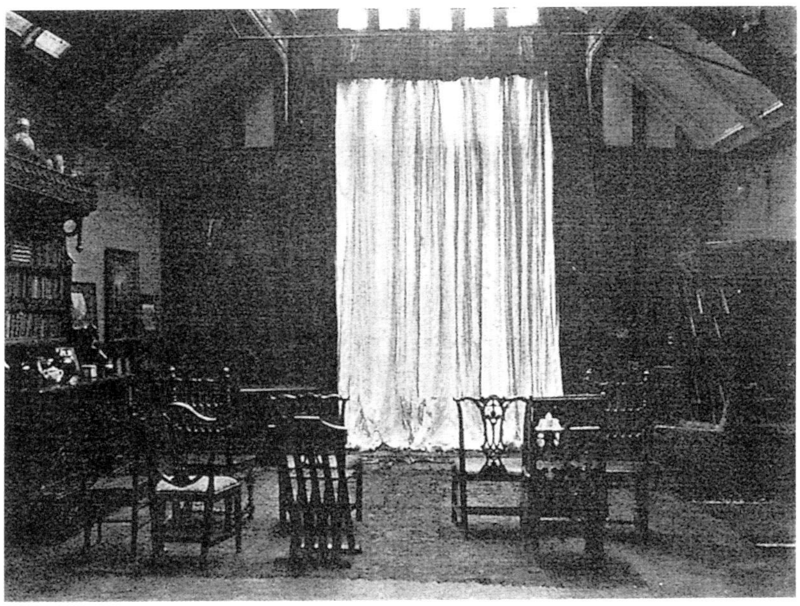

66 'Simple form of screen as used in the author's studio', from A. Wallace Rimington, *Colour-Music: The Art of Mobile Colour*, London: Hutchinson and Co., 1912, opp. p. 66.

THE LATEST CRAZE IN SCIENCE: THE

DRAWN BY OUR SPECIAL

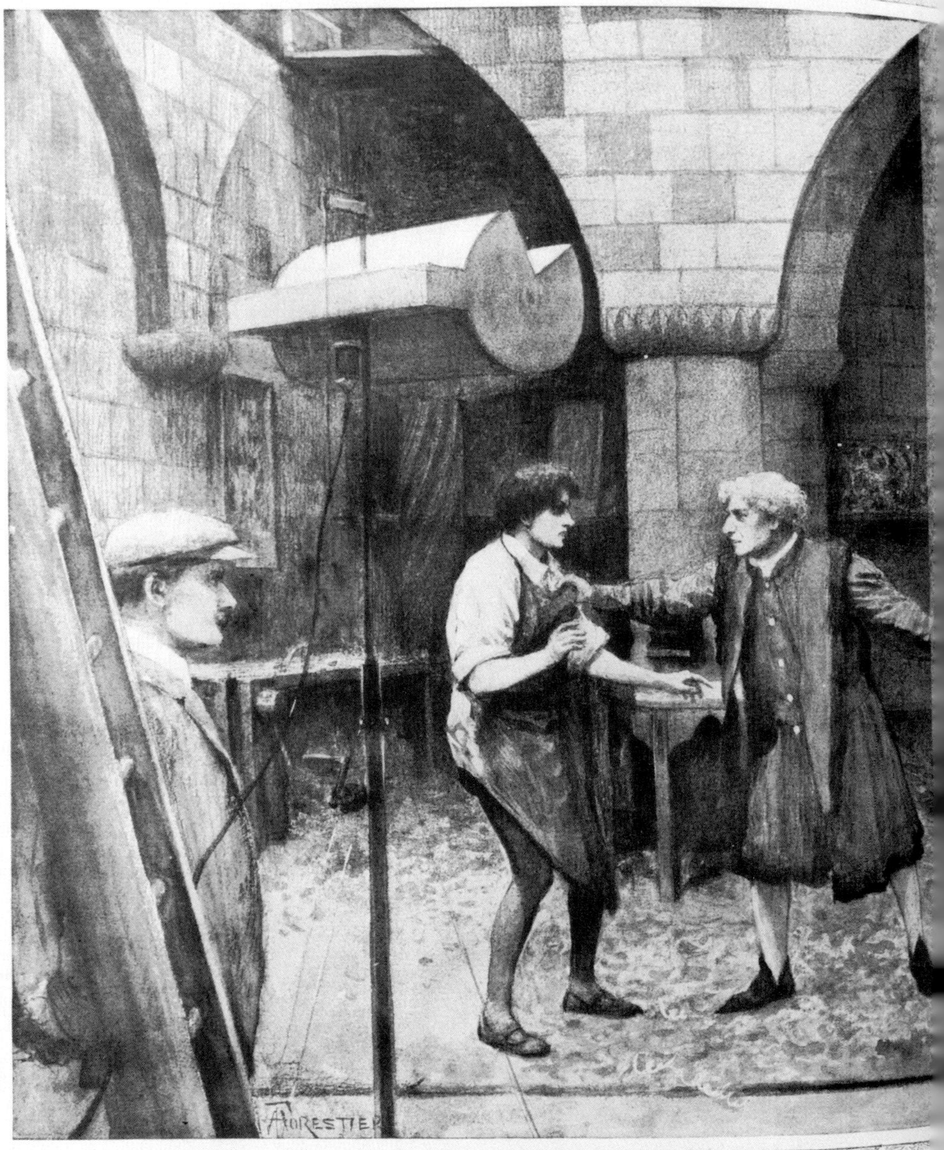

LIFTING THE SCIENCE OF CINEMATOGRAPHY INTO THE REGIONS OF HIGH AR
IN HIS OWN PICTUR

Sir Hubert von Herkomer, the famous painter, has realised that the cinematograph, or picture-theatre, has become a permanent and influential part of the national life, and the
it is highly desirable that it should be lifted out of the region of crude and occasionally vulgar sensationalism up to a higher level of artistic quality. At "Lululaund," his house a
Bushey, he has for many years had a well-arranged little theatre, and of late he has been vigorously engaged in preparing for production a number of picture-plays, with the a
of a small army of photographers, electricians, carpenters, and scene-painters. Many of the scenarios are rehearsed in the beautiful grounds of his house. He has engage

CINEMATOGRAPH TAKEN UP BY AN R.A.

ARTIST, A. FORESTIER.

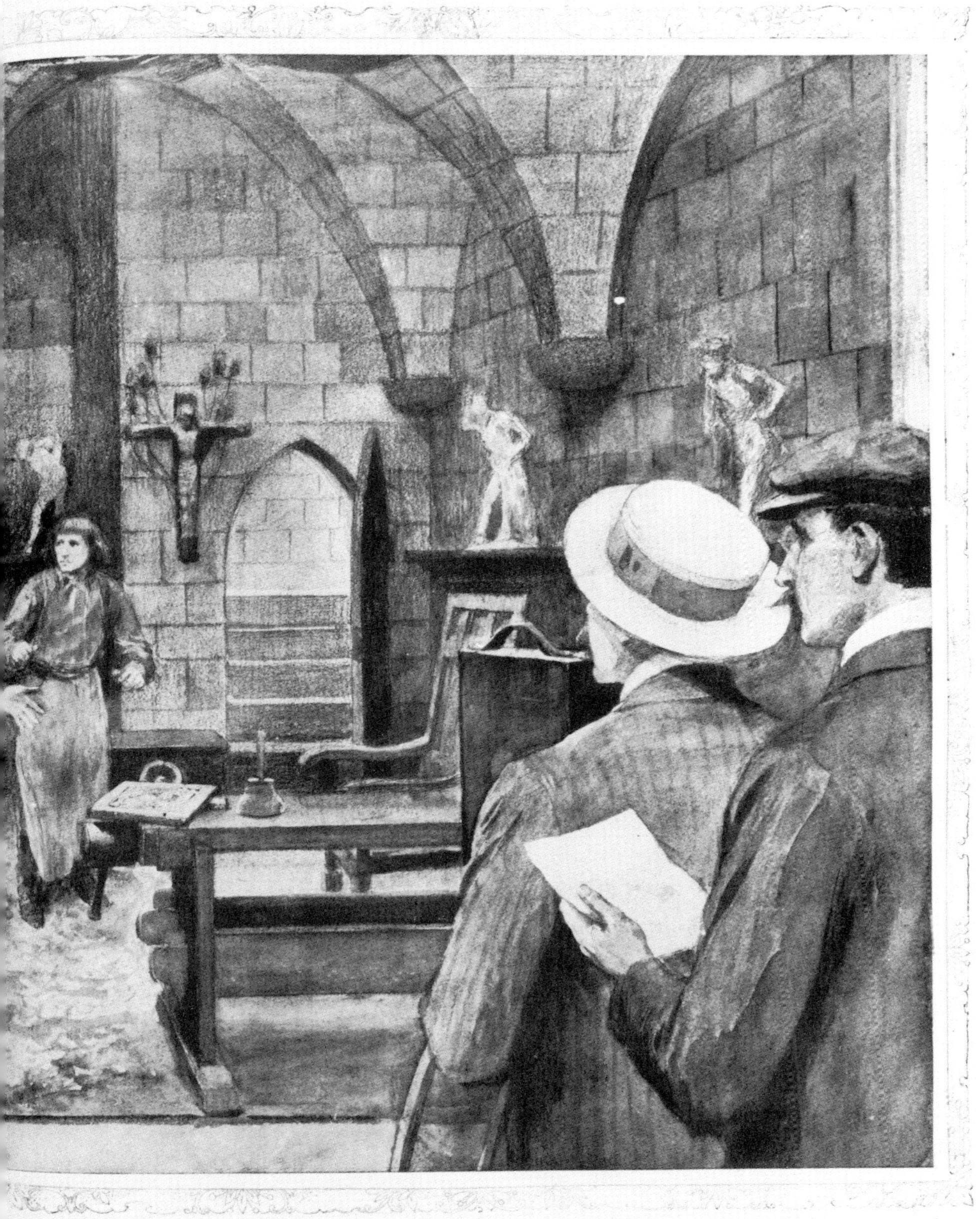

SIR HUBERT VON HERKOMER TAKING A LEADING PART IN "THE OLD CARVER," THEATRE AT BUSHEY.

a company of actors and actresses who have shown particular aptitude for cinematograph work, and he himself also takes a part in some of the pieces. In the above drawing, for instance, he is seen in the leading rôle of a picture-play entitled "The Old Carver," the scene of which is laid in a mediaeval workshop of the fourteenth century The master-carver discovers that his daughter has eloped with his chief workman, and the illustration shows him interrogating the other apprentices as to the whereabouts of the missing couple. In the foreground are the cinematograph-operators and their apparatus. "The Old Carver," it is understood, is to be produced in public picture-theatres this autumn.

67 'The Latest Craze in Science: The Cinematograph taken up by an R.A.', *Illustrated London News*, 2 August 1913, pp. 170–71.

THE RISE of the FILM.

Professor Sir Hubert von Herkomer's Cinematographic Endeavours at Bushey

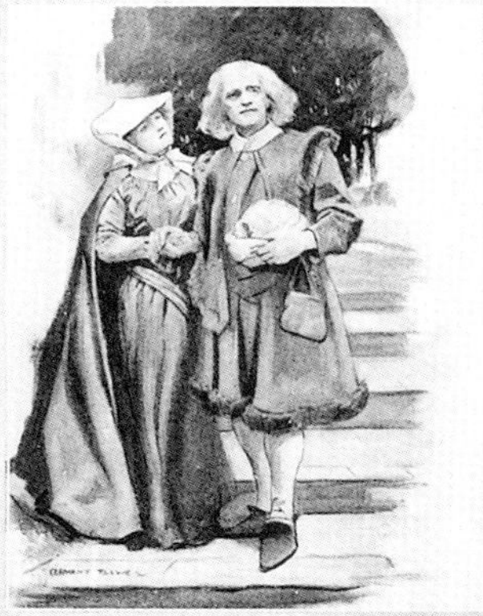

As an Old Woodcarver

Professor Sir Hubert von Herkomer acts the part of the old woodcarver himself in a mediæval drama

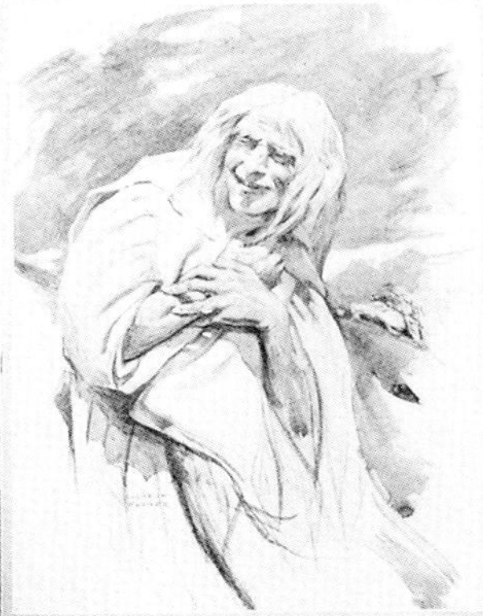

As a Witch

Professor Sir Hubert von Herkomer acts the name-part in a film entitled "The White Witch"

It is certainly a sign of wonderful progress in the past and of promise for the future when an artist of Professor Sir Hubert von Herkomer's standing takes such an interest in cinematography as his theatre at Bushey shows. Sir Hubert has been thinking of the wonderful possibilities of the cinematograph for the last year or so, and about six months ago decided to start the actual making of films himself. He has fitted up a glass theatre large enough to take two scenes at once, and has also built elaborate houses and scenes of the fourteenth century for two of his most important scenarios. The professor's own work now is as a kind of super-manager; he edits and criticises the films generally, and in the evenings discusses with his son, Mr. Siegfried Herkomer, who is his manager, the dramatic possibilities of the scenarios and the general arrangement of the scenes. The professor sometimes has a rehearsal before breakfast, then works on the portraits of a couple of sitters, again rehearses in the evening, and after dinner there may be a projection of the morning's work on the screen.

The staff are at present engaged on some very varied scenarios. Sir Hubert is very enthusiastic about the splendid settings and backgrounds he is able to find at Bushey; already his famous house has been used with great effect. The professor himself acts the principal parts in *The Old Woodcarver* and *The White Witch*, his "make-up" being most effective in the two plays. The stories are really charming ones and allow Sir Hubert full play for his dramatic abilities. Mr. Siegfried Herkomer and his assistant, Mr. Cielery, look after the practical side of the stage-managing and the general film business. Some of the Bushey films, it is hoped, may be seen in the early autumn.

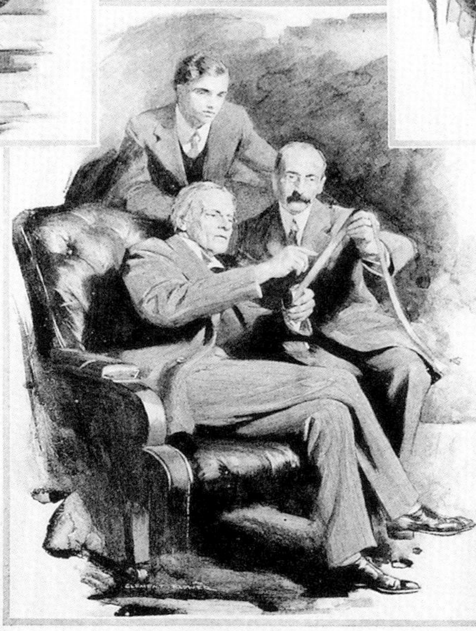

Professor Sir Hubert von Herkomer and his son (on right holding film) examining results of the morning's work

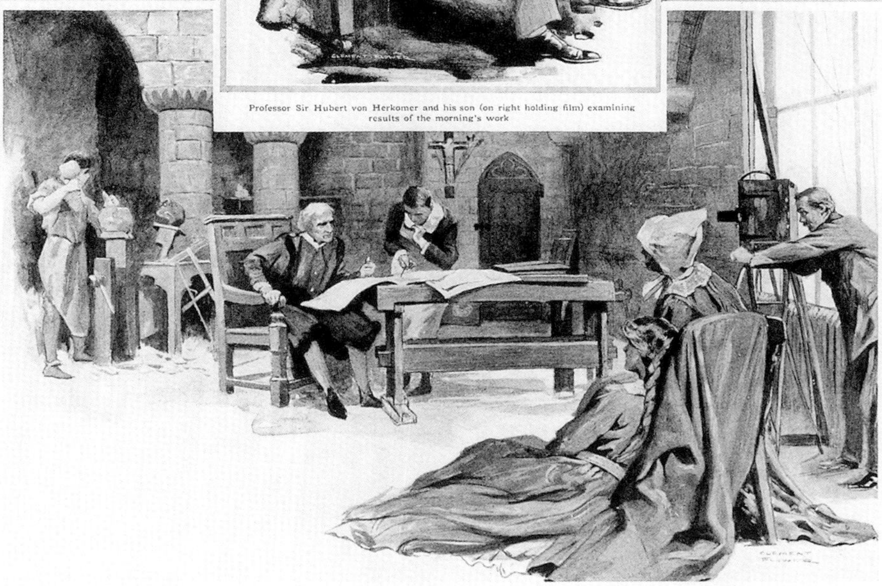

Taking a Film of "The Old Woodcarver" in Professor Sir Hubert von Herkomer's New Cinema Theatre at Bushey

These illustrations have been specially drawn for "The Sphere" by Clement Flower

68 'The Rise of the Film', *Sphere*, 2 August 1913, p. 138.

some technical experience of the medium, having worked for a time with the Pathé film company, and so the old theatre on the Herkomer estate was converted into a film studio, with a glass roof, studio stage, workshops, dressing rooms and a processing and viewing area.

In an illustrated article on 'The Rise of the Film' (plate 68), published in the *Sphere* in August 1913, Herkomer's role in the Film Company was described as: 'a kind of super-manager; he edits and criticises the films generally, and in the evenings discusses with his son, Mr. Siegfried Herkomer, who is his manager, the dramatic possibilities of the scenarios and the general arrangement of the scenes'.[19] The article paints a picture of time spent seamlessly crossing between still and moving images – rehearsals before breakfast, filming in the morning, portrait painting after lunch and a projection of the morning's shoot after dinner. This vivid evocation of Herkomer's working day demonstrates the need for an integrated history of visual culture. Film and art cohabited in these early years. Moving pictures were establishing an independent idiom but it was on the base of existing pictorial languages and cultural forms. The chains of association across cultural forms can be demonstrated by the linguistic shifts and connections in descriptions of Herkomer's work in different media. He started his career as an artist in black and white and regarded the cinematograph as an extension of this graphic art. His theatrical productions were called pictorial-music plays and his film-making was described as picture-theatre. Although nobody in this period confused illustration, painting, theatre and film, there were critical points of overlap where different representational practices leaned on or borrowed from other forms in order to define their cultural identity and value.

The Herkomer Company made eight films, none of which survives,[20] but still photographs of the sets and the published script for the first film give a good idea of what they were like (plate 69).[21] Herkomer's company made costume dramas,

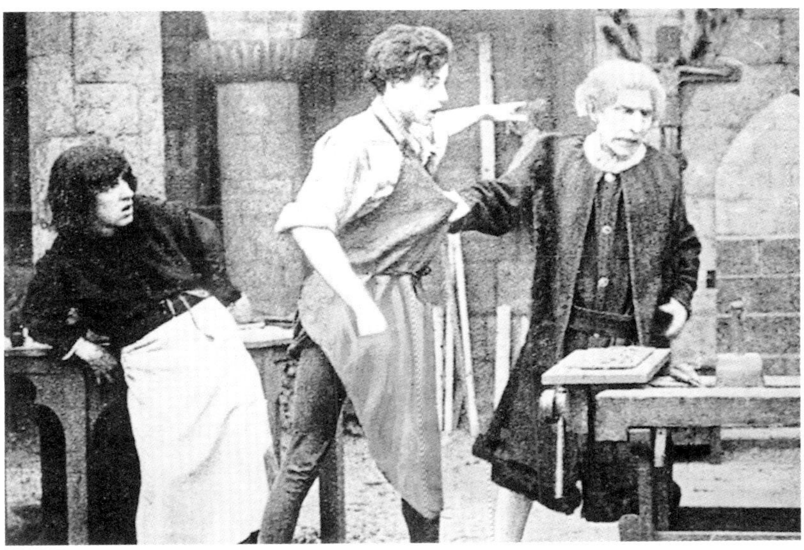

69 Still photograph from *The Old Wood Carver* (1913), taken from J. Saxon Mills, *The Old Wood Carver from the Cinematograph Film conceived and produced by Sir Hubert von Herkomer, R.A., and Siegfried Herkomer*, London: Stanley Paul and Co., 1914.

theatrical-style melodramas, with titles such as *The Old Wood Carver* and *The Highwayman's Honour*, which were distributed in Britain and the United States. In his published statements on film, Herkomer described moving pictures as the medium of the future but the only way he could theorise this role was by reference to paintings. He stated: 'The moving picture is action emphasised in pictorial form. It is nature revivified'[22] and elsewhere that 'A well-projected image on the screen requires so little elucidation and conveys so much more in a clearer way than the written or spoken word. And we all love pictures, don't we?'[23] In the right hands, film could realise more effectively than painting art's traditional role of educating and ennobling the public. Herkomer's platform was that films should be technically well executed, artistic and morally sober. He wanted to rid the cinematograph of its associations with sensationalism – its silly jokes and blood-curdling stories – and elevate it to a respectable art form.

Herkomer's intervention in the art of film came at a critical moment in the development of the medium. By the second decade of the twentieth century, film had moved on from its makeshift beginnings in fairgrounds and shop-fronts and had established sophisticated systems of distribution and exhibition and had begun to settle into the first purpose-built cinemas. There was a growing demand for motion pictures and the film industry was consolidating its position as the leading producer of commercial mass entertainment.[24] Yet as film exhibition in Britain grew, so too did anxieties about the nature and quality of this new cultural form and its possible impact on its audiences. Although film might have left the music halls, it seemed to many observers to have taken the worst vulgarities of music-hall performance with it. Films addressed the lowest cultural and moral standards and there seemed little, in terms of either individuals or organisations, that promised to regulate or improve this situation. This was precisely the significance of Herkomer's move into film-making and the cultural debates surrounding it. Herkomer represented the injection of artistic and moral value that British film badly needed.

In a long, polemical letter to the *Daily Telegraph* in 1912, Herkomer alleged that the picture palace smacked more of the gin palace than the art gallery; this was generating a low-class audience and it was now vitally important to draw the wealthier middle classes to this powerful new art form.[25] He advocated artistic sobriety in the choice of film subjects which, he suggested, could be drawn from the best examples of English literature such as Tennyson and Browning. Film could thus assume the role of high art as a didactic cultural form that could improve and calm its audiences, rather than excite and pander. These are familiar and well-trodden arguments, drawing on nearly a century of debates on the forms and influences of mass urban culture and the distinctions between productive recreation and reckless amusement.[26] Film had altered the landscape of leisure in modern urban society, creating new mass audiences vulnerable to temptation and corruption. If the film-makers, distributors and exhibitors could not be trusted to regulate themselves, then a public censor was required to take responsibility for and make judgements about the acceptability of film content.

For the first decade of cinema there was little direct legislation aimed at regulating public morals and controls were generally directed towards issues of health and safety.[27] Nevertheless, there was a significant and vocal outcry about cinema's damaging influence on mass audiences. Sex and sensation in moving pictures threatened a new generation of working-class youth; there were too many films of women undressing that were able to reach mixed and susceptible audiences with no regulation or quality control. Herkomer thus joined the growing ranks of politicians and commentators who were calling for a formal system of film censorship. In 1913, the same year that Herkomer made his move into film production, the British Board of Film Censors (BBFC) was established, headed by G. A. Redford, who had formerly worked as a stage censor in the office of the Lord Chamberlain.[28] The Board was, in fact, proposed and financed by the film industry itself, in order to avoid the imposition of central government censorship that some local authorities had been advocating. Censors were given few guidelines but were empowered to issue films with certificates. Local authorities also retained significant influence over the regulation of film exhibition and cinema licensing.

A few months after the BBFC had started its work in January 1913, *The Times* carried a lengthy article examining the fascination of the cinematograph for modern audiences.[29] Unlike the picture gallery or the church, which required some effort from the visitor before yielding their pleasurable effects, the picture palace offered 'immediate escape with the least possible expenditure of energy'. No work was required by the imagination and the constantly changing succession of images removed the need for concentration. In this insightful account of the pleasures of the first cinemas, the author reserves judgement about whether or not the evident power of the experience is cause for alarm and speculates about how this cultural form should be classified: 'Whether . . . we are fumbling towards some new form of art which is to have movement and shape, to be like life and yet to be selected and arranged as a work of art, who can say? In the meantime we have a fury for seeing and remain happy, greedy and terribly indiscriminate.' In 1913 the cultural value of film was up for grabs, poised between the status of being a new art form or being relegated as worthless amusement; the creation of the board of censors was a strategic move in the direction of cultural respectability. Not surprisingly, therefore, Herkomer's move into film was generally welcomed by the industry. Just at the moment when it had decided to take action about its shaky reputation, Herkomer offered the patina of high cultural capital and that magical quality, 'taste'.

Herkomer exploited his artistic identity in promoting his films, which were advertised as being 'the most artistic moving pictures yet produced, perfect in every detail',[30] and critics often emphasised this quality in their reviews. The *Bioscope* described scenes from *The Old Wood Carver* as 'equal in their artistic effect to any picture that we have seen' and anticipated a beneficial influence on future film-making.[31] Following his death in March 1914, the *Kinematograph and Lantern Weekly* observed that 'the association of his name with the film business added lustre to it from an artistic point of view' and reminded its readers of: 'an artistic touch, a something almost indefinable, in the work when screened, which marks it out as the product of a mind used to expressing itself in many media, and always with success'.[32] *The Times* obituary confirmed that 'he had lately devoted himself to bringing a new art, or rather a new invention – the cinematograph – under the jurisdiction of the highest taste.'[33]

This correction – an invention, not an art – is exactly the point. The cinematograph was a cultural form that could have gone in a number of directions; it was the aggregate of years of development in optical technologies but where was it to be situated on the prevailing social and cultural register? Herkomer saw that it could be a popular art form; he had begun his career as a black and white artist for the illustrated press and he regarded the cinematograph as a captivating new medium for the creation of narrative and the artistic arrangement of monochrome tones. He wanted high content, not low, and he drew on existing critical languages to hammer out a theoretical position for film. Herkomer had a pictorial (or, perhaps, picturesque) conception of moving pictures and was part of a pictorialist tradition in British photography that drew on theatre and painting and constituted a distinctive approach to cinema in the first decades of the twentieth century.[34] He saw cinematography as a way of mobilising artistic images and of setting composed *tableaux* into motion. Film liberated the static single-point perspective of his painting and created a sequence of pictures on the move.

In his popular 1913 book, *Practical Cinematography and its Applications*, Frederick A. Talbot reviewed recent developments in film production and singled out Herkomer's work as being of special interest. In a discussion over several pages, Talbot explained what was distinctive about Herkomer's films, admiring his indifference to sensational action, his attention to detail in sets and costumes and, above all, his subtle use of the black and white medium. By avoiding glaring lighting and garish make-up, Talbot suggested, Herkomer had extended the tonal range of the images. Acting styles in Herkomer's films were also slower and less exaggerated and, as a result, the films had greater naturalism and seriousness; they were the output of 'the combination of artist and producer'.[35] Herkomer's film career lasted less than a year but his influence on British film-making in this period spread beyond the actual films that were produced and had a symbolic significance. The neglect of this aspect of his work by film and art historians is to be deeply regretted. Herkomer died on film: his funeral procession was filmed and shown the same evening to audiences at the cinema in King Street, Watford, close to his old home in Bushey.[36]

the rural adventure machine

Years before Herkomer had turned his attention to film, he had encountered the potential of modern mobility through the motor car. The history of film and the history of the motor car mirror each other. As Kristin Ross has shown in her outstanding account of France in the 1950s and 1960s:

> the two technologies reinforced each other. Their shared qualities – movement, image, mechanization and standardization – made movies and cars the key com-

modity-vehicles of a complete transformation in European consumption patterns and cultural habits.

Much of that transformation involved a change in perception, a change in the way things were *seen*.[37]

Ross describes this change in seeing in terms of 'perception-in-movement': 'The automobile and the motion it creates become integrated into the driver's perception: he or she can see only things in motion – as in motion pictures.'[38] With railway and motor travel, viewers no longer belongs to the same space as the objects they perceive; they become more detached and passive and, as images stream continuously across their frame of vision, their viewpoint becomes that of the machine that moves them through the world.

The optical synergy between motor-car travel and motion pictures is neat and convincing for the period from the 1920s but the early years of the twentieth century represented a widely different moment in the history of those technologies. Standardisation was not yet a feature of film production and, as argued in earlier chapters, speed could not yet be understood as a consistent or absolute phenomenon. It would be more accurate in reference to this earlier period to speak of a hesitant 'coming into movement', a mobilisation, rather than a physical experience of continuous speed, both in relation to motoring and moving pictures.

In the mid-1890s the motor car and the cinematograph both made their formal public debut. In 1895 the Lumières mounted the first public exhibition of their Cinématographe and within months other inventors were coming up with their own versions of moving pictures. In 1896 in Britain legislation acknowledged the triumph of the automobile by abolishing the requirement that all vehicles using public roads should be preceded by a person on foot and should not exceed a speed of 4 miles per hour (mph). The speed limit was raised to 12 mph and in November 1896 the first London to Brighton run was organised on what became known as 'emancipation day', to celebrate the passing of the Act into law.[39] In 1903 the Motor Cars Act introduced a licensing system, along with speed limits of 20 mph and penalties for infringement.

Herkomer quickly abandoned his horses and carriages and embraced the motor car. He bought luxury cars such as the best Daimlers and joined the early and great enthusiasts in the new temporal and spatial world of motoring (plate 70). For many of these pioneering motorists, the car was the symbol of 'a restless and hurried age',[40] which offered an almost magical access to the past and to the future. As one writer put it, the motor car 'flattens out the world, enlarges the horizon, loosens a little the bonds of Time, sets back a little the barriers of Space'.[41]

For Rudyard Kipling – a passionate supporter of motoring in these years – his motor car allowed him to discover the geography and history of England. Motor travel was thus not simply a means of transport, it was a form of time travel in which the motorist moved across centuries as they drove along the lanes of the countryside. Kipling described this intense engagement with the past as a kind of spirit communication: 'In England the dead, twelve coffin deep, clutch hold of my wheels at every turn, till I sometimes wonder that the very road does not bleed.'[42]

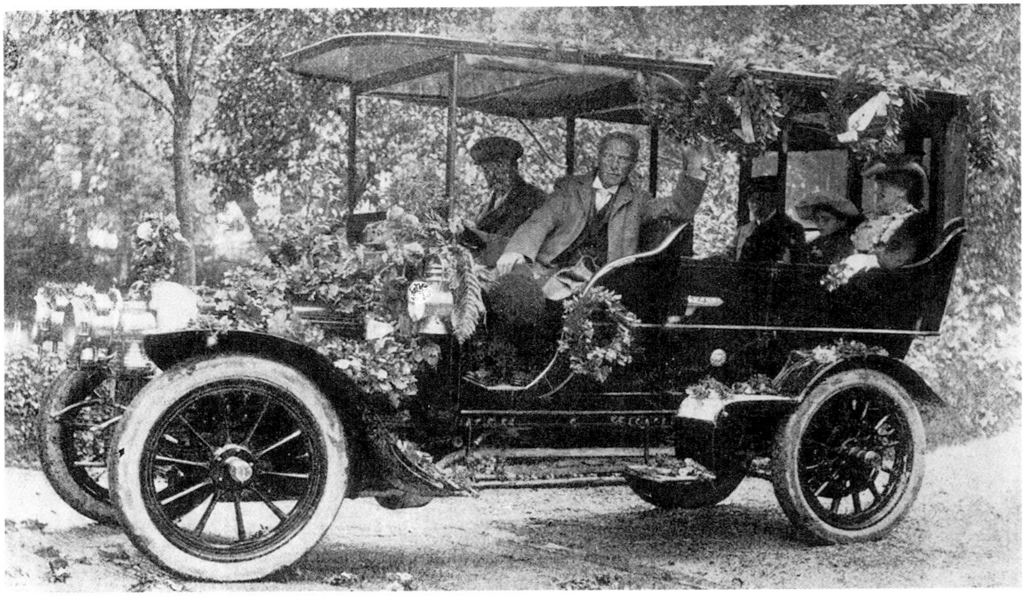

70 'Professor von Herkomer and his Family in his 28 h.p. Daimler at a Fete given in his Honour at Landsberg, Bavaria', *Motorist and Traveller*, 19 April 1905, p. 429.

The motor car in this period offered a new type of subjectivity – privileged, individualistic and phenomenological. Early drivers spoke of the physical pleasures of motorised speed; in a letter of 1904 an aristocratic lady motorist enthused: 'There is no sensation so enjoyable . . . as driving in a fast motor. The endless variety of scenery; the keen whistle of the wind in one's face . . . create an indescribable feeling of exhilaration and excitement.'[43] The experience of the early motorist was a highly embodied one; many referred to the almost human connection between driver and machine and drew on the concept of the horseless carriage to evoke the image of the car as an animate beast. This physical embodiment of motion differentiated the experience of motor-car travel from the speed of the express train. A writer in 1904 described the difference in this way: 'It is, I think, a combination of intense speed with the sensation of smallness, the lightness, the responsiveness of the thing that carries you, with the rushing of the atmosphere upon your body and of the earth upon your vision.' Motoring charged all the senses; the same writer evoked the sound of the road: 'every stone, telegraph post, and house that you pass close by makes a sharp sound, like the whizz of the Mariner's cross-bow. And to your exalted, expanded senses the noise of movement is heavenly music, the wind like wine of the gods.'[44]

* * *

motorised vision

Many writers on motoring compared the multifarious pleasures of driving with the joyless pragmatism of a railway journey. On a train, the passenger's attention was focused exclusively on departure and arrival; what lay in between was a matter of indifference.[45] In a car, by contrast, every yard was important and was travelled consciously and intensely. Most writers gave the same explanation for this difference: where the railway track presented the most direct route and was uninterested in the surrounding landscape, the road drew the motorist into an intimate and sensual relationship with the most ancient and picturesque parts of the country. Things seen from the window of a train represented the ugly side of modern life: 'The coalshed or the chimney of the heating apparatus is turned towards us in the train, and not the best line of gables or the old lych gate.' It was as though the rail passenger was 'looking at the brocade of the landscape on the wrong side'.[46]

The automobile offered individual motorists the freedom to choose when and where they travelled and the pace and tempo of their journey. Every writer in these early years agreed that the natural environment of the motor car was thus the countryside, rather than the city; the open road rather than the congested street. To this extent, the motor car was seen as a rural adventure machine and its pleasures were intimately connected to those of a newly emergent national identity based on the rediscovery and preservation of the British countryside. It was a conservative and nostalgic vision of the nation made possible by the latest innovations in motorised transport. In the years around 1900, the automobile took an elite class of motorists from the city to the country, where a powerful and enduring version of modern identity was forged. Along with the cinematograph and the motor car, a third element in this narrative made its first public appearance in 1895, the National Trust for Places of Historic Interest and Natural Beauty, dedicated to the conservation of a particular conception of the natural past, representing a specific set of aesthetic and moral values. Its visual rhetoric belonged to the pastoral tradition and favoured winding lanes and hedgerows; manor houses and inns; cottages and churches. And if this was not exactly the ideal environment for the unpredictable technology of early motoring, it was one whose rediscovery and survival were seen to depend on the interest of the motorist.

This imaginary construction of the nation through its past was commodified and marketed, for example, through the pages of new journals such as *Country Life*, the first issue of which appeared in 1897, and the new well-off motorists were the ideal consumers and disseminators of this vision of Britain.[47] As Patrick Wright has argued, this conception of national heritage represented 'above all a modern past', that is, one rooted in the exigencies of the present.[48] The motor car was an essential part of this formation: it opened up the places that became the landmarks of the topography of heritage and enabled a new kind of 'touring', a use of space and time, that became the standard for the exploration of this modern past. In the previous chapter, 'Animating the Everyday', it was suggested that the temporality of urban modernity was rich and varied and more complex than many recent accounts of modern life have allowed. Here I am arguing that modernity also took place in the spaces of the countryside and that the reinvention of rural life, through the experience of motor travel, was a fundamental aspect of the perception of the modern in the early years of the twentieth century.

Set free in rural England and drawing on the emergent discourse of heritage and national identity, motor driving offered a changed visual perception, a different way of seeing, that was dependent not only on the motion of the viewer motorist but also on the perceived values of the places through which they drove. As Alfred Harmsworth, later Lord Northcliffe, the press baron, creator of the *Daily Mail* and motor enthusiast, put it in 1902: 'The voyager by road thinks less of a great expanse of scenery, bounded though it may be by the long waving line of mysterious hills, than he does of *the thousand sights of beauty and interest under his eyes*' (my emphasis).[49]

A continuous, unfolding and framed vision gives way to a rapid succession of images; perhaps it is possible to define this shift as a move from a panoramic to a cinematic aesthetic. Such a claim would be neat and convenient, too easy; the relationship between speed and sight requires some further qualification. The motorist writers of the early twentieth century were fitfully attempting to capture the nature of new technological experience but the technology itself was still unstable. As many pages were devoted to breakdowns, 'side-slips' and punctures as to the joys of the open road. Stopping was as much a part of early motor travel as was continuous motion.

For all those who celebrated the exhilaration of speed, there were others who loved the motor car for its varied motion and its creation of leisurely, individualised travel. James Hissey, the author of a number of motoring guidebooks to Britain, described how he would 'dally where the scenery, places, and people pleased me, and, by grace of the speedy car, I would hasten over comparatively uninteresting stretches of country. I would start forth with all England before me and take the fortune of the road.' Hissey advocated a variable pace of whimsical roving, determined by the pursuit of the picturesque: 'the spirit of wider roving took possession of us – not precisely a spirit of speed, but one of progress – we would fare forth, with fewer stops on the way, into a fresh country, and, having reached it, resume our leisurely exploring'.[50] In fact, with its varied and capricious pace, the motor car seemed to Hissey to be more like horse-drawn transport than railway travel:

> It is not necessary because you elect to travel by car to emulate the rush of the railway; you can meander about in a car in as leisurely a fashion as though you were driving a horse . . . we meant to see and enjoy the country we passed through, not to obtain fleeting and soon-forgotten visions of it; otherwise express trains would have conveyed us from place to place as well.[51]

However, these accounts of leisurely motorised exploration are punctuated with euphoric episodes of speed, when Hissey tires of or is uninterested in the landscape and wants to experience the physical rush of letting the motor out and travelling at speed:

the spirit of speed took possession of us, the fascination and the frenzy of speed for speed's sake; the rush through the air, mocking the bird in its flight . . . We had escaped from the fetters that bind man to earth; we were intoxicated with a new-born sense of splendid freedom; without exertion or effort we lightly skimmed the ground; we rode on the wind as it were . . . We were rushing into infinity; 'distances, changes, surprises' greeted us in rapid succession as we sped along over the wild, sweeping wolds.[52]

It is impossible to say which of these motoring practices – roving or speed – yielded greater pleasure; it seems as though it was the capacity for both styles of motion that was the special charm of the motor car in these years. What is clear, however, is that speed did not suit the picturesque; the tempo of the modern pastoral was more leisurely and required seeing the landscape as a sequence of moving pictures. Fast speeds turned the countryside into what Hissey described as 'hurrygraphs' – indistinct impressions that rendered the picturesque redundant.[53]

This was the world of motorised travel and vision in which Herkomer lived and worked. Herkomer did not simply own cars, however; he sponsored motor-races and reliability trials and designed the medals and trophies for the winners. In April 1905, as a promotion for the Munich Reliability Trials, which he was sponsoring later that summer, the journal the *Motorist and Traveller* carried a profile of Hubert von Herkomer, R.A. – Motorist. Buried within this stiff and somewhat lifeless interview is Herkomer's clearest articulation of motorised perception. He explained that motoring was part of his life for three reasons, health, pleasure and utility, and specified: 'The pleasure is seeing Nature as I could in no other way see it; my cars having "tops", I get Nature framed – and one picture after another delights my artistic eye.'[54] Herkomer still seeks frames and pictures but now they press themselves on his vision in rapid succession, while the hood and glass front of his car create a screen for Nature's moving images. The article pronounced him 'A born artist and [a] born motorist' and reported that he had also designed and modelled the silver trophy for his Munich trials (plate 71). He described its appearance to the journalist: '[It] represents a beautiful youth leaning forward holding a wreath – "the Spirit of the Motor-Car" . . . Beyond is a female figure leaning back in graceful ecstasy: she represents "the Joy of Speed".'[55]

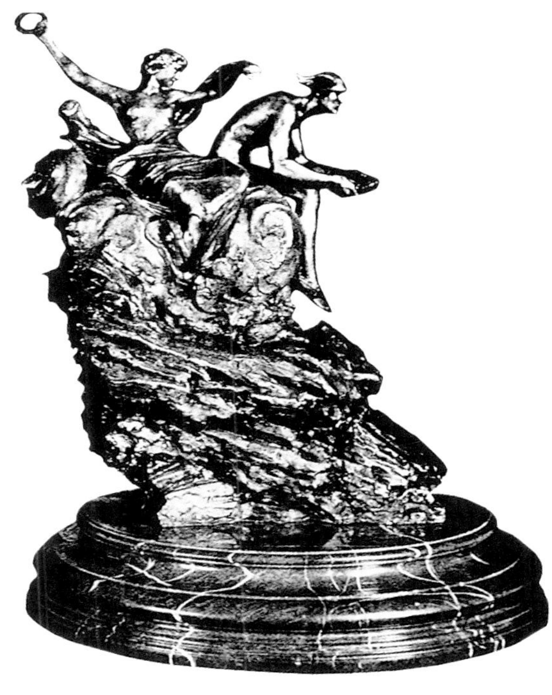

71 Hubert von Herkomer, 'The Herkomer Trophy', 1906.

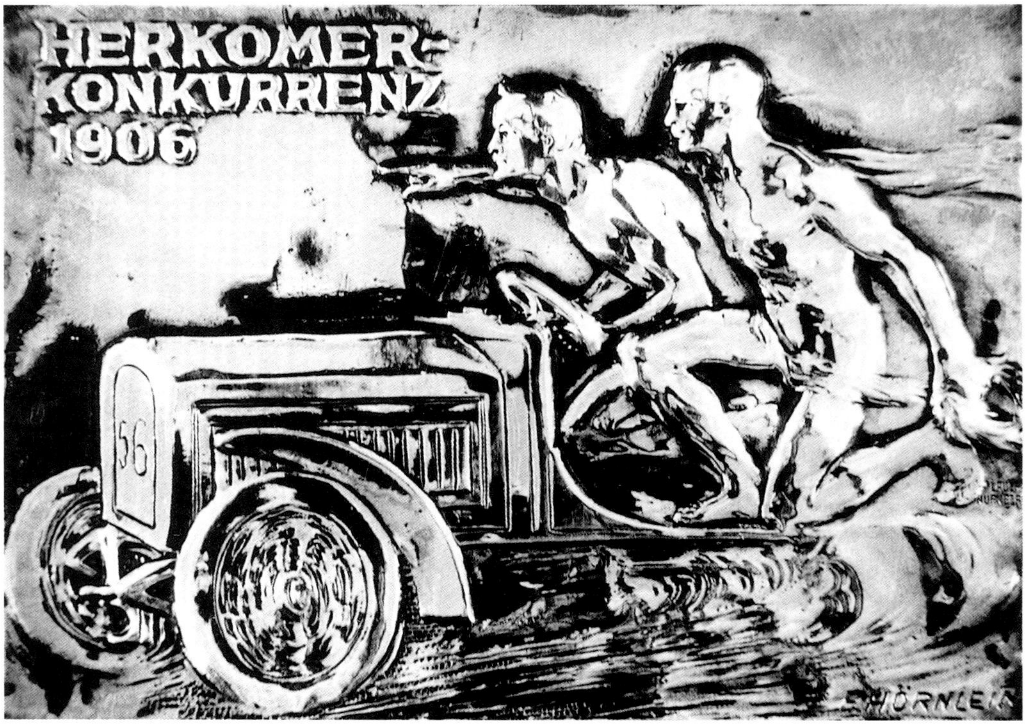

Herkomer also designed a silver plaque for the event showing two male nudes with streaming drapery on a speeding racing car (plate 72). These trophies show Herkomer's continuing interest in symbolism and in the use of unclothed figures as personifications of abstract values. He had adopted the conventional female nude as artistic muse for the School of Art's magazine, the *Palette* (plate 74) and later drew on the same iconography for his Film Company logo (see plate 58). For Herkomer, the female nude embodied his three passions – paintings, films and fast cars. His most extraordinary reworking of this theme was a 1905 design for a menu card (plate 76), which he later adapted into a silver medal (plate 73).[56] It shows a bound female nude, strapped to the front of a motor car, much like Herkomer's own Daimler, with the German words for 'The Future' ('Die Zukunft') imprinted on the sash round her middle. Although the figure takes the position of the single, powerful headlight that

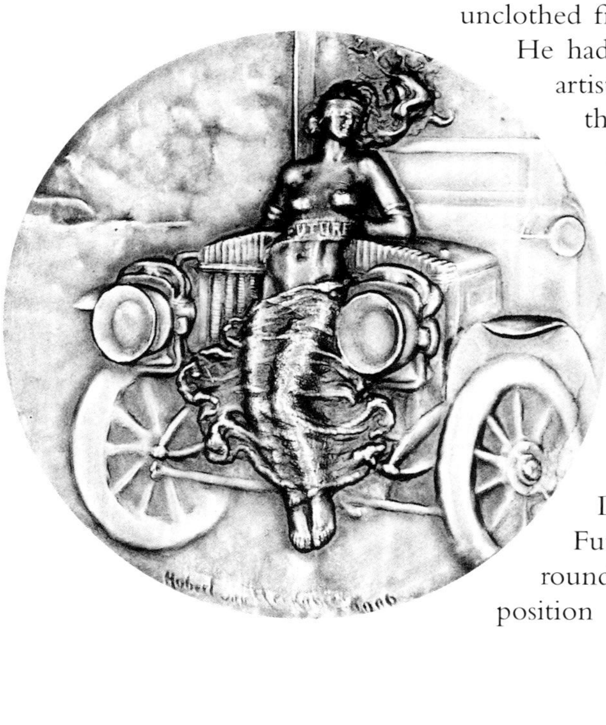

74 (*right*) Cover of the *Palette*, June 1887, from Hubert von Herkomer, *My School and My Gospel*, London: Archibald Constable and Co. Ltd, 1908, facing p. 50.

72 (*facing page top*) Hubert von Herkomer, 'Herkomer Konkurrenz', 1906. Private collection.

73 (*facing page bottom*) Hubert von Herkomer, 'The Future', 1906. Silver medal.

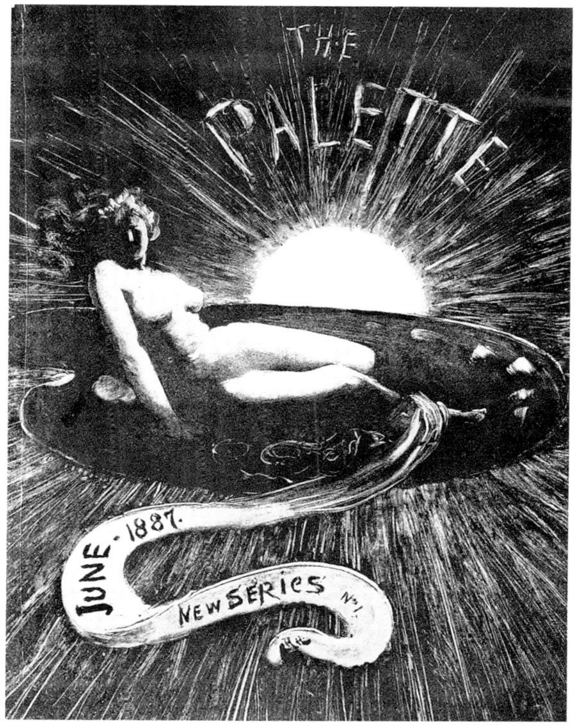

motorists were advised to carry when driving on dark nights,[57] she is blindfolded, a condition which is reinforced and compensated for by the two large, staring lamps on either side of the bonnet. Here the female figure represents the Future, the Spirit of the Motor-car and the Joy of Speed. Yet it is an unseeing light, captive and borne relentlessly towards an unknown future. The image belongs, partially, to the same world of speed as that of the phantom ride film discussed in chapter 1, with the camera tied to the front of the train creating a new kind of mobilised vision. In nearly every respect, however, Herkomer's vision fails to achieve the sensational representation of movement evoked by the films. The seeing eye of the camera is here blinded and the face is turned away from the onrushing speed and images. Rather than being placed in the position of the camera or, indeed, the motorist and being offered a visual analogue to the physical experience of speed, the viewer's position is reversed and he or she is shown the pictorial symbol of speed. The image is essentially motionless and the spectator is given the view of a pre-filmic, pre-motoring visual culture. 'The Future' deploys a confusing and unresolved iconography that stretches the coherence of the allegorical nude to its symbolic limits. The lines of the transparent drapery, hair and blindfold, the sketchy treatment of the wheels and road, attempt to give an impression of the car's movement, but there is little sense of speed. Herkomer could not find a pictorial language to depict speed; his still images simply could not convey the mobilised world of the twentieth century.

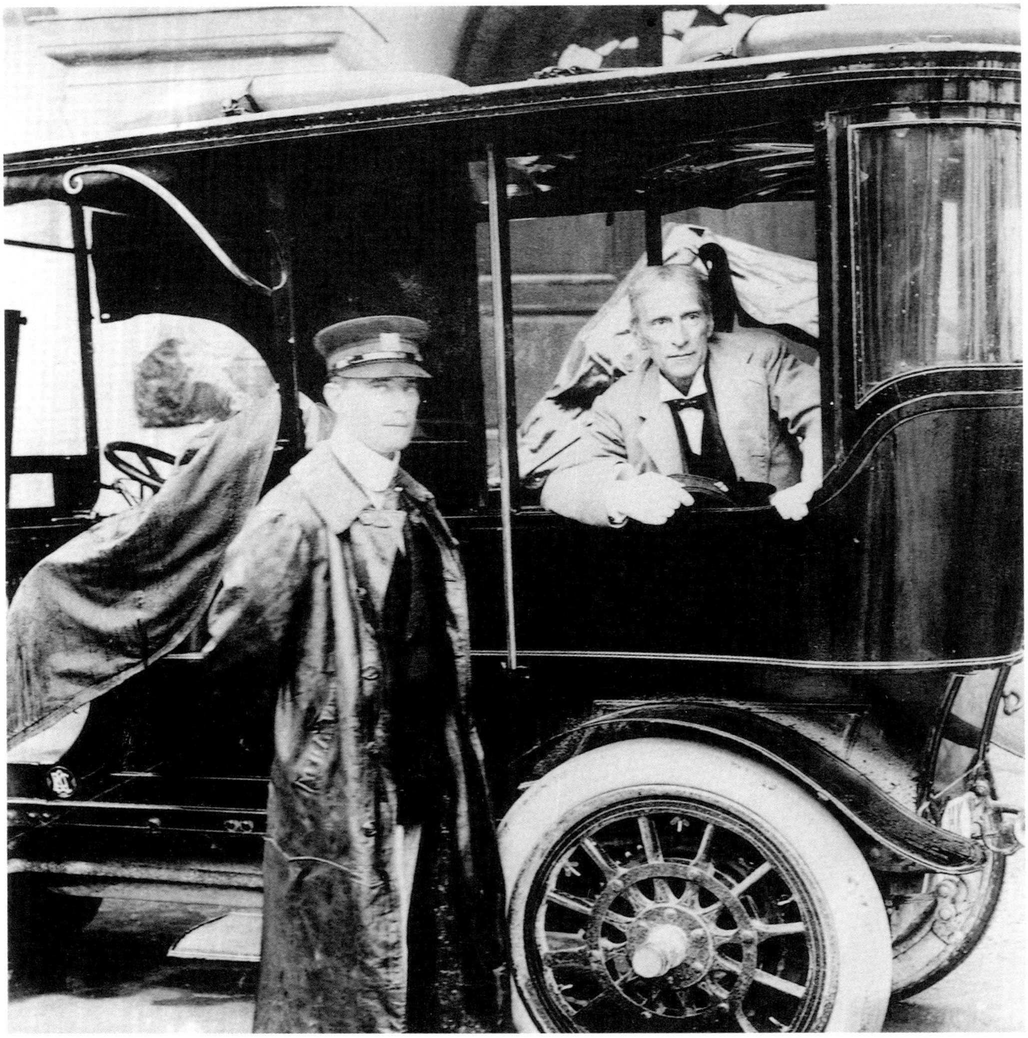

75 Herkomer with his chauffeur.

The motor car was a staple of Herkomer's art practice in the twentieth century (plate 75): it enabled him to move between his home and the metropolis, to work on a number of different projects at once and to bring sitters to his studio in Bushey. Further, like many others of the motoring elite in this period, Herkomer found the motor car was much more than an efficient and fast mode of transport; he believed it had changed his way of seeing. In 1911 he wrote: 'I never knew England . . . before I had a car. It has enlarged my horizon, and given *air* to my very existence.'[58] This sense of personal expansion is two-fold; it describes both a new understanding of Englishness through its countryside and a new mode of perception, an enlarged capacity for empathy and aesthetic appreciation. At the end of his life, Herkomer suffered repeated and severe periods of ill health. In 1912, when

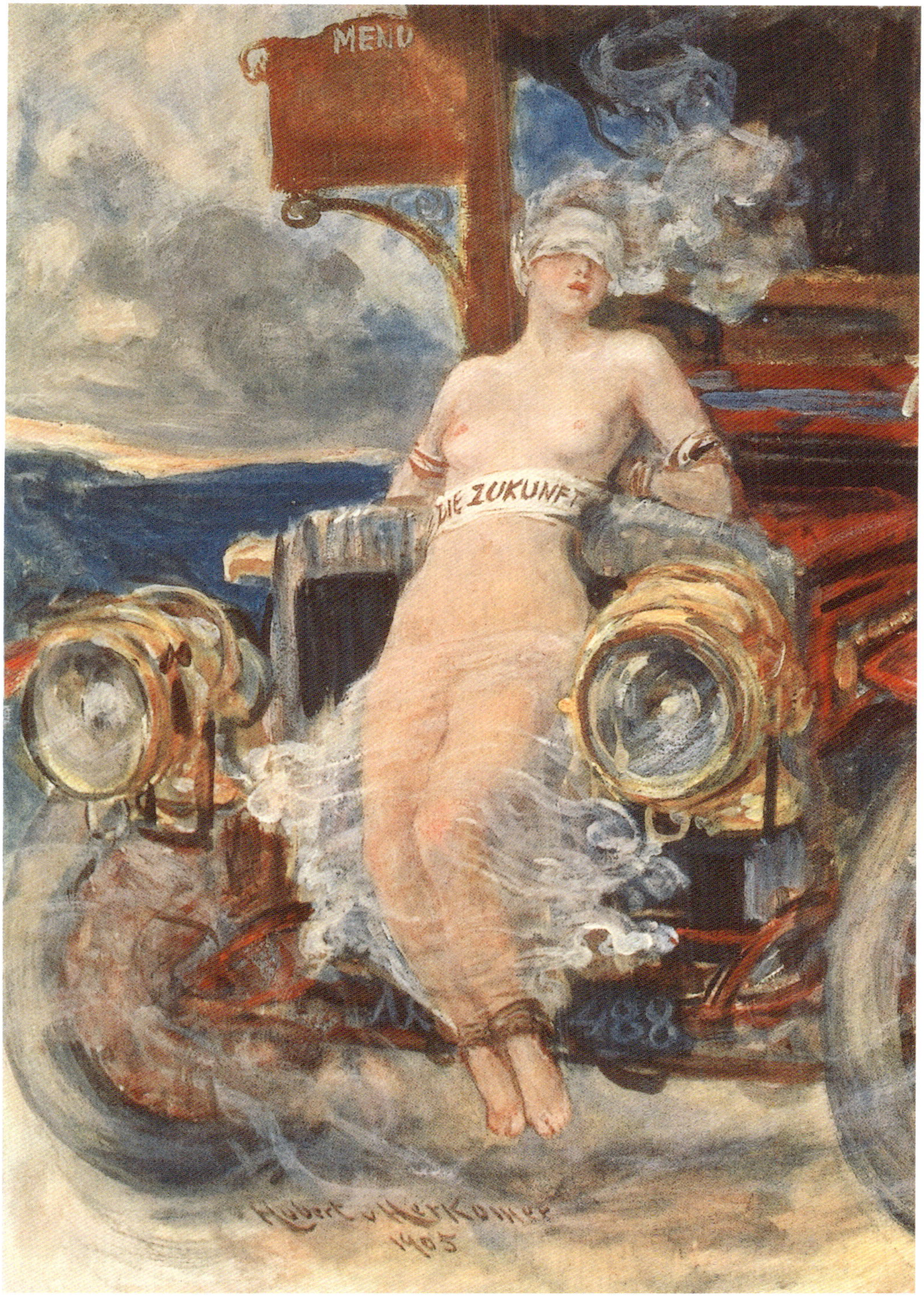

76 Hubert von Herkomer, *Die Zukunft* (*The Future*), 1905. Photogravure on menu card, 24.1 × 16.5 cm. Yale Center for British Art, Gift of Hans and Agnes Platenius.

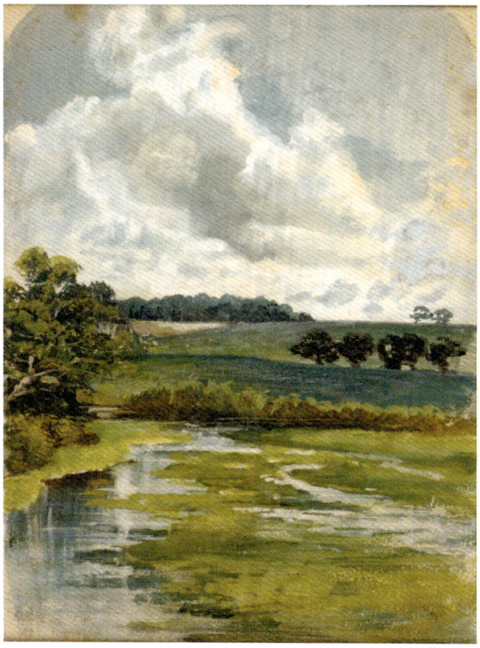

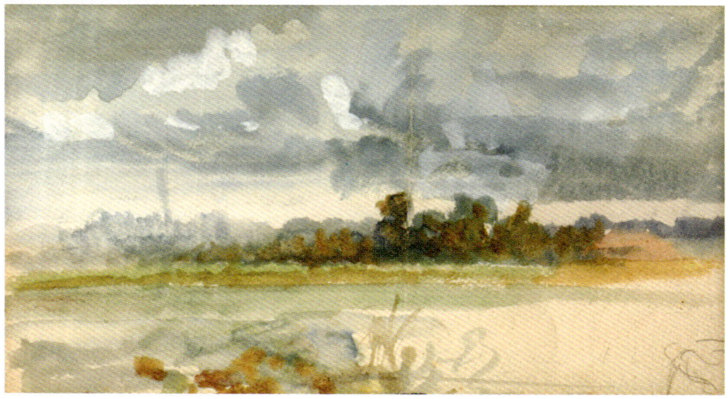

78 Hubert von Herkomer, 'Landscape Sketch', *c.*1912. Watercolour, 101 × 184 cm. Southampton City Art Gallery.

77 (*left*) Hubert von Herkomer, 'Landscape Sketch', *c.*1912. Watercolour, 247 × 177 cm. Southampton City Art Gallery.

he was recovering from an operation on his stomach, he undertook a tour of England in his Daimler, driven by his chauffeur. During this time he produced a series of landscape sketches that are generally supposed to have been made while he was on this motor tour (plates 77 and 78).[59] Describing the view from his motor car some years earlier, Herkomer referred to 'a kaleidoscope of images that positively amount to an apotheosis of nature'.[60] It is as though he could imagine or verbalise a different vision, coming out of the experience of motor travel, but could not resolve this into a developed pictorial language. Perhaps the 1912 sketches are freer and looser than Herkomer's usual style but this could be put down to the watercolour medium, or the fact that they were working studies, rather than finished pieces. Yet even the metaphor of the kaleidoscope is constrained as a figure of modern vision.[61] A succession of changing patterns coalesces with pleasing aesthetic results. In a sense, this had always been Herkomer's artistic method and until his death, in film and in art, he never deviated from the final goal of picturesque composition.

In *The System of Objects*, Jean Baudrillard described the impact of the speed offered by the modern motor car on contemporary subjectivity: 'Speed's effect, by integrating space and time, is one of levelling the world to two dimensions, to an image; it loses its depth and its becoming; in some ways it brings about a sublime immobility and a contemplative state. At more than a hundred miles an hour, there's a presumption of eternity.'[62] This idea that the automobile reduces the world to a kind of projected image that induces in the spectator a passive euphoria has become a maxim of post-modernism. However, it will not do as an historical account of the relationship between technology and vision. The case of Hubert von Herkomer and other motor-car enthusiasts of the early twentieth century makes it clear that in this first period the experience of motorised speed was quite different from that of their late twentieth-century counterparts. Rather than being an automated 'out of body' experience,[63] the first motorists wrote of a highly physical encounter with the speed of the car and invoked an intensely sensory relationship between motor and body. As shown in chapter 1, early film audiences were also not the passive recipients of detached visual spectacles and it is likely that moving pictures were an affective form of communication that created a motivated public response.[64]

Immersion in pure and constant speed was not the technological world of Herkomer. Motion in the early years of the twentieth century was concerned with mobilisation and velocity – in other words, the transformation from stasis to movement and the varied states between. It encompassed acceleration, pause, motion and arrest. In the same way that some of the earliest film shows started with a still image which then began to move and favourite special effects included altering the speed of the film, or reversing it, the pleasure of motor speed was most vividly expressed in terms of cessation and the after-shock of movement. Take, for instance, the following passage, written in 1904:

> Once we stopped, drawing up by the fragrant roadside; and as the pulses of the engine died away, so died away the strange sensation of giant, divine life with which its breath had endowed us . . . Inert and dead reposed the magic carriage . . . its devouring life resolved into a few hundredweights of metal, a few gallons of petrol, a few coils of wire . . .[65]

The way of seeing generated in the early years of these technologies was thus not cinematic in its recent sense. Images did not appear to dissolve into continuous flow but, as Herkomer described, they retained their individual pictorial integrity in rapid succession. What is fascinating about this moment is that it represents the point at which still images become mobilised but also when both still and moving images retain their perceivable autonomy.

Contemporaries tried to find ways to capture the distinctiveness of this new vision. James Hissey, whose career as a travel writer spanned more than two decades, from the age of the horse-drawn carriage to the apotheosis of motorised transport in the years of the First World War, exemplifies these faltering attempts to describe how seeing changed from the perspective of a motor car. He generally avoided speeds that blurred the passing landscape and aimed at what he described in 1906 as 'extended' vision: 'Our town-tired eyes, limited in range for the larger portion of the year by a narrow horizon of streets, squares, and houses, rejoiced in an unaccustomed freedom of vision . . . It is good to exercise the eye in far seeing, it is a tonic to the sight.'[66] This is a rural as much as it is a motorised vision and at this point Hissey shares precisely the same visual register as Herkomer when he referred in 1911 to his enlarged horizon.

Hissey frequently ascribed the optical effects of motorised movement to the visual effects of the landscape itself, as though there was a spatial and temporal affinity between the mutability of nature and the motion of the motor car. Passing through West Sussex he described the marshes 'green and golden in the glance of the sun, and purple-grey where the vast cloud-shadows in fast succession floated over it, giving a sense of life and briskness to the scene: movement on a gigantic scale without sound' (p. 8). This passage shares some of the qualities of film but is not properly filmic. Hissey's visual experience is of a sequence of intermittent views in which individual frames or moments are still discernible but have been set in motion. He wrote: 'As you motor on, the green country on either hand . . . flits by like so many beautiful pictures. The prospect is always changing; the distance is ever opening out. It is all so dreamy, yet so breezy, bracing, and exhilarating' (p. 228). The mesmerised state of Baudrillard's post-modern motorist is here shattered by the introduction of the bracing conditions of the early open-top motor cars.

Fast speeds brought a different corporeal experience and what was usually referred to as a 'reduction' in vision. In 1907 the writer and motoring enthusiast Max Pemberton concluded: 'We desire to see the country, and have discovered that we cannot see it when we are travelling at forty miles an hour.'[67] Only rarely is it possible to find an account of speeding motorised vision that abandons the framed picture and articulates a different aesthetic, more akin to the phantom ride: 'One horizon succeeded another in rapid, bewildering succession. Our eyes were on the distance – only that could we discern clearly – the wonderful distance that ceaselessly came rushing to us. For a time a strange illusion took place; it was as though the car were standing still, and the country it was that went hurtling past.'[68] In this passage, at the end of Pemberton's book, the traveller returns home; he accelerates and turns his gaze from the side to straight ahead and it is at this moment that he exchanges the experience of the picturesque motorist for that of the phantom ride spectator. Motorised vision, as a distinct mode of mobilised seeing related to the visual world of film, was slow to develop. It was not until 1917 that Hissey acknowledged the presence of cinematographers as well as photographers in the English countryside and described the surrounding landscape as 'living pictures'.[69]

79 Harry Tate in 'Motoring'. The Raymond Mander and Joe Mitchenson Theatre Collection.

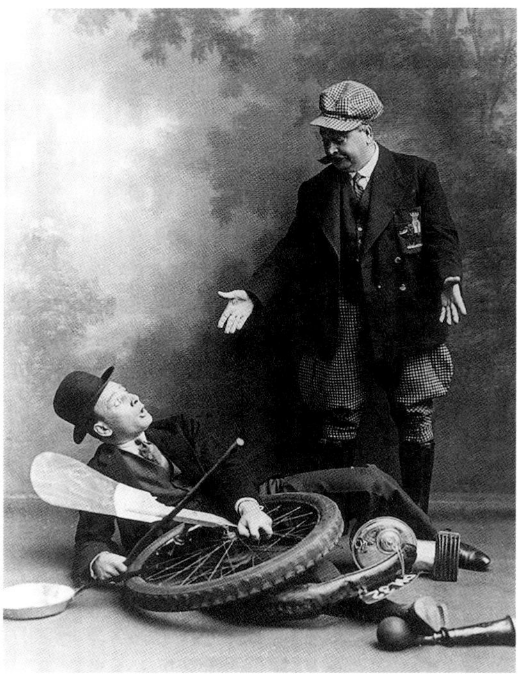

In fact, the first film-makers had taken to the motor car at about the same time as Herkomer and Hissey but had created a far different version of early motoring from that provided by decorous gentlemen and lady motorists. Theirs was a knockabout, music-hall vision of

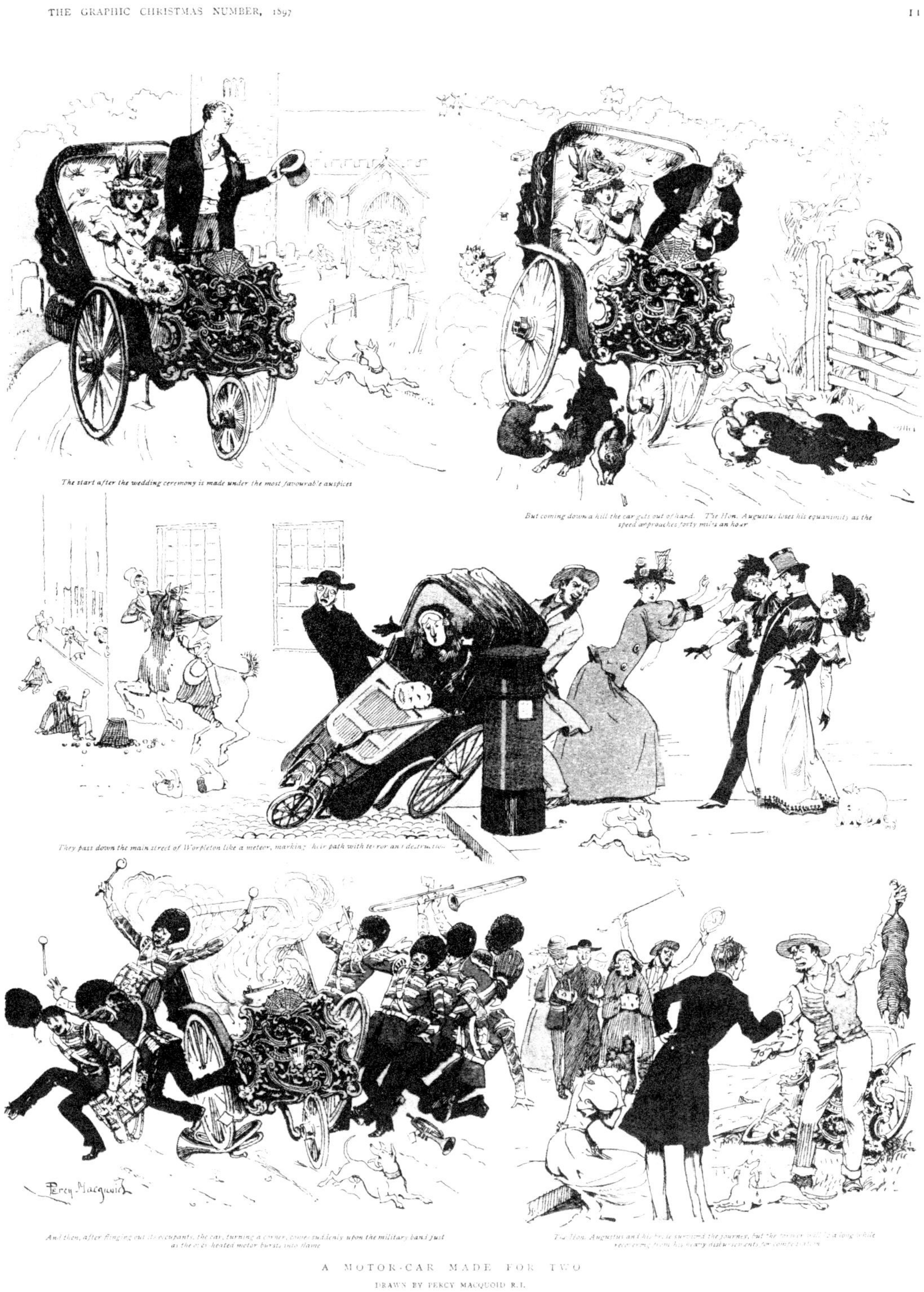

80 Percy Macquoid, 'A Motor-Car Made for Two', *Graphic*, December 1897, p. 11.

the motor car and its drivers. The machines were unreliable, the motorists reckless law-breakers and pedestrians usually hapless victims. Other forms of popular imagery also exploited the comic violence of the motor car in these years. Shortly after the 1896 legislation and the 'emancipation' of motor cars, the *Graphic* published a full-page comic strip titled 'A Motor-Car Made for Two', showing the havoc caused in a rural town and nearby countryside by a runaway automobile (plate 80). This scenario became the basic narrative for theatrical and film representations of motoring in the following years. The well-known music-hall performer Harry Tate created a sketch called 'Motoring' that became his first big success (plate 79).[70] Tate played a hopeless chauffeur who not only fails to start the car but also ultimately wrecks it. Many years later, his son described how his father's major sketches were created in response to current social themes and how acts were performed in venues where the subjects had greatest relevance to their audiences. The 'Motoring' sketch was always on the programme at Birmingham, he recalled, because of the car manufacturing industry there.

Cecil Hepworth set up his own film company in 1899 at Walton-on-Thames. His father had been a magic lanternist and with this background and his own experience with the first cinematographers, Hepworth developed an inventive approach to film-making that made his company pre-eminent in the British industry in the years up to 1914. Hepworth had a keen awareness of timing and comic effects and in his *ABC of the Cinematograph*, published in 1897 and the first British book on the subject, he recommended careful programme planning and the selective use of trick camera effects, in order to hold the audience's attention.[71] These elements feature in Hepworth's 1900 film *Explosion of a Motor Car*, in which a car carrying four passengers on a country road drives towards the camera and suddenly explodes (plate 81).[72] The bodies of the passengers are hurled into the air and disappear. A policeman arrives on the scene and searches the sky with a telescope; as he looks, the body parts fall back to earth and he collects them together. The motor car provided the perfect mechanical alibi for the dismemberments and fragmentations of the body that were the subject of many early trick films, including the enchanted pictures discussed in chapter 2, but it also added a piquant note of contemporaneity, rendering what was still at the time an elite modern pastime, ridiculous in the eyes of its working-class audiences. In the extraordinary Hepworth film *How it Feels to be Run Over*, also made in 1900, the scene is a country road. A horse-drawn cart passes by and then a motor car is seen rapidly approaching the camera (plate 82). The occupants of the car become extremely agitated as they see the cart in their path but it is too late. The car rushes towards the spectator, the screen is covered with stars and the words 'Oh! Mother Will be Pleased' appear.[73] Only film in this period would have attempted to show what it felt like to be run over, just as only film would imagine the visual impact of being strapped to the front of an express train speeding towards a tunnel. This was the nature of its inventive and occasionally anarchic encounter with contemporary speed. Film sought new ways of seeing the familiar, the strange and the new.

81 *(facing page left)* Cecil M. Hepworth, *Explosion of a Motor Car*, 1900. Frame stills.

82 *(facing page right)* Cecil M. Hepworth, *How it Feels to be Run Over*, 1900. Frame stills.

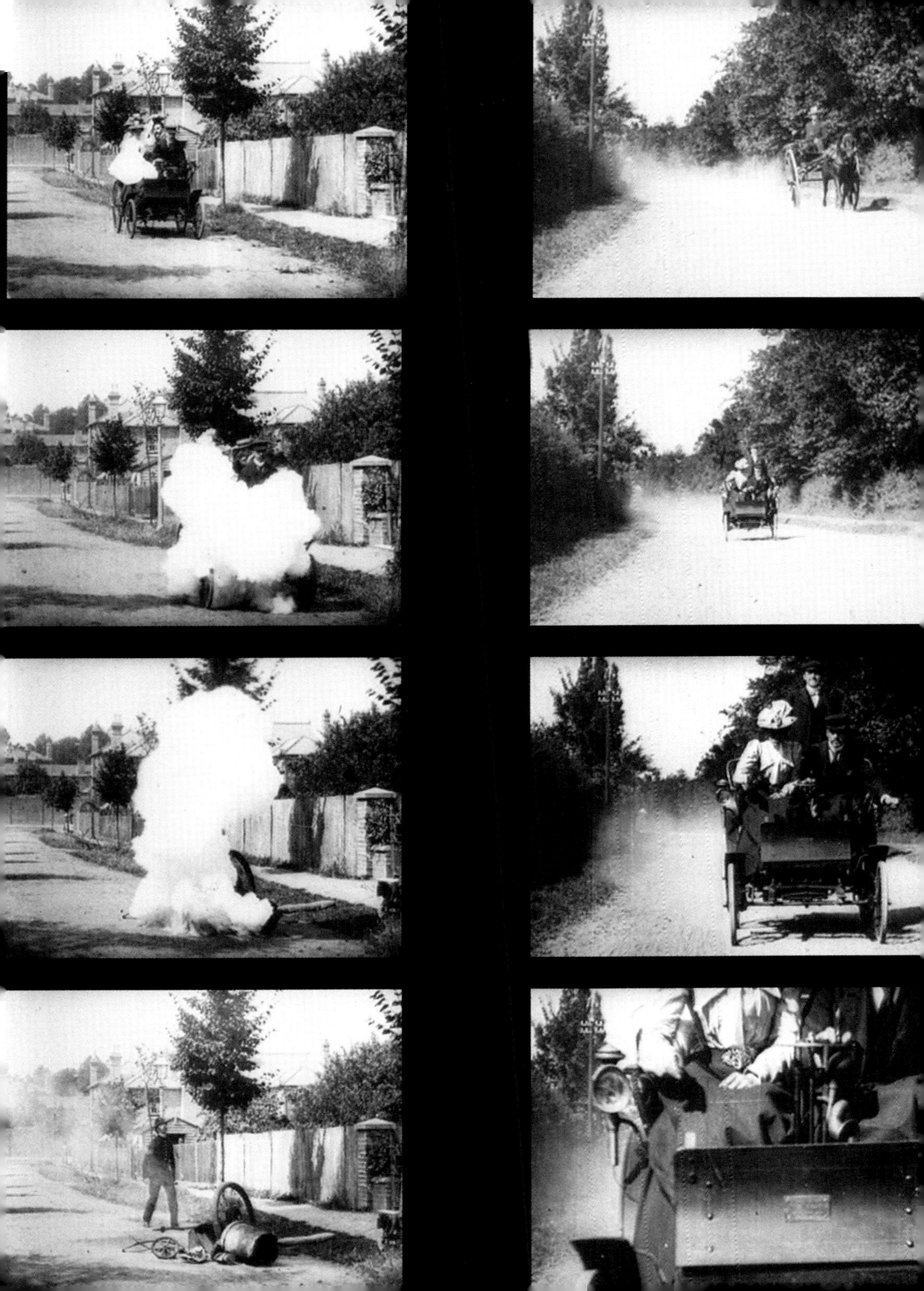

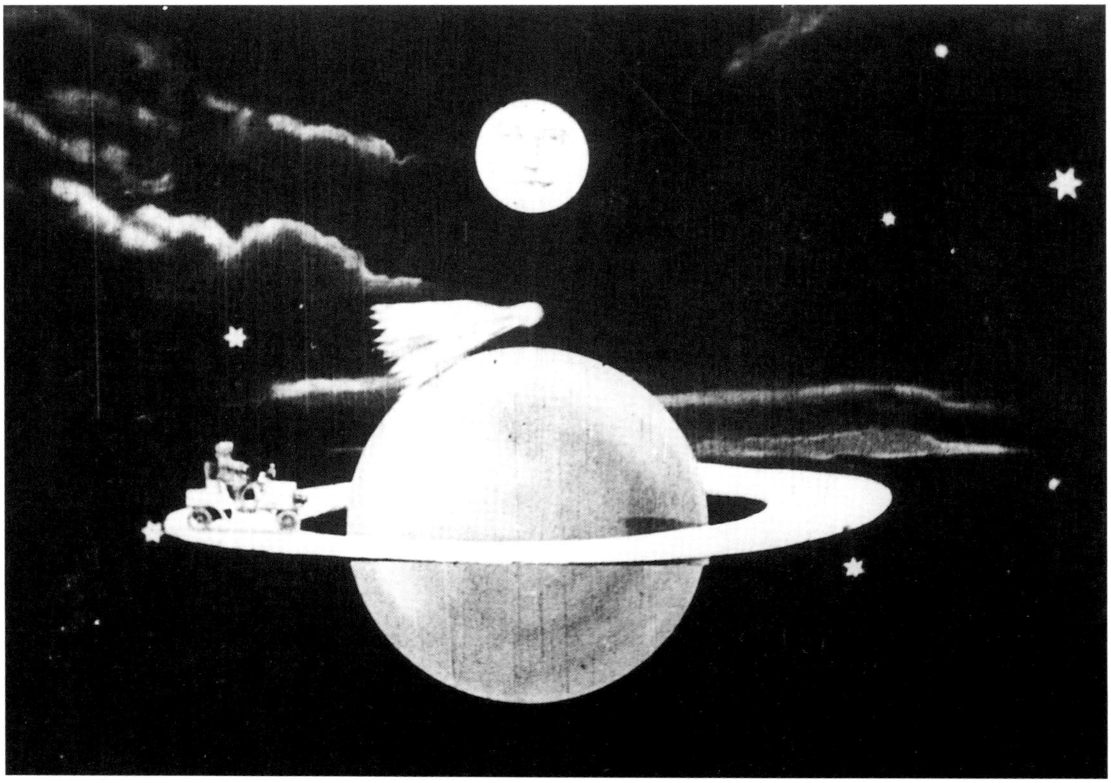

83 Robert Paul, *The ?Motorist*, 1906. Frame still.

The driver in *Explosion of a Motor Car* was Hepworth himself and he was evidently an enthusiastic if somewhat reckless driver.[74] It was in order to curb the excesses of drivers such as Hepworth that the 1903 Motor Car Act introduced licensing and penalties for exceeding the speed limit. These regulations also offered new opportunities for comic episodes relating to the motorist's encounter with the law. Robert Paul's 1906 film *The ? Motorist* is perhaps the most imaginative vision of this scenario, combining the reckless motorist narrative with astronomical fantasies (which will be discussed in chapter 6). A couple are seen speeding in a motor car; they run over a policeman who is signalling them to stop and continue until they reach a public-house. The car drives up the front of the building into the sky and the heavens; it drives round the circumference of the sun and the rings of Saturn (plate 83).[75] Eventually, the car falls from the sky and back to earth, where it drops through the roof of a building that turns out to be a law court. The car continues its journey out of the court, chased by a policeman, a magistrate and other officials. In order to avoid arrest, the car is magically transformed into a countryman's cart, until the couple have made their escape and it turns back into a motor. In these trick films motor-car technology is dangerous and unpredictable and its users are impetuous and irresponsible. Rather than ennabling a decorous roving and expansion of vision, the motor car is represented as a violent intrusion into the English countryside, generating speed and dust that blind passers-by and representatives of the law and that leaves devastation in its wake (plate 84).[76]

In the years from 1896 to 1906, motor-car ownership grew at an extraordinary rate. In 1904 the number of motor cars registered in the United Kingdom was 18,000 and by 1905 it had increased to 31,000.[77] Yet this remained a world in which the horse-drawn cart co-existed with the motor car, both in the cities and in the countryside, and in which the experience of motoring – in physical and conceptual terms – was still in the process of being formulated and given representation.

The motors and films of Hepworth and Paul seem a world away from those of Herkomer. Herkomer was at the elite, cutting-edge of motoring. The speed trials and endurance events that he sponsored in Munich involved the aristocratic motorists of Europe and America and his stately Daimler, with its reliable chauffeur, were the antithesis of the lunatic drivers that populated early film. Moreover, Herkomer's engagement with pictorial motion was from the perspective of high art and its associated cultural and moral values. His experiments with pictorial-music plays and mobile colour-music were undertaken in order to expand the formal possibilities of art and its narrative capacities. Around the end of 1912, Herkomer began to show films at his house in Bushey and shortly afterwards he

84 'A Quiet Sunday In Our Village', *Punch, Or the London Charivari*, 6 June 1906, p. 412.

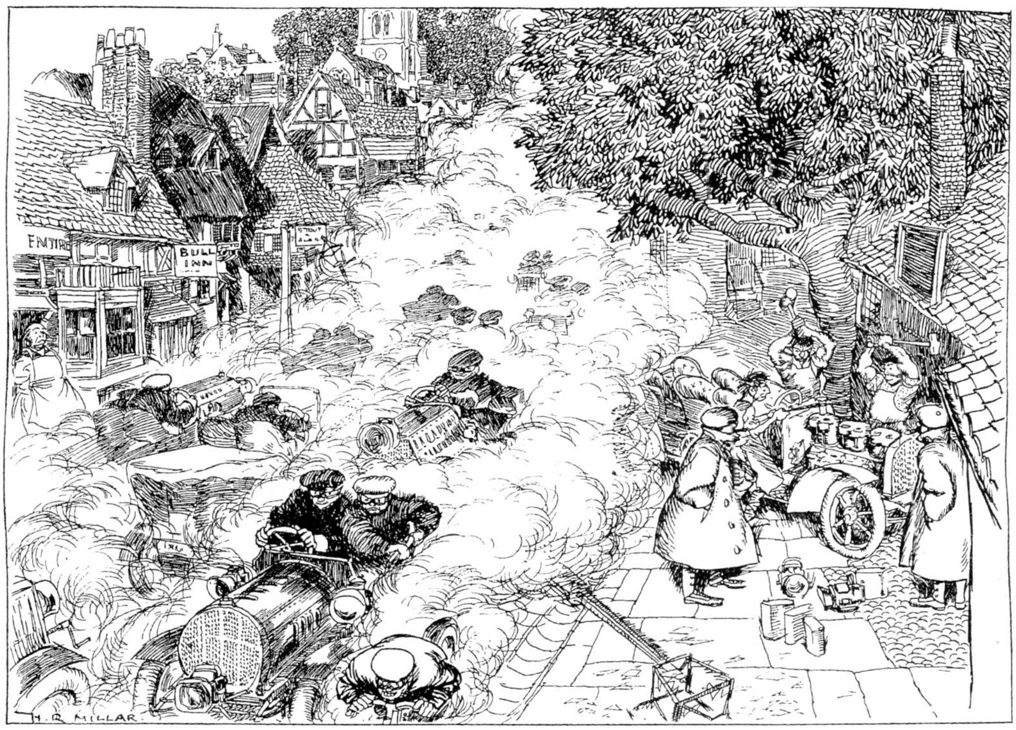

converted his theatre into a film studio and began making films.[78] His agenda was to create an alternative film idiom to that of the low and sensational films that he believed dominated the medium in its second decade. It was a fortuitous and timely move, allowing him to assume the mantel of artistic taste and sobriety within the film business, just as the British Board of Film Censors was created.

Herkomer was not the exception to the mainstream of motoring and film-making but nor was he entirely typical. His usefulness and interest to historians now is because of his intermittent and uneven interface with strictly linear, progressive histories of modern media and technology. His career suggests that these histories need to be reconfigured so that they can allow for a personality like Herkomer, who worked across high and popular culture, in a range of traditional and new media, and brought advanced and conservative views to his work. Herkomer's cultural identity is like Serres's account of the modern motor car, an ensemble of solutions 'dating from different periods'. Moreover, this model might also be used in order to understand the historical period around 1900 generally. Serres has suggested: 'Time is paradoxical; it folds or twists; it is as various as the dance of flames in a brazier – here interrupted, there vertical, mobile, and unexpected.'[79] Doesn't this sound like the motion of the motor car, as it rediscovered national identity in the English countryside or suddenly drove off into outer space in the visual imagination of early film? This, surely, is the pace of Herkomer's fitful engagement with the velocities of twentieth-century culture and technology. Let Herkomer stand as a rich and expressive case study of the exhilarating inventiveness of British visual culture at the beginning of the twentieth century.

earthly and astral bodies

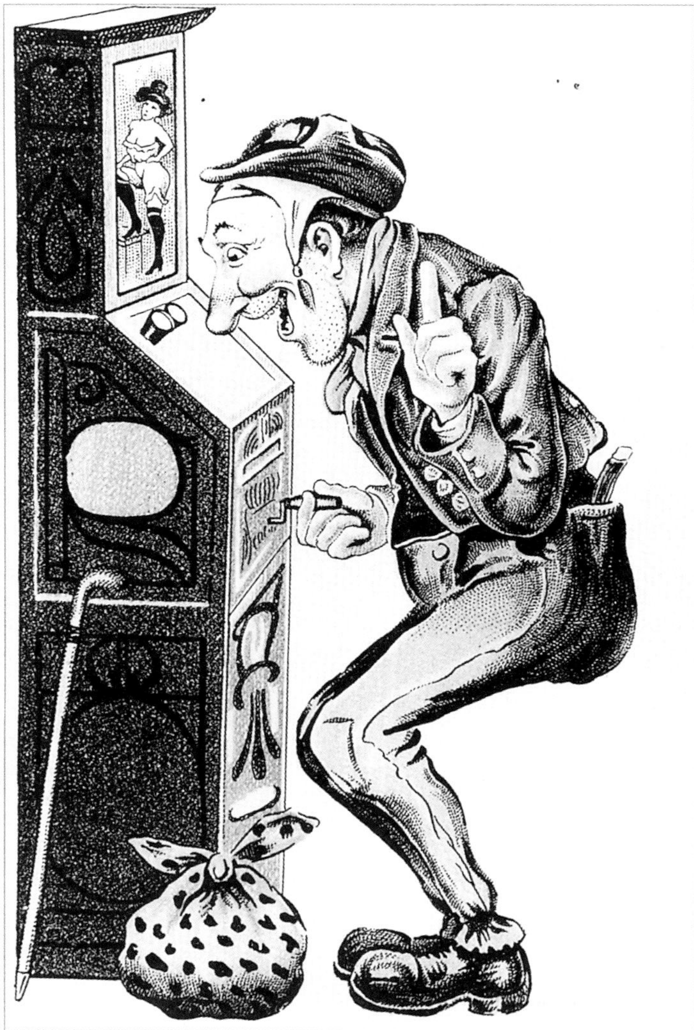

85 Anonymous coloured line cut, *c.*1900.

5 strip: moving bodies in the 1890s

> What happens when what you see, even though from a distance, seems to touch you with a grasping contact, when the matter of seeing is a sort of touch, when seeing is a *contact* at a distance?
>
> Maurice Blanchot, *The Gaze of Orpheus* (1981)[1]

moving images: moving bodies

The boundaries between still and moving images, between the inert and the animated, were eroded by a range of new optical technologies throughout the nineteenth century. Even before this period of optical invention, however, the enchantment of the magic lantern lay largely in its capacity to endow images with movement and flow. In the hands of the skilful lanternist, slides could be drawn through the lantern gate to suggest a continuous, unfolding scene and, as the previous chapters in this book have shown, the moving image was a part of visual culture long before the advent of photography and film. Developments in optical science and technology occurred with extraordinary rapidity in the nineteenth century. Patents and copyrights were registered at a spectacular rate, as inventors found new ways of exploiting the mechanism of the eye in order to create the illusion of movement and to engage the fascination of the viewer.

In the light of this long history of the moving image, the question remains of the significance and distinctiveness of film. The historiography of the moving image offers two key ways of addressing this issue. The first unapologetically foregrounds the emergence of cinema and relegates the entire range of non-filmic Victorian visual culture to the category of 'pre-cinema', as more or less successful precursors on the inexorable path to the invention of film. The second approach offers an alternative epistemology that positions film as simply one more form, or medium, in an ongoing history of optical devices that created the illusion of movement and life, from the magic lantern to instantaneous photography and computer-generated imagery. In order to approach accurately the historical significance of film as a distinctive mode of visual imaging, it is necessary to navigate these two extreme and media-centred accounts and find another interpretation. While it is true that many of the conceptual and technological components of film were already present in earlier optical media, it is also clear that in terms of the social and cultural reverberations of these technologies, film was not just one more device in a long and undifferentiated history. One should seek to recognise and understand the specific cultural and individual affects that were created when the early films were projected life size onto screens and the ways in which they shifted the landscape of visual culture in the years around 1900. The spread of film in public life had an impact on debates concerning the visual image and its audiences that had been evolving since the popularisation of photography. Questions concerning the constitution of large audiences, social respectability, responsibility and cultural value, all of which had been exercised earlier in the century, took on a renewed and urgent life at the end of the 1890s. Film altered the parameters and urgency of these issues and shifted relationships between the different forms of visual media in the period.

The representation of the human body has been at the heart of the visual arts in the West since classical antiquity. At once a symbol of ideal, pure beauty and a sign of fallen corruption, the visual representation of the body has been constituted both as the aim and the offence of art, its highest attainment and its greatest degradation. At any given historical moment, the imaging of the body thus brings together current attitudes towards the power and purpose of the visual image and concentrates debates on the sometimes fraught relationship between viewer and image and between living body and the body in representation. Is the represented body a force for good or harm? Does it and should it arouse the viewer: stimulate or pacify, render the onlooker all body or all mind? The configuration of these questions shifts in relation to changing historical factors such as prevailing religious beliefs, political influences or economic variations; it also responds, however, to the nature and form of the image itself. Expectations and interpretations of an image of the body will vary greatly depending, for example, on whether it is a unique painting or a reproduced print. The mechanical reproduction of the image was thus a key moment in the history of the body in representation, creating new, broader audiences and shifting the associated public debates on the influence and morality of the visual image. Photography also had a profound and permanent effect on the historical perception of the body imaged.[2] From its inception, photography was imbued with an ideology of realism and authenticity; the photographic image was believed to represent reality and to address the viewer in a particularly direct and unmediated way. Accordingly, photographic images of the body were assumed to be more arousing than images of the body in other, more 'artistic' media. From the 1840s, the apparent immediacy and accuracy of the photographic image was believed to endow it with a potentially pornographic intent and although the production of sexual arousal in the viewer was manifestly not the single purpose of photography, it seemed to many nineteenth-century and twentieth-century commentators that it was a peculiar proclivity or susceptibility of photographic images of the body.[3]

Compared with paintings, drawings and prints, the photographic image was perceived to be a relatively unmediated form of representation, both in terms of its production and of its consumption, enabling direct access not simply to an image but to the represented object itself. If the object in question was the body, then the photograph was believed to afford the viewer direct access to that body and to sexual arousal with a minimum of interference from the medium itself. Here, then, was a brave new world of sexualised representation.

This set of debates, generated by the advent of the still photographic image, had far-reaching implications for film's representation of the male and, particularly, the female body in the late 1890s. Film took the authenticity and address of the photographic image one momentous step further, offering mass audiences the visual pleasure of watching bodies, projected on a large scale, moving in real time. The erotic spectacle of the body in representation was set in motion, enabling an unprecedented expansion of sexualised gestures, actions and *mises-en-scène*. Given the significance of the debates concerning sexual representation and the moving image to the subsequent history of film, an examination of the early manifestations of these themes in relation to the first films is a productive area of study. It draws the late Victorian and Edwardian audiences of film to the centre of the analysis and introduces humour, innuendo and sexual desire as vital historical dimensions in the development of visual culture in the period.

As seen in chapter 1, the mobilisation of the visual image in early film and the mobilisation of the viewer were profoundly implicated with each other. The history of early cinema is punctuated with anecdotes about its audiences leaping from their seats in terror or touching the screen in disbelief, so convinced were they by the realism of the projected image. Among the early subjects made by the Lumières and included in their first public programmes was *The Arrival of a Train at the Station*. Although other views of everyday life were also shown at these public screenings, it is the train film that has come to exemplify the astonished physical reactions of cinema's first audiences and which, in turn, have taken on the status of a founding myth in the history of the medium.[4] It is striking that these stories of agitated and demonstrative viewers appeared almost as soon as the films themselves and tracked the early years of their development, to the point of becoming the subjects of comic films such as Robert Paul's *The Countryman and the Cinematograph*, described in the first chapter, in which the naïve and immature viewer becomes so involved in what he sees and identifies so strongly with the images that he can no longer distinguish between himself and the figures and stories on the screen (see plate 97). As the film historian Stephen Bottomore has argued, 'The projected film image was the closest copy of the real world that had yet been achieved by technology.' Many of the early caricatures and films about the cinema took its astonishing realism as their theme and frequently, as in Paul's film, by having a character 'confuse the screen with reality'.[5]

In the presence of animated pictures, it was claimed, the viewers themselves became animated, a corporeal analogue of the images on the screen. Films, these sources suggest, created a newly embodied, visceral and physically motivated audience. These stories are important, not because they accurately record cinema's impact on its first public but because they give cinema its syntax, its origins, a genealogy. Whether or not audiences actually moved, the experience of viewing images was understood to incriminate a bodily response. Movement was always immanent, if not performed. Looking, in these early years, was corporeal and viewing was embodied.

Here I want to hold onto the ghosts of these early viewers as a metaphorical device. They testify to a radical reconceptualisation of space and subjectivity that was taking place in the 1890s, in which the optical technologies that converged in projected moving pictures forced a different understanding of the psychology of perception and of the relationship between viewing body and the object of representation. It was in the consumption of images of the disrobing body that the sensory and phenomenological implications of the new media became most focused and, in this setting, there were two types of animated bodies: first, the moving bodies seen through peepholes and on the screens of late Victorian visual culture; and second, the bodies of viewers as they experienced a particularly intense form of embodied, haptic spectatorship.

eyes and bodies (looking and feeling)

The historiography of cinema studies has been dominated by the triumph of the eye, by the framing of the cinematic experience in terms of a kind of disembodied looking, driven by the pleasures of scopophilia, the desire for pleasurable looking. In their present, mature phase, cinema audiences have grown out of their early uninhibited physical responses and are concerned with the indulgence and management of the gaze. Cinema, it is suggested, has abandoned its sensory promiscuity and has realised its definitive function as an ocular form of representation and mode of address.

Let me return, however, to that brief, but iconic, film strip of the train pulling into the station and the reactions of its startled audience. As the film historian Tom Gunning has convincingly shown through his concept of the 'cinema of attractions', agitation was an integral part of the attraction of the new medium.[6] The early film projections came partly out of a tradition of magic theatre and illusionism and audiences were used to and expected a pleasurable oscillation between unbelievable effects and the latest mechanical technology. Gunning has shown how film presentations exploited precisely this dual audience expectation. Thus, the gimmick of beginning a film exhibition with a frozen, still image, which could then be cranked into life as the projector started up, was part of this play on the audience's amazement and credulity. This moment of coming into movement and the audience's response was the true spectacle of the early film shows, which played to the audience's willingness to be astonished, or moved, by the moving image. It was a modern form of cultural consumption, in which viewing became a dynamic exchange among film, projectionist and audience.

Most importantly, the body was the medium through which the viewing experience was expressed. This was an immediate and non-contemplative mode of

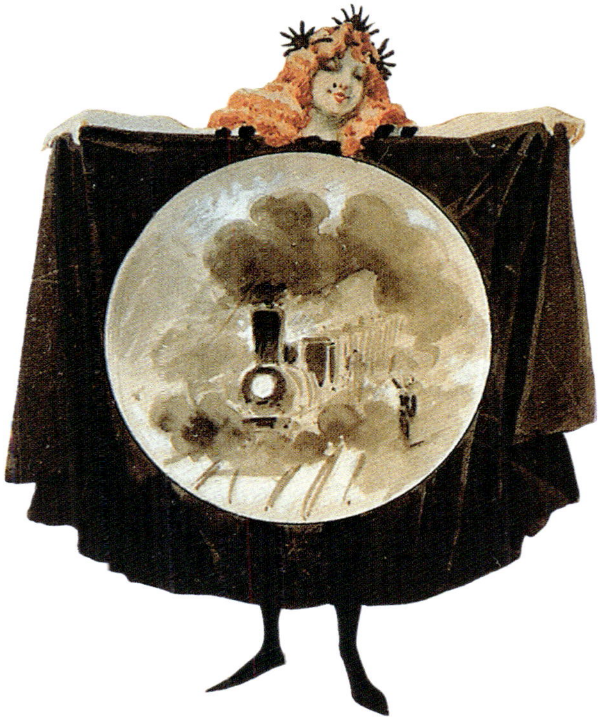

86 Unused design for a Lumière poster, n.d.

viewing, a form of entertainment which sought gut reactions. In an early design for a Lumière poster (plate 86), the train appears as if projected on or, equally possible, as emerging from a woman's abdomen. Image, screen and viewer have become mutually absorbed and the space between them has imploded as the body becomes the screen. The woman's body is eviscerated, emptied out, and is then filled with the projected image, which draws the viewer's gaze deep into its pictorial space. This different perception of viewing was in direct opposition to the traditional Kantian ideal of the detached contemplation of beauty. If art promoted the intellectual and contemplative consumption of the image in which the body had been trained not to look, then film and the optical machines of the mid- and late nineteenth century reintroduced the viewer's body as an integral part of their attraction – and never more intensely than when the object of representation was the body.

This is not to exclude the opportunities for embodied vision in the arts of painting or sculpture; indeed, a number of artists and theorists in the nineteenth century were exploring the possibilities of absorbed spectatorship and a more multi-sensorial understanding of the art object. It is to argue, however, that physical arousal and a tactile visuality were the very stuff of early film and defined its mode of address and the condition of its viewers. Moving pictures animated their viewers if not literally, then certainly metaphorically and this agitation took on a particular quality and significance when the images in question were of sexualised bodies set in erotic narratives, albeit of no more than a minute or two. The argument is made manifest in a cartoon called 'The Improved Magic Lantern or Cinematograph', which was published in 1906 in the French comic journal *Le Rire* (plate 87). It shows the reactions of the same audience to two different film subjects. The first, a cavalry charge, has the figures scattering in all directions to get out of the way of the oncoming horsemen. The second, 'Bedtime of the Parisian Lady', shows the female members of the audience physically restraining the men, who have pushed their hands through the screen in order to get hold of the image of the corseted woman in her boudoir. Attraction and terror are the two extreme states of this fictional film audience. In addition, however, the cartoon articulates other key ideas about early film and its audiences. Whereas the terrifying image unifies

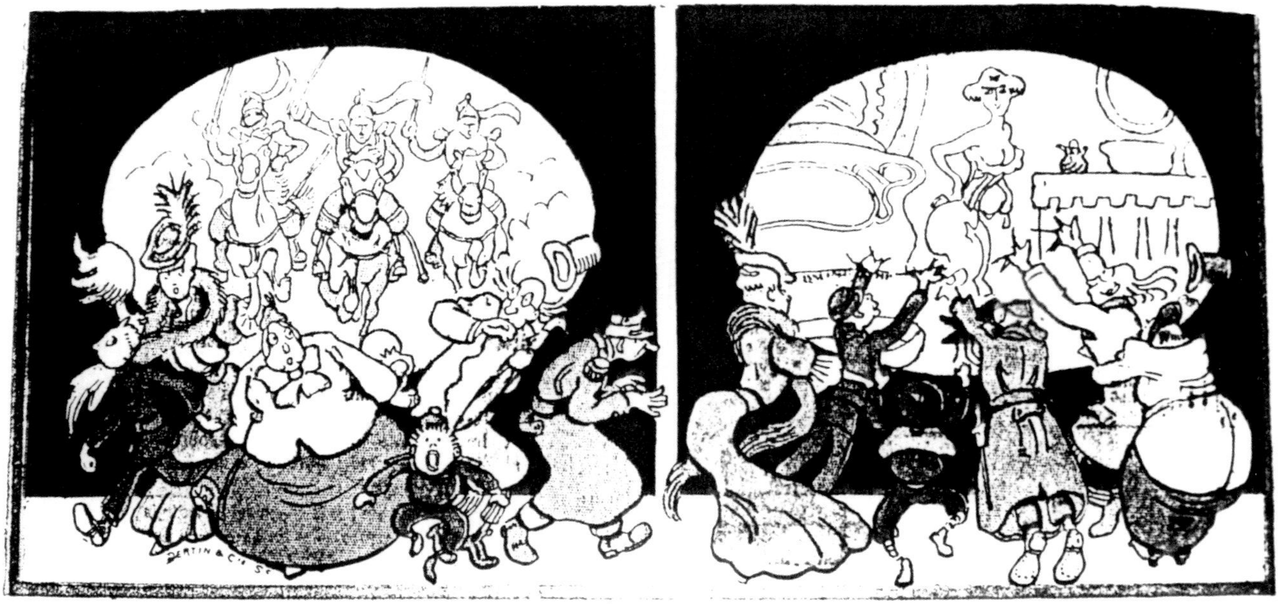

87 Henri Avelot, 'La Lanterne magique améliorée ou cinémtographe', *Le Rire*, 28 July 1906.

the audience, the erotic image splits the audience along lines of gender. Moreover, the motion created by the cavalry charge is centrifugal, as the figures scatter to get out of the way of the horses, whereas the movement generated by the erotic image is centripetal; it draws the men into its centre, its core. The Parisienne smiles out, unseeingly, to everyone and to no one and the men react by tearing at the screen that supports the image. 'Tear' may seem the appropriate description of some of the marks made on the screen but 'bury' seems a more accurate account of the action of the youth on the left who plunges his fingers into what has become the fleshy thickness of the image. The erotic images of film reduce everything – each element of the viewing experience – to the values and drives of the sexualised body. Here the audience and even the flat screen assume a corporeal immediacy that eradicates any vestige of intellectual reflection or bodily repression.

corporeal eyes

The most significant feature of the new optical machines of the nineteenth century was that they were meant to be touched and held, to be physically connected to their viewers. The phenakistiscope, for instance, was a device with a disc, painted with objects or figures in successive stages of motion, with small slits between the images (plate 88).[7] By spinning the disc in front of a mirror and looking through the slits from the back of the disc, the viewer was able to see a moving image

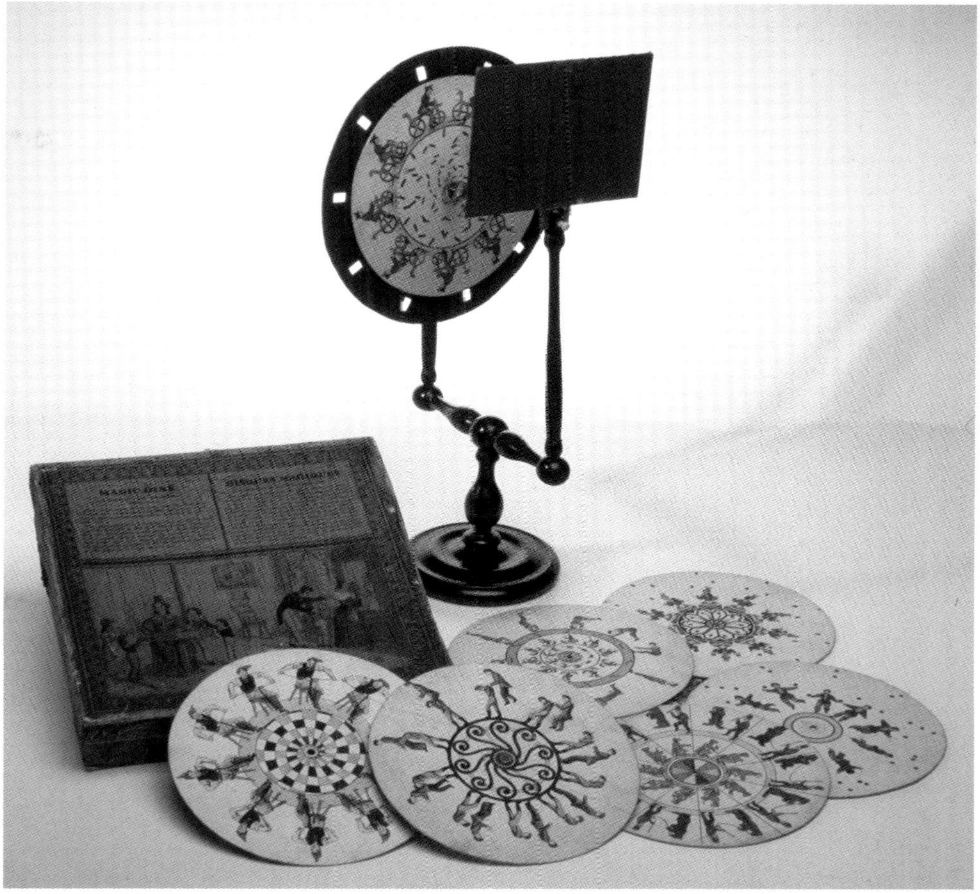

88 A phenakistiscope magic disk, *c.*1840. Courtesy of University of Exeter Library (Bill Douglas Centre).

reflected in the glass. Taking its name from the Greek for 'deceptive view', the phenakistiscope was an intimate toy, intended for use by one person at a time and with a close proximity of viewer, instrument and image. The zoetrope, the 'wheel of life', also drew on nineteenth-century concepts of the persistence of vision and worked on a similar principle to the phenakistiscope, but could be used by more than one viewer at once (plate 89). Pictures were drawn or printed on paper strips that were placed round the inside of a drum that had slits pierced in its upper section. The drum was rotated and when looked at through the slits, the pictures formed a moving image. Again, the viewer's face had to be close to the image and the illusion of motion was created, in part, by the action of the viewer, who could also control the movement of the image by determining the speed of the disc or drum. These kinds of devices were not designed for a detached gaze or to be looked at from afar and the images created did not belong in an art gallery, with a decorous public who had been taught not to touch. They occupied a liminal space between domestic entertainment and scientific diversion and, as Jonathan Crary has demonstrated in his book *Techniques of the Observer*, they were handled and oper-

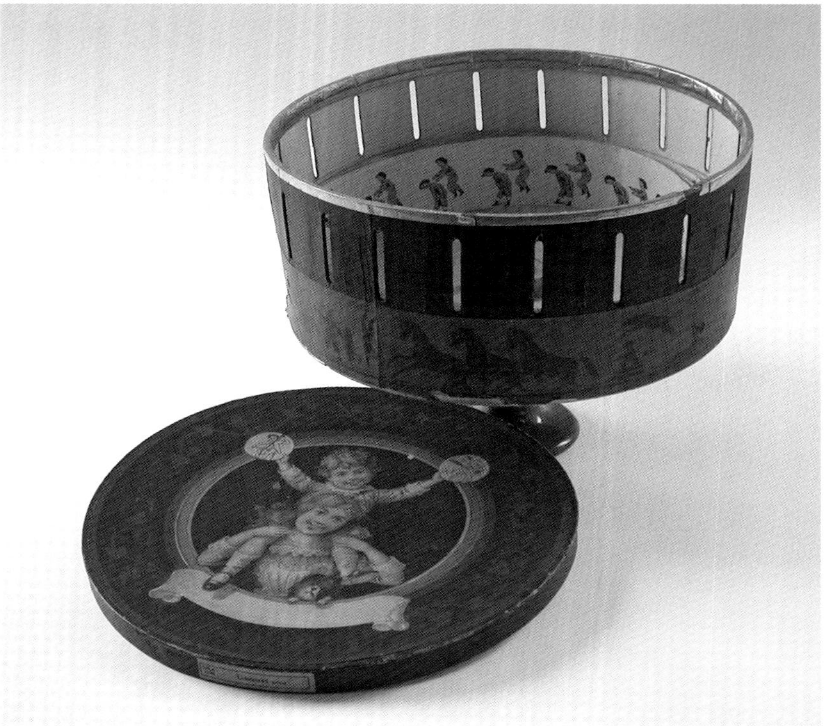

89 A zoetrope, n.d. Courtesy of University of Exeter Library (Bill Douglas Centre).

ated by the viewer user in an experience that eroded the distinctions between gaze and body, and body and machine.[8]

This intensely tactile experience of image viewing was a distinctive quality of visual imagery throughout the nineteenth century, across a range of media that drew on some of the most advanced optical technologies of the period and some of the most simple. At the end of the 1890s spectators could watch a serpentine dance performed by the American dancer Löie Fuller, or one of her imitators, on stage, on film or on the pages of the *Motograph Moving Picture Book*. Although the book was the least technically innovative of these options, it created the most explicitly tactile relationship between dancer and viewer (plate 90). The viewer was instructed to place a special transparent sheet in a cardboard frame, supplied with the book, exactly over the picture of the dancer. A precise match was essential and the user was advised to practise initially on a trial abstract image. When an exact fit had been achieved, the user was told to use the middle finger of the left hand as a pivot and to 'vibrate' the transparency from side to side and thus set the serpentine dancer in motion. The serpentine dancer was not the only plate in the book but it was the only illustration of the human figure and although animating a water mill would also, no doubt, have been a source of pleasure, it might not have held the same frisson as the motion of the shimmying dancer, whose body responded to the agitation of the plastic sheet on the paper. The devices used to move photographic images were not usually as basic, or direct, as the handling

SEE THAT THE TRANSPARENCY LIES FLAT AGAINST THE PICTURE.

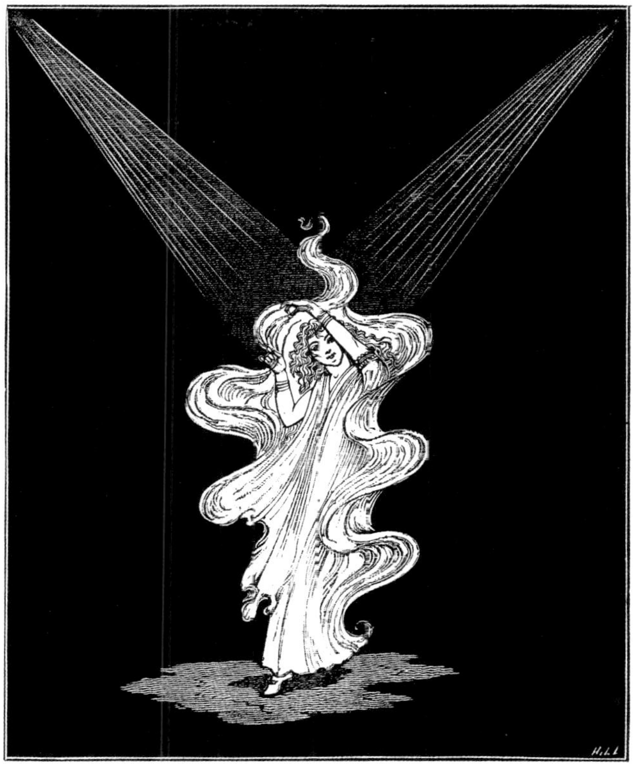

THE SERPENTINE DANCER.

INSTRUCTIONS.—Same as for the preceding picture.

90 'The Serpentine Dancer', from *The Motograph Moving Picture Book*, London: Bliss, Sands and Co., 1898.

required by the *Motograph* images, but the principle of a form of vision that was inseparable from tactile apprehension and physical contact remained a more or less implicit attraction of visual representations of the eroticised body throughout this period.

Devices for viewing new forms of mass, still photography also engaged the viewer in a highly absorbed physical relationship. The stereoscope exploited binocular vision by presenting two slightly discrepant images, which when looked at through the viewer, converged in a single, three-dimensional image. The eye and the body were equally implicated in the production and consumption of the stereographic image. As Crary puts it, popular, modern technologies of vision such as the stereoscope plunged the viewer into a 'newly corporealized immediacy of sensations'. He concludes: 'The body that had been a neutral or invisible term in vision was now the thickness from which knowledge of the observer was obtained. This palpable opacity and carnal density of vision loomed so suddenly into view that its full consequences and effects could not be immediately realized.'[9]

To many writers in this period, the effects of depth and three-dimensional space presented in the stereograph, along with the experience of total absorption created by the hood of the viewing device, made looking at the image essentially like the physical sensation of being in space or in the presence of actual people or objects. For this reason it was frequently used for tourist scenes, where the inaccessibility of the location could be overcome and the place made real at a distance by the immersive effects of the stereoscopic photograph. Stereography seemed also to inaugurate a new mode of viewing, one that involved the body as much as the eyes. In a study of the stereoscope published in 1904, Albert E. Osborne noted: 'It is not enough to look passively, but some self-activity of the right kind is necessary . . . as we look at the scene through the stereoscope, we should not only think of the position of these objects, but make *hand motions*, or *head motions*, to emphasize our *feelings* of the position of each.'[10] The perception of the stereographic image was thus described as a kind of physical mimicry in which the eyes triggered the body and a set of actual moves were performed. This convergence of mental and physical responses was also noted by the experimental psychologist Oliver Wendell Holmes, who described how 'the mind feels its way into the very depth of the picture' and imagined a situation in which eyesight was violently assaulted by the realism of the scene: 'The scraggy branches of a tree in the foreground run out at us as if they would scratch our eyes out.'[11] The physicality of viewing stereoscopic images was unique, its advocates claimed, and made this experience different from looking at images 'in a gallery or on the screen'.[12] There was no surface in the stereograph; surface yielded to spatial depth and to an experience of physical presence within the fictional space of the representation. Visual impressions gained from the stereoscope were 'such as we should get if we went there in body'; these were images that not only addressed the imagination but also produced 'corporeal eyes'.[13]

It is impossible to ignore the wonder and excitement of these accounts of stereographic viewing. What differentiated this type of image from other media was its effect on the viewer of actual physical presence. The implications were unavoidable. If this technique was effective for the representation of natural scenes, what might its power be in relation to images of the body and, more especially, of the body displayed for sexual consumption? How would corporeal eyes respond to the body presented for erotic display?

The consequences of this new embodied gaze may not have been fully grasped in the middle of the nineteenth century but Charles Baudelaire surely inferred the new role of the body and its cultural fall-out in his critique of photography published in 1859. He wrote:

> It was not long before thousands of pairs of *greedy* eyes were *glued* to the peepholes of the stereoscope, as though they were the skylights of the infinite. The love of obscenity, which is as vigorous a growth in the heart of natural man as self-love, could not let slip such a glorious opportunity for its own satisfaction.[14]

For Baudelaire, the connection between mass photography and the obscene was inevitable and inescapable, a natural development of the medium and its audience. Nearly fifty years later, commentators expressed a similar sense of inevitability concerning the link between sexual arousal and 'animated pictures'. In 1898 the *Photographic Times* protested about the vulgarisation, by particular individuals, of the new animated photography, suggesting that such a development was an inevitable outcome of the extreme naturalism of the technology and its images. Drawing an analogy with the history of stereoscopic photography, it observed:

> Stereoscopic photography, which a short time ago was as popular as its animated relative of the present time, was peculiarly adapted, by the wonderful appearance of solidity which it gives to the photographs, for perversion to the uses of the unprincipled. It was so perverted and to-day it is dead, practically . . . There is the same possibility in animated photography and there is, unfortunately, the same tendency to make use of it.[15]

Throughout the nineteenth century, the emergence of new visual technologies – mass production prints, photography, film – was repeatedly associated with the indulgence of consumer desires for cheap, mass sexual imagery. The extreme naturalism and illusion of solidity associated with stereoscopic and, later, animated photography, along with the intensity of the viewing experience, seemed to make them especially well adapted to the production of sexualised images of the body. In the stereoscope there was a perfect synergy between the supply of and the demand for sexualised vision. The viewer not only participated in the generation of the image but seemed also to eliminate entirely the boundaries between them. Baudelaire imagined a viewer hungry for, craving, the image, and eyes not just pressed but glued to, inseparable from, the image-making device. These greedy, corporeal eyes haunted the nightmares of cultural campaigners and legislators throughout the early history of film.

Vision and touch are not easily separated in these pre-cinematic forms of photographic technology. As Linda Williams has suggested:

> First of all there is the new tactility of the image itself; the mass-produced image is accessible to handling in a way that painting, for example, is not. It is passed around from hand to hand, pinned up, and, in the case of erotic and pornographic images, often physically present as incitement to masturbation and other sexual acts. Second, there is the tactility of the body's engagement with the particular apparatus of vision.[16]

The stereoscope and other devices such as the mutoscope were significant because they offered the possibility of total immersion in semi-private sexual reverie. They sold the pleasures of the peepshow or, more properly, the keyhole.

It is worth pursuing this question of the pleasures of the peepshow because it may provide a link between the experience of still and moving images and of viewing hand-held and projected images. Peepshows have a long history and a simple technology.[17] They consist of an enclosed box, with a hole for the spectator's eye and a flap for light to enter. By the eighteenth century they had become a popular form of entertainment and later developments included scene changes and clockwork figures. The special appeal of the peepshow was that, unlike other forms of public amusement, it offered the viewer a private pleasure: a glimpse of a closed, hidden scene and the possibility of seeing secrets. Bent over and peering into the eyehole, the viewer was offered a particularly acute and physical form of voyeurism.

In *Being and Nothingness* (1943), Jean-Paul Sartre chose the situation of the spy at the keyhole in order to describe utter loss of self in human actions: 'My attitude . . . has no "outside"; it is a pure process of relating the instrument (the keyhole) to the end to be obtained (the spectacle to be seen), a pure mode of losing myself in the world, of causing myself to be drunk in by things as ink is by a blotter.'[18] This evocation of total absorption in the act of looking (of being drawn and soaked up 'as ink is by a blotter') begins to convey the extent to which looking can be a bodily experience. For Sartre, the whole being is absorbed in the act of looking through the keyhole; it is a particular type of gaze that, for its duration, renders the viewer a pure and powerful subject. There is, however, another stage to the episode. Suddenly, while the voyeur is at the keyhole, he hears a footstep in the corridor behind him. Immediately, he is robbed of his imagined and omnipotent invisibility and becomes aware of himself as object, as another might see him and his actions and it is at this moment that he recognises his guilt and shame. The experience of the keyhole viewer is thus an aching oscillation between powerful absorption and shameful objecthood and between loss of self in the act of viewing and the recovery of embarrassed self-awareness. Sartre's allegory of the keyhole voyeur explains, in part, the pervasiveness of nineteenth-century images of peepshows in which the male viewer, bent over the peephole, his eye pressed against the opening, to consume better the scene within, is the victim of crime (plate 91). The viewer is so absorbed by the world in the box that he is unaware of the world outside. The space around the peepshow in these nineteenth-century images is always highly animated and potentially dangerous. It is as though the physical motivation of the oblivious viewer has been displaced onto the figures round him and the dangerous secrets of the scene within have been projected out of the box, rather than having been contained within its four sides.

The potent attractions of the peepshow were infinitely enhanced by the possibilities of interactive motion. With the mutoscope came an advanced version of the updated peepshow (see plate 3). As seen in chapter 1, the mutoscope was a kind of mechanical flip book, made of cards bound into books, which gave the impression of movement when turned by a mechanical device. The viewer peered through the eye-piece and could control the speed and direction of the movement by the turn of a handle. Not surprisingly, perhaps, the mutoscope, with its combination of peephole and moving images, became a popular and ubiquitous form of entertainment. For a penny, viewers in mutoscope parlours and at the end of the seaside pier could decide how fast to turn the handle, when to linger and when to speed up. From its first appearance, the mutoscope became associated with smutty pictures, usually featuring semi-naked women. Yet if the moving bodies of the flip book cards tested the boundaries of acceptability, so too did the behaviour of their audiences. As one inspector reported to a Select Committee in 1908, boys and girls 'were indulging in all sorts of indecent acts among themselves . . . two were looking round and picking out the different machines which bore the most seductive titles and which they thought contained the worst pictures'.[19] The mutoscope was an adaptable and pragmatic response to the demands of popular entertainment at the end of the nineteenth century and its keyhole attractions survived well into the twentieth century. It exemplifies the type of viewing apparatus that cohabited with lantern slides, postcards, film projection and other visual media in the late Victorian period. Yet, if the viewing machine can be said to have enlisted an embodied mode of looking, is it still possible to speak of haptic and corporealised viewing when the image is no longer physically handled by the viewer but is seen as projection? It is a question of what happens to the body of the viewer of the projected image.

I am unconvinced that the emergence of projected moving images in the 1890s signalled the switching on of detached sight and the switching off of corporealised vision. The first years of cinema were a period of visual miscegenation. Film entered

91 John Doyle, 'Political Showbox', 1840. Lithograph, 36.8 × 29.2 cm.

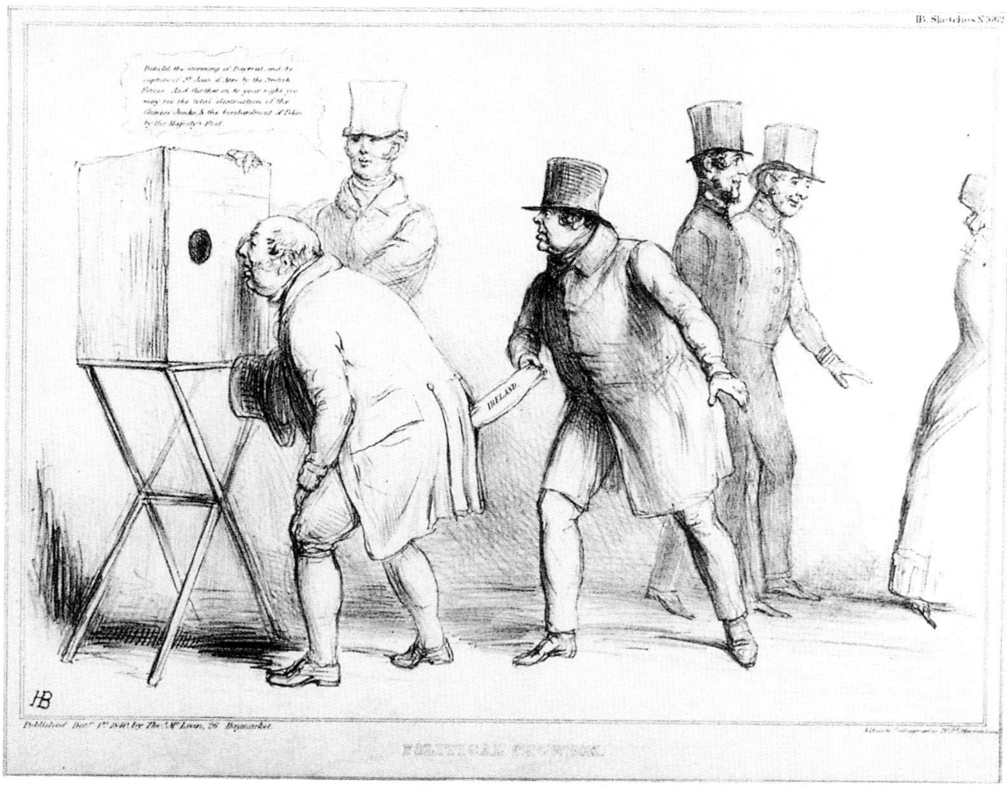

a developed and complex commercial and cultural world in which the boundaries between media were porous and in which audiences brought to film their music-hall manners and fairground expectations. The cultural context of early film reinforced what phenomenology tells us about the nature of visual perception. As the film theorist Vivian Sobchak has clearly put it, vision 'always implicates a sighted body rather than merely transcendental eyes . . . This is a vision that knows what it is to touch things in the world, that understands materiality.'[20] The viewing experience no longer involved a static object viewed by a passive spectator but could be defined as a dynamic activity involving an act of vision and a viewing body. It is this model of looking that is most appropriate to the experience of early film and that is enacted in the anecdotes referred to at the beginning of this chapter. Movement, in this context, refers not only to the images projected on the screen but also to an immanence within the body of the viewer. As Maurice Merleau-Ponty showed in the *Phenomenology of Perception*, sight is not something that can be detached from the embodied viewer in a material space. Sight is never only sight; it draws in the other senses – hearing, touch, smell and taste. 'My entire bodily existence is implicated in my vision.'[21]

While it is true that this conception of embodied viewing is not unique to film – indeed, that it is possible to develop this model in relation to spectatorship across a range of visual media – it is also the case that the specific conditions pertaining to the exhibition and consumption of film in the years around 1900 enhanced the possibilities for 'corporeal eyes' and made the function of the body in looking explicit. I am arguing, then, for the centrality of the body – the projected body and the viewing body – in the first years of cinema. Indeed, it is possible to make this point more emphatically and, taking the cue of feminist film historians such as Linda Williams, Gertrud Koch and Giuliana Bruno, to identify an inherent, structural link between an embodied cinematic gaze and corporeal investigation.[22] For Bruno, there is an 'epistomological relation between the cinematic eye and the anatomist's eye'.[23] Taking as her case study the first Neapolitan movie theatre, opened in 1901, she examines the proprietor's move from the public display of anatomy lessons, performed on wax models, to the screening of films. The anatomy lesson was, according to Bruno, the natural precursor of cinema. Both shared a common phantasmatic terrain, based on a mobile and 'dissecting gaze' and a fragmentation of the represented body.[24] The cinematic gaze offered the possibility of penetrating the visceral interior of the body and produced a corporeal form of visuality that dissolved the traditional separation of viewer and image.

The intense scrutiny of bodily mass and the drive to go beyond the body's surface and make visible the invisible is also the subject of Linda Williams's discussion of Muybridge's sequence photography and, specifically, his fetishisation of the female body in *Animal Locomotion* (1887; plate 92). Muybridge's eleven-volume study of men, women, children and animals performing set actions and recorded, using a battery of cameras, in a sequence of instantaneous photographs, is described by Williams as part of the 'prehistory' of hard-core pornography.[25] For audiences, the pleasure of watching these images set in motion, or projected in a lecture hall using

92 (*facing page*) Eadweard Muybridge, 'Miscellaneous Phases of the Toilet', *Animal Locomotion*, 1887, plate 498. Collections of the University of Pennsylvania Archives.

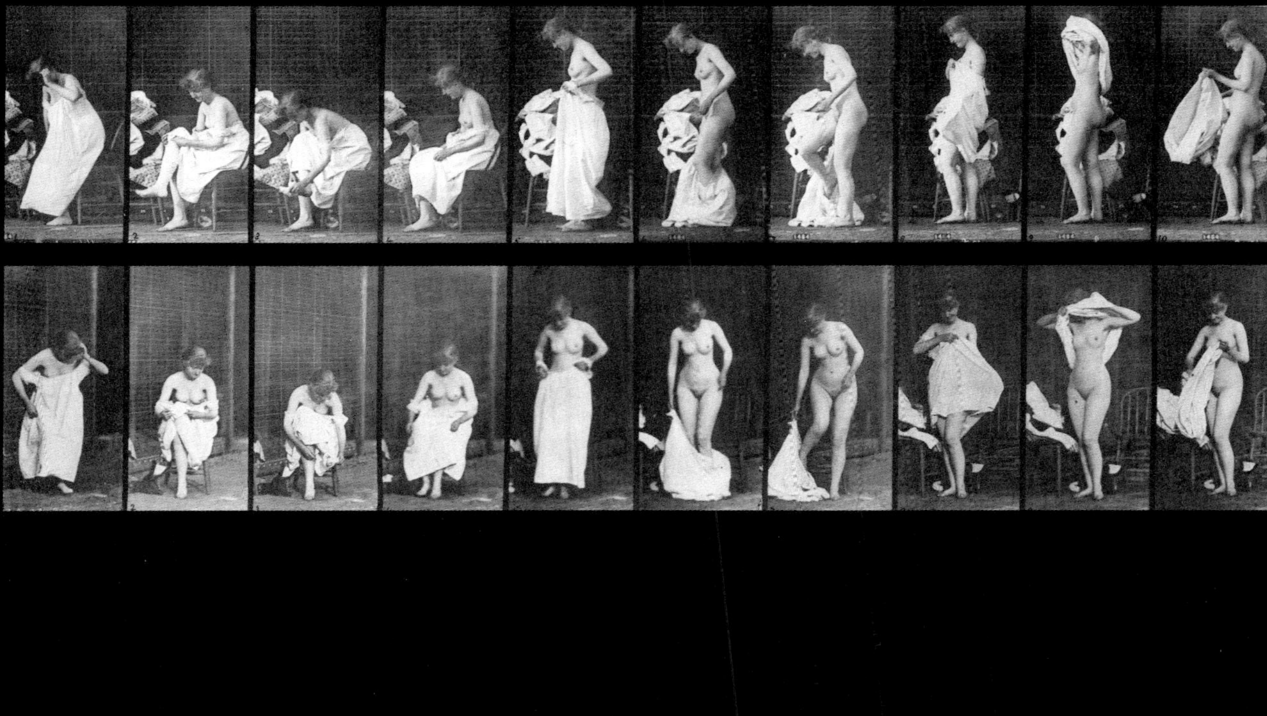

his motion-picture machine, the zoopraxiscope, was more than scientific, it was also sexualised and corporeal and introduced a new kind of representation of the female body that was both voyeuristic and fetishistic. The revelation of the body, Williams argues, was an intrinsic part of the prehistory of film and became a fundamental structure of the cinematic apparatus. Far from sounding the death knell of animated photography, as predicted in 1898 by the *Photographic Times*, the 'implantation of perversion' became cinema's social and cultural mission.

In her outstanding work on the history of film pornography, Williams moves from the work of late nineteenth-century pioneers such as Marey and Muybridge to the earliest instances of sexually explicit hard-core films.[26] There is, however, another route that this history can take, one that is prompted by a number of plates in *Animal Locomotion* in which Blanche Epler, Muybridge's favourite model, is shown in the act of disrobing (see plate 92).[27] Viewing machines, motion-picture cameras and moving bodies converge in the logic of the strip and I want to focus these issues through a discussion of the short film *A Victorian Lady in her Boudoir*, which was made in 1896 and is symptomatic of an entire genre of early films showing women undressing (plate 93).[28]

strip

It is no accident that the word 'strip' refers both to the first ribbons of perforated film and to the ritual performance of staged nudity. There is a compelling synergy between these two meanings. What better demonstration of the power of the movies than to take those climactic moments of transformation from clothed to unclothed and make them move, to project them to an audience hungry for spectacle, for whom looking was a proleptic experience of touch, taste and smell?

Live performance had wrestled with prohibitions regarding nudity and movement for more than a century. As seen in chapter 2, the *tableau vivant* was a device for freezing a group of performers in an artistic arrangement. It was a popular form of home entertainment but was adapted for public amusement in the form of *poses plastiques*, in which figures in flesh-coloured body stockings struck classical poses or imitated pictures or statues. In their prohibition of movement, the most respectable *tableaux vivants* were obsessed with even the most minute possibilities of motion. Static bodies in artistic arrangements were generally acceptable in public performance; the problems arose in relation to nudity in motion and the associated fears of animated bodies in the auditorium.

Whether or not one classifies a film like *A Victorian Lady in her Boudoir* as pornography is less interesting than how the work can be seen as a culmination of the related developments concerning technology, movement and the body that have been discussed in this chapter.[29] Indeed, sources from the period such as memoirs, newspapers and the photographic press, parliamentary reports and the outpourings of political and moral pressure groups, suggest that there was little consensus concerning the definition of obscenity, or of the distinctions between closely related categories such as vulgarity, bawdiness or vice. It seems perfectly possible that what one audience, or segment of an audience, might have found offensive, another might have enjoyed as harmless, if ribald, fun. Historians risk losing much of the nuance of late Victorian and Edwardian popular culture if the question of sexual humour is neglected.

Following a spate of arrests for the traffic in obscene photographs, the *British Journal of Photography* observed that 'some living pictures have been exhibited at some of the music halls, which, if not exactly indecent, were extremely vulgar. It is a great pity that such a thing should be, as it will tend to bring this class of picture, now so popular, into disrepute among respectable people.'[30] The language is significant. A line is drawn between indecency and extreme vulgarity – perhaps, here, a distinction between a moral and an aesthetic judgement. The article concedes that the films in question are 'not actually obscene' but they do seem to go beyond the taste of respectable audiences. Other terms that were frequently used in this debate were 'risky' and 'suggestive'. The *Photographic News* reported on a display which:

> wound up with one or two of those 'undressing' scenes in which the female form divine is gradually exposed to view, that are of such a nature that one does not care to have them exhibited in the presence of ladies . . . we noted that some of the latter immediately left the room when the last 'turn' was put on.[31]

Some, it should be noted, but evidently not all, of the ladies left the room. The question remains as to whose experiences represented the moral norm, those who left the room or those who stayed to watch the film.

The equivocal nature of these images and the attendant uncertainty regarding their cultural meaning were also articulated by individual viewers in these years. Sydney Race was a Nottingham clerk who kept a journal in the 1890s, recording his visits to shows and circuses in the region. In the late 1890s he was in his teens; he attended Anglican events, without being devout, and was involved with the management of his local Mechanics Institute. He was educated and engaged with the everyday life of leisure around him.[32] On Thursday 10 June 1897 he recorded a late visit to the Nottingham Cinematograph. The entry is worth quoting at length, both for its description of the films concerned and his reactions to them:

> But the scene which some of the audience were on the lookout for, though of which, when we entered, we had not the slightest knowledge, was called 'The Model's Bath'. A woman – we could detect a large smile on her face – divested herself of her skirt and other outer objects of clothing and appeared in her white drawers and chemise and when the picture expired was just dancing a jig. Dose number two: the girl was in a large white night dress which had fallen down from the breast disclosing a well developed 'frontage' and was in search of a 'flea'. After one or two dives she appeared to catch and squeeze it in her fingers and then she flopped it into a bath. Here an attendant came up and pulled off the white thing while the lady displayed a fine pair of calves in black stockings and darkness – in time to hide greater disclosures – opportunely covered the screen.

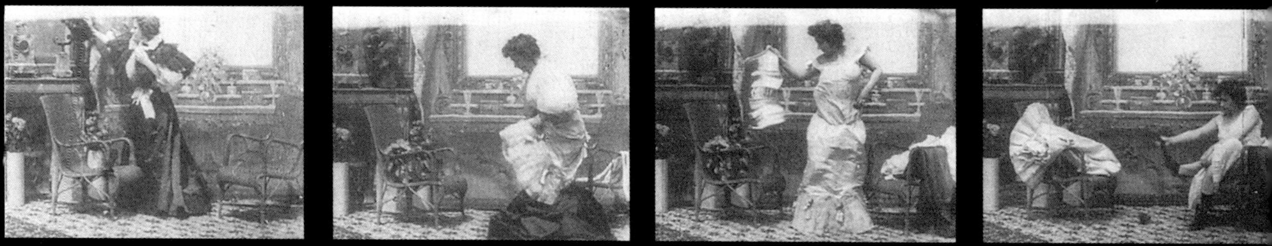

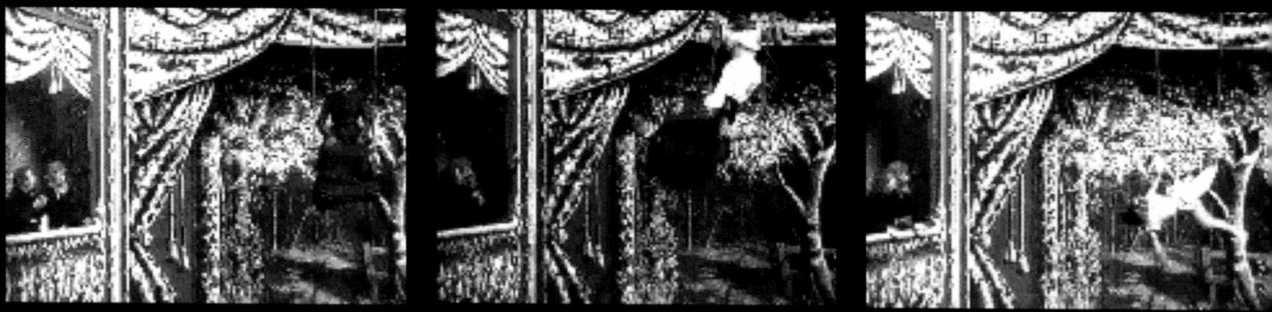

> It was a dirty and suggestive exhibition though we really saw no indecency. I notice on the bills of this and Radford and Chappell's show some scenes – including one called 'The Bride's Dilemma' – which show to what base uses the Cinematograph can be put and shady characters who posses [sic] one will need very close surveillance to keep them from public mischief. I am glad it was late at night when we saw the thing and that no lady was with me.[33]

The three subjects mentioned by Race – 'The Model's Bath', 'The Flea' and 'The Bride's Dilemma' – are all known to historians from film archives and trade catalogues and seem to typify a genre of non-explicit erotic films made and distributed in this period.[34] Race notices details such as a woman's smile in one film or the gesture of groping down the front of a chemise to find a flea in another; and while there is a tone of concern and disapproval, he is clear that these films are not indecent. Dirty and suggestive, certainly, but not that legalistic definition of obscenity, 'indecent'. The films circulate in a grey world of cultural ambiguity, of shady characters and public mischief, in which women should not participate but do.

Anecdotes from the period suggest that adaptable exhibitors could show risqué films in a range of venues; it was the context that mattered and that anchored the cultural identity of the subject. Robert Paul recalled, perhaps apocryphally, showing a film of Löie Fuller's Serpentine Dance in a chapel as *Salome Dancing before Herod*.[35] Sensation could be played up or down, however, depending on whether the films were seen in music halls, fairgrounds or mutoscope machines or the notorious smoking concerts. The smoking concert was an all-male gathering, possibly drawn from political or trade associations, that provided the eponymous smoking and entertainment. Yet it was not the only outlet for erotic films of this kind and it is likely that the tag 'smoking concert film' was sufficient for distributors to promote an appropriate subject to potential exhibitors in a variety of venues.

What is at least clear from this *mêlée* of opinions is that films such as *A Victorian Lady in her Boudoir* contributed to the growing call for a public censor to take decisions concerning acceptability and non-acceptability for audiences and that, for the time being, responses were highly varied and unpredictable. Equally evident, however, is the fact that film companies immediately comprehended the marketing potential of this genre of films and drew on its illicit associations in order to target an economically important consumer group. The Warwick Trading Company catalogue for 1901 described a film called *The Bridegroom's Dilemma* as: 'An excellent film, full of surprise and illusions, the exhibition of which will certainly be welcomed at any Smoking Concert or Stag Party. Space forbids a detailed description.'[36] The critical issue here is what is not said. The contents of the film are left to the purchasers' imagination and their skills at deciphering marketing language and programme design. It is most unlikely that there would have been

93 *(facing page top)* *A Victorian Lady in her Boudoir*, 1896. Frame stills.

94 *(facing page bottom)* Edwin S. Porter, *Trapeze Disrobing Act*, 1901. Frame still, courtesy of Library of Congress, Motion Picture, Broadcasting and Recorded Sound Division.

any sexually explicit material in the film; it was more a question of context and innuendo.

Twenty-first-century viewers of *A Victorian Lady* will be struck by its mundaneness. This is not the world of provocative dance or striptease. A woman comes into her boudoir and strips to her underclothes. There is only one, fleeting moment of address to the camera and the woman throughout appears remarkably indifferent to and even weary of the performance. It is simply strip. The space of this boudoir/set is the space of the peepshow, with its enclosed box and hidden scenes, but now it can also be projected for group consumption. In this respect, it is a display of the erotics of the medium. The strip is a sequence of moments united and 'narrativised' by the movement of the body. It stages the sexualisation of the body, layer by layer, frame by frame.

Unlike a still image, the strip film mobilises the disrobing and reveals the becoming sexual, the coming into nakedness. It is a study in physical transformation and of the temporality and process of the clothing and unclothing of the body, as in the extraordinary *Trapeze Disrobing Act* (Edison, 1901) in which a trapeze artist, suspended on a bar, disrobes to her leotard (plate 94).[37] In an essay on striptease, Barthes described it as a performance concerned precisely with the nature of temporality and its erotic rendering: 'It is only the time taken in shedding clothes which makes voyeurs of the public'.[38] This is important because it makes explicit the link between time and eroticism that is embodied in the act of strip. There is necessarily, therefore, a strong narrative element in the act and representation of striptease, created by the removal of layers, the gradual revelation and the viewer's waiting and longing to see.[39] Nakedness brings strip to an end. The art of strip is thus to defer this moment for as long as required – by the time of the performance or the length of the film – as the woman is caught between partial concealment and revelation.

Barthes makes another observation in this essay that may begin to draw out the particular qualities of *A Victorian Lady in her Boudoir*. He differentiates the polished gestures of professional striptease from the technical awkwardness of the amateur performance that constantly threatens to falter into immobility and to disrupt the artistic alibi of the thing. At one point in the film someone behind the camera seems to tell the woman to keep moving, to keep it going, keep it professional. To stop is to introduce a fatal hiatus in the fantasy being played out on the screen with its own rhythm of revelation and deferral. Time is of the essence in strip; its erotic power is produced through postponement of the final revelation and narrative closure. So desire is waylaid and transfixed (as Peter Brooks has put it[40]) by the process of unveiling. Those narrative moments along the way – the layers and details and expressions, the suspensions and reversals – represent the most intense moments of visual pleasure. The layers of undergarments, with their lace trims and exquisite complexity of fastenings, do not represent a coy prudishness in the sexual meaning of this film; they are its narrative drive.

Women's underclothes became highly elaborate in the late 1890s and early 1900s.[41] There was an accumulation of individual items that were subjected to

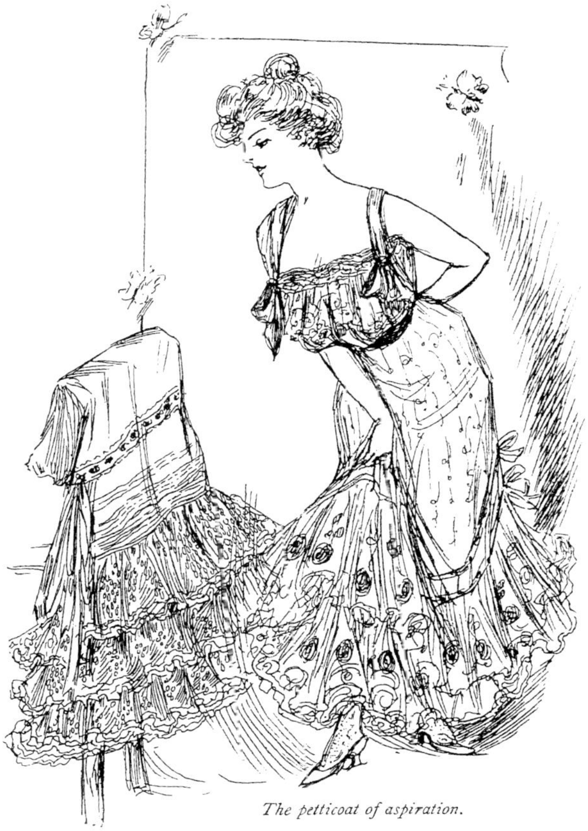

The petticoat of aspiration.

95 'The petticoat of aspiration', from Mrs Eric Pritchard, *The Cult of Chiffon*, London: Grant Richards, 1902, p. 33.

increased amounts of ornamentation. The style of lingerie, choice of colours, mode of combination and occasions for use were discussed in detail in journals such as the *Lady's Realm*, where they were drawn into a revision of mid-Victorian accounts of respectable femininity and matrimonial life. In *The Cult of Chiffon*, published in 1902, the author defined lingerie as an essential female charm and part of a wife's repertoire of respectable flirtation (plate 95).[42]

The corset, in particular, had become a highly nuanced semiotic system of its own, registering, in its style and decoration, a range of social and sexual details about its wearer. Having weathered the attacks on tight lacing from dress reformers at the end of the nineteenth century, the corset continued to represent fashionable, sexual femininity in the years around 1900. The form of the woman's corseted body made visual 'a system of compression and restraint'[43] and represented the softness of the body pulled in and made hard, enclosed and contained. The artifice of the clinched waist and curving breasts and hips also invoked its opposite, the removal of the restraint and unbinding of the body that, in this context, constituted a form of erotic release. Moreover, as David Kunzle has suggested, this oscillation between binding and loosing could be 'deliberately controlled, prolonged and postponed'.[44] In effect, then, the corset observes the same rules of desire as the strip.

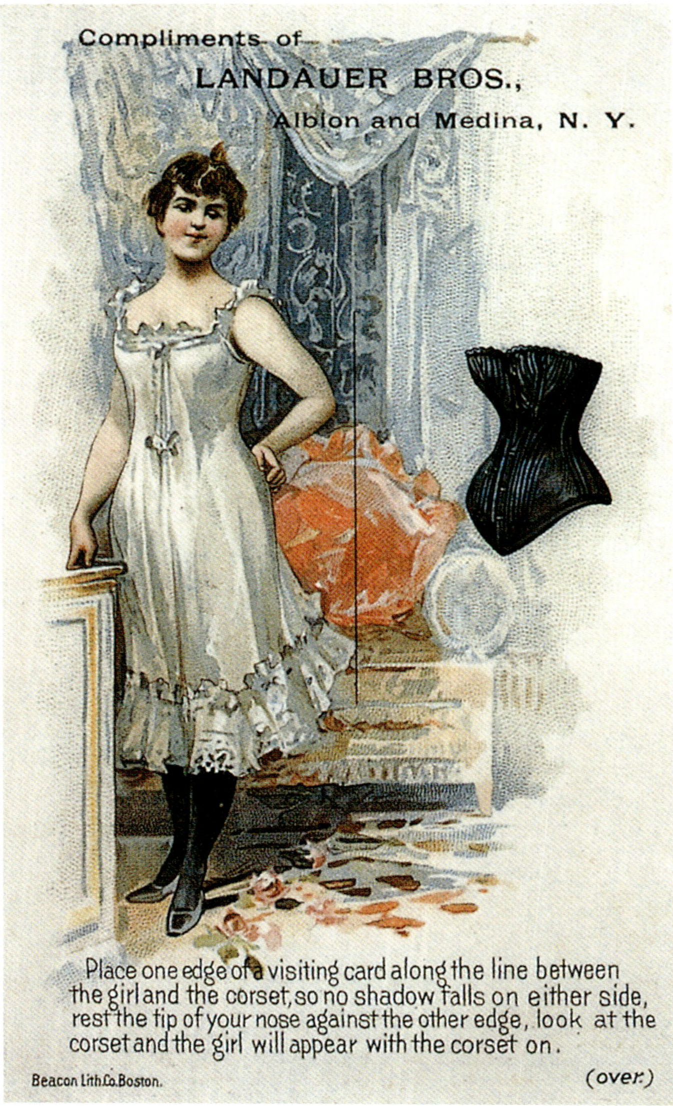

96 Trade card for Ball's corsets, 1880s. Collection of Valerie Steele.

It is historically utterly consistent that Freud should have begun his long investigation of the fetish in precisely these years. In his first discussion of the subject in 'Three Essays on the Theory of Sexuality', published in 1905, he described the structure of the fetish in the following terms: 'What is substituted for the sexual object is . . . some inanimate object which bears an assignable relation to the person whom it replaces and preferably to that person's sexuality (e.g., a piece of clothing or underlinen). Such substitutes are with some justice likened to the fetishes in which savages believe that their gods are embodied.'[45] The undergarment is perhaps the most literal form of fetish object. Underclothing had touched the warmth of the body; it was part of the body but also hid the traumas of sexual

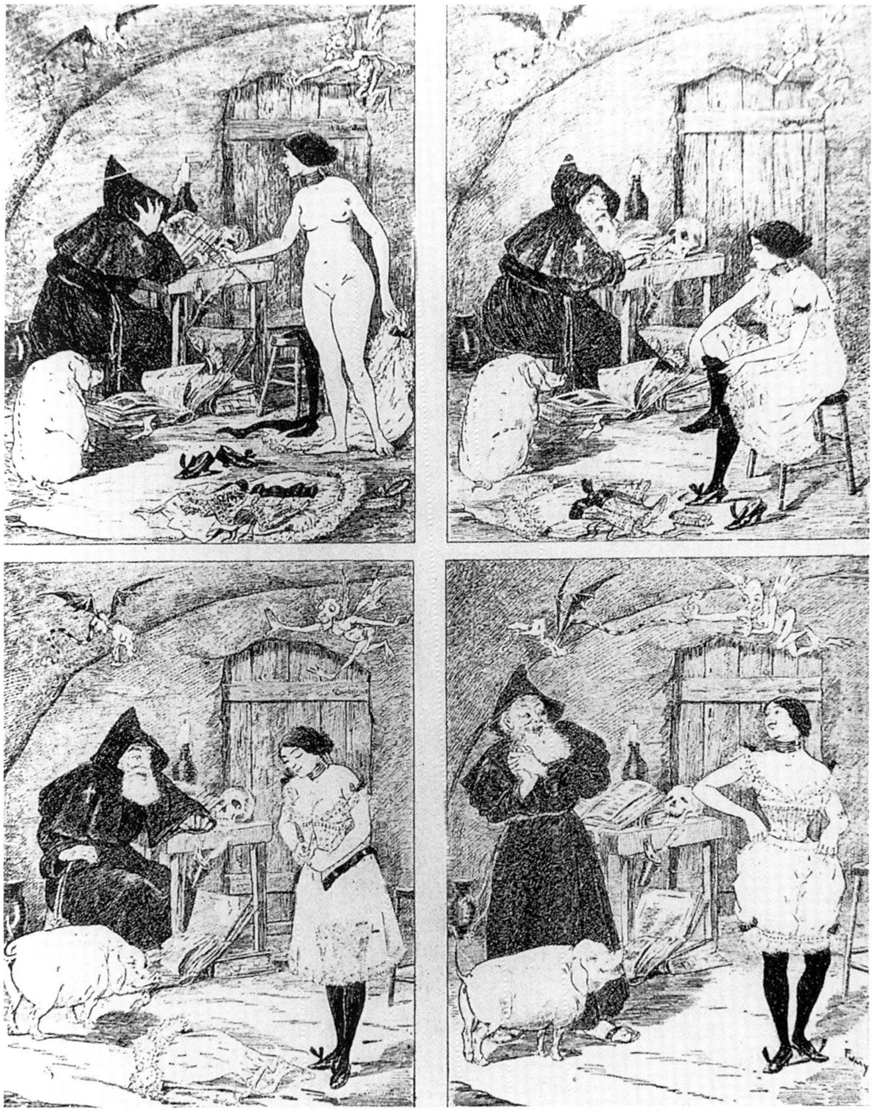

97 'The New Temptation of Saint Anthony', 1895. Collection of Valerie Steele.

difference within folds and drapes of textile and frill. It embodied the power of sexual difference but never ultimately revealed it.

Those sensual layers of underclothing – sensory not just in terms of their look but also in their tactility and their invitation to hear the rustle of chiffon, lace and cotton – were the perfect sexual substitutes. Lingerie addressed both the gaze and the body of the viewer in precisely the way that cinema produced an embodied spectator. In her outstanding study, *The Corset: A Cultural History* (2001), the dress historian Valerie Steele illustrates a trade card for an American corset company that invites the viewer to 'place the corset on the girl' by playing with optical illusion (plate 96). The viewer is told to 'Place one edge of a visiting card along the line between the girl and the corset . . . rest the tip of your nose along the other edge, look at the corset and the girl will appear with the corset on.'[46] The distinction between viewer and image collapses in the moment that the viewer presses his or her nostrils to and attempts to focus on the edge of the card.

To the extent to which *A Victorian Lady in her Boudoir* plays with these themes it is a knowing work of representation. It is also humorous; one can imagine a playful projection of the strip film that slows down or accelerates critical moments of action and that, along the lines of a trick film format, reverses striptease to dresstease.[47] Steele also illustrates a contemporary French caricature that encapsulates the skein of ideas that I have been considering here. In *The New Temptation of Saint Anthony*, 1895 (plate 97), the scholarly saint and his downcast pig are shown oblivious to the temptation of the naked woman in his cave but become increasingly excited as she puts on her underwear and finally stands triumphant in chemise, drawers and stockings.[48]

So, in spite of, or perhaps because of, its banality, I want to stake a big claim for the strip film. It is eroticism's counterpart to *The Arrival of a Train at the Station*. Both perform the power of the new technology of the moving image. They enact transformation: the station is empty, the train arrives; the woman is dressed, she removes her clothes. And they both address the gut, not the intellect.

touching with one's eyes

At the end of the nineteenth century, cinematography demanded new accounts of the psychology of perception; those derived from painting and still photography were no longer adequate.[49] Although codes concerning the representation of sexual difference in the high art nude seemed to change little over a century, painting was not immune to the changes taking place in other visual media and it is difficult to over-estimate the effect of moving images on late Victorian culture generally.

The nude, and most particularly the female nude, has always been a troublesome subject for fine art. This is precisely the point of the nude: to test the boundaries of morality and artistic propriety, to play with convention and sensation at once. Photography and more especially film shifted the debate up a few gears. In his published memoirs on this period, Cecil Hepworth recalled that 'there came a small but apparently growing quantity of short films which were said to be intended for "smoking room" exhibition. They were only a few at first but, like the small black cloud no bigger than a man's hand, they seemed to us to be ominous.'[50] To some, the history of film was also the history of its clandestine, erotic other that tracked and kept pace with the growth of the medium and could not be prized away. Here was a medium that had introduced a new way of showing and looking at the female body. In its review of photographic trends for the year 1897, *Photogram* put its finger on the problem with unusual directness and clarity. Commenting on a number of films such as *The Temptation of St Anthony*, *A Bride Unrobing* and *A French Lady's Bath*, sold by the dealer Philipp Wolff (plate 98), it stated:

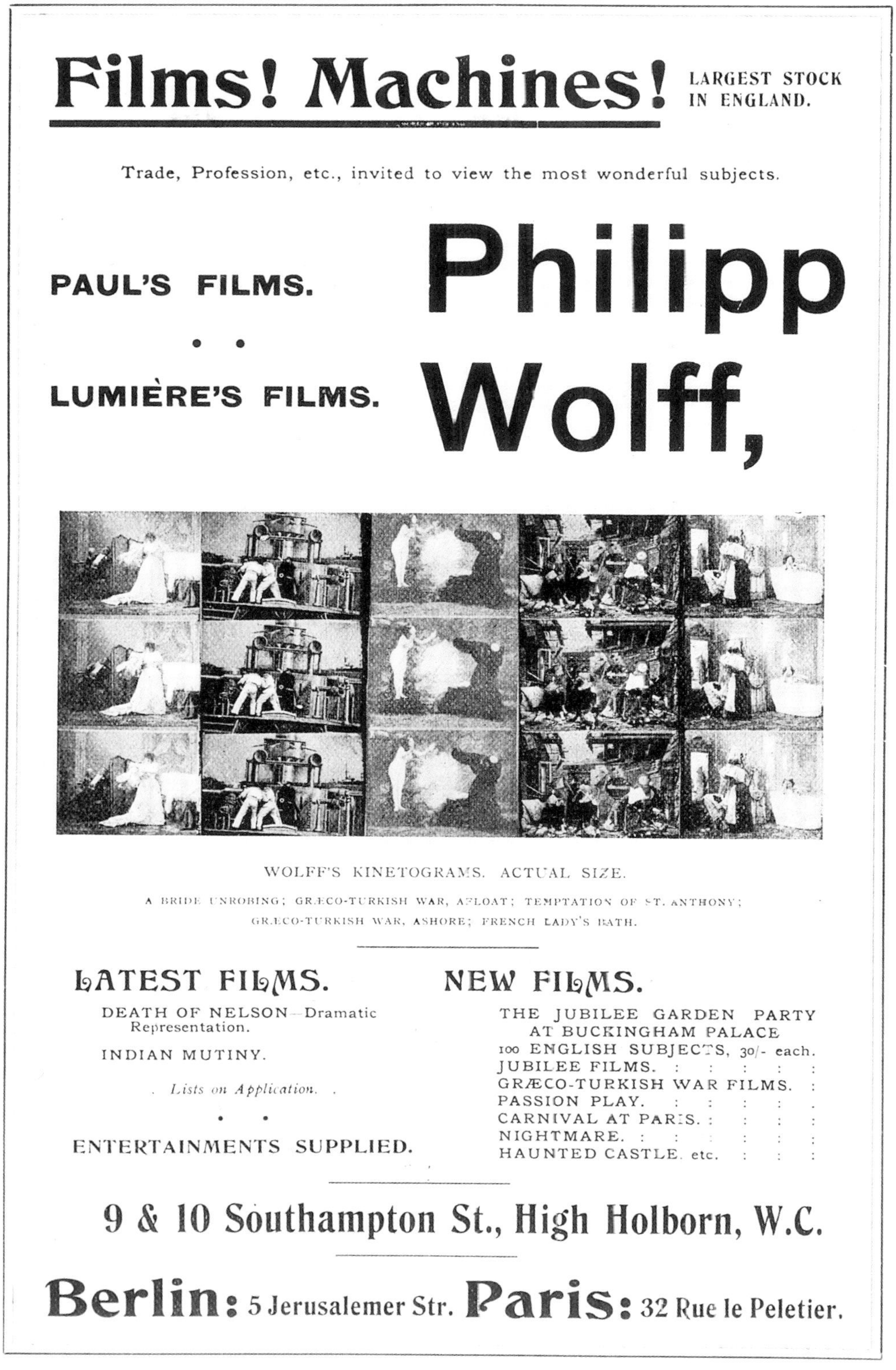

98 Advertisement for Philipp Wolff, *Photogram*, 1898, p. iii.

> Kinetography has hardly claimed, and certainly has not been recognised as having any artistic pretensions, and yet it has revived, in a very practical manner, the old question of how far the public exhibition of the nude is admissible . . . [The] separate pictures are such as would be accepted at an exhibition of paintings, calmly viewed by all classes of society, and reproduced in our strictly moral weeklies. But when the subjects are projected in rapid succession, giving a certain illusion of life, their eligibility for public exhibition becomes very doubtful.[51]

It was a view that was repeated frequently in these years; for example, in 1899 a Member of Parliament, Samuel Smith, feared the 'nude female figures represented [on film] . . . as the pictures are all moving, it makes them the more dangerous in their influence'.[52] The content of the individual frames was not the problem; looked at individually, they might almost be taken for pictures at an art exhibition. It was the medium that was creating the obscenity, the fact that the pictures, the bodies, were moving and seemed more likely, therefore, to exercise a dangerous influence on their excited and susceptible audiences.

Motion clearly enhanced the authenticity and the realism of the images concerned but it was more than a question of degrees of verisimilitude. In the years around 1900, the specific motion of projected films was believed to elicit a distinctively physical viewing experience, in which looking became a kind of touching. Furthermore, as the film historian Antonia Lant has shown, this concern with the spatial properties of representation was not unique to cinema but was also a feature of art theory in the period, playing a significant role in the emerging discipline of art history.[53] In *The Problem of Form* (1893), the German sculptor and theorist Adolf von Hildebrand analysed the spatial qualities of perception in the visual arts and, specifically, the experience of proximity and distance in sculptural form.[54] Distant perception was aligned with a sense of the entirety and flatness of an object but when the object was close to the observer, it appeared fragmented and required greater eye movement and a kinetic mode of viewing in order to make the object coherent.

Hildebrand's differentiation of visual and kinaesthetic perception was developed by the Viennese art historian and curator Alöis Riegl, in his formulation of optic and haptic modes of vision.[55] Where optic perception defined the distant view, haptic perception was analogous to the sense of touch; it was a mode of vision that involved the synthesis of disparate sensory experiences and that was almost tangible, a projection of touch.

The first years of film were thus part of a broader historical investigation of spatial perception in relation to the visual arts and media. Moreover, as seen in chapter 1, in the emergent field of psychology writers such as James Sully were attempting to demonstrate the interdependence of tactile and visual perception: 'movement and touch are from the outset coming in to modify the visual experience . . . The space-perception of the eye is even in its most elementary form complicated by references to active touch.'[56] The moving pictures of film provided further evidence for these scientific and aesthetic opinions. Here were observers who seemed to be the literal physical embodiment of the imbrication of sight and touch; who fled from images of charging cavalry and dug their hands into the screen that supported the representation of a disrobing woman.

It was a time of immense possibilities in the visual arts, when visual media were seen as a related continuum and the act of viewing was being radically reconceived. However, it was a brief moment. The unpredictability of film's audiences was short-lived and by the second decade of the twentieth century spectators were learning to sit in their seats and behave; the great age of cinema had arrived.

6 lumen and the celestial archive of images

> . . . in the intermediate points of space are the pictures of the events which have happened in every moment . . . actually extended in space . . . the universe encloses the pictures of the past, like an indestructible and incorruptible record containing the purest and clearest truth.
>
> Anon. [Felix Eberty], *The Stars and the Earth* (1846)[1]

astronomy and the visual imagination

G. F. Watts's *The Sower of the Systems* (1898–1903) is one of the boldest works of art produced in the late Victorian period (plate 100).[2] Taking its structure from the form of the spiral, the canvas pulses with the energetic force of the brushwork. Gold and yellow pigments are dragged across the surface and then cluster in dense, crusty pyrotechnic pools. Passages of blue momentarily cohere to take on the form of the twisted shoulders of a massive striding figure that swiftly loses its solidity and dissolves into the spiralling lines and points of paint. The picture has form and structure but they belong to the aesthetics of astrophysics, rather than of art. It is about the nature of creation but transcends the limits of Christianity and institutional religions. The painting testifies to the impact of nineteenth-century stellar astronomy on the late Victorian and Edwardian visual imagination.

Watts was one of those giants of the Victorian art world whose long career involved him in every key debate concerning the visual arts in the period.[3] From his commitment to the mural decoration of the new Palace of Westminster in the 1840s and 1850s through to his ambition to commemorate British achievement and individualism in a grand series of portrait paintings, and the donation of his work to the nation, Watts remained committed to the public importance of great art and to its mission to express noble ideas. This lifelong project, along with his absorption of European symbolism, goes some way towards explaining the astonishing look of *The Sower of the Systems* but it does not account for it entirely. To be sure, the subject has grandeur and the artist explores pictorial form in order to embody this idea; but Watts could not have arrived at this particular solution without an awareness of recent developments in astronomy and the extraordinary implications

99 Isaac Roberts, 'Nebula V 37 Cygni' (detail of plate 107).

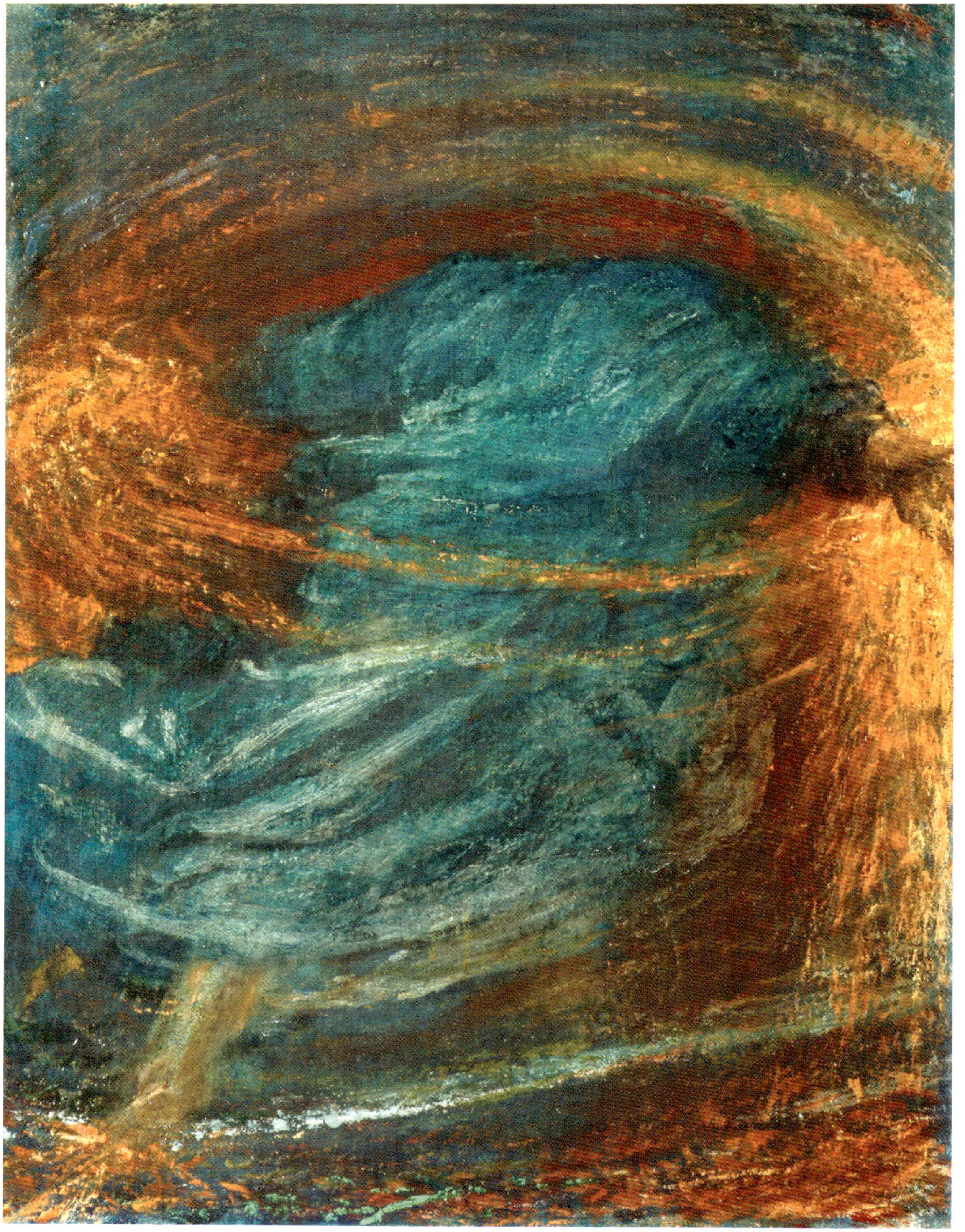

100 G. F. Watts, *The Sower of the Systems*, *c.*1902. Oil on canvas, 66 × 53.3 cm. Watts Gallery, Compton, Surrey.

they held for conceptions of mass, scale, form and light. This is what the artist is seeking to express in the endlessly spiralling tracks of paint – the pictorial equivalent of pure energy and absolute physical creation. Watts's painting belongs to a different pictorial order from the crude personifications of *The Evening Star* (1872; private collection) by his contemporary, Edward Burne-Jones; it is a style of painting that responds to its subject matter and, in so doing, transcends the norms both of painting in this period generally and the work of the artist himself.

The spiral structure of star groups had been recognised by astronomers as early as the 1840s and although the numbers of these identified forms grew dramatically throughout the century, they remained enigmatic and fascinating. It seemed to many that these beautiful stellar forms held the key to the first moments of planetary creation and that the entire solar system had originated from a spiral nebula. In 1857 an article on 'astro-photography', published in *Photographic Notes*, explained the significance of these astronomical images: 'These nebulae exhibit the appearance of a burning catherine wheel, revolving about its axis, and throwing off from its centre bent radii of luminous matter . . . [leading] to the conclusion that they may be systems in the process of formation!'[4] The delicate beauty of the gaseous spiral belied its sublime energy and the awful rotations that, it was claimed, formed new planets and hurled them into space. By the end of the nineteenth century, it was suggested that when two rotating nebulae followed paths close to each other, they created tidal forces that stretched their forms and fragmented their outer edges. These fragments finally broke off from the main body of the nebula in a spiral direction, dragging clouds of gaseous particles with them. For astronomers in this period, nebulae represented the 'earliest stages of star-life' and 'the birth of suns'.[5] Knowledge, in this instance, seemed to increase, rather than to dispel wonder. To see the nebulae through the powerful lens of a telescope was to make the invisible visible and to be given the power to look back on time and to witness the creation of the world. According to his wife, Mary Seton Watts, the veiled figure at the centre of the nebula in *The Sower of the Systems* projected 'stars, suns and planets' from its hands.[6] If this is a vision of a Supreme Being, then it is one that is refracted through an understanding of the universe derived from contemporary astronomy.

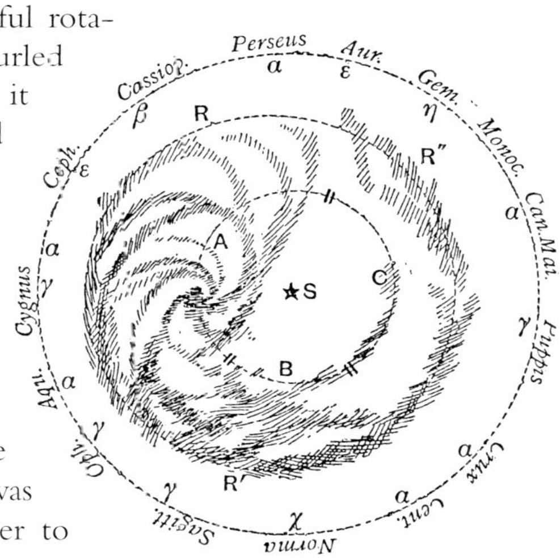

101 'The Galactic Spiral', from Agnes Clerke, *The System of the Stars*, 2nd edn, London: Adam and Charles Black, 1905, p. 344, fig. 37.

The spiral was the definitive visual form of the firmamental zone and gives the structure to Watts's daring image of the origins of creation. Reduced to the simple forms of a sketch (plate 101), by the late nineteenth century the spiral was a pictogram representing the primal energies of the universe. In this way, the complexities of the galaxy could be condensed in a single, comprehensible pictorial code and could be absorbed into the visual language of the arts in this period, both in their most ambitious elevated forms and in the rowdier types of popular entertainment.

There is one more, possibly fictional, element in the genesis of Watts's picture that draws together the extremes of high art and popular media. According to his wife's memoirs, the form of the picture was partly inspired by watching the rays of light thrown on his bedroom ceiling by a night-light.[7] In this reference to the magical, phantasmatic qualities of the projected image, Seton Watts draws on a long tradition of the power of the beam of light on the imagination that has been a recurrent theme throughout the pages of this book.

The imagination of the dozing child, the feverish adult or the creative artist is possessed by the luminous images and shadows cast by the lantern in a darkened room. In a semi-conscious state, familiar surroundings are made strange; images are at once real and fantastic, tangible and transparent. Marcel Proust returned to the motif of the beam of light repeatedly in his evocation of Swann's intense memories of childhood in the first volume of *In Search of Lost Time*. Sleep, for Proust's narrator, is a state that ruptures everyday perceptions of time and space, shattering the ego and hurtling the subject out of earth's orbit and among the stars. Memory retrieves being and identity, recovering the heaviness of the body and the familiar shape of rooms. Proust's most resonant images of this experience of lost and regained consciousness are drawn from natural and artificial illumination, at times a shaft of daylight through curtains but, more often, the coronas and rays of light cast by oil-lamps and night-lights. Recalling his childhood years in Combray, Swann remembers a magic lantern that had been set up in his bedroom: 'it substituted for the opaqueness of my walls an impalpable iridescence, supernatural phenomena of many colours, in which legends were depicted as on a shifting and transitory window'. The lantern's images dissolve the safe familiarity of the room, creating an extreme unease in the anxious boy. Its images shift seamlessly between taking on a life of their own and being caught within the material conditions of their production. Knights, damsels and castles are confined by the oval frames of individual slides, even as they take possession of the boy's fantasy world. A projected horseman advances 'across the window-curtains, swelling out the curves and diving into their folds',[8] while his cloak and face glide over and absorb the banal forms of the bedroom, such as the door-knob. These images cast a translucent veil of mystery and beauty over the familiar contours and appearances of the everyday.

The magical power of the projected image is unique to the medium. A beam of light, thrown out from the slide or film projector, bears sequences of images that reconstitute and take form when the light meets an opaque surface. Projected images are at once solid and transparent, able to simulate palpable, three-dimensional objects in space, while draping themselves diaphanously over the lines and shapes of the supporting surface. The beam of light is a powerful sign of memory and the visual imagination. It transmits ghost images, figures that live only through the power of the projective apparatus and that die as the picture vanishes. Projected in darkness, the cone of light traces the genesis of the images from projector to screen. It is spellbinding and full of promise. It bears an archive of images

– pleasures and terrors, stories from the past and from the future, the entire history of worlds. In Giuseppe Tornatore's 1989 film *Cinema Paradiso*, a film director recalls his childhood in a Sicilian village and his friendship with the projectionist at the local theatre. The magic that cinema brings to the boy and his community is captured in shots of the child gazing up at the beam of light emanating from the projection box. Motes of dust and curls of cigarette smoke swim in the white cone of light that eventually coalesces in the captivating images of film romance, westerns and comedy. The cultural resonance of the beam of light packed with images has been part of the magical power of projected images for centuries and developing technologies have served only to enhance this effect.[9]

By the end of the nineteenth century, projectors still bore strong connections to their earliest technological predecessors but the intensity of the projection and the range of images produced were constantly developing. In the context of late Victorian astronomy, however, the beam of light, the luminous bearer of enchanted images, took on an entirely new and sublime significance. Unfettered by conventional concepts of time or space, planets and stars were imagined as gigantic projecting devices, throwing beams into outer space that bore entire histories of worlds and civilisations. If modern astronomical photography could capture images of stars that had died thousands of light years before, then it might be possible, from certain points in the galaxy, to see the earth's past, borne on a continuous ray of light, projected into space. At the end of the nineteenth century these ideas were fantastic but potentially more realisable than ever before.

Astronomy in the nineteenth century was a photographic system of knowledge that expanded the late Victorian visual imagination. It drew on the old magical associations of ancient optical devices, to which it added the wonder of the most recent advances in photography, physics, chemistry, artificial illumination and lens production. It revealed the invisible, it overwhelmed the eye and the mind and could offer to those who desired it unprecedented evidence of a Supreme Intelligence. This is the vortex of ideas to which Watts's painting, *The Sower of the Systems*, belongs. The Leviathan striding across the canvas has both the translucency and the tangibility of the projected image. Hurling stars, suns and planets in its wake, it is the embodiment of a divine creator. In her annals of his life and work, Watts's wife recalled a preparatory drawing for the subject, in which Watts had made circular scribbles and had pierced the centre of the paper with his pencil, creating 'a great void'.[10] However, rather than a void, the artist had created an aperture, an opening for light. In the painting also, pigment comes as close to becoming a beam of light as at any time in the history of British art.

Latin has two terms for light, *lux* and *lumen*. *Lux* refers to the brightness of shining bodies, such as the light of the sun. *Lumen* describes a source of light, a lamp or aperture through which light penetrates and directs its beam. Astronomy and the visual imagination were ignited by both *lux* and *lumen*. A new form of perception was created in the second half of the nineteenth century that went far beyond the vision of the eye. It was a matter of the power of a beam of light to reach into the past of visual media and take it light years into the future.

living pictures on dead pages

To gaze from the earth at the evening sky is to witness an ever-changing succession of views, minutely altered patterns of light and dark that shift with the earth's rotation. It is like looking at a sequence of pictures, astronomical chronophotographs, that plot the structures and mechanisms of the heavens. Viewers today know that what we see are only the closest and most visible forms in space and that beyond lie further galaxies that exceed any comprehensible human scale. Our conventional conceptions of time are also thrown into disarray by the image of the night sky, for we know that the celestial light we observe started its journey in the past and that what is visible now may already have disappeared completely. What happens, then, when these extraordinary visions are represented in a photograph, caught within the rectangular borders of a black and white print that is held in the hand or reproduced on a page? Ann Thomas has described the peculiar contradictions of astronomical photographs:

> They reduce the immensity of the universe to the familiar scale of photographic paper . . . and yet the vast expanses of both space and time which these images represent . . . lie completely outside our everyday experience of viewing the world around us.
>
> Astronomical photographs describe macrocosms beyond human scale . . . Celestial light reaches us from a multitude of sources, such as distant galaxies, dying stars, forming stars, nearby stars, planets and passing comets in a variety of intensities and forms . . . All of this occurs against a black background, without perspectival reference points or any markers of scale.[11]

What Thomas captures here is the remarkable nature of celestial photography and its paradoxical creation of containable images of what are the most unimaginable forms and ideas. It demonstrates the particular power of visual representation and its ability to draw the reader, or viewer, away from any textual framing, deep into its own layers of pictorial meaning. It is a form of visual seduction of a willing viewer, one who is only too ready to become absorbed and transported by the visual image, to abandon reading for looking and to relinquish the actual and to embrace the imaginary.

Perhaps the best way to explore these ideas historically is to take an instance when readers of the nineteenth-century periodical and serial press were confronted with a new mode of visual representation, a new, powerful pictorial order that offered unprecedented imaginative scope and possibilities. The reproduction of astronomical photographs in the popular scientific press and related publications presented readers with just such an historical shift or hiatus. Although the interpretation of these images drew on existing conventions of the sublime to try to account for the immensity of what was shown and what could be seen in photography's engagement with astronomy, it was a new version of the sublime, an astrophysical sublime, if you like. Yet even this updated, modern sublimity could not contain all the viewing possibilities for the images that were being reproduced on the pages of books and journals in the last decades of the nineteenth century.

I want to focus on how the visual imagination responded to and worked on these images: how it drew on already existing knowledge and ideas to comprehend the new; how it sought to hold wonder and understanding, amazement and reason, in a pleasurable union; and how it was able to liberate viewers and transform their conventional, everyday experiences of time and space.

To begin at an end. What is it like to look at an image of the universe that no one has seen before, one that changes conceptions of existence, that uses the most advanced technologies but which is already thousands of years out of date? We today know what this is like, we have experienced this, because for a number of years we have been able to look at colour pictures of distant celestial forms, created from data produced by the Hubble Space Telescope and reproduced in daily newspapers and other media. The image of the 'Butterfly Nebula' was printed in London's daily newspaper, the *Evening Standard*, on 29 April 2004 (plate 102). It was placed in the middle of reports on specifically metropolitan issues such as crime levels, house prices, traffic charging and local elections. Then, on page 7, was a different order of headline, 'Riddle of a Dying Star'. Yet it is the image that arrests and detains. It is spectacular; the golden wings of dust, formed as the star dies, spread and glow, before fading into the surrounding black space. The image is surely

102 'Riddle of a Dying Star', *Evening Standard*, 29 April 2004, p. 7. Solo Syndication Ltd.

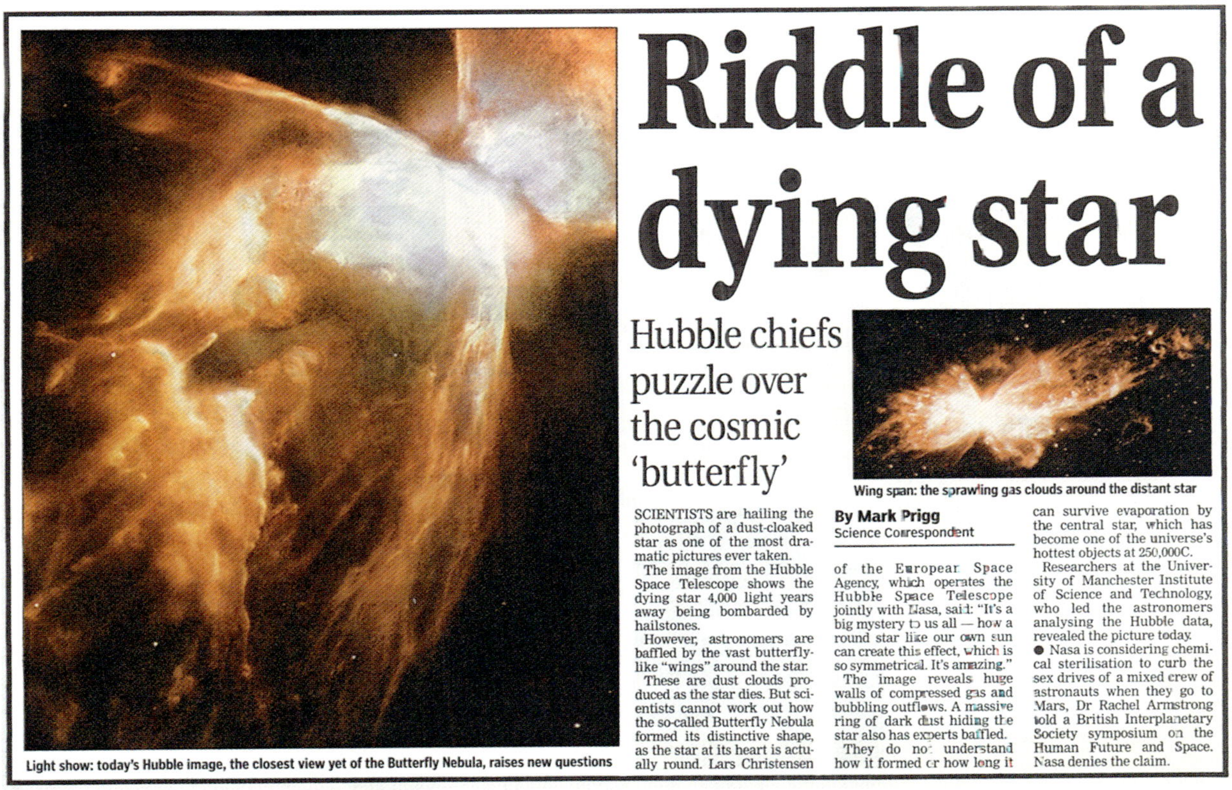

Riddle of a dying star

Hubble chiefs puzzle over the cosmic 'butterfly'

Light show: today's Hubble image, the closest view yet of the Butterfly Nebula, raises new questions

Wing span: the sprawling gas clouds around the distant star

By Mark Prigg
Science Correspondent

SCIENTISTS are hailing the photograph of a dust-cloaked star as one of the most dramatic pictures ever taken.

The image from the Hubble Space Telescope shows the dying star 4,000 light years away being bombarded by hailstones.

However, astronomers are baffled by the vast butterfly-like "wings" around the star.

These are dust clouds produced as the star dies. But scientists cannot work out how the so-called Butterfly Nebula formed its distinctive shape, as the star at its heart is actually round. Lars Christensen of the European Space Agency, which operates the Hubble Space Telescope jointly with Nasa, said: "It's a big mystery to us all — how a round star like our own sun can create this effect, which is so symmetrical. It's amazing."

The image reveals huge walls of compressed gas and bubbling outflows. A massive ring of dark dust hiding the star also has experts baffled.

They do not understand how it formed or how long it can survive evaporation by the central star, which has become one of the universe's hottest objects at 250,000C.

Researchers at the University of Manchester Institute of Science and Technology, who led the astronomers analysing the Hubble data, revealed the picture today.

● Nasa is considering chemical sterilisation to curb the sex drives of a mixed crew of astronauts when they go to Mars, Dr Rachel Armstrong told a British Interplanetary Society symposium on the Human Future and Space. Nasa denies the claim.

as beautiful as anything that the history of art can offer; it is reminscent of and easily surpasses the wonder of J. M. W. Turner's abstract studies of light and colour.

As the reader looks back into this image, he or she must try to comprehend the scale of what is seen, the distances that are involved and the temporal implications of looking at an image that was already 4000 light years out of date when it was taken and that might already no longer exist. These thoughts, provoked by the Hubble image, detain the reader of the newspaper. They create a different kind of imaginary space and turn the reader into a viewer, a speculator, perhaps. Such thoughts just begin to unfold the meaning and significance of the picture. The point is this: while the visual imagination might be triggered by the headline and accompanying article, it is not defined or contained by them and moves deep into the pictorial signification of the image. For a time, the gaze is detached from the black border and white margins of the newspaper page and becomes immersed in the image. It is as though the point of view shifts from a place outside the page to somewhere within the image.

While it would be reckless to suggest that the late Victorian 'frame of mind' and the early twenty-first-century 'frame of mind' are the same, or that one can understand the responses of viewers more than a century ago simply by reflecting on one's own responses, there are some points of contact between these two historical moments. Both are involved in a major transformation and expansion of the forms of available visual media. Developments in photographic technology in the 1880s enabled unprecedented visual representation of both the visible and the invisible world; similarly, the last two decades have seen today's visual environment transformed by digital imaging and the creation of new forms of virtual reality and visual omniscience. Moreover, these two moments are not historically divorced or distinct from each other; they should be seen as related episodes within a broader history of modern visual media. Today, as in the 1890s, there has been a huge increase in the dissemination of forms of knowledge. At both times, the production of knowledge and the cultivation of wonder are not antithetical but seem to stimulate and enhance each other.

By the 1890s the developments that had affected astronomical research in the second half of the nineteenth century, largely as a result of photography, were reaching a wider and more popular audience. Unquestionably, this new-found popularity was a consequence of the growth of the Victorian periodical and newspaper press and the proliferation of titles keen to cover the latest astronomical events and controversies. An article published in 1898 and titled 'Newspaper Astronomy', commented that:

> Hardly one of the last runs through a volume does not contain one or more articles on astronomical subjects; hardly an issue of any great weekly is barren in this regard; every daily paper is anxious for the news concerning current astronomical events, eclipses, discoveries of comets, erection of observatories etc. while many make the publication of astronomical articles a regular and prominent feature.[12]

This was published in a monthly journal called *Popular Astronomy*. Started in 1893, it carried the descriptive sub-heading 'Plainly Worded and Largely Untechnical in Language. Amply Illustrated'. It can be said with some justification, therefore, that the journal had a large stake in the growth of popular interest in astronomy that its own article describes. However, although it catered to a non-specialist, or non-professional, audience, its articles often assumed a significant degree of prior knowledge and technical familiarity and certainly did not 'talk down' to their readers. So, for example, the issue for October 1898 included one of the more thorough and detailed surveys of astronomical photography published in this period, written by its greatest advocate and practitioner, E. E. Barnard.[13] Journals such as these were clearly able to address different sub-groups, representing varying degrees of scientific knowledge, within their general readership. The language was not always untechnical but the attraction of ample illustration cut across these different interest groups and could appeal to and draw together readers with diverse forms of knowledge.

The history of astronomy in the second half of the nineteenth century is of the gradual replacement of the human eye by the photographic lens. During photography's first decade, the daguerrotype and collodion on glass processes limited its potential for astronomical research. In 1851 a daguerrotype of the moon was awarded a prize and received rapturous praise at the Great Exhibition and the eclipse in May 1851 – the very month in which the exhibition opened in Hyde Park – was seen as an unprecedented opportunity for amateur astronomers to capture the stages of the eclipse photographically. Generally, however, celestial objects and events posed different and extreme technical challenges to the new medium.[14] The huge distances involved required long exposure periods, during which the photographic plate was subjected to poor light and the constant movement of the objects being photographed. A number of these problems were overcome by the late 1870s with the introduction of the new dry gelatine plates that were far more sensitive and could be applied to telescopes at night, to photograph distant stars and nebulae. In 1887 an international collaboration was set up to create a complete map of the stars from observatories all over the world. The subsequently unfinished *Carte du Ciel* marked the zenith of photographic ambition in this period.[15]

Photography made the development of the new astronomy possible. It did away with the individual vagaries and peculiarities of looking with the eye and recording with the hand and replaced them with the unwavering and penetrating gaze of the photographic exposure. Photography literally brought to light celestial objects that had previously been invisible to the naked eye.

In the same period, spectroscopy finally took astronomical research into the new age of astrophysics (plates 103 and 104).[16] By putting a glass prism in front of the camera lens, each star image could be spread out and visually translated into a spectrum of ultra-violet and infra-red bands that offered an abstract visualisation of the chemical composition of any given celestial body. Properly decoded, these linear and chromatic sequences revealed the composition, temperature and velocity of the

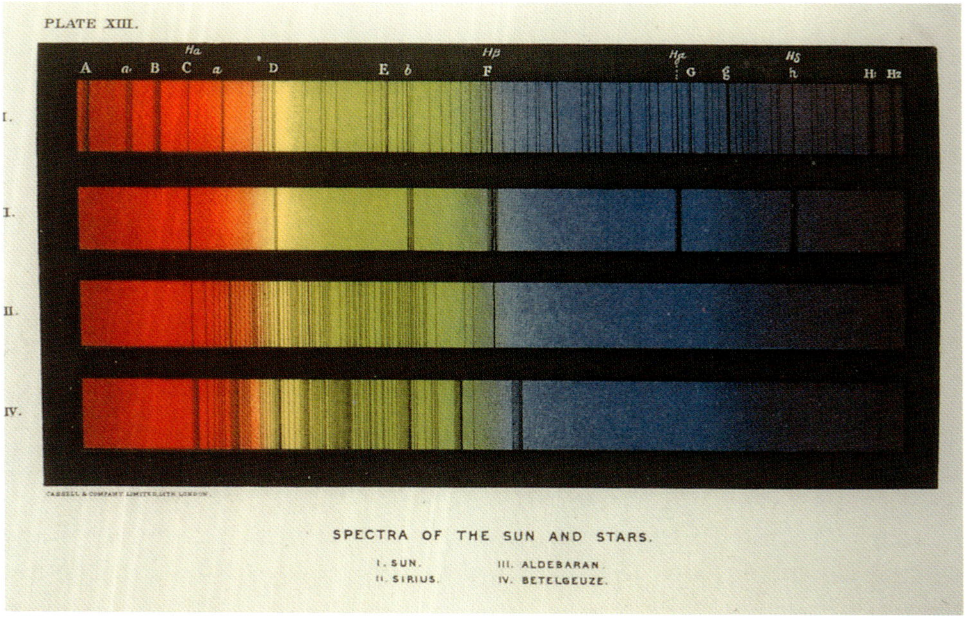

103 'Spectra of the Sun and Stars', from Robert S. Ball, *The Story of the Heavens*, rev. edn. London, Paris and Melbourne: Cassell and Co., 1897, plate XIII.

104 'Stellar Spectra', *Knowledge*, vol. 20, 1 March 1897, opp. p. 78.

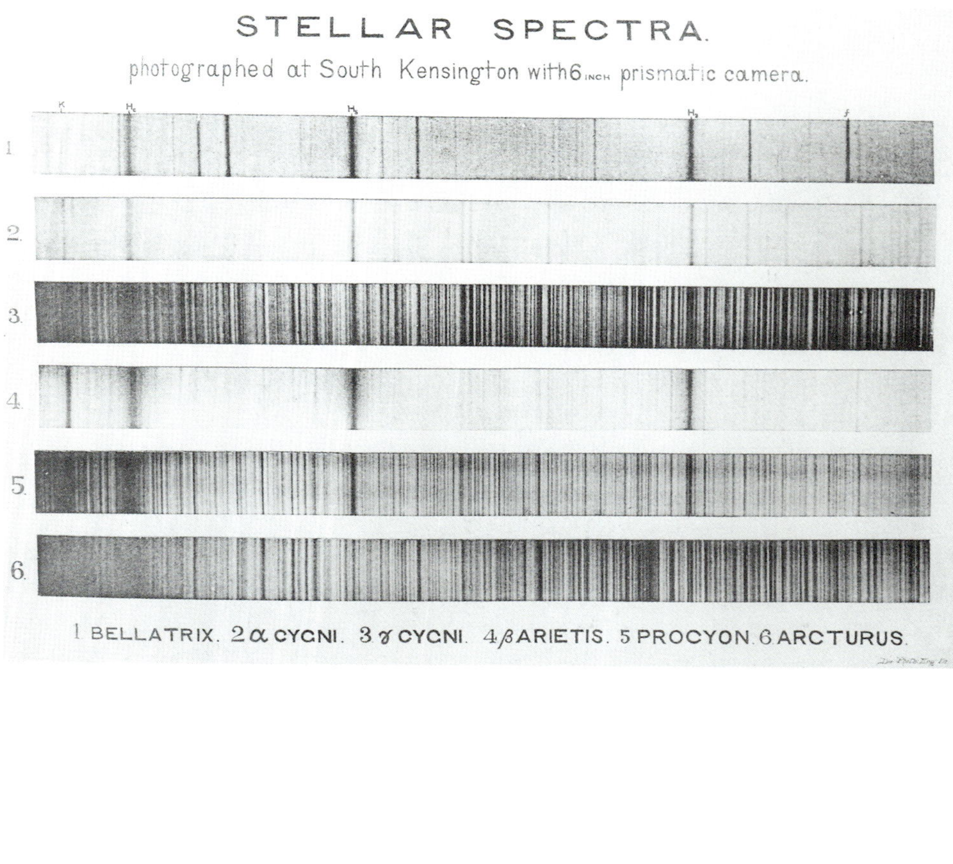

stars; yet they remained uniquely poised between the domains of knowledge and the imagination and were treated both as objects of immense beauty and the source of unprecedented scientific information. In spite of their dependence on the latest astronomical technology, spectra were also treated as if they were enigmatic messages from distant civilisations, traces of other worlds that required archaeological deciphering, rather than scientific analysis. Describing recent stellar spectra, made at the Observatory at Harvard, as 'starry hieroglyphs', an article published in *Knowledge* in 1898 went on to speculate:

> they hint at so much of revelation as to the secrets of world life: they have like an inscription in unfamiliar characters and in an unknown tongue, so plainly a message to tell if we could but interpret them. At such interpretation we have indeed made our first attempts: the riddle is not all unread; we have spelled out a word . . . here and there, and, like Cleopatra's soothsayer, can say:
>
> 'In Nature's infinite book of secrecy
> A little I can read.'[17]

If this interpretation of spectroscopy seemed too pagan, or even blasphemous, then the sublime groups of lines and colours were easily restored to a Christian narrative of the wonders of God's universe. The prodigious astronomer and committed Christian Richard A. Proctor saw the spectra as evidence of a divine design in which the earth was simply one small element; his study of the subject, *The Spectroscope and its Work* (1877), was published and distributed by the Society for Promoting Christian Knowledge.[18]

The new astronomy was a visual science; it went beyond the observation of the human eye and used photography to create new images of objects that had never before been seen. These images might have remained in the possession of a small, highly specialist audience were it not for an historical convergence of the advances in photography and developments in the reproduction of black and white and, later, colour photography in books and periodicals. From the 1880s, improvements in the direct reproduction from photographs enabled a much higher quality of picture resolution. Photographic illustrations in this period tended to occupy separate pages from text and engraved images, so that the half-tones could be concentrated on dedicated printing plates. The stage was set for the high-quality reproduction of astronomical photographs that were related to the main body of the publication but were also set apart and thus prone to a different order of consumption.

A photograph of the moon, reproduced in the general science journal *Knowledge* in 1897, nearly half a century after the prize-winning daguerrotype at the Great Exhibition, was a triumph of advances in both the manufacture of optical instruments and in printing methods (plate 105). Together, they produced a representation of the moon of extreme sensitivity and clarity. In the accompanying article full details were given of the lenses, plates and exposure times but, set apart on its own page, the photograph takes over and creates its own visual environment. The high quality of the image and the fine, smooth paper on which it is printed invite

SOUTH.

WEST.

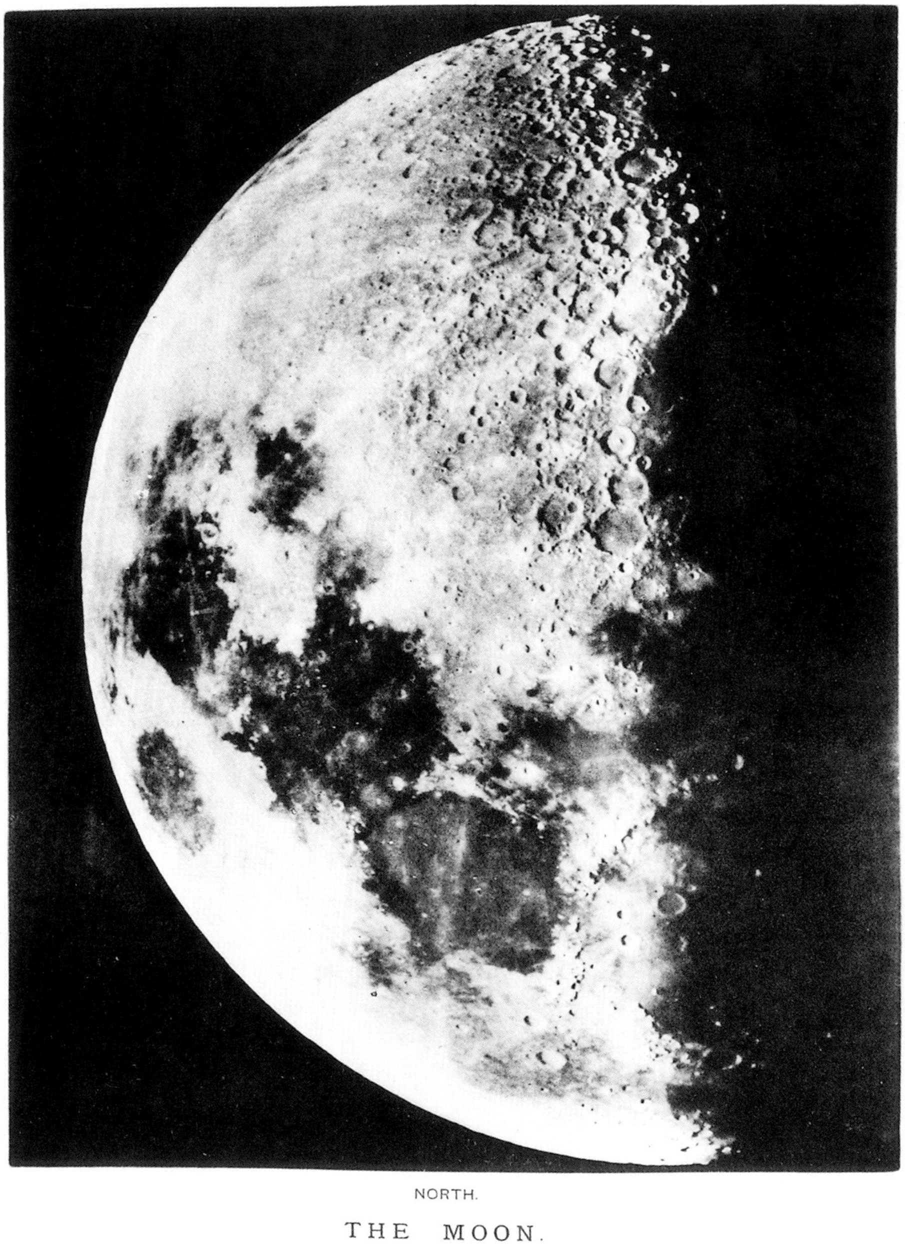

EAST.

NORTH.

THE MOON.

AGE, 9d. 10h. 7m. 1897, MARCH 12th, 10h. 3m. Greenwich Mean Time.

Enlarged, by the kind permission of the Astronomer Royal, from a Photograph taken by Mr. T. LEWIS, F.R.A.S., with the 28-inch Refractor of the Royal Observatory, Greenwich.

105 T. Lewis, 'The Moon', *Knowledge*, vol. 20, 1 November 1897, opp. p. 261.

the reader to inspect the lights and shades of the lunar surface, to touch its cool expanse, to wonder at the detail and speculate about what lies hidden by the lunar night.

By the late 1890s photographic images of the moon were reasonably familiar to an interested public but the main focus of astronomical photography from the 1880s was galaxies, the distant and faint stars and gaseous nebulae that had previously been barely discernible but were then transforming scientific conceptions of the extent of the universe (plates 106 and 107). These images revealed billions of brilliant dots of light and hazy, swirling clouds of gas, surrounded by deep darkness. Stellar photography was able to capture accurate, intelligible images of the galaxy far beyond the possibilities of any hand-drawn rendering of a telescopic view. Furthermore, over and above this aspect, it also created images of unprecedented dramatic beauty that could be circulated around large audiences.

Annexed on its own sheet, the image had the power to exceed and break free of its framing contexts. The articles on the facing page are eliminated from the frame of vision. White margins, headers and captions lose their significance as the viewer's gaze is drawn into the astounding forms and celestial masses in the photograph. This is not image *and* text or image *in* text; it is the power of the image itself, overwhelming any surrounding textuality. Moreover, astronomical photography is unlike other forms of photographic imagery. It defies what is described as the 'indexicality' of the photograph; it is not simply a trace of a thing in the visible world but makes visible that which cannot be seen by the naked eye. In this way, astronomical photography belongs to the world of X-rays and spirit photography, the domain of the sublime imagination.

For a majority of astronomers, then, photography was a powerful and versatile tool that had transformed their discipline; it was, as Agnes Clerke described it, the 'Ariel to Astronomy's Prospero'.[19] Clerke was one of a number of women who made a major contribution to astronomy at the end of the nineteenth century. She was an innovative scientist but also a prolific writer and populariser. For Clerke, the photographic plate was a perfect eye and an ideal observer. 'The promptly fatigued living retina', she wrote, 'is left far behind by the imperturbable gaze of a sensitised plate . . . By *looking long enough* [the photographic plate] can see anything there is to be seen.'[20] Here was a new and enhanced form of vision, one that had opened up a new field of research beyond the habitual range of visual accessibility and that made images of objects which otherwise could not be seen. The conclusion was astounding: the depiction of the invisible world had been realised.

The most fascinating aspect of this material, however, was the shift from an acknowledgement of photography's scientific possiblities to an imaginative encounter with the resulting images. Camille Flammarion, the French astronomer, polymath and psychic researcher, epitomises more than any other figure in this period the fusion of scientific investigation and fantasy. For Flammarion, photography was the key to making this leap of imagination from astronomical obser-

NEBULA HERSCHEL V 14 CYGNI.

By ISAAC ROBERTS, D.Sc., F.R.S.

S.

P.

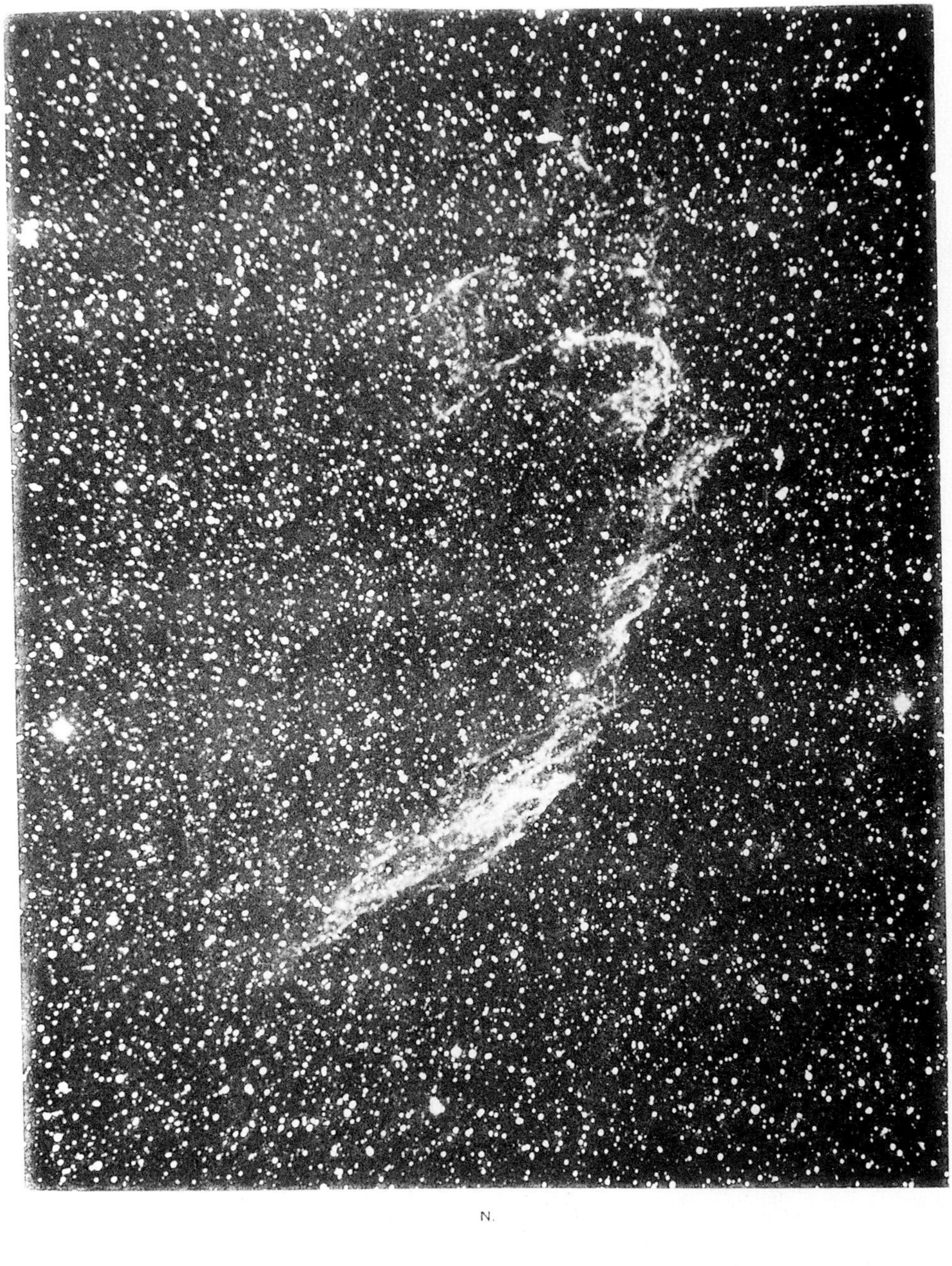

F.

N.

106 Isaac Roberts, 'Nebula Herschel V 14 Cygni', *Knowledge*, vol. 20, 1 September 1897, opp. p. 218.

NEBULA H V 37 CYGNI.

By ISAAC ROBERTS, D.Sc., F.R.S.

S

P 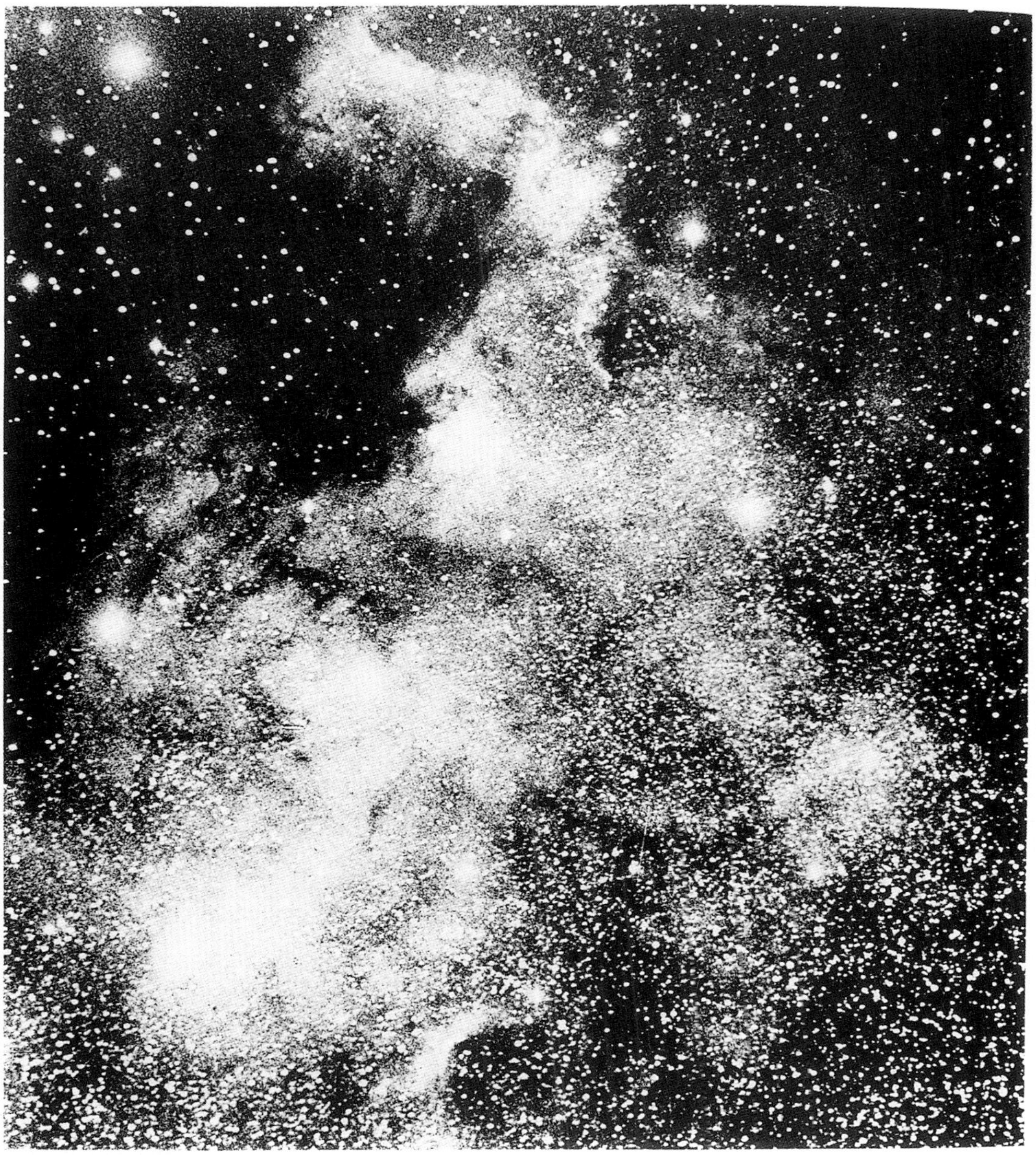 F

N

107 Isaac Roberts, 'Nebula V 37 Cygni', *Knowledge*, vol. 21, 1 November 1898, opp. p. 253.

vation to empathetic identification. In his best-selling book, *Popular Astronomy*, he went beyond Clerke's formulation of 'making visible' and speculated that the astronomical photograph might have still more secrets to yield. Reflecting on the experience of looking at lunar photographs, he wrote:

> these photographs contain, in a latent state, all that exists on the surface of the moon. *If there are inhabitants, they are there* . . . and it is difficult to resist a certain emotion when we hold one of these photographs in our hands, and when we are told . . . that a sufficiently high magnifying power might permit us to perceive them.[21]

Although Flammarion was describing the particular haptic experience of handling a photograph, one should perhaps recall the equally tactile experience of reading an illustrated periodical, of turning pages or lifting the volume to scrutinise visual details at closer range, eliminating all else from the fascinated, speculative gaze. For Flammarion and for other viewers of astronomical photographs in this period, immersion in the image became a form of imaginative transportation. The camera, he wrote, draws observers to Infinitude and '*leaves us there*'.[22]

In Flammarion's case, to look at a photographic image of the moon was to detach oneself from the everyday things of the earth and to embark on the first stage of an endless celestial voyage. Space and the imagination were perfectly conjoined in the astronomical photograph: 'Space has no bounds. Whatever be the frontier which we may assign to it in thought, our imagination immediately flies across this frontier, and, looking beyond, still finds space. And although we cannot comprehend the infinite, each of us feels that it is easier to conceive space as unlimited than to imagine it limited.'[23] The camera and the telescope created images of a new order of sublimity that liberated the visual imagination and enabled it to roam through the immensity of the universe.

More prosaic advocates of astronomical photography conceded that some of the power and beauty of the images was a result of instrumental and chemical distortion. Sir Robert Ball, another of the great astronomical popularisers of the period, acknowledged that the plates (plate 108) 'owe a part of their beauty to the fact that the negatives have been reduced in their bright central portions which are inevitably over-exposed during the long time that is required to photograph the faint outlying portions of the nebula'.[24] Yet this does not seem to have diminished the pleasure that these images offered to both specialist and general audiences. Faced with two visual renderings of the nebulae in the Pleiades – the graphic chart with textual key (plate 109) or a photograph by a skilled astronomer like Isaac Roberts (plate 110) – it is not difficult to imagine the immediacy and impact of the photograph over the diagram. Photography offered the promise of immersive proximity, the collapse of the immense distances between terrestrial observer and celestial body.

The cover of Ball's *The Story of the Heavens*, issued in monthly parts in 1897, shows exactly how optical instruments drew together planets and stars and men (plate 111). The telescopic image, refracted through prisms, or caught on the photo-

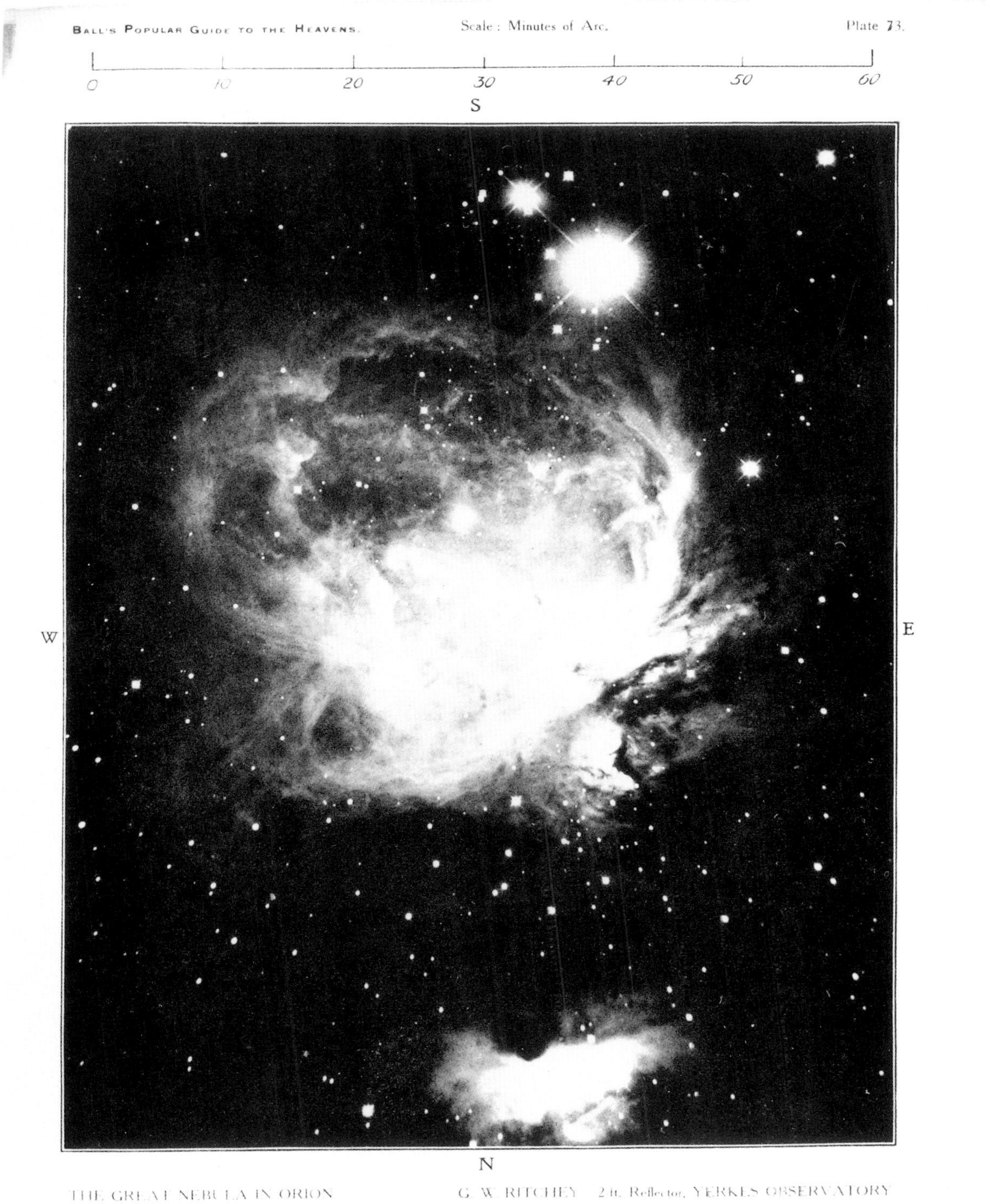

108 G. W. Ritchey, 'The Great Nebula in Orion', from Robert S. Ball, *A Popular Guide to the Heavens*, London: George Philip and Son, 1905, plate 73.

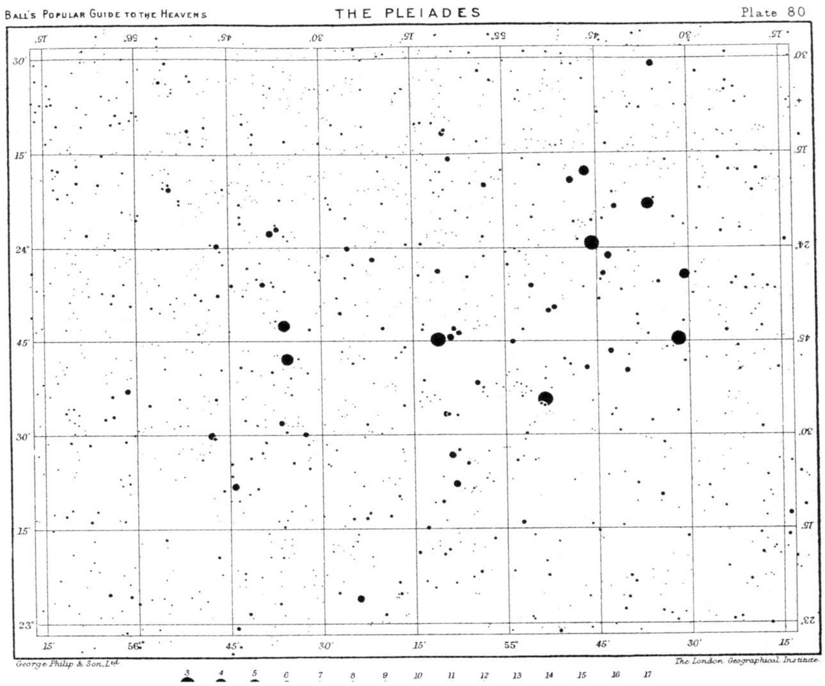

109 'The Pleiades', from Robert Ball, *A Popular Guide to the Heavens*, plate 80.

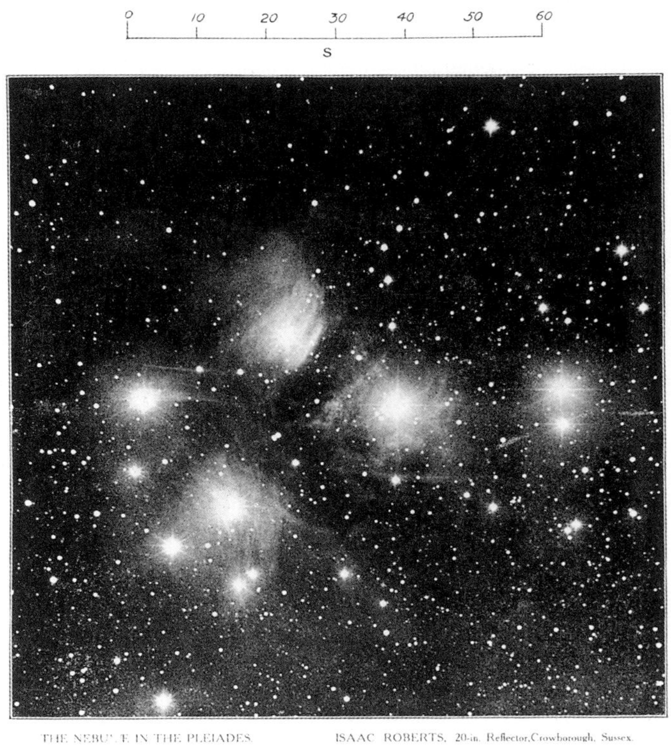

110 Isaac Roberts, 'The Nebulae in the Pleiades', from Robert Ball, *A Popular Guide to the Heavens*, plate 79.

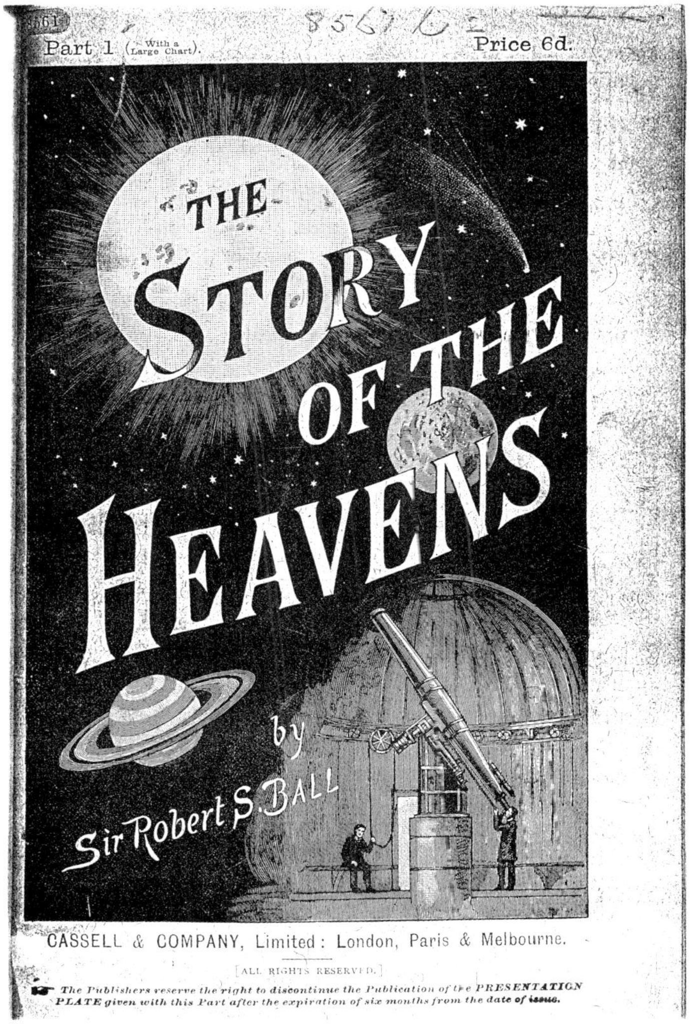

111 Robert S. Ball, *The Story of the Heavens*, rev. edn. London, Paris and Melbourne: Cassell and Co., 1897, Part 1, cover.

graphic plate, brought the universe within scientific and imaginative reach. Planets and stars seemed close enough to touch. Like the microscopic image, the telescopic image radically transformed scale and distance. Distant worlds, which were beyond the visible, were brought within optical and conceptual grasp. As one French cartoonist put it, on the occasion of the construction of the giant telescope for the 1900 Paris World's Fair, the image of the moon would seem so close that it could be served up on a plate (plate 112).

The conceptual collapse of immense distances brought about by astronomical photography marked both the expansion and the limit of human understanding. As Robert Ball put it:

> It is believed that some of these nebulae are sunk in space to such an appalling distance that the light takes centuries before it reaches the earth. We see these

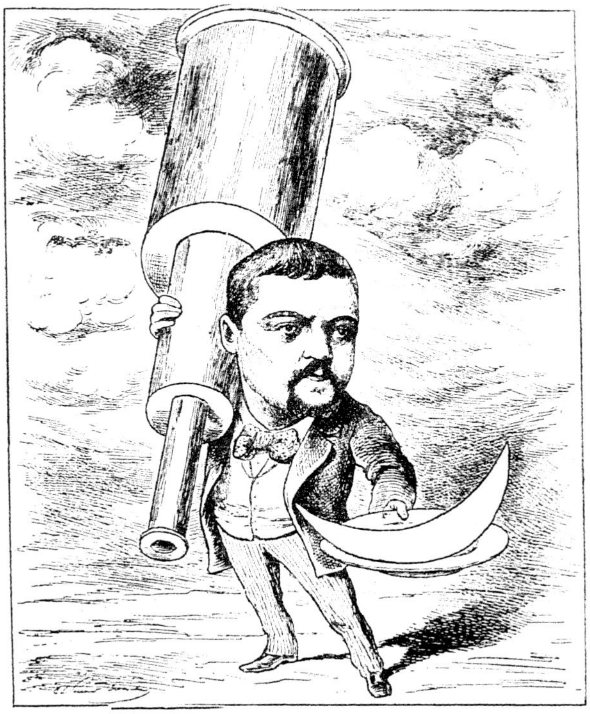

112 'La lune à un mètre', *L'Exposition de Paris (1900) publiée avec la collaboration d'écrivains spéciaux et des meilleurs artistes*, vol. 2, Paris: Libraire Illustré, 1900, p. 3.

nebulae, not as they are now, but as they were centuries ago. At this climax we bid farewell to the nebulae. We have reached a point where man's intellect begins to fail to yield him any more light, and where his imagination has succumbed in the endeavour to realise even the knowledge he has gained.[25]

In the stellar photography of the 1890s, conventional codes of pictorial legibility were shattered; perspective, light and colour could not be relied upon to decipher and comprehend what was represented. The photographic image opened up a new visual and imaginative field. Groups, systems and streams of stars were captured against an undifferentiated ground of space and immense distances were eradicated on the flat surface of the picture. To the observer, the most distant galaxies seemed provocatively close and it was possible to imagine oneself in this space, immersed in its strange illegible immensity and close to the sublime.

Thomas Hardy captured the awesome nature of telescopic images of the stellar universe in the descriptions in his novel *Two on a Tower*, of nights spent in an astronomical observatory by two doomed lovers, Lady Constantine and Swithin St Cleeve. Hardy drew on his reading of popular astronomical authors such as Richard Proctor to evoke the wonder and erotic intensity experienced by the couple as they scan the heavens. 'Then, by means of the instrument at hand, they travelled together from the earth to Uranus and the mysterious outskirts of the solar system . . . till the ghastly chasm which they had bridged by line of sight was realized by Lady Constantine.'[26]

a trip to the moon

The peculiar experience of viewing astronomical images was expressed in terms of a highly mobile point of view. In many astronomical publications of this period what starts from a terrestrial viewpoint moves quickly to a place somewhere else in the solar system or galaxy. It is as though the astronomical imagination cannot be contained by an earthbound perspective but must inevitably take flight in order to adopt the viewpoint of other planets and galaxies – to see as they see. For Flammarion, every act of astronomical observation was an 'interplanetary journey' and its termination 'a return to Earth'. Flammarion could not remain earthbound when he looked at the heavens and his books are peppered with illustrations of imaginary views of the earth as seen from other planets.[27]

In James Nasmyth and James Carpenter's *The Moon: Considered as a Planet, a World and a Satellite* (first published in 1874), there is a chromolithograph of a solar eclipse 'as it would Appear as seen from the moon' (plate 113). The book includes a range

113 'Aspect of an Eclipse of the Sun by the Earth as it would Appear as seen from the Moon', from James Nasmyth and James Carpenter, *The Moon: Considered as a Planet, a World and a Satellite*, 4th edn, London: John Murray, 1903, frontispiece.

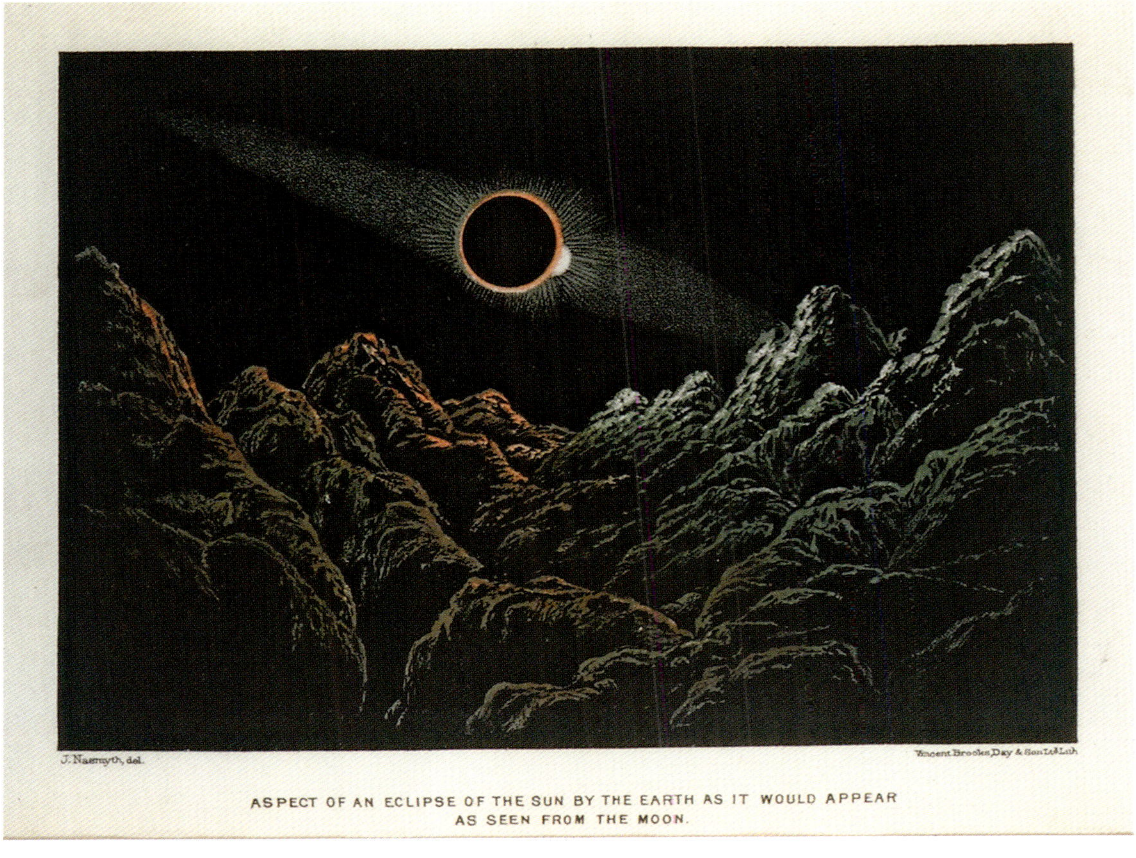

of photomechanical reproduction techniques, among them wood engravings, lithographs, photogravures and Woodburytypes, and is based on the authors' observation and visual documentation of the moon. However, they cannot be tied to earthbound observation. They are drawn to and transport the reader viewer to the lunar surface from where they observe the solar eclipse.

In a marvellous hybrid form of illustration, they made plaster of Paris models of the moon's surface from drawings by Nasmyth, which were carefully lit to simulate lunar conditions and then photographed for reproduction (plate 114). These images of the plaster lunar sets construct a viewpoint on the moon's surface. The viewers – one would perhaps need to refer to them at this point as spectators – are set down among the craters and volcanic mountains, looking across the landscape, rather than down on it.

In their chapter 'The Moon as a World', there is a section called 'A Flight of Fancy', in which Nasmyth and Carpenter clearly articulate the compulsion of this lunar point of view. It marks a significant shift in sensibility:

114 'An ideal sketch of "Pico", an isolated lunar mountain 8000 feet high, as it would probably appear if seen by a spectator located on the Moon', from James Nasmyth and James Carpenter, *The Moon*, plate XXI.

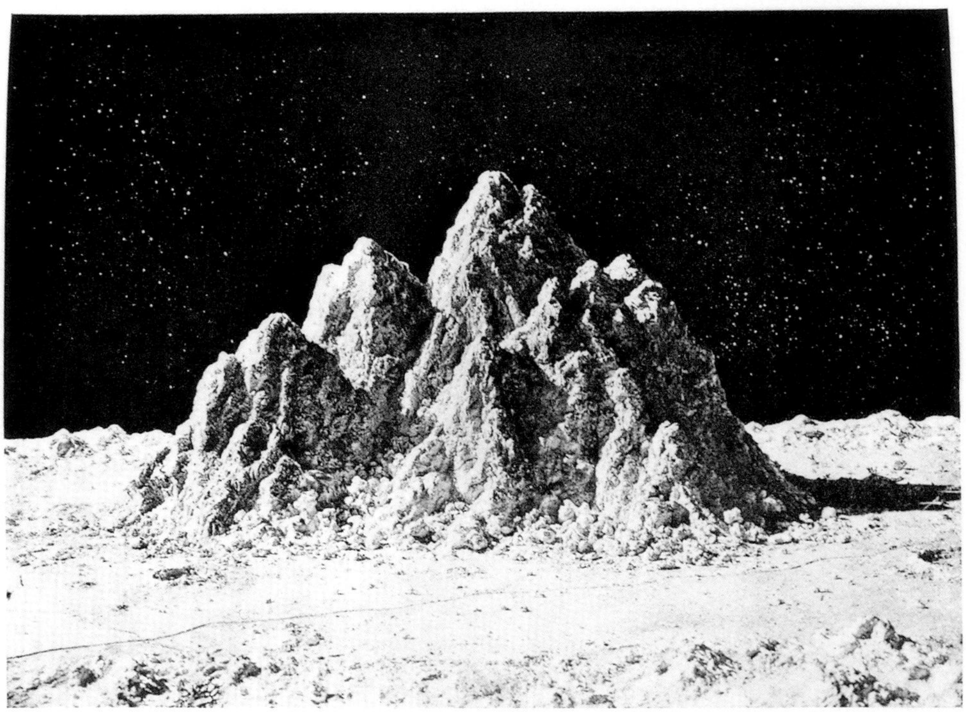

PLATE XXI.—An ideal sketch of "Pico," an isolated lunar mountain 8000 feet high, as it would probably appear if seen by a spectator located on the Moon.

> It may be urged that, in depicting the moon from such a standpoint . . . we are describing scenes that never have been such in the literal sense of the word, since no eye has ever beheld them . . . Although it is impossible for a habitant of this earth fully to realise existence upon the moon, it is yet possible, indeed almost inevitable, for a thoughtful telescopist – watching the moon night after night . . . to identify himself so far with the object of his scrutiny, as sometimes to become in thought a lunar being. Seated in silence and in solitude at a powerful telescope, abstracted from terrestrial influences, and gazing upon the revealed details of some strikingly characteristic region of the moon, it requires but a small effort of the imagination to suppose oneself actually upon the lunar globe . . . and under these circumstances there is an irresistible tendency in the mind to pass beyond the actually *visible*, and to fill in with what it knows must exist . . . Where the material eye is baffled, the clairvoyance of reason and analogy comes to its aid.[28]

This is a critical piece of writing, describing as it does the actual process of imaginative transposition from telescopic observer to lunar being. Surely it is possible to substitute the still observatory for a quiet, darkened room and an earnest reader poring over the pages and transfixed by the images of an astronomical journal or book. In the words of Nasmyth and Carpenter, it is almost inevitable for such an observer to so identify with the object of scrutiny that the point of view is transfigured.

Moreover, all the senses are engaged in this experience, not simply sight. As the chapter continues, Nasmyth and Carpenter evoke the bodily impressions of lunar conditions such as extreme cold and heat and the cracking and grating produced by the expansion and contraction of the moon's crust, which can be felt rather than heard because 'dead silence reigns on the moon'.[29] For the authors, the reader or observer has been turned into a space traveller and moon walker whose imagination has been freed from the limits of the possible and inhabits the domain of cultural fantasy.

The lunar observer looks back at the earth and, as Richard Proctor states in the 1886 edition of his study *The Moon*, from this position: 'they have an object of contemplation utterly unlike any known to our astronomers'[30] (plates 115 and 116). Proctor places his readers on the surface of the moon; they become 'lunarians', moving around the lunar landscape and gazing at the one celestial body that is not visible from the earth, the earth itself. Plates illustrate the phases of the earth as seen from the lunar station and, for the devoutly Christian Proctor, it is a view whose majesty recalls the sight shown to Satan by Uriel from the sun.

If the putative late Victorian follower of astronomy also had a taste for popular commercial entertainment, then the fantasy of a space journey, or a trip to the moon, might have been encountered elsewhere. In 1887 a popular, multi-media lecture called 'A Trip to the Moon' was touring Europe and America.[31] Starting with a reconstruction of a solar eclipse, viewed from a lake just outside Berlin (plate 117), the scenario shifted to a view of the moon from a distance of about five

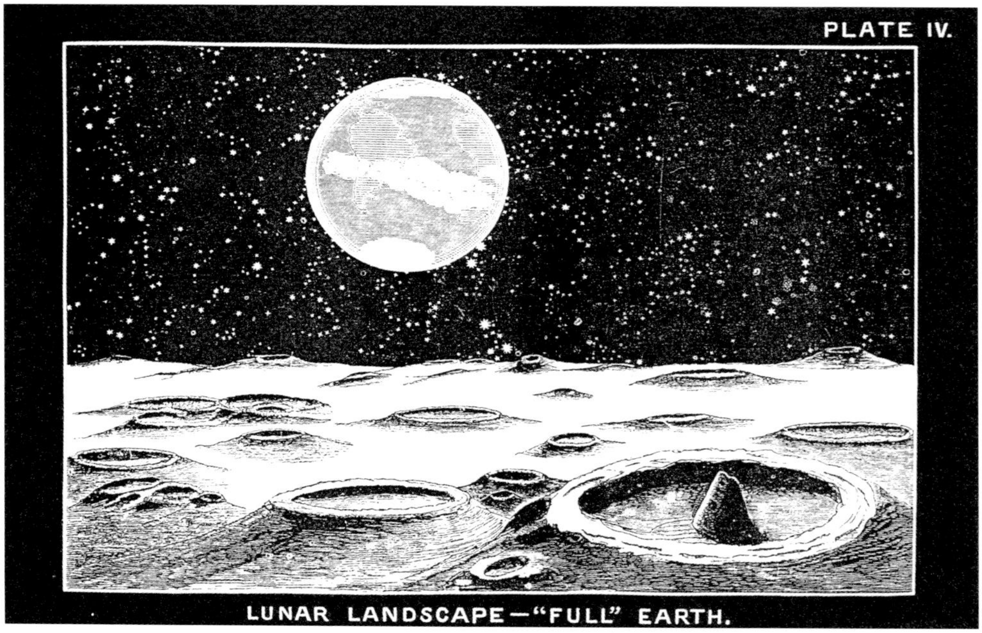

115 'Lunar Landscape – "Full" Earth', from Richard A. Proctor, *The Moon: Her Motions, Aspect, Scenery and Physical Condition*, 3rd edn, London: Longmans, Green and Co., 1886, plate IV.

116 'Lunar Landscape – "New" Earth', from Richard Proctor, *The Moon*, plate V.

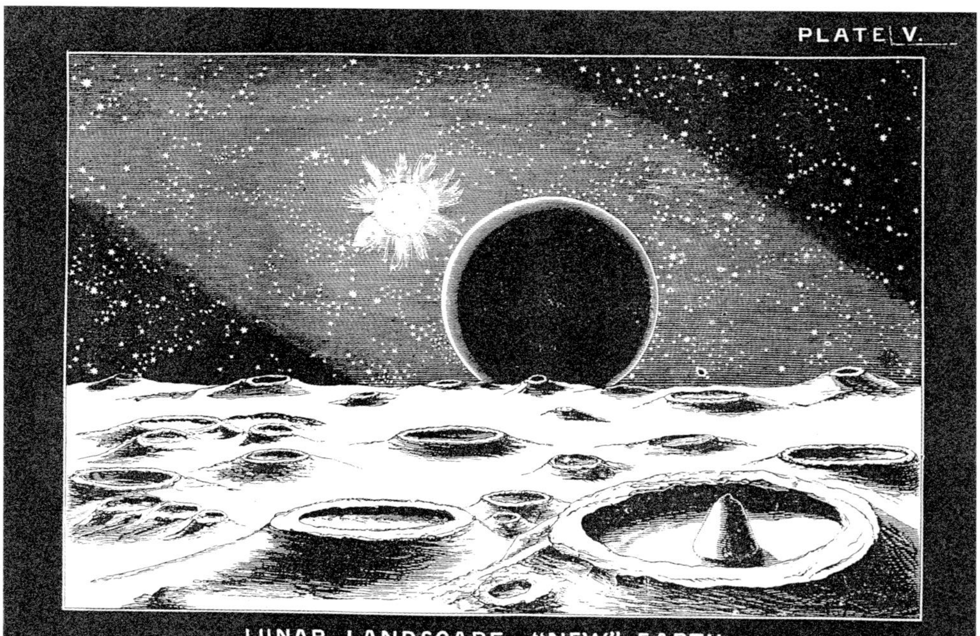

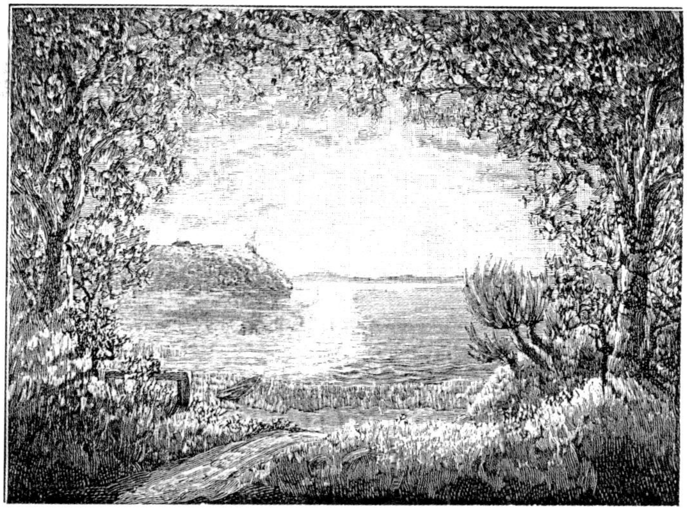

117 'Sunrise on the Havel, near Berlin, August 19, 1887', from Albert A. Hopkins, *Magic: Stage Illusions and Scientific Diversions Including Trick Photography*, London: Sampson Low, Marston and Co., 1897, p. 348.

thousand miles and then from a distance of just two and a half miles above the lunar surface. Through a combination of plaster models, painted backcloths and the most advanced stage machinery and lighting, the spectacle took the viewer from the picturesque shores of the lake to the sublime terrain of the moon (plate 118). Returning to earth, the effects of sunset, moonrise and a lunar eclipse were depicted in sequence and, if the viewer's imagination was still over-excited by the trip to the moon, it was finally calmed by a series of lantern views of local beauty spots.

Astronomy provided the subject matter for many forms of late Victorian performance and optical entertainment. Its appeal was two-fold: it was highly didactic and also wildly spectacular. Many of the astronomical photographs were turned into lantern slides for illustrated lectures and magnified to four or five feet in diameter. In this form, they found a perfect synergy in the brilliance of the lamp projection in a darkened room and the luminosity of the celestial subject matter. Efforts

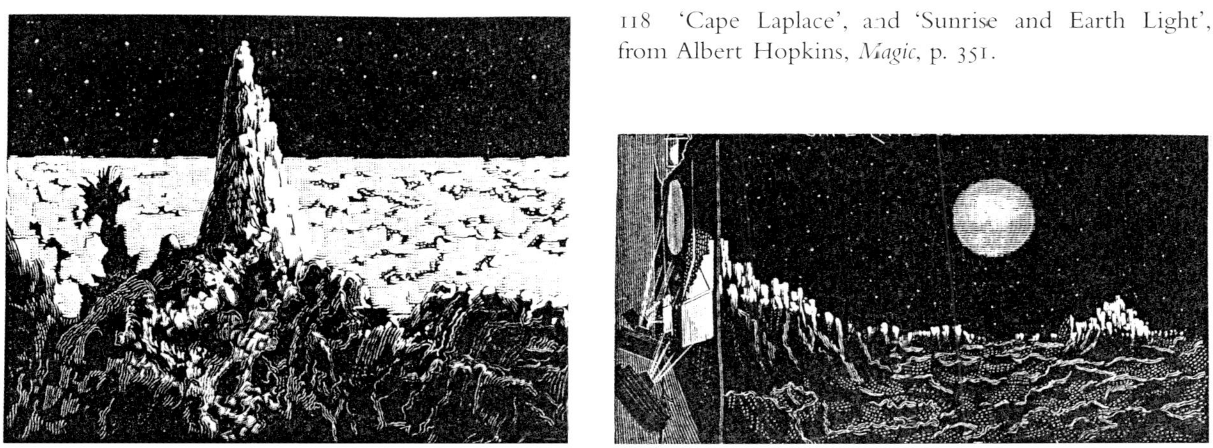

118 'Cape Laplace', and 'Sunrise and Earth Light', from Albert Hopkins, *Magic*, p. 351.

to improve the quality of the screen by whitewashing the sheet or using new silver-surfaced screens enhanced the quality of the projected light and intensified the attraction of looking at astronomical images in the form of lantern slides.[32]

The 1900 Paris World's Fair offered visitors a number of astronomical attractions. The Giant Telescope, located in the Palace of Optics, produced views of the moon magnified ten thousand times, so that the observer was brought within fifty to sixty miles of the surface. As the construction of the huge telescope, with its immaculate lens, progressed the French press marvelled at its precision and its promise to bring *la lune à un mètre* (see plate 112). Photographic images of the stars were also projected from the telescope onto giant screens, to audiences comfortably seated in a large theatre.[33] The Palace of Optics and its diverse attractions were a paean to recent technological developments in glass production. From the astronomical uses of the giant telescopic lens to the hilarious distortions of a hall of mirrors, the Palace was a revelation of the wonders of enhanced sight. Still photographs and films, in black and white and in colour, were projected to rapt audiences, while lecturers explained their scientific significance. Light and shadow, colour and reflection provided the raw materials for the magic performed by the instruments in the Palace of Optics. The bodies of visitors were manipulated in each of the exhibition halls, deformed on the surfaces of distorting mirrors and wrenched from the earth on a space journey that, if it did not actually bring the moon within one metre, certainly took the visitors visually within a few miles of its surface.

Even more spectacular was the Celestial Globe, a gigantic sphere, 145 feet in diameter, supported on four giant arches, whose interior was decorated with astronomical and mythological figures (plates 119 and 120). Illuminated at night, the interior of the glowing globe could be seen throughout the Exposition grounds.[34] Inside the globe, elevators and staircases took visitors to a second sphere representing the planetary system. Visitors took up positions at the centre, on a miniature earth, from where they watched models of the sun, moon, stars and comets, while the earth slowly revolved. To enter the Celestial Globe was to embark on a voyage to outer space, to be placed somewhere between the surface of the earth and the surrounding planets. It was literally a moving experience, which was enhanced by accompanying music, some of which had been specially composed for the attraction. Visitors fatigued by their virtual journey were offered refreshments in a large café, also located within the sphere.

The ubiquitous and apparently inexhaustible Camille Flammarion was instrumental in the planning and realisation of the Celestial Globe. He had been a vocal contributor to the public debate about the astronomical attractions in the Paris World's Fair from their inception in the late 1890s. His vision was grand and wildly ambitious and he was openly dismissive of the more modest plans proposed for the Giant Telescope and Celestial Globe. Specifically, Flammarion proposed an extravagant cinematographic presentation that drew on previous performances and descriptions of 'A Trip to the Moon' but which went much further in its visionary scope.[35] The scenario opens with a sunset on earth; the moon is seen to rise and there is an eclipse. Then the viewer is taken to the moon, which gets lighter

119 *(facing page)* View of the 1900 World's Fair, Paris.

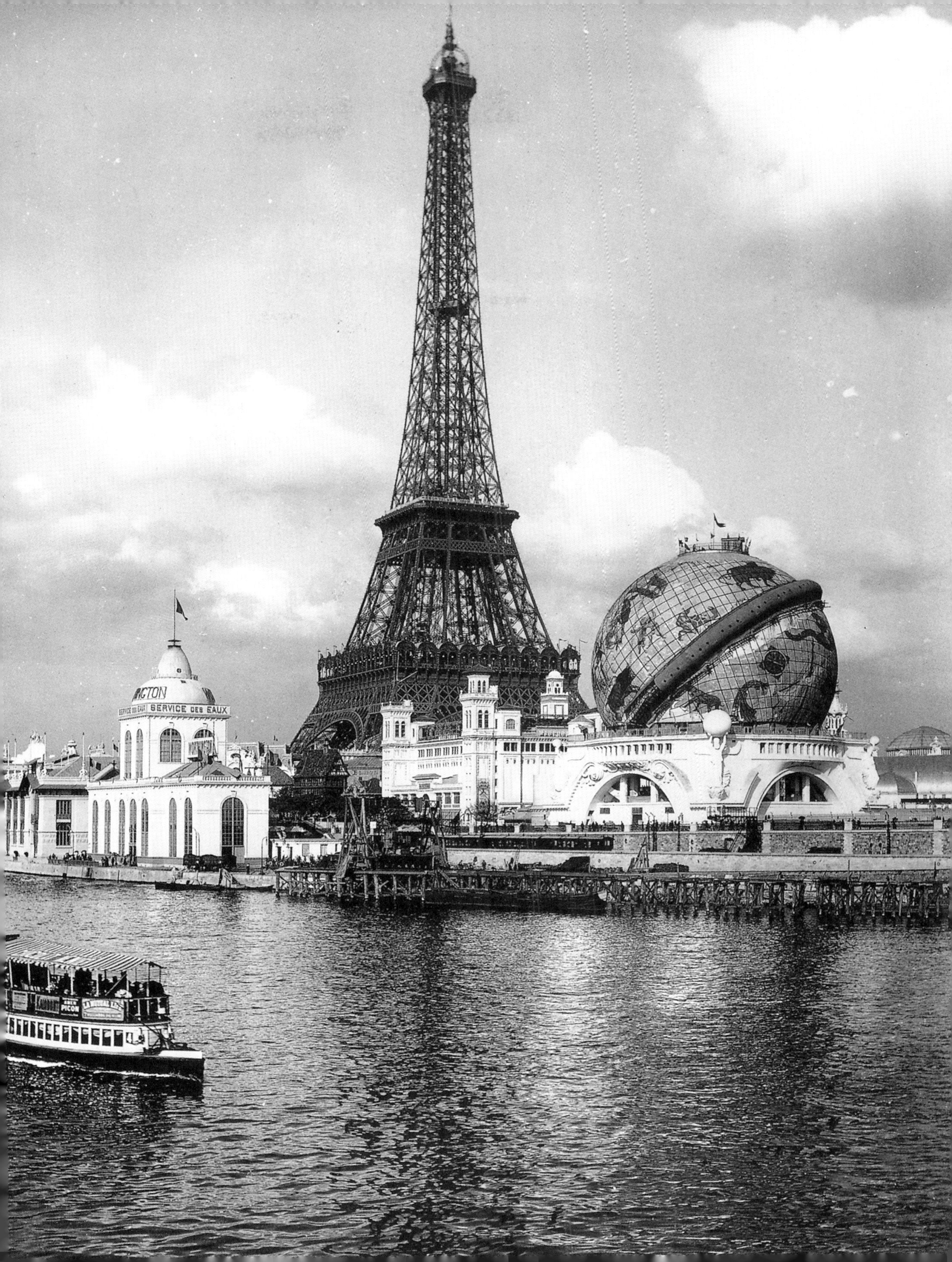
SERVICE DES EAUX

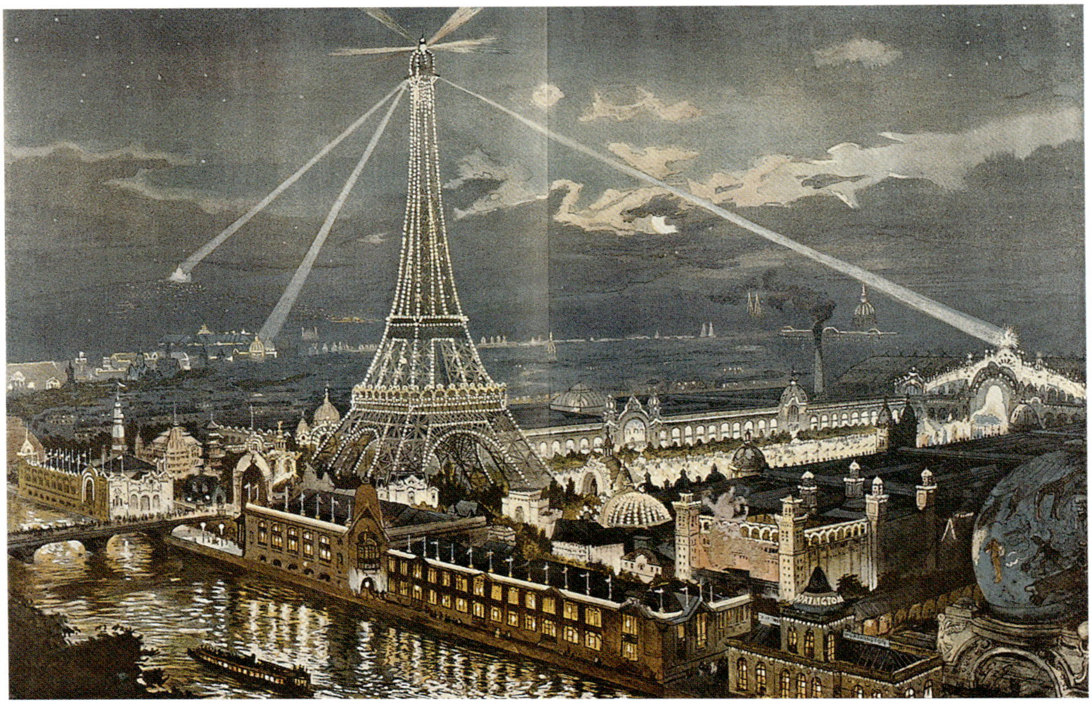

120 'Les fêtes de nuits à l'exposition – les illuminations des Palais du Champ de Mars', *L'Exposition de Paris (1900)*, vol. 1, supplement, no. 29.

and bigger on approaching, an effect achieved by integrating telescopic views with the repertoire of film images. Next the visitor sees the earth from the moon and returns to earth to observe the galaxy. A journey to the planets and stars follows, along with images of the transit of Venus, shooting stars and further eclipses of the sun and moon. Had this exhilarating film of a journey through the cosmos been made, it would have been the most exceptional visualisation of the astronomical viewer as space traveller and explorer for many years; sadly and perhaps inevitably, Flammarion's immense imagination encountered financial and bureaucratic obstacles and the project was abandoned.

Multi-media lectures and Exposition exhibits offered a far more embodied experience of celestial fantasy than the flat images printed on the pages of the periodical press but they prepared the ground for the imaginative consumption of astronomical images in the period. H. G. Wells drew on and satirised this array of astronomical media in his 1901 science-fiction novel *The First Men in the Moon*. Describing the spaceship's approach to the moon, the narrator comments: 'I take it the reader has seen pictures or photographs of the moon, so that I need not describe the broader features of that landscape'; but as it lands on the surface he adopts the tone of a lunar observer: 'And now we could see, what no eye on earth will ever see.' The mobility of point of view is absolutely central to Wells's narrative and indeed to the late Victorian astronomical imaginary as a whole.[36]

Astronomy liberated the technological and cultural imagination in this period. At amusement parks like Coney Island, which have been described by the historian John Kasson as 'laboratories of the new mass culture', 'A Trip to the Moon' featured as one of a range of kinaesthetic experiences on offer to a heterogeneous urban public.[37] In precisely the same years, the first film-makers drew on astronomy as the vehicle for their most creative fantasies. The quality that many of these early fictional films capture is the conjoining of the archaic and the new in the popular fascination with astronomy. Their imagery belongs to both ancient mythology and contemporary science, to the worlds of astrological star charts and of stellar photography, often resulting in an anarchic and visually astounding *mêlée* of signification. Discovery and mystery are bound together in these films. The astronomer is a necromancer, whose telescopic lens reveals that the universe is, after all, an animated host of celestial personifications. It is the world of the man in the moon and astrological divination, in which the austerity of modern astrophysics is unravelled in minutes. This contact with the ancient wonder of the heavens also characterises the popularisers of astronomy in the second half of the nineteenth century. Although Flammarion was responsible for some of the most important scientific discoveries about the nature of double stars, he could not resist reiterating that the geographical configuration of the moon's surface looked like the head of a man or woman (plate 121).[38] It was this irreverence and continuing adherence to old superstitions that made modern astronomy a fertile source for cultural appropriation and the popular imagination.

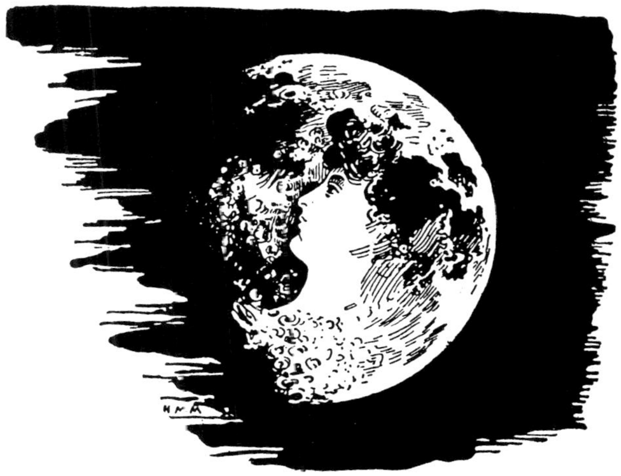

121 'Woman's Head in the Moon', from Camille Flammarion, *Astronomy for Amateurs*, London: T. Fisher Unwin, 1905, p. 238, fig. 67.

In Georges Méliès's *The Astronomer's Dream* (*La lune à un mètre*, 1898), an astronomer is seated in an observatory in which a number of magical transformations take place.[39] He begins to observe the moon through a large telescope and, suddenly, the face of the moon, with rolling eyes and gaping mouth, appears in his laboratory. It opens its mouth and swallows the telescope; the astronomer tries to retrieve it from the ghastly moon mouth, which then spits out two little boys (plate 122). The moon recedes into the middle distance, from where it continues to mock the astronomer with its grinning mouth and rolling eyes. Without warning, the ghastly head disappears, to be replaced by a starry sky and a crescent moon bearing a veiled female figure. As the astronomer begins to observe this scene through his telescope, the veiled figure appears in his laboratory. A series of outlandish transformations occurs, culminating in the reappearance of the giant, grinning moon face that swallows up the astronomer and spits him out in bits and pieces, along with fragments of other

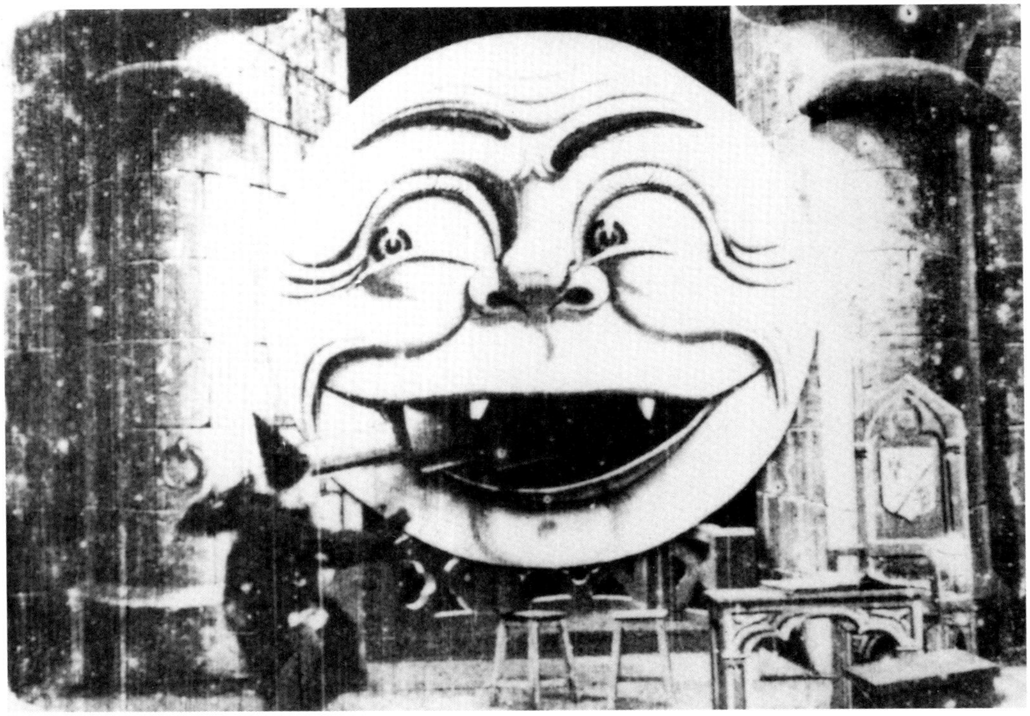

122 Georges Méliès, *The Astronomer's Dream (La lune à un metre)*, 1898. Frame still.

characters from the film. The astronomer is finally, magically, reconstituted and left bewildered and overwhelmed at his desk. Whenever the astronomer looks at an object or figure through his telescope, it appears abruptly, through stop-motion substitution, in his laboratory. To look through the telescopic lens in this film is to eradicate entirely the distance between observer and celestial body and the ensuing tussle between the moon and the astronomer is an hysterical enactment of the collapse of a fixed point of view and of measurable distance, described earlier in this chapter in relation to other visual media in this period. It is a compelling depiction of an old astronomy in a new medium.

Méliès's *A Trip to the Moon* of 1902 is startling for a number of reasons, not least because of its length, which at twenty-one minutes distinguished it from most films of the period that lasted little more than a few minutes.[40] It also marks the apogee of Méliès's trick effects, which are woven into the film's narrative of a scientific journey to explore the moon. The means of transport for the astronauts is a rocket shell, fired from a huge cannon. When the shell is fired, it lands right in the eye of the man in the moon (plate 123). This spectacular and memorable image can be read as a symbolic vision of the end of an astronomical science based on the transcription of the observation of the eye and the triumph of a new astronomy based on the superior gaze and representational capacities of the camera lens.

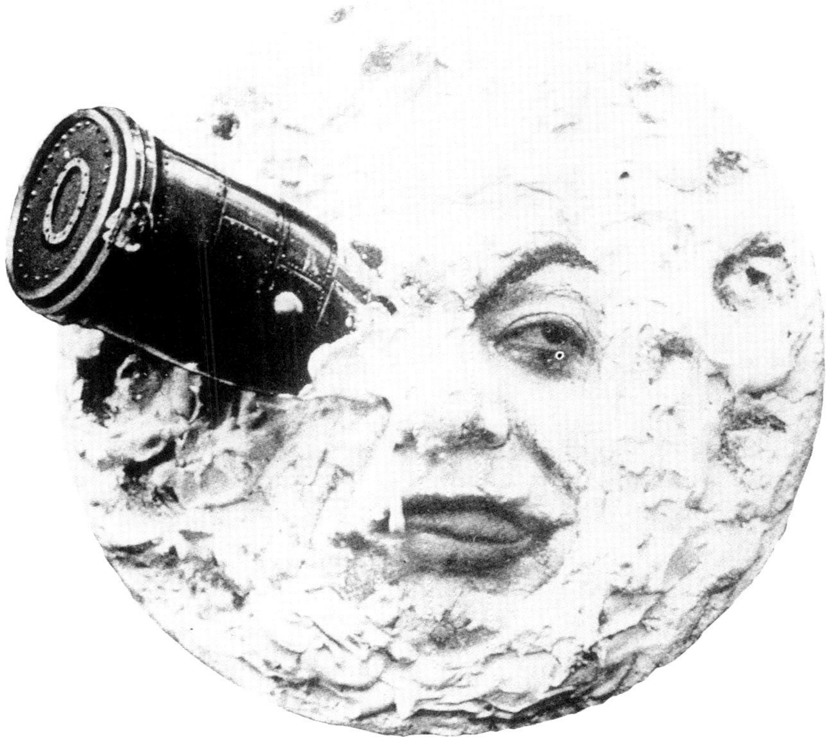

123 Georges Méliès, *A Trip to the Moon*, 1902. Frame still.

At close range, the anthropomorphic moons and stars of early films are harbingers of mayhem, in the same way that the animated figures in enchanted paintings bring chaos to the world they take possession of. In *Love by the Light of the Moon*, an Edison film made in 1901, a courting couple stands on a balcony, with a full moon in the sky. Inevitably, its face begins to change and to interfere with the romantic canoodlings on the balcony. It grins, it frowns, it winks conspiratorially as they caress and then begins to get bigger and closer, as though on a spring. The couple kiss and the woman jumps up, alarmed by the sudden appalling proximity of the girning moon; she faints in her lover's arms and he fans her with his hat. This simple visual joke draws on the audience's immediate familiarity with the idea of the moon 'à un mètre' and its readiness to see the heavens as a subversive counter-space to the terrestrial world of romantic love or astronomical science.

Outer space was also an easy setting for an erotic interlude, featuring star-girls in tutus. In the Pathé Frères film *The Girl in the Moon* (1904), a woman in an acrobat's costume performs pirouettes and balletic somersaults against a black background scattered with stars and a crescent moon. In contrast to this piece of astronomical vaudeville, the beauty of the celestial woman becomes the alibi for a much more complex fantasy narrative of space travel in Gaston Velle's *Voyage autour d'une étoile* (Pathé Frères, 1906). Here, the elderly astronomer falls in love with a star-girl whom he spies through his telescope. He decides to go to her, travelling inside a giant bubble that floats into space among the stars, all of which are, in fact, the faces of beautiful women. The astronomer finds his star-lady, with a chorus of dancing 'starlets' and he joins her in her star. Finally he is expelled from this celestial paradise by an angry Jove-like figure. He falls through the sky, holding an open umbrella, until he is impaled on a spinning weather vane, with a hen – the Pathé logo – on the top.

Paintings, photographs, lantern slides, multi-media performances, amusement rides and films reveal the richness of the encounter between astronomy and the visual imagination at the end of the nineteenth century. Here were pictures that absorbed the viewer and offered an immersive experience of the visual image that disturbed the idea of a fixed viewing position. They created a dynamic, kinetic viewer whose point of view was just as likely to be that of the lunarian or martian as that of an inhabitant of earth. There is, however, one further detour to make on this space journey, which concerns what celestial travellers saw when they looked back at the earth.

lookback time

When mid-Victorian viewers first looked at photographs of distant stars, galaxies and nebulae, the most profound impact of this encounter concerned everyday assumptions of time and duration. They were conscious that the light which was recorded on the photographic plate might have emanated from space thousands of light years before and that the systems represented might already have changed dramatically or even disappeared entirely. The phrase that is used to describe this collapse of conventional notions of past, present and future in astronomical observation is 'lookback time'. Flammarion described the phenomenon clearly in *Popular Astronomy*:

> There is here, then, a surprising *transformation of the past into the present*. For the star observed, it is the past – already vanished. For the observer, it is the present, the now. The past of a star is strictly and positively the present of the observer . . . What we believe we see now in the stars is already past; and what is now being accomplished we do not yet see.[41]

The import of this apparently matter of fact statement is considerable, unfastening unitary notions of duration and subjectivity. Initially, the implications of these ideas were elaborated in philosophy and science but they also found their way into popular culture and provided a rhetoric for comprehending the significance and future role of the new medium of film. This route from specialist to popular discourse can be traced through the work and powerful imagination of Flammarion. Although he was an outstanding and, in some ways, exceptional figure in scientific circles in the period, he also represented more widely held attitudes towards the visual culture of astronomy and was an effective and successful populariser of these ideas. He never lost his sense of astonishment and wonder at the sights of the heavens. In his *Astronomy for Amateurs* the language of marvel continually surfaces in his prose; he refers to 'an astonished gaze' and 'the dazzled eye'.[42] Knowledge and fascination were entirely compatible in Flammarion's astronomy; science, for him, was founded on an appreciation of the sublime beauty of the heavens.

Flammarion was born in 1842; he moved to Paris with his family as a child and worked first as an engraver and then as an astronomer. He later founded the French Astronomical Society and established the journal *L'Astronomie*. At the Paris Observatoire he held a number of positions and made special studies of the moon, Mars and double stars.[43] This research did not interfere with his prolific writing and he became a central figure in the growth of amateur and popular astronomy in the period. Flammarion had a spectacular vision of the universe that was inflected by his interest in psychic research and spiritualism. In the early years of the twentieth century he was engaged with equal vigour in astronomical research and séances and counted among his colleagues mediums as well as scientists. For Flammarion these were complementary, rather than contradictory, fields of study; what they shared was a commitment to worlds beyond the visible and known limits of observation.[44] X-rays and spectroscopy had demonstrated the existence of previously unseen forms and bodies of knowledge and, to Flammarion, the belief in psychic forces was no more extraordinary than the belief in scientific forces such as 'the influence of the moon on the sea . . . [or the revelation] of the chemical constituents of a star by the analysis of its light'.[45] He anticipated a future religion based on a scientific understanding of psychical facts.

As a communicator Flammarion embraced a range of visual media to enhance his public lectures. From the start, he used the magic lantern to illustrate his lectures and almost from its first appearance he was eager to exploit the possibilities of the cinematograph.[46] To this extent, he was part of a greater historical shift from the representation of the planetary system through the small-scale mechanical model, or orrery, to the projection of large, two-dimensional images on a hemispherical dome, the planetarium.[47] A slow development, rather than a sudden change, the move was from a hand-operated, three-dimensional device that was used to demonstrate the movement and relations of astronomical bodies, to an optical medium, housed in a special building for public viewing. The modern planetarium was thus part of the history of projected moving images and cinematic culture.

In 1898 the *Amateur Photographer*, along with other specialist and general press, reported two film projects that Flammarion had recently demonstrated to the public.[48] The first used a series of exposures, taken at regular intervals during one night, on a single strip of film, to depict the changing sky from sunset to sunrise. In the short period of projection, his film showed the viewers the gradual appearance of the stars, moonrise and the motion of astronomical bodies that had occurred during the sixteen hours of darkness on one winter's night. Flammarion's visual imagination could not remain fixed to the earth for long, however. The second application was demonstrated to members of the French Astronomical Society and involved a model of the earth on which was represented the various land and water masses. Set against a dark background, studded with stars and illuminated by an intense light to simulate the light of the sun, the globe was set in motion and filmed and in two minutes executed a single rotation representing the earth's motion over twenty-four hours. The audience was thus offered a view of the earth as seen from the moon and a day truncated in order to fit the time of a length of film. Where films of street life, in the same years, were capturing fragments of the everyday in real time, the astronomical film played with time and point of view. If street films placed the viewer on the street and among its diverse rhythms and social types, the astronomical film took the viewer on a sublime phantom ride, in which the unseen mode of transport was astral projection rather than a railway engine.

Flammarion's interest in the projection of moving images went far beyond simply using film as an additional medium for disseminating his astronomical research. He identified a profound conceptual link between the images produced by the beam of the projector and the spectacles of the heavens. If the magic lantern or cinematograph generated a constant series of changing views, then this was precisely the nature of the sights that were offered to the astronomical observer. Space was thus filled with light images being successively and endlessly projected from different celestial bodies. He wrote:

> As the aspect of worlds changes . . . we can represent this aspect as escaping into space and advancing in Infinitude to reveal itself to the eyes of distant beholders. Each aspect is followed by another, and so on successively; and it is as if a series of waves bearing from afar the past of worlds should become present to observers ranged along its passage![49]

If space is thus imagined as a kind of multiplex cinema, receiving and transmitting the histories of every world in existence, then who is the audience for these images? This is the point (on the same page) at which Flammarion develops the idea of 'lookback time' from the perspective of a spirit traveller in space.

> If from the earth we see a star, not as it is at the moment we observe it, but such as it was a hundred years previously, so from this star its inhabitants see the earth after a delay of a hundred years . . .
>
> A man, a spirit, leaving the earth, either by death or otherwise, this year and transported in some hours or days to a great distance, would see the earth of former times . . . for the aspect of the earth would not arrive where he was till after a long delay.
>
> There is here neither a vision . . . nor a marvellous or supernatural action, but an actual, positive . . . and uncontestable fact; what has been for a long time the past for the earth is only the present for a distant observer in space . . . Events vanish for the place which brings them forth, but they remain in space.

This remarkable vision of cosmic image banks and celestial viewers was clearly explicable for Flammarion in terms of his spiritualist beliefs, but he conceived the astronomical imagination anyway as a virtual interplanetary journey and often referred to telescopic observation as celestial travelling. Even the most elementary photograph could trigger his kinetic imagination; at the end of *Popular Astronomy* he wondered whether anyone could look at such images 'without feeling himself transported towards this first stage in celestial voyages and detached from the vulgar things of earth?'[50]

on a beam of light

The vision of light images travelling from the earth into space and bearing a continual record of the planet's history in its smallest details was proposed in the first half of the nineteenth century by the German philosopher and biographer Felix Eberty. In *The Stars and the Earth; Or, Thoughts upon Space, Time and Eternity*, first published anonymously in 1846 and later revised and enlarged by Richard Proctor, Eberty precociously imagined God as an ominiscient viewer, watching the pictorial history of the world as it is transmitted and extended into space.[51] The universe was thus like a vast and indestructible visual archive, with pictures of every single event in the earth's history carried on 'the wings of a ray of light'.[52] Moreover, if this divine observer began his viewing on a star of the twelfth magnitude, for example, and moved with immense speed in the direction of the earth, reaching the sun in one hour, he could 'run' the history of the earth from Abraham to the present, in the same amount of time. The velocity of the celestial viewer determined the speed of the images and created a highly interactive viewing experience. He could slow down to enjoy moments in the world's history at greater leisure and accelerate or 'fast forward' through less engaging periods and events.[53] The observer's varied travel along the ray of light images – with acceleration, slow motion and even stop-motion – created, according to Eberty, 'a *Microscope* for time'.[54]

For Eberty, writing half a century before the cinematograph, the paradigmatic optical device through which he conceived the power of the beam of light was the magic lantern; but his conception of the heavenly succession of images was far in excess of any sequence of changing views obtainable from that source. He referred to the 'rushing stream' and 'whirling procession of these consecutive images'.[55] This was a spectacular celestial cinema for the eyes of a divine spectator.

The limitations of the magic lantern as the technological generator of this fantastic beam of light were acknowledged by Eberty when he described the production of a picture from a magic lantern. Rather than seeing the image reconstituted and spread across a screen or wall, he preferred the moment at which the image was concentrated in a single point of light. The ray of light was thus the bearer of images to a viewer with a heightened sense of vision; a projecting surface was no longer necessary.[56] In his later, revised edition of *The Stars and the Earth*, Proctor also drew attention to the inaccuracies in Eberty's consideration of lantern-image projection. The issue, in reality, was less a matter of the magic lantern than of Eberty's vision of projected moving images being in advance of available optical technology. As later commentators have acknowledged, this was a filmic vision. In one of the earliest histories of film, published in 1899, Henry Hopwood referred in his last pages to Proctor's edition of Eberty and to Flammarion's reworking of the theme. Here was a future, megalomaniacal role for film – the creation of 'an eternal and universal living picture of all past events'.[57] An American newspaper confirmed that the fabulous vision of the history of the universe carried on a ray of light had indeed been made possible by the invention of the kinetoscope.[58] In this utopian, even magical, version of the future of film, the beam of light becomes a conveyor of images to audiences of divine celestial beings.

It was Flammarion's creative reworking of these ideas, however, that brought them to the greatest public attention. *Lumen* was first published in 1872, after which it went through many French editions, before being published in English in its final form in 1897. It consists of a number of dialogues between a teacher, the eponymous Lumen – the source of light – and his pupil and interrogator, Quaerens – the seeker of knowledge. The central conceit is that of Lumen's soul, freed from his body at the moment of death and leaving the earth to travel through the heavens. From this viewpoint the spirit traveller looks back at the earth and sees its past events projected, as though on a beam of light, into space. Depending on the velocity of the traveller, the earth's history can be observed at different speeds and for different periods of time. Lumen describes his observation of earth from the star world Capella, seventy-two light years away, and his experience of watching events from both his own life and from history unfold before him. The ray of light is like a belated courier, bringing news from a distant country of events that happened when he left, seventy-odd years ago. Lumen adds: 'the light . . . brings, not written news, but photographs, or, strictly speaking, *the real aspect* of the country from [*sic*] whence [it] came. We see this living picture such as it appeared, in all its aspects, at the moment when the luminous rays shot forth from the distant orb.'[59]

There is thus a constant relay of images into space; each appearance is followed by another in an endless sequence. Movement through space is thus conceived as a passage across a succession of zones in which the visible history of the earth is 'spread out as in a scroll'.[60] It is impossible not to see this conception of space and psychical optics other than in cinematic terms, with the earth images projected from the planet in a succession of frames, like a strip of film. It is clear that Flammarion thought in visual terms and presented his research through optical devices. For a creative thinker in the 1870s it was not a huge imaginative leap to move from the still photograph to dissolving lantern slides to continuously moving images, or 'living pictures', as film was also first called. As successive terrestrial photographs are projected and imprinted in space they constitute a kind of celestial archive of the history of the world. Lumen tells his pupil: 'we shall have in a ray of light, or rather in a jet of light, composed of a series of distinct pictures in juxtaposition, the aerial register of the history of the Earth'.[61] If this breathtaking conception were not enough, he goes on to evoke a colossal heavenly screen, a Celestial Globe surpassing any didactic entertainment that the 1900 Paris World's Fair could come up with. The images emanating from earth, he suggests, might encounter in space stars whose surface was so sensitised that they could fix the image and 'Thus terrestrial events might be printed on a dark globe . . . a sort of continuous photograph of successive events.'[62]

To an extent, these were also the imaginative terms of early cinema. The beam of light was an image with great creative possibilities, figuring both the present and future roles of optical technologies. More than the reconstituted, large-scale images that ended up spread across screens, it was the presence of an apparently endless succession of pictures, carried in the beam of light between projector and screen, that symbolised the potency of the new medium. In many visual representations of film from this period, the beam is imagined as a tangible, material presence, crossing the dark spaces of the tents, halls and auditoria that constituted the homes of early cinema. In an 1896 advertisement for a 'mutagraph' show at the Egyptian Hall, London, the projector is relegated to the bottom right-hand corner and the screen is excluded entirely (plate 124). It is the cone of light that is of greatest importance and that contains the miscellany of animated pictures. Life is in the beam of light and, for a moment, the film spectator shares in the visual omniscience of Lumen and the divine and ultra-terrestrial viewers of astronomy and science fiction.

The repetition of the beam of light as a motif for the diverse attractions and possibilities of film in the years around 1900 is striking. In 1901 the British Muto-

124 'Egyptian Hall Daily at 3 & 8. Animated Photographs. The First and Finest in London'. Advertising poster, C. J. Culliford, 1896.

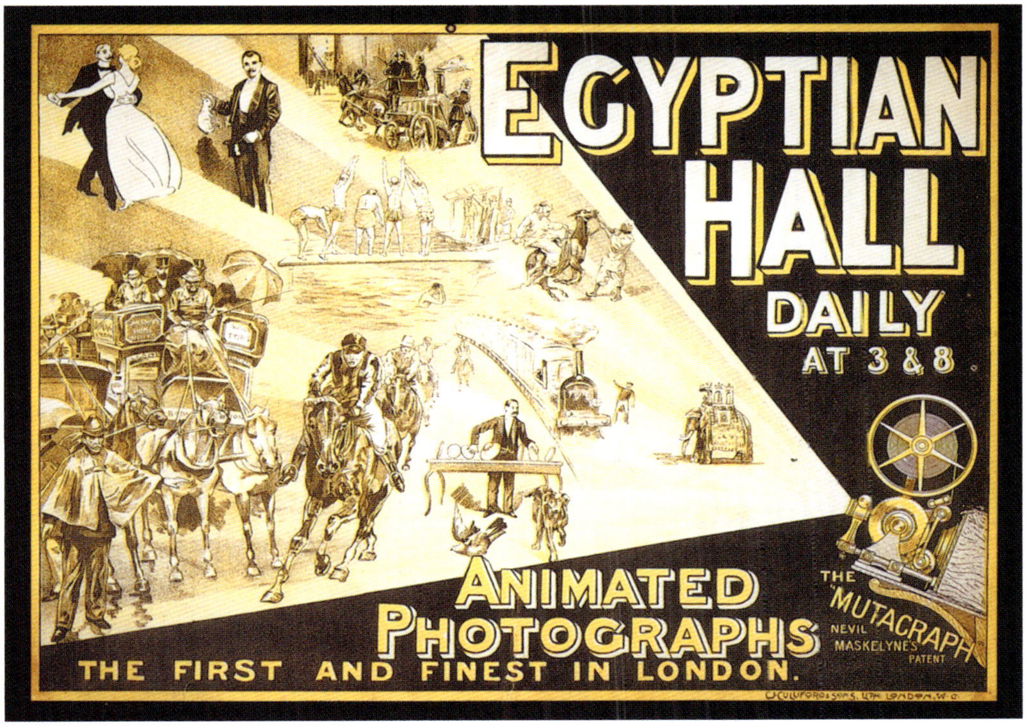

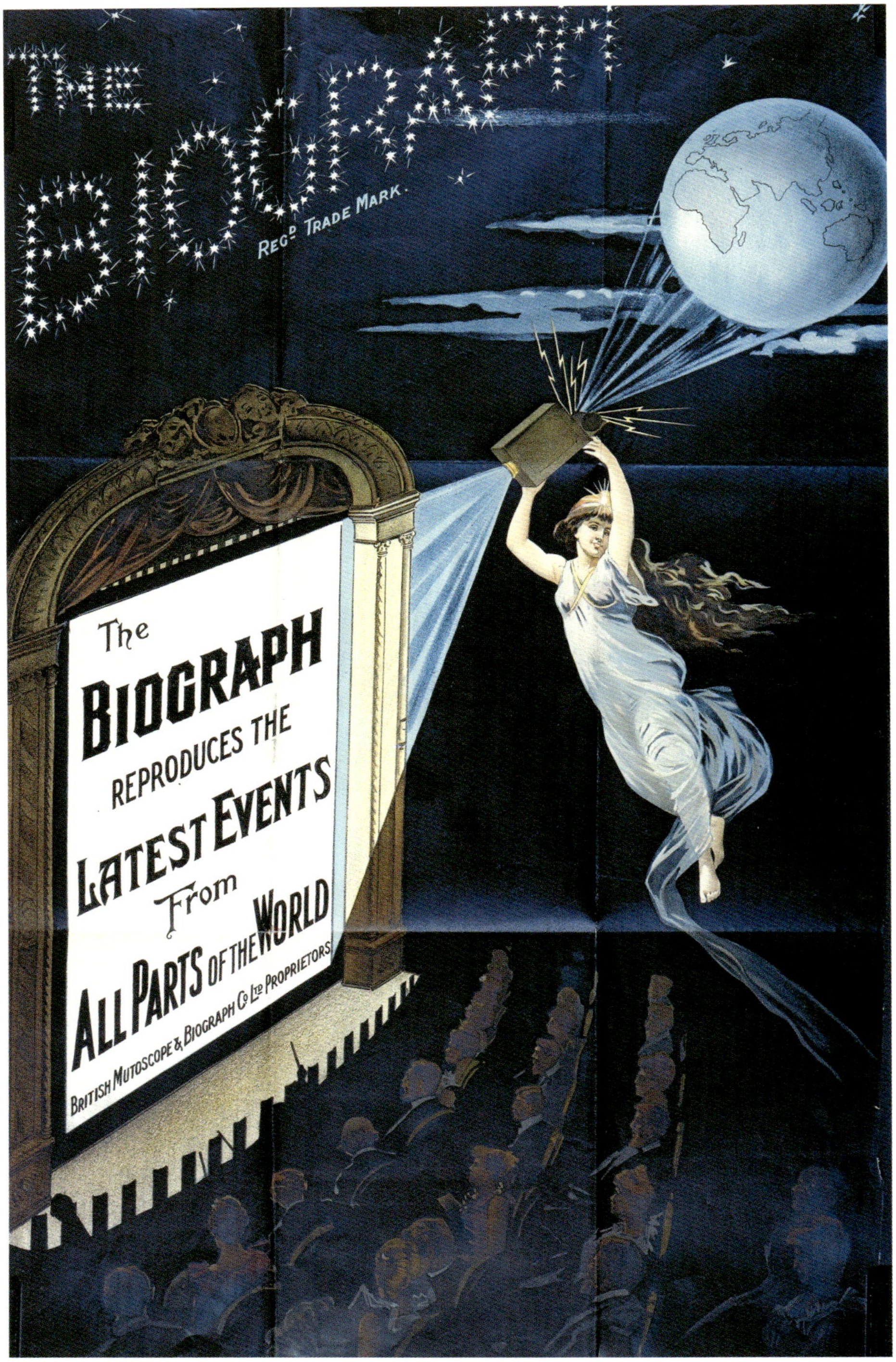

125 'The Biograph Reproduces the Latest Events from All Parts of the World. British Mutoscope & Biograph Co. Ltd. Proprietors'. Advertising poster, 1901. National Archives, COPY1/171/f261.

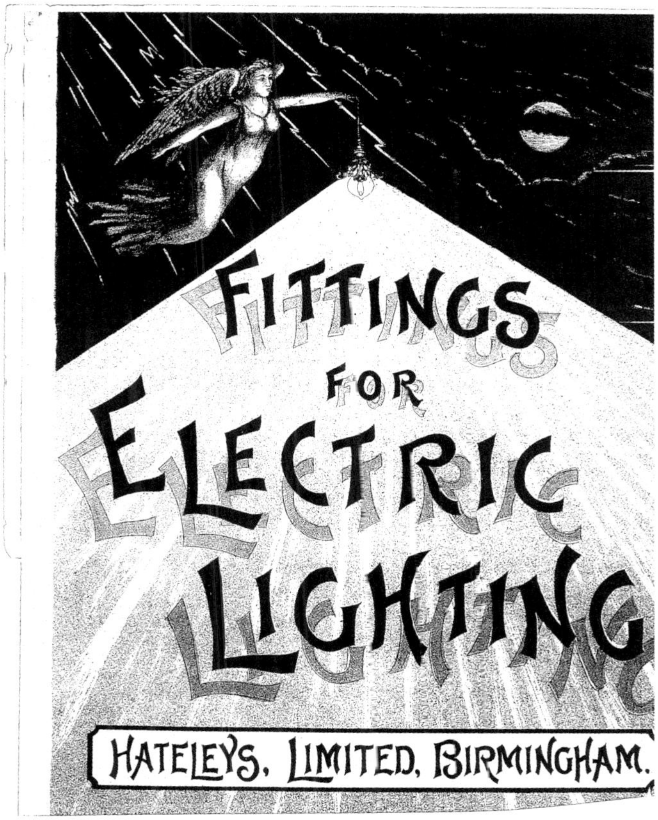

126 Design for a cover of a book entitled 'Fittings for Electric Lighting', February 1899. National Archives, COPY1/147/F121.

scope and Biograph Company registered a design for an advertising poster at Stationer's Hall (plate 125). It shows a female figure, in diaphanous drapery, holding a camera-cum-projector that receives beams of light from the earth and transmits them onto a stage screen. The word 'Biograph', the company trademark, is lit up in stars and the setting appears to be the night sky, rather than the interior of an auditorium. One might speculate about what this female figure represents – perhaps the spirit of film and modern technology, or the symbol of astronomy and its liberation of the creative imagination at the end of the nineteenth century. In more than one sense, however, the figure is simply a support, a caryatid, bearing the weight of a beam of light in which is carried the entire history of the world.

Rays of light, borne by allegorical female figures, were ubiquitous in the electrical and optical cultures of the *fin de siècle*. A design for the cover of a book of electrical fittings included a winged female figure, surrounded by flashes of lightning, holding an electrical lamp in whose powerful beam the title is illuminated (plate 126). More spectacularly, the Palace of Electricity at the 1900 Paris World's Fair was crowned with a sculptural group, representing the genius or spirit of electricity (plate 127).[63] A statue of a naked woman, with flowing hair and raised arms, stands above a pediment of glass and electric light bulbs. Behind her there is a stag-

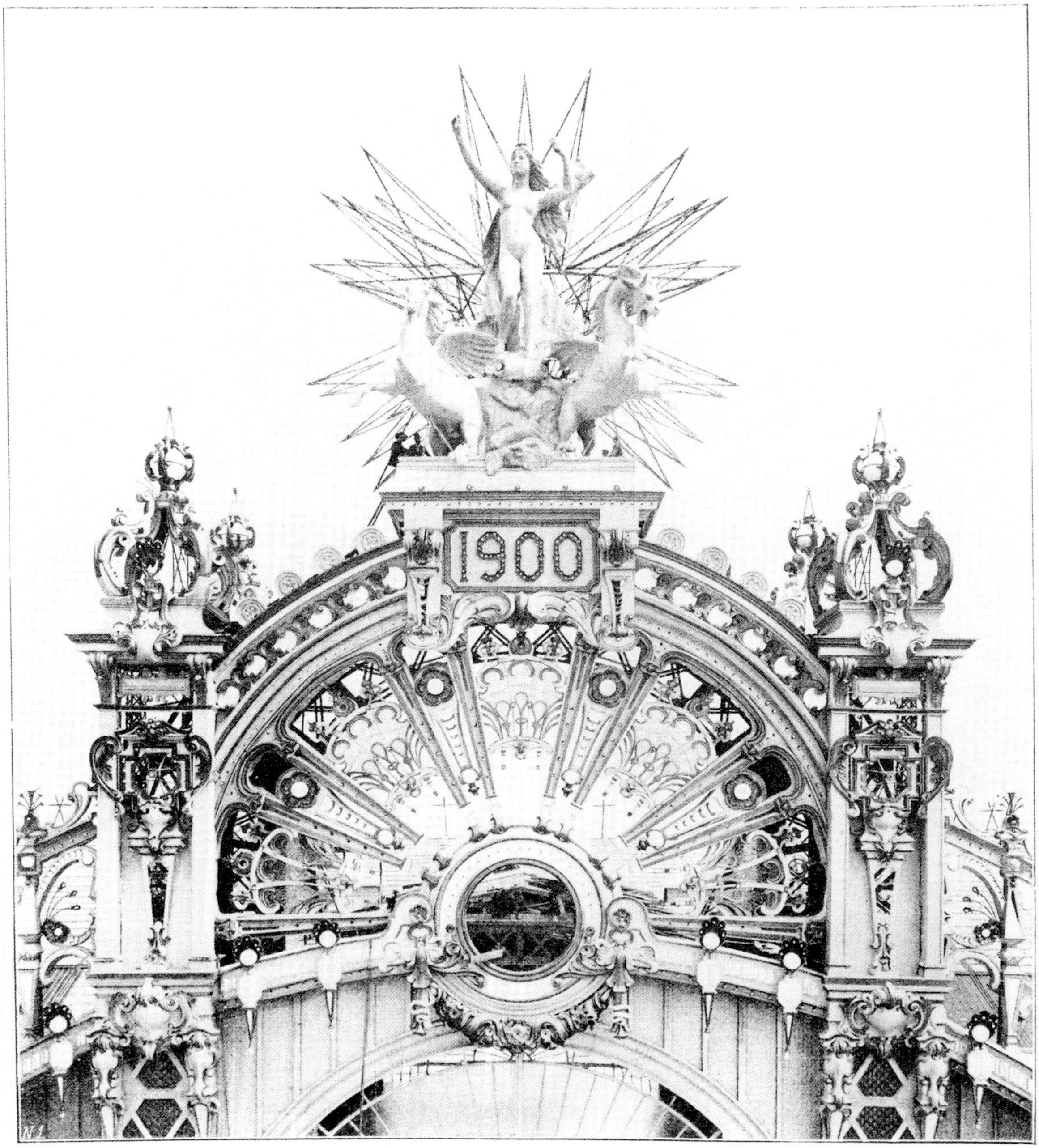

127 'Motif qui couronne le Palais de l'Electricité', *L'Illustration*, vol. CXV, 26 May 1900, p. 337.

128 (*facing page*) Advertising poster, London, 1900. National Archives, COPY 1/149/f267.

gering three-dimensional star whose points shoot out in all directions with jagged precision. Of course, the impact of this arrangement was greatest at night, when the Palace of Electricity was illuminated and the whole of Paris was covered by a network of beams of light. A colour poster of the Exposition at night shows beams of light converging at the top of the Eiffel Tower, from where further beams are sent out into the cloudy night sky (see plate 120). It is a nightscape that defines the power of modern technology through the beam of light and the hubristic ambition of man to illuminate the heavens.

This interpretation begins to unpack the iconographic significance of the conical beam of light in this period. In a template poster for the Salle de l'Etoile, the allegorical girl is there, along with the camera projector and an empty, neutral beam of light that will carry the images of any show that the venue needs to promote (plate 129). The beam is an adaptable medium, the bearer of comedy, tragedy, fantasy and reality. It brings the past and the future into the present of the audience. Thus the celluloid opponents in a boxing match, projected at a music hall, seem to hover somewhere between lens and screen (plate 128); they remain 'in' the beam of light and as tangible as that section of the film's audience who are also caught up in the magical illumination of the projected beam.

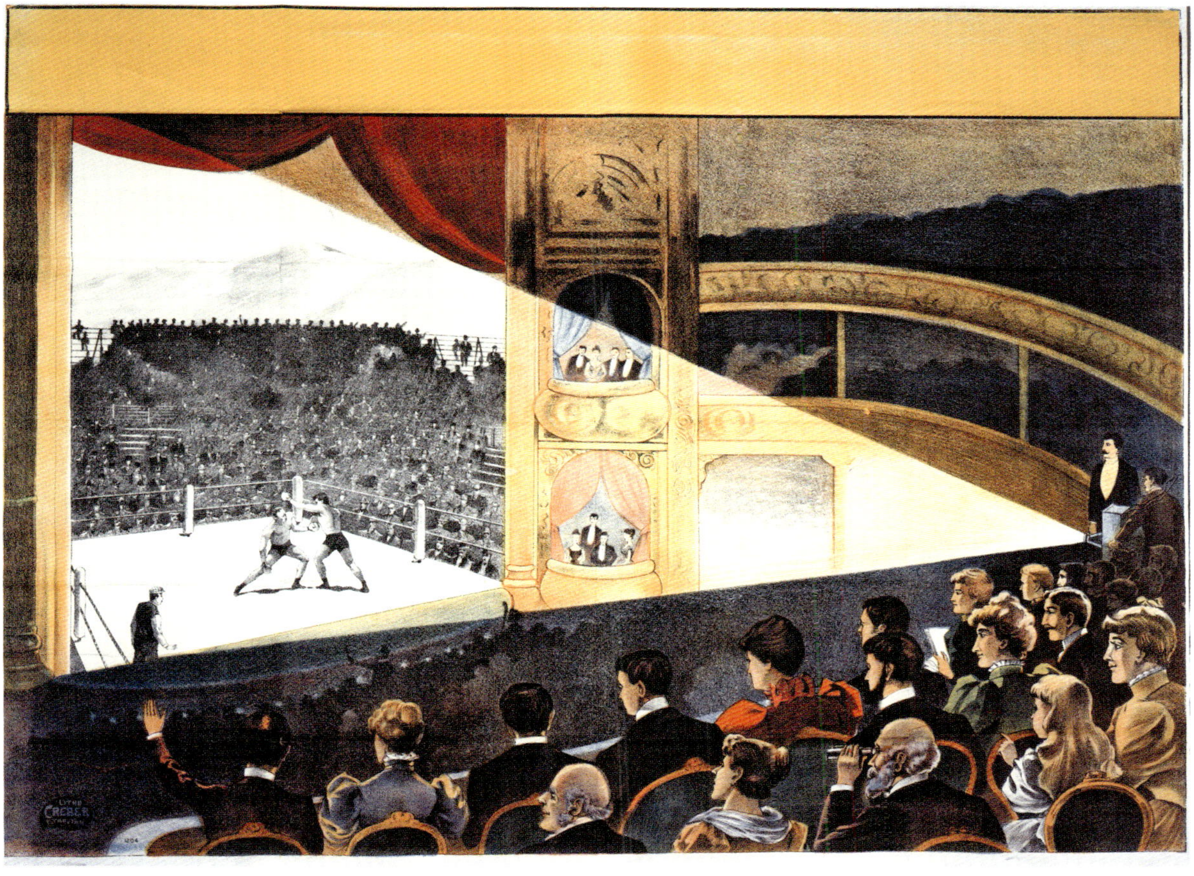

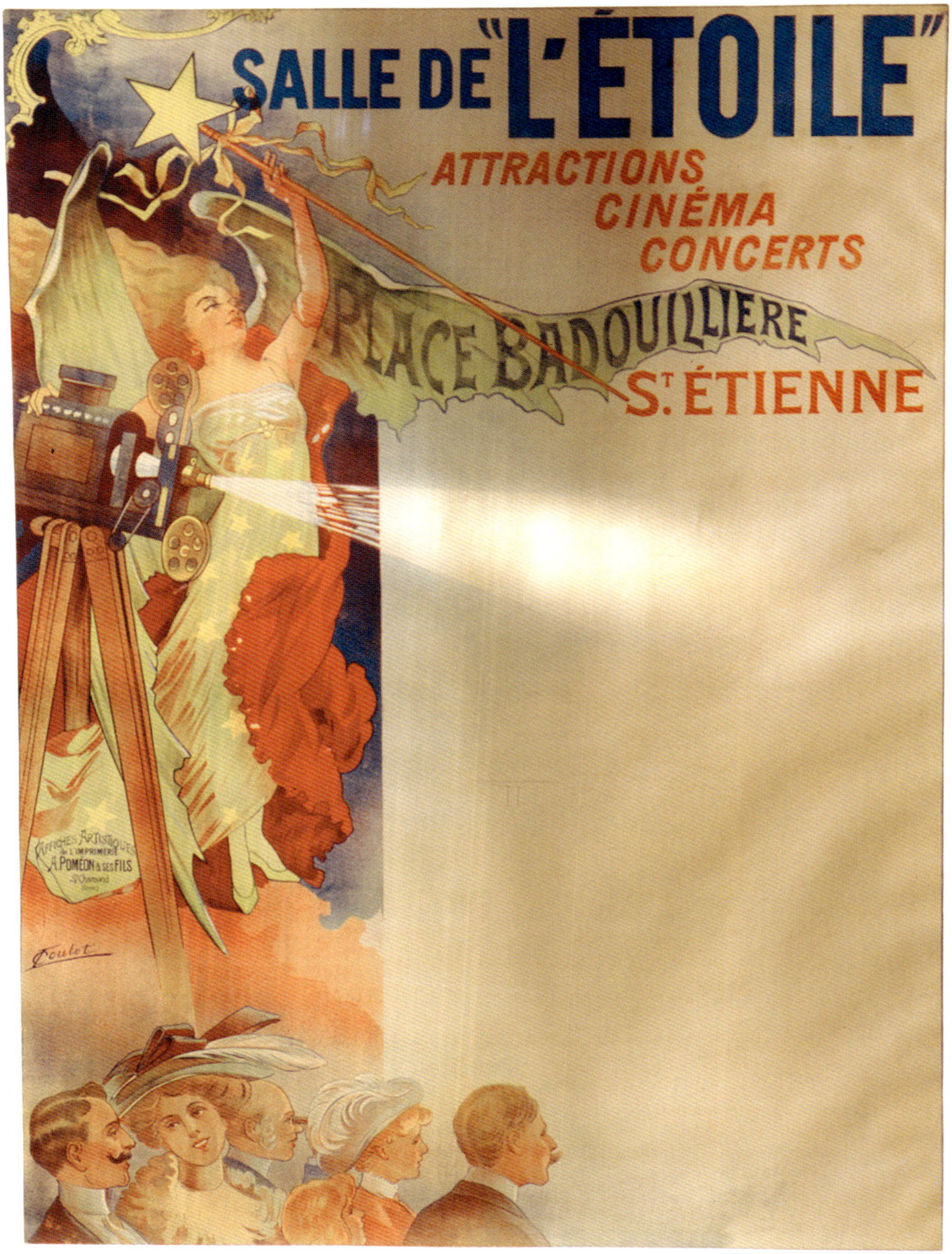

129 'Salle de "l'Etoile" attractions, cinéma, concerts'. Advertising poster, Paris, 1900. Werner Nekes Collection.

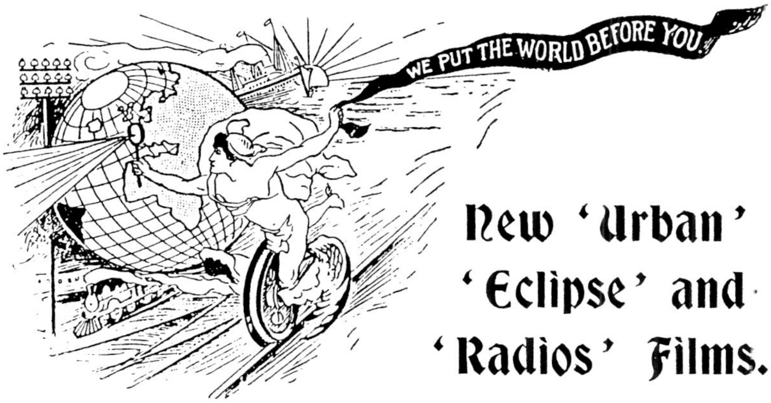

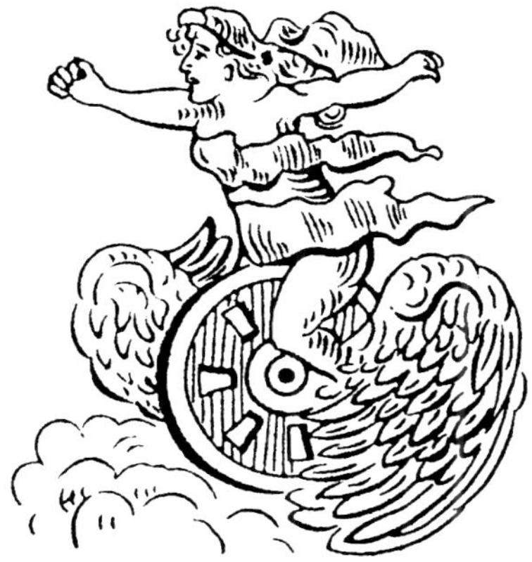

130 (*above left*) 'New "Urban", "Eclipse" and "Radios" Films'. Company logo, Charles Urban Trading Company, 1908. British Film Institute, National Film Archive Cataloguing Department.

131 (*above right*) 'Drawing of a figure on a winged wheel'. Copyright registration for Harry Saunders, Woodyer, 74 Faulkner Street, Manchester, 16 November 1900. National Archives, COPY3/137, p. 167, no. 1666.

It is hardly surprising, then, that the film-maker and distributor, Charles Urban, chose a variation on this theme – albeit a somewhat obscure one – as his company logo in the early 1900s (plates 130 and 131). In this image, a male figure – a type of Mercury with winged heels – rides a monocycle, whose wheel is also the reel of film.[64] He holds a banner with the slogan 'We Put the World Before You' in one hand and a magnifying glass that projects a beam of light in the other. Behind him there are images of modern technology, such as telegraph poles and a steamship, and the earth. Urban's speciality was educational films and, specifically, what he described as 'micro-cinematographic' studies of germs and microbes.[65] The magnifying glass represents Urban's novel approach to scientific film and provides the structural link between the earth and the rays of light that issue from it. In this context, therefore, the magnifying glass also evokes the filmic 'microscope for time' that Felix Eberty had imagined in the 1840s.

All the themes that have been discussed thus far – astronomy, illumination, cinematography and the gendered allegorical body – come together, finally, in the figure of Loïe Fuller. Fuller was an American-born dancer who devised a distinctive style of performance that involved the manipulation of lengths of cloth round her body, illuminated by multi-coloured spotlights. It was a type of dance that broke with the conventions of classical and popular choreography and that focused on the formal effects created by the interplay of the constantly moving fabric and changing lighting. Following an appearance at the Folies Bergère in 1892, when she performed this 'Serpentine Dance', she came to the attention of artists such as Toulouse-Lautrec and Jules Chéret, who used the mobile forms and colours created by her dance as the inspiration for their art in the 1890s (plate 132).

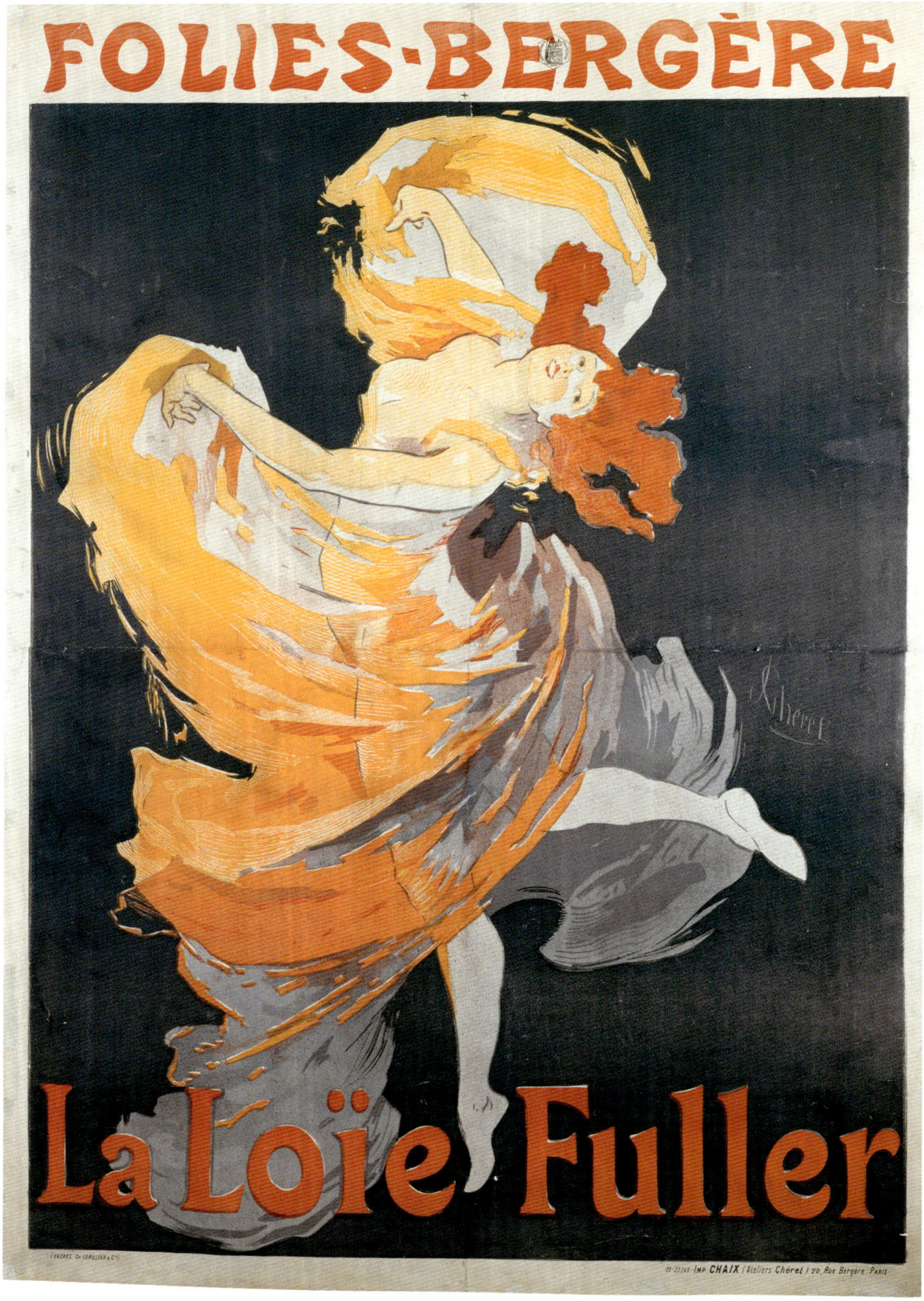

132 Jules Chéret, 'Folies-Bergère: La Loïe Fuller', 1893. Victoria and Albert Museum, London.

Although creators of sculpture, paintings and prints turned to Fuller as the subject of their art, there was an even greater synergy between Fuller's performance style and the moving images of film.[66] Fuller's dance created a fluid and kaleidoscopic spectacle of modern motion in which the female body was simultaneously on show and erotically concealed by the veils and clouds of swirling drapery. As Tom Gunning has suggested, Fuller's performance was a further instance of early film's fascination with motion and transformation, which was also demonstrated in subjects such as rough seas, phantom rides and the trick films of Méliès and Pathé.[67] What was distinctive about Fuller's performance of the body in motion, however, was its quality of formal abstraction and its use of colour and lighting. Drawn by its unique kinetic qualities, a number of film-makers made versions of the Serpentine Dance, performed either by Fuller herself or by one of her many imitators. Both Edison and Lumière also hand-tinted their Fuller films so that as the film was projected it became a celluloid analogue of the shifting patterns of shape and colour created by Fuller's performance itself (plate 133).

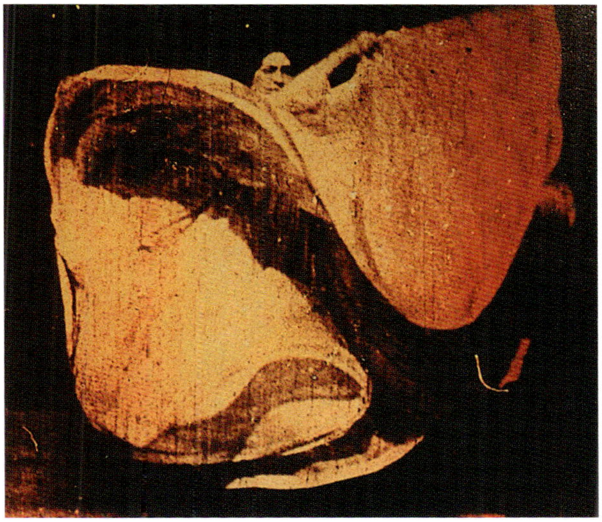

133 Thomas A. Edison, *La Danse Serpentine*, 1895–1902. Hand-tinted still.

Up to this point, Fuller must be acknowledged as a particularly influential, modernist intervention in the early film genre of contemporary theatrical performance. There is, however, a further twist in her story that brings her into direct contact with the astronomical imagination. As well as the famed Serpentine Dance, Fuller devised variations on that routine, which she named after natural forms such as the lily and the butterfly. These themes included performances named after astronomical phenomena such as 'Aurora boréale' and 'Firmament' (plate 134).[68] Illuminated by coloured beams of light, projected onto her moving body by oxyhydrogen projectors, Fuller became a personification of the heavens, a dancing nebula who

134 'A Sunshine Effect in the "Firmament Dance"', from Marcus Tindal, 'Queen of all Dancers', *Pearson's Magazine*, December 1901, p. 596.

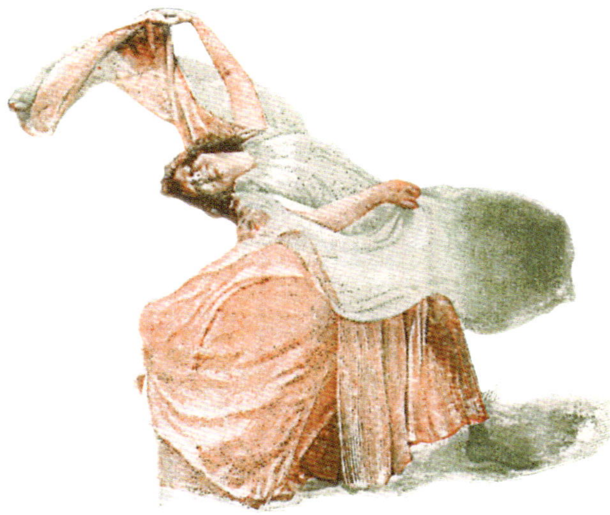

captured in contemporary performance the exquisite beauty of modern astrophysics. Among the large audiences that admired Fuller's art was Flammarion, who was captivated by her celestial performance and invited her to dance at his observatory.[69] For the astronomer, Fuller must have seemed like the living embodiment of his own celestial spirit traveller, Lumen. Together, Fuller and Flammarion were a perfect realisation of the poetic fantasy of modern astronomy.

the sublime archive of images

To return, now, to the reader of the astronomical press with whom this chapter began, settled into a comfortable chair, in a darkened room, on a winter's evening, turning the pages of the latest issue of *Knowledge* or *Popular Astronomy* or opening the next instalment of Robert Ball's *The Story of the Heavens*. The beam from a reading light focuses his attention on a new photograph of a distant nebula and he begins to wonder about time and space. Perhaps it is the weeks and months following the celebrations for Queen Victoria's Diamond Jubilee in July 1897 and the reader wonders how this historical moment will be remembered in hundreds or thousands of years' time; or even whether there are others, elsewhere in the universe, watching the ceremonial processions in 'lookback time'. Flammarion had also speculated about this experience of watching the dead move and live when he imagined Lumen on the star world Capella, watching the events of his own childhood: 'this whole troop of children had ceased to exist. But I saw them such as they were at the moment the ray of light left the Earth, which only reached me at the present time.'[70]

These fictional questions were given a new relevance by the development of film. Within months of the first public exhibitions of moving images, the potential of the medium as a new form of archiving and as an historiographical recording system was being discussed.[71] In an article published in 1897 and entitled 'What the Biograph is Doing for the Future Historian', one New York newspaper claimed that the Biograph 'will abolish the past, or rather, the past will speak through it to the present, and a thousand years will be unto this marvelous device of man's brain as a single day'.[72]

The role of film as an outstanding medium of historical preservation was immediately understood and in the same Jubilee summer of 1897, the British Museum agreed to accept films of recent public events, in order to create a secure archive of the past for the future. In the press, articles imagined the experience of future historians watching the moving simulacra of the last years of the nineteenth century; of future generations seeing their dead forbears smiling out at them from the screen. This was the true power of film: its capacity to haunt the future with moving traces and fragments of the past.

This hubristic vision of an eternal and universal living picture of past events brought its inevitable nemesis. The future was uncertain and all the imperial pageantry of the Jubilee days could not prevent future ruin and downfall. Perhaps,

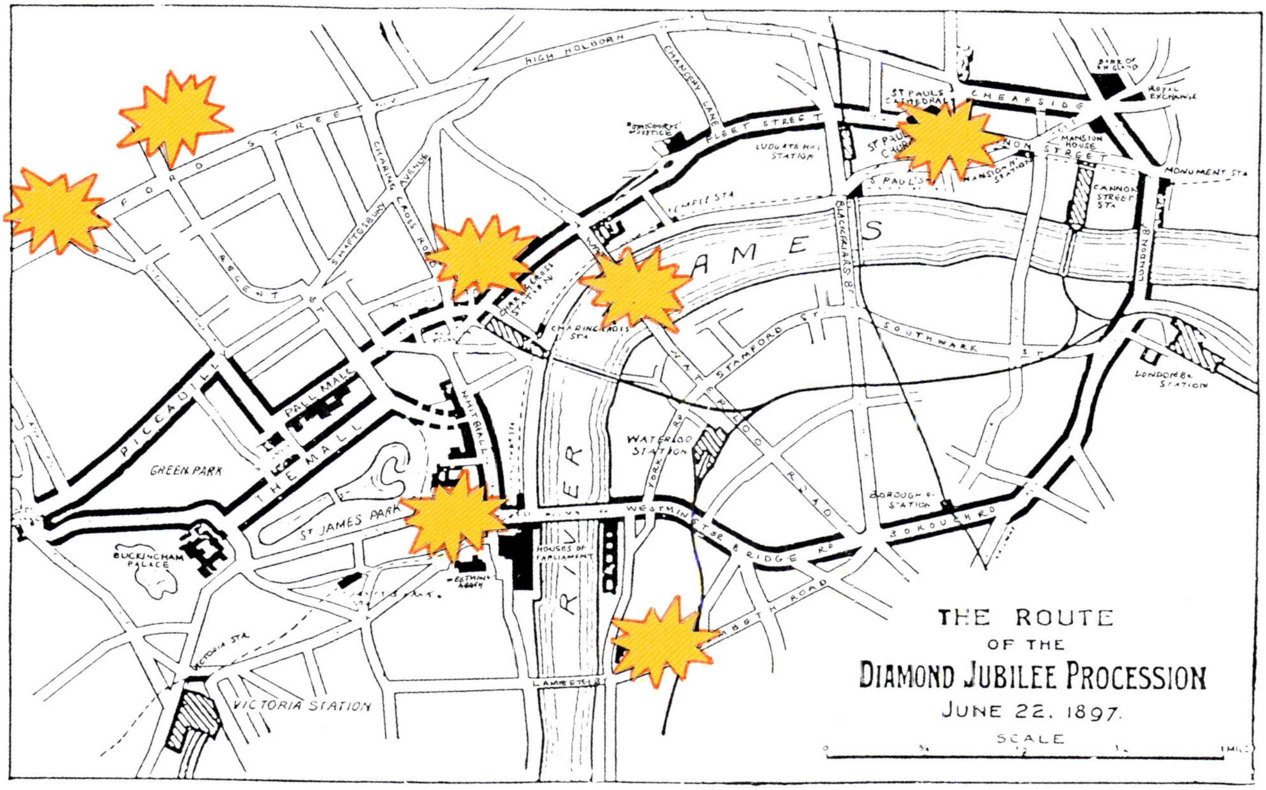

135 'The Route of Queen Victoria's Diamond Jubilee Procession, 22 June 1897'. With markings of Martian explosions from 'War of the Worlds', added by Lynda Nead.

the eponymous 'reader' also entertains these thoughts, as the latest findings of the American amateur scientist Percival Lowell are made public. From his observatory in Arizona in 1894, Lowell confirmed earlier reports that the dark markings seen on the surface of Mars were canals, artificial waterways constructed by intelligent beings and definite evidence of intelligent life on that planet.[73]

The reader turns from these pages and picks up the most recent issue of another journal, published in October 1897. It is *Pearson's Magazine* and in the latest instalment of H. G. Wells's 'War of the Worlds', London is described in the month of the Jubilee, devastated by the attacks of Martian firepower.[74] As film cameramen had recorded for posterity London decked in bunting and garlands of flowers for Victoria's Diamond Jubilee, readers of *Pearson's Magazine* could visualise the same streets, St Paul's cathedral itself, lying in ruins and choked with red Martian weed (plate 135). This was one horrifying conclusion to the sublime archive of images. The present was haunted by its fears of the future and the past would forever possess the future through its filmic preservation. Those extra-terrestrial viewers might not turn out to be as benign as the gentle spirit-traveller Lumen.

notes

introduction

1 'Where the Past Speaks', *New York Mail and Express*, 25 September 1897, as cited in *Biograph Bulletins 1896–1908*, compiled with an introduction and notes by Kemp R. Niver, Los Angeles: Locare Research Group, 1971, p. 28.

2 See Michel Serres, *Atlas*, Paris: Editions Juilliard, 1994, and Michel Serres and Bruno Latour, *Conversations on Science, Culture and Time*, trans. Roxanne Lapidus, Ann Arbor: University of Michigan Press, 1995. For an excellent discussion of Serres's metaphors of history see Steven Connor, 'Topologies: Michel Serres and the Shapes of Thought', *Anglistik*, XV, 2004, pp. 105–17, and www.bbk.ac.uk/english/skc/topologies.

1 velocities of the image c.1900

1 Alexander Bain, *The Senses and the Intellect* (1855), 4th edn, London: Longmans, Green and Co., 1894, p. 253.

2 *Punch* had made other suggestions for enhancing the visibility of pictures at Royal Academy shows; see e.g. 'How to Get a Little More Space for Pictures at the Royal Academy. Suggestion Gratis to the President and Council', *Punch*, 23 May 1900, p. 366, in which it was proposed that a trench be dug to create a new lower-ground tier of paintings and to make the ground level a viewing platform for the higher tiers.

3 For example the cartoon 'The Automatic Dentist Will No Doubt Follow the Amputation Machine', *Punch*, 23 April 1898, p. 191.

4 Walter Benjamin, 'The Work of Art in the Age of Mechanical Reproduction', *Illuminations*, ed. with an introduction by Hannah Arendt, trans. Harry Zohn, London: Fontana, 1973, p. 240.

5 Jay David Bolter and Richard Grusin, *Remediation: Understanding New Media*, Cambridge, Mass., and London: M.I.T. Press, 1999, p. 15.

6 On the history of the Ferris wheel see Norman D. Anderson, *Ferris Wheels: An Illustrated History*, Bowling Green, Ohio: Bowling Green State University Popular Press, 1992. For an account of the modern Ferris wheel as a contradictory manifestation of modernity see Paul Overy, 'Re-inventing the Wheel – Speed in Slow Motion: The London Eye (Millennium Wheel)', *Visual Culture in Britain*, IV, no. 2, 2003, pp. 21–40.

7 On the shift from a rhetoric of improvement to spectacular amusement in World Fairs see François Robichon, 'L'attraction, parergon des expositions universelles', in *Le livre des expositions universelles 1851–1989*, Paris: Union Centrale des Arts Décoratifs, 1983, pp. 315–28, and Lieven de Cauter, 'The Panoramic Ecstasy: On World Exhibitions and the Disintegration of Experience', *Theory, Culture and Society*, X, no. 4, 1993, pp. 1–23.

8 On the shift from spectator to participant through the mechanical attractions of the amusement parks see John F. Kasson, *Amusing the Million: Coney Island at the Turn of the Century*, New York: Hill and Wang, 1978, pp. 7–8.

9 For details of the *trottoir roulant* see *Harper's Guide to Paris and the Exposition of 1900*, London and New York: Harper and Bros., 1900, pp. 145, 189–90. See also Richard D. Mandell, *Paris 1900: The Great World's Fair*, University of Toronto Press, 1967, p. 63 and fig. 39, and *Le livre des expositions universelles*, p. 112.

10 Description given in *The Warwick Trading Company Ltd 1901 Catalogue*, p. 220, in its account of its film, 'Panoramic View of the Moving Sidewalk at the Paris Exposition' (no. 7513b). The experience of standing still on a moving sidewalk today is still occasionally one of impatience at being overtaken by pedestrians and of speeding up the process by walking on the moving belt.

11 On the history of the escalator see www.inventors.about.com/library/inventors/blescalator; www.otis.com/aboutotis/elevatorsinfo; Jason Goodwin, *Otis: Giving Rise to the Modern City*, Chicago: Ivan R. Dee, 2001, pp. 105–7, and illustration of a Manhattan street escalator *c.*1900.

12 See John H. Barr, *Kinematics of Machinery: A Brief Treatise on Constrained Motions of Machine Elements*, New York: John Wiley and Sons; London: Chapman and Hall, 1899, pp. 1–3, and Charles William MacCord, *Kinematics: A Treatise on the Modification of Motion, as Affected by the Forms and Modes of Connection of the Moving Parts of Machines*, New York: John Wiley and Sons, 1883, p. 3.

13 Einstein's Special Theory of Relativity was first published in 1905, the General Theory of Relativity in 1916. I shall not consider Einstein's radical reconceptualisation of space and time here. My argument is that Einstein's theories had not yet made an impact on the more established, practical sciences in the early years of the twentieth century. A helpful guide to the historical implications of the theory of relativity can be found in J. B. Kennedy, *Space, Time and Einstein: An Introduction*, Chesham: Acumen, 2003. See also Nick Huggett, ed., *Space from Zeno to Einstein: Classic Readings with a Contemporary Commentary*, Cambridge, Mass., and London: M.I.T. Press, 1999.

14 MacCord, *Kinematics*, p. 3; see also Barr, *Kinematics*, p. 3.

15 F. Reuleaux, *The Kinematics of Machinery: Outlines of a Theory of Machines*, trans. and ed. Alex B. W. Kennedy, London: Macmillan and Co., 1876, p. 19.

16 Ibid., p. 34.

17 Ibid., p. 22.

18 Barr, *Kinematics*, p. 13.

19 Charles William MacCord, *Velocity Diagrams: Their Construction and their Uses. Intended for All who are interested in Mechanical Movements*, New York: John Wiley and Sons; London: Chapman and Hall Ltd., 1901, pp. 1–2.

20 The best recent source on Marey is Marta Braun, *Picturing Time: The Work of Etienne-Jules Marey (1830–1904)*, Chicago and London: University of Chicago Press, 1992. For an account of Marey's photographic experiments in the context of motion pictures see Deac Rossell, *Living Pictures: The Origins of the Movies*, Albany: State University of New York Press, 1998, esp. pp. 31–42 and 48–54.

21 Illustrated in Braun, *Picturing Time*, p. 37, fig. 20.

22 There is an extensive literature on the history of optical devices; for a good recent source see Barbara Maria Stafford and Frances Terpak, *Devices of Wonder: From the World in a Box to Images on a Screen*, Los Angeles: Getty Research Institute, 2001.

23 A useful account of this notion and an alternative explanation are given in Joseph and Barbara Anderson, 'Motion Perception in Motion Pictures', in Teresa de Lauretis and Stephen Heath, eds, *The Cinematic Apparatus*, London and Basingstoke: Macmillan, 1980, pp. 76–95.

24 See e.g. C. Francis Jenkins, *Animated Pictures: An Exposition of Chronophotography, its Present Scientific Applications and Future Possibilities and of the Methods and Apparatus employed in the Entertainment of Large Audiences by Means of Projecting Lanterns to give the Appearance of Objects in Motion*, Washington, D.C.: C. Francis Jenkins, 1898, esp. p. 45. An important revision of 'persistence of vision' was given by Hugo Münsterberg, *The Photoplay: A Psychological Study*, New York and London: D. Appleton and Co., 1916.

25 On the phenomenon of visual flicker in early film see Bill Nichols and Susan J. Lederman, 'Flicker and Motion in Film', in de Lauretis and Heath, *Cinematic Apparatus*, pp. 96–105.

26 See the cameras advertised in the *Warwick Trading Co. Ltd 1901 Catalogue*, p. 10. Film companies in this period commonly produced catalogues giving a synopsis of every film and advertising them for sale.

27 Ibid., p. 18.

28 Jenkins, *Animated Pictures*, pp. 77–8.

29 The British film pioneer Cecil Hepworth recommended reversal: 'the effect is extremely funny. It is a variation of the usual order of things which, if confined to once in an evening, is sure to raise a laugh. Cecil M. Hepworth, *Animated Photography: The ABC of the Cinematograph. A Simple and Thorough Guide to the Projection of Living Photographs, with Notes on the Production of Cinematograph Negatives*, London: Hazell, Watson and Viney Ltd.,

1897, p. 87. The *Lantern Record*, 6 January 1899, p. 1, recommended soldiers marching and men diving as particularly suitable for reversal.

30 R. W. Paul's *Rough Sea at Dover* (Great Britain, 1895) was one of the hits of Edison's first screening and the *Warwick Trading Co. Ltd 1898 Catalogue* listed a number of 'sea films', including nos 5018 and 5022. See also *A Selected Catalogue of the Best and Most Interesting 'Hepwix' Films Manufactured Only by Hepworth & Co.*, London: 1903, p. 24: 'No. 124 "Breaking Waves" Of all the myriads of subjects which have come within the ken of the cinematographic lens, none is more beautifully shown than the breaking waves on the seashore.'

31 See Henry Peach Robinson's discussion of this issue in *Picture-Making by Photography*, London: Hazell, Watson and Viney Ltd., 1902, ch. XIII 'On Sea and Shore'.

32 For a helpful discussion of audience behaviour in relation to changes in film form and conditions of exhibition see Lise Shapiro Sanders, '"Indecent Incentives to Vice": Regulating Films and Audience Behaviour from the 1890s to the 1910s', in Andrew Higson, ed., *Young and Innocent? The Cinema in Britain 1896–1930*, Exeter: University of Exeter Press, 2002, pp. 97–110. See also David Robinson, *From Peep Show to Palace: The Birth of American Film*, New York: Columbia University Press, 1996.

33 The most frequently cited publication of this term is Tom Gunning, 'The Cinema of Attractions: Early Cinema, its Spectator and the Avant Garde', *Wide Angle*, VIII, nos 3–4, 1986, pp. 63–70. André Gaudreault has also developed this conceptualisation of early cinema in a number of articles; see e.g. 'Showing and Telling', in Thomas Elsaesser and Adam Barker, eds, *Early Cinema: Space, Frame, Narrative*, London: British Film Institute, 1990, pp. 274–81. For a helpful summary of revisionist approaches to narrative in early cinema see Lynne Kirby, *Parallel Tracks: The Railroad and Silent Cinema*, Exeter: University of Exeter Press, 1997, pp. 102–4.

34 See Gunning's own revision of the term in '"Now You See It, Now You Don't": The Temporality of the Cinema of Attractions', *Velvet Light Trap*, no. 32, Fall 1993, pp. 3–12, and the excellent historical argument given in Charles Musser, 'Rethinking Early Cinema: Cinemas of Attraction and Narrativity', *Yale Journal of Criticism*, VII, no. 2, 1994, pp. 203–33.

35 For a reading of Edwin S. Porter's film *Uncle Josh at the Moving Picture Show* (U.S., 1902) in terms of the spectator's assimilation of cinematic practice see Miriam Hansen, *Babel and Babylon: Spectatorship in American Silent Film*, Cambridge, Mass., and London: Harvard University Press, 1991, pp. 25–30.

36 This might seem the inevitable moment to introduce a discussion of Wolfgang Schivelbusch's much cited study *The Railway Journey: The Industrialization of Time and Space in the 19th Century* (Germany, 1977), Leamington Spa, Hamburg, New York: Berg, 1986. Schivelbusch argues that the experience of train travel produced a new kind of mobile, 'cinematic', perception. While acknowledging the significance of his work, this chapter moves beyond Schivelbusch to examine more closely the diverse concepts of velocity during this period and their relationships to visual media and modes of viewing.

37 Most histories of early cinema refer to the 'phantom ride' phenomenon. For an extended examination see Philip Codling, 'The Road becomes Alive: Moving towards an Understanding of the Phantom Ride', MA diss., British Film Institute and Birkbeck College, 1995, which informs my discussion. On the greater kinetic possibilities of images shot from a moving camera see Rudolf Arnheim, *Film as Art*, London: Faber and Faber, 1958, p. 154, and Arthur C. Danto, 'Moving Pictures', *Quarterly Review of Film Studies*, IV, no. 1, Winter 1979, pp. 15–19.

38 From the *Phonoscope*, August–September 1897, p. 6, as cited in Charles Musser, 'The Travel Genre in 1903–1904: Moving towards Fictional Narrative', *Iris*, II, no. 1, 1984, p. 53.

39 On the technical qualities of the Biograph see John Barnes, *The Rise of the Cinema in Great Britain: The Beginnings of the Cinema in England 1894–1901. Volume 2. Jubilee Year 1897*, London: Bishopsgate Press, 1983, p. 154; also Stephen Bottomore, 'The Panicking Audience?: Early Cinema and the "Train Effect"', *Historical Journal of Film, Radio and Television*, XIX, no. 2, 1999, pp. 187, 194. George R. Sims described a Biograph phantom ride film at the Palace in 'A Country Cousin's Day in Town', *Living London: Its Work and its Play, its Humour and its Pathos, its Sights and its Scenes*, 3 vols, London: Cassel and Co., 1902, II, p. 349.

40 *Era*, 30 October 1897, p. 19 as cited in Barnes, *Rise of the Cinema*, p. 145.

41 'At the Palace', *Punch, Or the London Charivari*, 6 August 1898, p. 57.

42 For an excellent and full account of Hale's Tours see Raymond Fielding, 'Hale's Tours: Ultrarealism in the Pre-1910 Motion Picture', in John L. Fell, ed., *Film before Griffith*, Berkeley, Los Angeles, London: University of California Press, 1983, pp. 116–30.

43 For an example of this earlier conception see David Brewster, *The Stereoscope: Its History, Theory and Construction*, London: John Murray, 1856, p. 41, fig. 56. Jonathan Crary has traced this new conception of seeing in relation to the work of Manet, Seurat and Cézanne in his outstanding study *Suspensions of Perception: Attention, Spectacle and Modern Culture*, Cambridge, Mass., and London: M.I.T. Press, 1999, to which I am indebted.

44 B. Joy Jeffries, *The Eye in Health and Disease. Being a Series of Articles on the Anatomy and Physiology of the Human Eye, and its Surgical and Medical Treatment*, Boston, Mass: Alexander Moore, 1871, p. 77.

45 On the impact of physiology on the development of British psychology see Kurt Danziger, 'Mid-Nineteenth-Century British Psycho-Physiology: A Neglected Chapter in the History of Psychology', in William R. Woodward and Mitchell G. Ash, eds, *The Problematic Science: Psychology in Nineteenth-Century Thought*, New York: Praeger, 1982, pp. 119–46.

46 On the history of psychology as a discipline see Woodward and Ash, *Problematic Science*; Robert Thomson, *The Pelican History of Psychology*, Harmondsworth: Penguin, 1968; Graham Richards, *Putting Psychology in its Place: An Introduction from a Critical Historical Perspective*, London and New York: Routledge, 1996.

47 Hermann von Helmholtz, *Treatise on Physiological Optics* (1867, rev. and enlarged 1910–11), ed. and trans. James P. C. Southall, 3 vols, Rochester, N.Y.: Optical Society of America, 1924–5. See R. Steven Turner, 'Helmholtz, Sensory Physiology and the Disciplinary Development of German Psychology', in Woodward and Ash, *Problematic Science*, pp. 147–66.

48 See Herbert Spencer, *The Principles of Psychology*, (1855), 3rd edn, 2 vols, London: Williams and Norgate, I, 1890, p. 404. In the following discussion I have concentrated on key texts that were republished throughout the nineteenth century; in the case of texts first published in the 1850s or 1860s, I have cited editions from the 1890s.

49 Bain, *Senses and the Intellect*, p. 252.

50 James Sully, *The Human Mind: A Text-Book of Psychology*, 2 vols, London: Longmans, Green and Co., 1892, I, pp. 237, 243–4.

51 William James, *The Principles of Psychology*, 2 vols, London: Macmillan and Co., 1890, II, p. 61.

52 Ibid., p. 173.

53 Ibid., p. 91. Other writers who examined this phenomenon included Spencer, *Principles*, I, p. 261; Silvanus P. Thompson, 'Optical Illusions of Movement', *Brain*, III, October 1880, pp. 291 and 296; James Sully, *Illusions: A Psychological Study*, London: C. Kegan Paul and Co., 1881, p. 57; Münsterberg, *Photoplay*, p. 61.

54 Sully, *Illusions*, pp. 50–51.

55 Thompson, 'Optical Illusions', pp. 289–98. See also the response to this research by Charles S. W. Cobbold, 'Observations on Certain Optical Illusions of Motion', *Brain*, IV, April 1881, pp. 75–81. Sully drew on Thompson's work in *Illusions*.

56 Spencer, *Principles*, II, p. 639.

57 James Sully, 'On the Possibility of a Science of Aesthetics', in *Sensation and Intuition: Studies in Psychology and Aesthetics*, London: Henry S. King and Co. 1874, pp. 336–72. Sully's essay on Burne-Jones's *The Mirror of Venus* is discussed in Kate Flint, *The Victorians and the Visual Imagination*, Cambridge: Cambridge University Press, 2000, ch. 9.

58 James Sully, 'Pleasure of Visual Form', *Mind: A Quarterly Review of Psychology and Philosophy*, n.s., XX, 18 April 1880, p. 185.

59 Grant Allen, *Physiological Aesthetics*, London: Henry S. King and Co., 1877, p. 2. See also Sully, 'Pleasure of Visual Form', p. 196, and Dr Colley March, 'Evolution and Psychology in Art', *Mind: A Quarterly Review of Psychology and Philosophy*, n.s., XX, October 1896, pp. 441–63.

60 See Münsterberg, *Photoplay*. On his work at Harvard see Matthew Hale Jr, *Human Science and Social Order: Hugo Münsterberg and the Origins of Applied Psychology*, Philadelphia: Temple University Press, 1980.

61 Hugo Münsterberg, *Psychology and Life*, London: Archibald Constable and Co., 1899, p. 152, from the ch. 'Psychology and Art', pp. 145–78.

62 For a biography of Lee see Peter Gunn, *Vernon Lee: Violet Paget 1856–1935*, London: Oxford University Press, 1964. See also Hilary

Fraser, 'Women and the Ends of Art History: Vision and Corporeality in Nineteenth-Century Critical Discourse', *Victorian Studies*, XLII, no. 1, autumn 1998, pp. 77–100. My thanks to Steven Connor for discussing his research on Lee's library, presently at the British Institute in Florence.

63 As cited in Gunn, *Vernon Lee*, p. 2.

64 Bernhard Berenson, *The Florentine Painters of the Renaissance: With an Index to their Works*, New York and London: G. P. Putnam's Sons, 1896, p. 4.

65 Ibid., p. 50.

66 Vernon Lee, review of Bernhard Berenson, *Florentine Painters*, in *Mind: A Quarterly Review of Psychology and Philosophy*, n.s., XVIII, April 1896, pp. 270–72. She continued her debate with Berenson in print in 'The Central Problem of Aesthetics' (1910), repr. in Vernon Lee and C. Anstruther-Thomson, *Beauty and Ugliness and Other Studies in Psychological Aesthetics*, London: John Lane, The Bodley Head, 1912, pp. 77–151.

67 V. Lee and C. Anstruther-Thomson, 'Beauty and Ugliness, I', *Contemporary Review*, LXXII, October 1897, pp. 544–69; 'Beauty and Ugliness, II', ibid., LXXII November 1897, pp. 669–88; repr. in Lee and Anstruther-Thomson, *Beauty and Ugliness*, pp. 156–239, in which Lee identified their separate contributions. Hereafter, page references to the 1912 reprint will be given in parentheses in the text.

68 A similar scanning of an image is given in Bain, *Senses*, p. 256. Of course, the concept of the eye 'reading' the image has been a staple of art historical method; see E. H. Gombrich, 'Moment and Movement in Art', *Journal of the Warburg and Courtauld Institutes*, XXVII, 1964, pp. 301–2.

69 See the questionnaire that they submitted to the Psychological Congress of 1901: Vernon Lee and C. Anstruther-Thomson, *Le rôle de l'élément moteur dans la perception esthétique visuelle. Mémoire et questionnaire soumis au quatrième congrès de psychologie*, Imola: Coopérative Typographique Edit, 1901.

70 'Aesthetic Responsiveness: Its Variations and Accompaniments. Extracts from Vernon Lee's Gallery Diaries, 1901–4', in Lee and Anstruther-Thomson, *Beauty and Ugliness*, pp. 241–350.

71 Lee, 'Central Problem', p. 137.

72 Münsterberg, *Photoplay*, p. 71.

2 the haunted gallery

1 On the statue as a living thing, stilled and needing to break free of its sculptural confinement, see Kenneth Gross, *The Dream of the Moving Statue*, Ithaca, and London: Cornell University Press, 1992.

2 On life and movement in the terminology of early cinema see Tom Gunning, 'The Ghost in the Machine: Animated Pictures at the Haunted Hotel of Early Cinema', *Living Pictures: The Journal of the Popular and Projected Image before 1914*, I, no. 1, 2001, pp. 3–17.

3 Sigmund Freud, 'The Uncanny', in *The Standard Edition of the Complete Psychological Works of Sigmund Freud*, trans. and ed. James Strachey, London: Hogarth Press and the Institute of Psycho-Analysis, XVII, 1955. Hereafter, page references to this edition will be given in parentheses in the text. In his essay, Freud acknowledges Ernest Jentsch's 1906 essay 'On the Psychology of the Uncanny'; Jentsch's work is discussed in Aura Satz, 'Puppets and Prosthesis', *New Formations*, special issue, 'The Prosthetic Aesthetic', no. 46, Spring 2002, pp. 103–18.

4 It is in this part of Freud's argument that he draws most heavily on Jentsch's argument, quoting his 1906 article concerning the uncanny, and 'doubts whether an apparently animate being is really alive; or conversely, whether a lifeless object might not be in fact animate' (p. 226).

5 Horace Walpole, *The Castle of Otranto: A Gothic Story*, 2nd edn, London: William Bathoe and Thomas Lownds, 1765, ch. 1.

6 For references to a number of these subsequent reworkings see David Eden, 'The Ancestors' Ancestor', in *Ruddygore: A Booklet to Commemorate the Centenary of the First Performance. 22 January 1887*, London: The Sir Arthur Sullivan Society, 1987, pp. 39–41.

7 Letter from Walpole to the Revd William Cole, 9 March 1765, quoted in C. D. Yonge, ed., *Letters of Horace Walpole*, 2 vols, London, Swann Sonnenschein and Co., 1891, II, p. 287.

8 On this phenomenon see Theodore Ziolkowski, *Disenchanted Images: A Literary Iconology*, Princeton, N.J.: Princeton University Press, 1977, p. 35, and Andreas Blühn and Louise Lippincott, *Light! The Industrial Age 1750–1900: Art and Science, Technology and Society*, London: Thames and Hudson, 2000, p. 122.

9 On various aspects of the history of

the magic lantern see Dennis Crompton, Richard Franklin and Stephen Herbert, eds, *Servants of Light: The Book of the Lantern*, London: The Magic Lantern Society, 1997; David Robinson, ed., *The Lantern Image: Iconography of the Magic Lantern 1420–1880. Supplement No. 1*, London: The Magic Lantern Society, 1997; Barbara Maria Stafford and Frances Terpak, *Devices of Wonder: From the World in a Box to Images on a Screen*, Los Angeles: Getty Research Institute, 2001.

10 The excitement and wonder of a magic lantern show performed by a skilful lanternist is still palpable today. I am grateful to meetings of the Magic Lantern Society for giving me the opportunity to be part of the audience at a number of such shows.

11 Memoirs of Alison Uttley, as cited in Lesley Gordon, *Peepshow into Paradise: A History of Children's Toys*, London: George G. Harrap and Co. Ltd, 1953, pp. 202–3.

12 'Un franc seulement et vous verrez des personnages grandeur nature s'agiter et vivre sous les yeux.' As cited in Elizabeth Ezra, *Georges Méliès: The Birth of the Auteur*, Manchester and New York: Manchester University Press, 2000, p. 1.

13 Walter Pater, *Studies in the History of the Renaissance*, London: Macmillan and Co., 1873, p. viii. Hereafter, page references will be given in parentheses in the text. For a good introduction to Pater's work see Laurel Brake, *Walter Pater*, Plymouth: Northcote House, 1994. I am grateful to Laurel Brake for her suggestions concerning the theme of animation in Pater's writing.

14 See Brake, *Pater*, pp. 44–5.

15 Walter Pater, 'Sebastian van Storck', *Imaginary Portraits*, London: Macmillan and Co., 1887, pp. 91–113. An outstanding account of the relationship of image and narrative in this story was given in S. Jöttkandt, 'Image, Metaphor, Action: Representing Walter Pater's "Sebastian van Storck"', paper delivered at 'Image and Text', Research Society for Victorian Periodicals 2004 Conference, University of Ghent, Belgium, July 2004. See the revised version in 'Effectively Equivalent: Walter Pater, "Sebastian van Storck", and the Ethics of Metaphor', *Nineteenth-Century Literature*, LX, no. 2, 2005, pp. 163–98.

16 See Henri Bergson, *Matter and Memory*, trans. Nancy Margaret Paul and W. Scott Palmer, London: Swann Sonnenschein and Co., 1911, pp. 178, 243.

17 For useful analysis of ekphrasis see Peter Wagner, ed., *Icons – Texts – Iconotexts: Essays on Ekphrasis and Intermediality*, Berlin and New York: Walter de Gruyter, 1996.

18 Bernadette Fort, 'Ekphrasis as Art Criticism: Diderot and Fragonard's 'Coresus and Callirhoe"', in ibid., p. 58.

19 Walter Pater, 'Denys L'Auxerrois', *Imaginary Portraits*, p. 88.

20 Walter Pater, 'A Novel by Mr Oscar Wilde' (*Bookman*, November 1891), repr. in J. Uglow, ed., *Walter Pater: Essays on Literature and Art*, London: Dent, 1973, pp. 142–5. The Poe story that Pater refers to is probably 'The Oval Portrait'; see *Three Tales by Edgar Allen Poe*, London: S. Wellwood, 1907, pp. 32–41.

21 Oscar Wilde, *The Picture of Dorian Gray*, London: Penguin, 1994, p. 166.

22 Ibid., p. 138.

23 Bernhard Berenson, *The Florentine Painters of the Renaissance. With an Index to their Works*, New York and London: G. P. Putnam's Sons, 1896, p. 55.

24 Vernon Lee and C. Anstruther-Thomson, *Beauty and Ugliness and Other Studies in Psychological Aesthetics*, London: John Lane, The Bodley Head, 1912, p 356. See also Lee's account of her visit to the Capitoline Museum on 10 April 1903 discussed in ch. 1, p. 40 above.

25 Ibid., p. 287. On Lee in the context of lesbian intellectualism in the late Victorian period see Burdett Gardner, *The Lesbian Imagination (Victorian Style): A Psychological and Critical Study of 'Vernon Lee'*, New York and London: Garland, 1987.

26 Vernon Lee, 'Amour Dure: Passages from the Diary of Spiridion Trepka', *Hauntings: Fantastic Stories*, London: William Heinemann, 1890, pp. 3–58; 'Oke of Okehurst; Or, The Phantom Lover', pp. 105–91.

27 Vernon Lee, 'Prince Alberic and the Snake Lady', *Pope Jacynth and Other Fantastic Tales*, London: Grant Richards, 1904, p. 41.

28 Vernon Lee, *Renaissance Fancies and Studies: Being a Sequel to Euphoria*, London: Smith, Elder and Co., 1895, p. 69.

29 Ovid, *Metamorphoses*, ed. with an introduction, trans. and notes by D. E. Hill, Warminster: Aris and Phillips Ltd., 1999, Book x, ll. 250–51. There are many interesting commentaries on Ovid's story; see e.g. David Freedberg, *The Power of Images: Studies in the History and Theory of Response*, Chicago and London: University of Chicago Press, 1989, pp. 340–44; John Elsner, 'Visual Mimesis and the Myth of the Real: Ovid's Pygmalion as

Viewer', *Ramus: Critical Studies in Greek and Roman Literature*, XX, no. 2, 1991, pp. 154–68.

30 See Nicholas Penny, 'Goddesses and Girls', *London Review of Books*, 2–29 December 1982, p. 20. For a helpful history of subsequent versions and interpretations of Ovid's story see Geoffrey Miles, ed., *Classical Mythology in English Literature: A Critical Anthology*, London and New York: Routledge, 1999, ch. 6.

31 Benjamin Tarnowsky, *The Sexual Instinct and its Morbid Manifestations from the Double Standpoint of Jurisprudence and Psychiatry* (1885), trans. W. C. Costello and Alfred Allinson, Paris: Charles Carrington, 1898, pp. 84–5.

32 See Havelock Ellis, *Studies in the Psychology of Sex*, 7 vols, Philadelphia: F. A. Davis, 1905, IV, *Sexual Selection in Man. I. Touch. II. Smell. III. Hearing. IV. Vision*, pp. 186–8; *Studies in the Psychology of Sex*, 4 vols, New York: Random House, 1936, III, pp. 11–12.

33 Ellis, *Studies*, 1905, p. 188.

34 On nineteenth-century versions of Pygmalion in which the figure returns to its marble state, see Gail Marshall, *Actresses on the Victorian Stage: Feminine Performance and the Galatea Myth*, Cambridge University Press, 1998, p. 23.

35 For analysis of the two series see Stephen Wildman, *Visions of Love and Life: Pre-Raphaelite Art from Birmingham Museums and Art Gallery*, Alexandria, Va.: Art Services International, 1995, pp. 301–9. For an interesting interpretation in relation to the erotics of artistic creativity see Caroline Arscott, 'Venus as Dominatrix: Nineteenth-Century Artists and their Creations', in Caroline Arscott and Katie Scott, eds, *Manifestations of Venus: Art and Sexuality*, Manchester and New York: Manchester University Press, 2000, pp. 109–25.

36 See Elsner, 'Visual Mimesis', pp. 155–7, and A. R. Sharrock, 'The Love of Creation', *Ramus: Critical Studies in Greek and Roman Literature*, XX, no. 2, 1991, pp. 170–71.

37 Pater, *Studies*, pp. 58, 65. For a reading of Michelangelo see Juergen Schulz, 'Michelangelo's Unfinished Works', *Art Bulletin*, LVII, 1975, pp. 366–73.

38 Normand's relentless completion of this figure included basing it on the *Venus de Milo* but reconstituting the arms of the classical statue. See Robert Upstone, catalogue entry for Ernest Normand, *Pygmalion and Galatea*, in Alison Smith, ed., *Exposed: The Victorian Nude*, London: Tate Publishing, 2001, p. 205.

39 The technique is described in Albert A. Hopkins, *Magic: Stage Illusions and Scientific Diversions including Trick Photography*, London: Sampson, Low, Marston and Co. Ltd., 1897, pp. 448–9, and in Walter E. Woodbury, *Photographic Amusements: Including a Description of a Number of Novel Effects obtainable with the Camera*, New York: Scovill and Adams, 1898, pp. 17–18.

40 For a detailed examination of the links between miraculous objects in early Christianity and myths of animation on the modern stage see Aura Satz, 'Off the Pedestal; On the Stage: Animation and De-animation in Art and Theatre', PhD thesis, Slade School of Fine Art, University College London, 2002.

41 The phrase is from Gail Marshall's account of uses of the sculptural metaphor on the Victorian stage, *Actresses*, p. 22.

42 Kenneth Clark, *The Nude: A Study in Ideal Art*, London: John Murray, 1956, esp. ch. V.

43 On the Hamiltons in Naples see I. Jenkins and K. Sloan, *Vases and Volcanoes: Sir William Hamilton and his Collection*, London: British Museum, 1996.

44 On the history of *tableaux vivants* see Richard D. Altick, *The Shows of London*, Cambridge, Mass., and London: Belknap Press of Harvard University Press, 1978, and Jack W. McCullogh, *Living Pictures on the New York Stage*, Epping, Essex: Bowker Publishing, 1981. On *tableaux* as domestic amusement see Mary Chapman, '"Living Pictures": Women and *Tableaux Vivants* in Nineteenth-Century American Fiction and Culture', *Wide Angle*, XVIII, no. 3, July 1996, pp. 22–52. In its music-hall context see Raymond Mander and Joe Mitchenson, *British Music Hall: A Story in Pictures*, London: Studio Vista, 1965.

45 On London County Council regulation of 'living picture' performances see Susan Pennybacker, '"It was not what she said but the way in which she said it": The London County Council and the Music Halls', in Peter Bailey, ed., *Music Hall: The Business of Pleasure*, Milton Keynes: Open University Press, 1986, pp. 120–40, and on the National Vigilance Association's attack see John Stokes, *In the Nineties*, New York and London: Harvester Wheatsheaf, 1989, pp. 76–82.

46 For an outstanding analysis of the interplay between suspended movement and mobility in *tableaux vivants* see Satz, 'Off the Pedestal', ch. 3, to which I am indebted.

47 G. J. Goodrick, *Tableaux Vivants and Living Waxworks, with Directions for Stage Management*,

London: Dean and Son, 1895, pp. 60 and 64, original emphasis.

48 The so-called 'Canova Pedestal' is discussed in McCullogh, *Living Pictures*, pp. 21 and 163 n. 6. On the Glyptorama see pp. 108, 112, 154–6.

49 Quoted in ibid., p. 108.

50 For a detailed discussion of the best arrangement and manipulation of curtains in amateur *tableaux vivants* see Goodrick, *Tableaux Vivants*, p. 43 and *passim*.

51 On Ducrow's life and career see A. H. Saxon, *The Life and Art of Andrew Ducrow and the Romantic Age of the English Circus*, Hamdon, Conn.: Archon Books, 1978.

52 Quoted in ibid., p. 152.

53 Roland Barthes, 'Diderot, Brecht, Eisenstein', in *Image–Music–Text*, selected and trans. Stephen Heath, London: Fontana, 1977, p. 70. See also Satz, 'Off the Pedestal', p. 83 and *passim*.

54 Edith Nesbit, 'The Ebony Frame', in *Fear*, London: Stanley Paul and Co., 1910, pp. 93–4. For a plot summary and descriptions of other stories of magic images see Ziolkowski, *Disenchanted Images*. For further references to fiction on this theme see Montague Summers, ed., *Victorian Ghost Stories*, London: Fortune Press, 1933.

55 W. S. Gilbert, *Pygmalion and Galatea: An Entirely Original Mythological Comedy in Three Acts*, London: Judd and Co., 1872. For discussion of Gilbert's treatment of the Pygmalion myth see Marshall, *Victorian Actresses*, pp. 56–63.

56 *Ruddigore* was first produced at the Savoy Theatre by D'Oyly Carte, January 1887. For the libretto see W. S. Gilbert, *Iolanthe and Other Operas*, with illustrations by W. Russell Flint, London: G. Bell and Sons Ltd., 1910, esp. Act II, pp. 144–54. For discussion of the haunted gallery scene see essays in *Ruddygore: A Booklet*. Note the spelling of the opera was originally *Ruddygore* but was changed for subsequent performances to *Ruddigore*. My thanks to Michael Symes for his help with research on this material.

57 Gilbert, *Iolanthe*, p. 148.

58 On pre-cinematic moving pictures see J. A. Sokalski, 'Living Motion Pictures: The Panoramic Stage and Pre-Cinematic Show Technology', *Living Pictures: The Journal of the Popular and Projected Image before 1914*, I, no. 2, 2001, pp. 59–68; Brigitte Peucker, *Incorporating Images: Film and the Rival Arts*, Princeton, N. J.: Princeton University Press, 1995.

59 See *Biograph Bulletins 1896–1908*, compiled with an introduction and notes by Kemp R. Niver, Los Angeles: Locare Research Group, 1971, p. 14.

60 See, e.g., 'Living Pictures' (American Mutoscope and Biograph Company, 1903), in ibid., p. 144.

61 See the catalogue description in *Urban and Eclipse Films*, London. Charles Urban Trading Co. Ltd., 1904–5, no. 1957.

62 '"Star" or Magical Films'. *Warwick Trading Co. Ltd 1901 Catalogue*, p. 60, no. 4156. The title is also advertised in Warwick's 1898 catalogue. Star Films was the name of Georges Méliès's production company.

63 The dismemberment of the female body in magic theatre and film is discussed at length in Lucy Fischer, 'The Lady Vanishes: Women, Magic, and the Movies', in John L. Fell, ed., *Film before Griffith*, Berkeley, Los Angeles, London: University of California Press, 1983, pp. 339–54, and will be considered later in this chapter.

64 From the *Warwick Trading Co. Ltd 1899 Catalogue*, no. 3059, as cited in John Barnes, *The Beginnings of the Cinema in England 1894–1901*. IV, *1899*, Exeter: University of Exeter Press, 1996, p. 230. For discussion of Smith's transformation films see Frank Gray, 'George Albert Smith's Visions and Transformations: The Films of 1898', in Simon Popple and Vanessa Toulmin, eds, *Visual Delights: Essays on the Popular and Projected Image in the 19th Century*, Trowbridge: Flicks Books, 2000, pp. 170–80.

65 My thanks to Jacqui Seargeant, Company Archivist of John Dewar and Sons Ltd., for kindly supplying material on the history of this campaign on which my discussion is based. The theme was also used in a proposal for an advertisement for Bovril in which a servant stands holding a tray of cups of Bovril in a statue gallery and the statues reach out for the cups; National Archives (Public Records Office), 16 February 1900, COPY 3/136, p. 30.

66 For a reference to this film see Richard Brown and Barry Anthony, *A Victorian Film Enterprise: The History of the British Mutoscope and Biograph Company, 1897–1915*, Trowbridge: Flicks Books, 1999, pp. 223–34 and 289. My thanks to Luke McKernan for his helpful comments on this film.

67 *Harry Potter and the Sorcerer's Stone* (Warner Bros, 2001); *Harry Potter and the Chamber of Secrets* (Warner Bros, 2002); *Harry Potter and*

the Prisoner of Azkaban (Warner Bros, 2004); *The Haunted Mansion* (Disney, 2003).

68 For an interesting account see Alex Owen, *The Darkened Room: Women, Power and Spiritualism in late 19th-Century England*, London: Virago, 1989. On spiritualism's relation to visual media see Tom Gunning, 'Phantom Images and Modern Manifestations: Spirit Photography, Magic Theater, Trick Films, and Photography's Uncanny', in Patrice Petro, ed., *Fugitive Images: From Photography to Video*, Bloomington and Indianapolis: Indiana University Press, 1995, pp. 42–71.

69 For an account of magic's critique and exposé of spiritualism see Dan North, ' "Exceedingly amusing, and in no way repulsive": Showmanship, Magic and Early Film', paper delivered at the conference of the AHRB Centre for Film and Television Studies at the University of Exeter, September 2002; see also his 'Special Effects and the Aesthetics of Illusion', PhD thesis, University of Exeter, 2003. From a different perspective, Harry Price, the psychical researcher, devoted his life to the exposure of fraudulent mediums and spirit photography; as seen in the exhibition 'The Magical Library of Harry Price: An Exhibition of Books, Archives and Artefacts from the Collection of a Psychic Investigator and Ghost Hunter', University of London Library, 19 April–30 October 2004.

70 See e.g. Professor Hoffmann, *Modern Magic: A Practical Treatise on the Art of Conjuring*, London: G. Routledge and Sons, 1874, which went through many editions into the 1920s. Harry Price Collection, University of London Library.

71 Hopkins, *Magic*, p. v.

72 Arprey Vere, *Ancient and Modern Magic: With Explanations of Some of the Best Known Tricks Performed by Messrs. Maskelyne and Cooke*, London: George Routledge and Sons, 1879, p. 95.

73 The term is used as the title for A. Roterberg, *The Modern Wizard*, Chicago: A. Roterberg, 1896.

74 The title of a chapter in ibid.

75 For a biography of Maskelyne and reproductions of related posters and printed material see www.ex.ac.uk/bill.douglas/Houdini.

76 Nevil Maskelyne and David Devant, *Our Magic: The Art in Magic. The Theory of Magic. The Practice of Magic.* London: George Routledge and Sons Ltd., 1911, p. 9.

77 Ibid., p. 22.

78 Ibid., p. 46. The entire passage is italicised in the original.

79 See George A. Jenness, *Maskelyne and Cooke: Egyptian Hall, London, 1873–1904*, Enfield: George A. Jenness, 1967, pp. 41–5.

80 From an advertisement for the Egyptian Hall in Charles Dickens, Jr, *Dickens's Dictionary of London*, London: Macmillan, 1879, as cited on www.victorianlondon.org/entertainment/magicians.

81 Hopkins, *Magic*, p. 376.

82 Ibid., p. 55.

83 See copies of the programme held in the Museum of London, Entertainment A1 file. My thanks to John Fisher and Michael Symes of the Magic Circle for their invaluable help and for allowing me access to the Magic Circle Library. Thanks also to Dan North for his generous suggestions for visual material.

84 The script of the blank-verse sketch, written by M. B. Spurr to accompany the illusion, is reproduced in David Devant, *Secrets of My Magic*, London: Hutchinson and Co. 1936, App. II. The relationship between magic spectacle and narrative is discussed in Dan North, 'Magic and Illusion in Early Cinema', *Studies in French Cinema*, 1, no. 2, 2001, pp. 70–79.

85 The illusion is explained by Devant in his chapter 'Famous Illusions Revealed', *Secrets*, pp. 90–91. See also S. H. Sharpe, *Devant's Delightful Delusions*, Pasadena, Cal.: Magical Publications, 1990, pp. 137–9, and David Devant, 'My Illusions', *Strand Magazine*, XLV, January 1913, pp. 24–33.

86 This point is also made in North, 'Magic and Illusion', pp. 72–3.

87 For a development of this theme see Erik Barnouw, *The Magician and the Cinema*, New York and Oxford: Oxford University Press, 1981.

88 Fischer, 'The Lady Vanishes', pp. 339–54. See also Linda Williams, 'Film Body: An Implantation of Perversions', in Philip Rosen, ed., *Narrative, Apparatus, Ideology: A Film Theory Reader*, New York: Columbia University Press, 1986, pp. 507–34, which revises a number of Fischer's arguments. Also on this theme Karen Beckmann, *Vanishing Women: Magic, Film and Feminism*, Durham, N.C.: Duke University Press, 2000.

89 Robert Paul, *The Hundred Best Animated Photography Films, in Every Variety of Subject*, London: 1900–01, p. 4. My thanks to Vanessa Toulmin for drawing this material to my attention.

90 For examples of trick films of this kind see 'The Artist's Dream: A Vision', *Warwick Trading Co. Ltd 1898 Catalogue*, no. 4165 (a Robert Houdin film); *His Masterpiece* (American Mutoscope and Biograph Company, 1903), listed in Kemp R. Niver, *Motion Pictures from the Library of Congress Paper Print Collection*, Berkeley and Los Angeles: University of California Press, 1967, p. 191, and Georges Méliès's *Delirium in a Studio*, 1907, described in John Frazer, *Artificially Arranged Scenes: The Films of Georges Méliès*, Boston, Mass.: G. K. Hall and Co., 1979, pp. 186–8.

91 Mary Ann Doane, *The Emergence of Cinematic Time: Modernity, Contingency and the Archive*, Cambridge, Mass., and London: Harvard University Press, 2002, p. 109.

92 For a suggestive discussion of early films of animators see Donald Crafton, 'Animation Iconography: The "Hand of the Artist"', *Quarterly Review of Film Studies*, IV, no. 4, Fall 1979, pp. 409–28.

93 See Niver, *Motion Pictures*, p. 5; Barnouw, *Magician*, p. 100.

94 *Urban and Eclipse Films*, 1904–5, no. 1964, n.p.

95 Titles taken from *1909 General Catalogue of Classified Subjects. 'Urban', 'Eclipse', 'Radios' Film Subjects, and 'Urbanora' Educational Series*, London: 1909, n.p., British Film Institute, National Film Archive.

96 Ibid., no. 2207.

97 Henri-Georges Clouzot used a similar technique in his film *Le Mystère Picasso* (1956). In this case, the paper was stretched upright, with the artist on one side of the screen and the camera on the other, so that Picasso's picture-making could be filmed with the marks appearing on the screen without the artist being visible. I discuss the significance of this technique in detail in 'Seductive Canvases: Visual Mythologies of the Artist and Artistic Creativity', *Oxford Art Journal*, XVIII, no. 2, 1995, pp. 59–69.

98 For more detailed accounts of Méliès's life see David Robinson, *Georges Méliès: Father of Film Fantasy*, London: Museum of the Moving Image, 1993; Frazer, *Artificially Arranged Scenes*, 1979; Elizabeth Ezra, *Georges Méliès: The Birth of the Auteur*, Manchester and New York: Manchester University Press, 2000.

99 See Robinson, *Georges Méliès*, p. 12.

100 See Ezra, *Georges Méliès*, pp. 28–30.

101 See Frazer, *Artificially Arranged Scenes*, pp. 75–6, and Ezra, *Georges Méliès*, pp. 51–2. See also Richard Abel, *The Ciné Goes to Town: French Cinema 1896–1914*, Berkeley, Los Angeles, London: University of California Press, 1994, pp. 61–4.

102 The phrase the 'king of cinema' is Ezra's, *Georges Méliès*, p. 58.

103 Other films that depict animated poster figures include *The Poster Girls and the Hypnotist* (1899), *A Midnight Phantasy* (1903) and *Kiss Me* (1904), all from the American Mutoscope and Biograph Company, and *Barnum's Handbag* (Walturdaw, 1904).

104 From Georges Méliès, *Mes mémoires*, 1938, as cited in Frazer, *Artificially Arranged Scenes*, p. 51. The incident is also described and quoted in Robinson, *Georges Méliès*, pp. 46–7.

105 My thanks to Lawrence Steigrad Fine Arts, New York, for their generous help with this image.

106 On the opening of the Haunted Gallery in 1918 see Ernest Law, *The Haunted Gallery at Hampton Court and its Associations with Shakespeare*, London: Hugh Rees Ltd., 1918; for earlier histories by Law see *A Short History of Hampton Court*, London: George Bell and Sons, 1897; *The Royal Gallery at Hampton Court Illustrated*, London: George Bell and Sons, 1898; *The New Historical Guide to Hampton Court with a New Historical Catalogue of the Pictures*, London: George Bell and Sons, 1900.

107 Maxim Gorky, review of the Lumière programme at the Nizhni-Novgorod Fair, originally published in *Nizhegorodskil listok*, 4 July 1896, reprinted in Colin Harding and Simon Popple, eds, *In the Kingdom of Shadows: A Companion to Early Cinema*, London: Cygnus Arts; Cranbury, N.J.: Fairleigh Dickinson University Press, 1996, pp. 5 and 6.

3 animating the everyday

1 Henri Lefebvre, *The Production of Space* (1974), trans. Donald Nicholson-Smith, Oxford: Basil Blackwell, 1991, p. 207. Andrey Tarkovsky, *Sculpting in Time: Reflections on the Cinema*, trans. Kitty Hunter-Blair, London and Boston: Faber and Faber, 1989, p. 68.

2 On the marvel of cinema for its first audiences see Tom Gunning's influential article 'The Cinema of Attractions: Early Cinema, its Spectator and the Avant Garde', *Wide Angle*, VIII, nos 3–4, 1989, 63–70.

3 Leo Charney, 'In a Moment: Film and the Philosophy of Modernity', in Leo Charney and Vanessa Schwartz, eds, *Cinema and*

the Invention of Modern Life, Berkeley, Los Angeles, London: University of California Press, 1995, p. 279. For a similar approach see Ben Singer, 'Modernity, Hyperstimulus, and the Rise of Popular Sensationalism', *Cinema and the Invention of Modern Life*, p. 73.

4 Georg Simmel, 'The Metropolis and Mental Life', in Kurt H. Wolff, ed., *The Sociology of Georg Simmel*, New York: Free Press, 1964, p. 410. For discussion of Simmel's work see David Frisby and Mike Featherstone, *Simmel on Culture: Selected Writings*, London: Sage, 1997; David Frisby, *Fragments of Modernity: Theories of Modernity in the Work of Simmel, Kracauer and Benjamin*, London: Polity Press, 1985; Mike Featherstone, ed., *Georg Simmel (A Theory, Culture and Society Special Issue)*, London: Sage, 1991; David Frisby, *Simmel and Since: Essays on Georg Simmel's Social Theory*, London and New York: Routedge, 1992.

5 Giuliana Bruno, *Streetwalking on a Ruined Map: Cultural Theory and the City Films of Elvira Notari*, Princeton, N.J.: Princeton University Press, 1993, p. 54. Simmel's essay is cited in a number of recent publications in relation to early cinema; see e.g. Lynne Kirby, *Parallel Tracks: The Railroad and Silent Cinema*, Exeter: University of Exeter Press, 1997, p. 144; Charney and Schwartz, *Cinema and the Invention of Modernity*, p. 2; and Clark Arnwine and Jesse Lerner, eds, 'Cityscapes: Introduction', *Wide Angle*, XIX, no. 4, October 1997, p. 2.

6 I discuss the statistical representation of London more fully in *Victorian Babylon: People, Streets and Images in Nineteenth-Century London*, New Haven and London: Yale University Press, 2000, pp. 14–16.

7 George R. Sims, ed., *Living London: Its Work and its Play, its Humour and its Pathos, its Sights and its Scenes*, 3 vols, London: Cassell and Co., 1901–3. For a concise account of Sims's work and of his urban motifs in particular see www.chriswillis.freeserve.co.uk/georgesims.

8 Mrs E. T. Cook, *Highways and Byways in London*, London: Macmillan and Co. Ltd., 1902, pp. 54 and 74. See also Laurence Gomme, *London in the Reign of Queen Victoria 1837–1897*, London: Blackie and Son Ltd., 1898.

9 Cook, *Highways and Byways*, pp. 18–19.

10 Henry James, 'London', *Essays in London and Elsewhere*, London: James R. Osgood, McIlvaine and Co., 1893, p. 32.

11 The technical developments in photography are given in most general histories of the medium. See, e.g., Helmut Gernsheim, in collaboration with Alison Gernsheim, *The History of Photography from the Earliest Use of the Camera Obscura in the Eleventh Century up to 1914*, London, New York, Toronto: Oxford University Press, 1955, and Beaumont Newhall, *The History of Photography from 1839 to the Present*, London: Secker and Warburg, 1982. For a nineteenth-century account of hand cameras see 'Detective and Hand Cameras. Issued as a Supplement to *Photography*, compiled and written by Walter D. Welford', *Photography*, 23 May 1889, pp. 3–11.

12 Quoted in Newhall, *History of Photography*, p. 489. The social and legal implications of instantaneous photography are discussed in the following excellent articles: Robert E. Mensel, '"Kodakers Lying in Wait": Amateur Photography and the Right of Privacy in New York, 1885–1915', *American Quarterly*, XLIII, no. 1, March 1991, pp. 24–45, and Tom Gunning, 'Embarrassing Evidence: The Detective Camera and the Documentary Impulse', in Jane M. Gaines and Michael Renov, eds, *Collecting Visible Evidence*, Minneapolis and London: University of Minnesota Press, 1999, pp. 46–64.

13 The emergence in the nineteenth century of forms of public behaviour which assumed both a physical and emotional distance is described in Richard Sennett, *The Fall of Public Man*, New York: W. W. Norton, 1976.

14 See e.g. 'Vanishing London', *British Journal of Photography* (hereafter *BJP*), 10 March 1899, p. 147.

15 The implications of the embodied viewing of stereoscopic photography are fully considered in Linda Williams, 'Corporealized Observers: Visual Pornographies and the "Carnal Density of Vision"', in Patrice Petro, ed., *Fugitive Images: From Photography to Video*, Bloomington and Indianapolis: Indiana University Press, 1995, pp. 3–41, and are discussed in chapter 5 below in the context of the representation of the moving body in this period.

16 Walter D. Welford, *The Hand Camera and how to use it*, London: Iliffe, Sons and Sturmey Ltd., 1899, p. 79. See also *The Photographer's Indispensable Handbook: A Complete Cyclopaedia upon the Subject of Photographic Apparatus, Material and Processes*, compiled by Walter D. Welford, London: Iliffe and Sons, 1887, p. 60, and *Photographic Times*, XXVI, July 1895, p. 63. The popularity of street scenes among hand-camera photographers is demonstrated by the

appearance in photographic society exhibitions of special sections devoted to 'Street and Town Life' or 'Street Characters and Incidents of Street Life'. See Roy Flukinger, Larry Schaaf and Standish Meacham, *Paul Martin: Victorian Photographer*, London: Gordon Fraser, 1978, p. 35.

17 On the limitations of studio and earlier outdoor photography in the context of instantaneous photography see 'Hints on Portraiture. Expression. By Joseph Mahlstick', *Amateur Photographer*, 17 July 1885, p. 234; Benjamin Wyles, 'Outdoor Portraiture and Groups', *Amateur Photographer*, 2 October 1885, pp. 406–7; 'Portraiture and Pose', *Photography*, 8 August 1889, pp. 461–2.

18 'The maxim to be observed in all street work is secrecy.' Welford, *Hand Camera and how to use it*, p. 81.

19 Advertisement in *The British Journal Photographic Almanac and Photographer's Daily Companion*, London: H. Greenwood, 1889, p. 763.

20 Women were targeted in terms of instantaneous photography's technical simplicity; its portability made it ideal for tourists on cycling tours. See Bill Jay, *Cyanide and Spirits: An Inside-Out View of Early Photography*, Munich: Nazraeli Press, 1991, pp. 219–58.

21 Walter D. Welford, *The Hand Camera Manual: A Beginner's Guide to Photography in its Connection with the Hand Camera*, London: L. Upcott Gill, 1893, p. 6.

22 Ibid., pp. 74–5.

23 Welford, *Hand Camera and how to use it*, p. 86.

24 See Peter Stallybrass and Allon White, *The Politics and Poetics of Transgression*, London: Methuen, 1986, pp. 2–3.

25 On the low status of commercial photography in the period see Elizabeth Anne McCauley, *Industrial Madness: Commercial Photography in Paris 1848–1871*, New Haven and London: Yale University Press, 1994.

26 On technology as prosthesis see Tim Armstrong, *Modernism, Technology and the Body: A Cultural Study*, Cambridge: Cambridge University Press, 1998.

27 'Spirit of the Times', *Photography*, 30 July 1891, p. 480; original emphasis.

28 'The Obtrusive Amateur', *Amateur Photographer*, 25 September 1885, p. 397.

29 'A Point of Law', *Photographic Times*, XXVI, 1895, p. 375.

30 'Hand Cameras. I', *Photography*, 16 April 1891, p. 242.

31 'A New Terror', *Photographic News*, 11 August 1899, p. 498.

32 'The Protection of the Public', *BJP*, 14 July 1899, p. 438, which appeals to decorum. Correspondence in the *Daily News* and the *Daily Telegraph* in 1895 called for a new law; see Jay, *Cyanide*, pp. 230–31. The debate in America and, specifically, the ground-breaking academic article on privacy by Warren and Brandeis in 1890 is discussed in illuminating detail in Mensel, 'Kodakers', pp. 24–5.

33 The situation in relation to copyright and photography following the Fine Arts Copyright Act, 1862, is discussed in Walter Arthur Copinger, *The Law of Copyright in Works of Literature and Art: Including that of the Drama, Music, Engraving, Sculpture, Painting, Photography, and Designs*, 4th edn by J. M. Easton, London: Stevens and Haynes, 1904. An action for libel by an individual against a camera club for taking an instantaneous photograph without consent while in a public thoroughfare is reported and discussed in the *BJP*, 16 December 1898, p. 809; 23 December 1898, p. 818; 3 February 1899, p. 75; 10 March 1899, p. 154; 14 April 1899, pp. 225–6.

34 English common law has continued to treat images as a question of property rather than privacy although the Human Rights Act of 1998 has begun to shift this principle. My thanks to Costas Douzinas for discussion on this subject.

35 'Persecuted by Photography', *BJP*, 14 July 1899, p. 435; 21 July 1899, pp. 450–51. See also Stephen Bottomore, 'Dreyfus and Documentary', *Sight and Sound*, LIII, no. 4, Autumn 1984, pp. 290–93.

36 For biographical accounts of Martin see e.g. Gernsheim, *History of Photography*, p. 342, and Flukinger et al., *Paul Martin*, *passim*.

37 Paul Martin, *Victorian Snapshots: Illustrated from Contemporary Photographs*, London: Country Life Ltd, 1939, p. 19.

38 Ibid., p. 22.

39 *BJP*, 23 December 1898, p. 818.

40 Paul Martin, 'Blocked-Out Lantern Slides', *Amateur Photographer*, 6 November 1896, p. 374.

41 Ibid., p. 375.

42 T. C. Hepworth, *The Camera and the Pen*, London: Percy Lund Humphries and Co. Ltd, 1897, p. 29. T. C. Hepworth was the father of Cecil Hepworth, a leading figure in British early silent cinema.

43 On the use of local crowd scenes as openers for film shows see Vanessa Toulmin, Patrick Russell and Simon Popple, eds, *The Lost World*

of Mitchell and Kenyon: Edwardian Britain on Film, London: British Film Institute, 2004.

44 Sims, *Living London*, 1901, I, p. 3.

45 Asa Briggs, *Mass Entertainment: The Origins of a Modern Industry*, Adelaide: Griffin Press, 1960, p. 9.

46 For an indication of the early popularity of film for all classes of society see 'Notes and News', *Amateur Photographer*, 10 April 1896, p. 314, on the cinematograph at the Empire Theatre.

47 An Empire Theatre programme is reproduced in John Barnes's classic study, *The Beginnings of the Cinema in England 1894–1901*. 1, *1894–1896*, Exeter: Exeter University Press, 1998, p. 101. The Museum of London also has an excellent collection of London music-hall and theatre programmes from the period.

48 See advertisements for Paul's Theatrograph and Animatograph in the *Era*, e.g. 30 May 1896 and 13 June 1896, which are referred to in Colin Sorensen, *London on Film: 100 Years of Filmmaking in London*, London: Museum of London, 1996, p. 14. Paul's marketing techniques in this year are discussed in Frank Gray, 'Robert Paul in 1896: Innovation, Success and Wonder', in Claire Dupré la Tour, André Gaudreault and Roberta Pearson, eds, *Le cinéma au tournant du siècle* (*Cinema at the Turn of the Century*), Quebec: Editions nota bene, 1999, pp. 337–45.

49 On the attraction for audiences of local actuality films see Robert C. Allen, 'Contra the Chaser Theory', in John L. Fell, ed., *Film before Griffith*, Berkeley, Los Angeles, London: University of California Press, 1983, p. 109.

50 The literature on the Lumière cinema is now extensive; for discussion of Lumière actuality cinema see e.g. Robert C. Allen, 'Vitascope/Cinématographe: Initial Patterns of American Film Industrial Practice', in Fell, *Film before Griffith*, pp. 144–52; Barnes, *Beginnings of Cinema*. 1, *1894–1896*, pp. 87–107 and 267–72; John Barnes, 'Filming Scenes in the United Kingdom for the Cinématographe Lumiére', in Christopher Williams, ed., *Cinema: The Beginnings and the Future. Essays marking the Centenary of the First Film Show projected to a Paying Audience in Britain*, London: University of Westminster Press, 1996, pp. 60–62; Erik Barnouw, *Documentary: A History of the Non-Fiction Film*, Oxford and New York: Oxford University Press, 1974; Richard M. Barsam, *Non-Fiction Film: A Critical History*, Bloomington and Indianapolis: Indiana University Press, 1992; Noël Burch, *Life to Those Shadows*, trans. and ed. Ben Brewster, London: British Film Institute, 1990. On the question of narrative and Lumière actuality films see Marshall Deutelbaum, 'Structural Patterning in the Lumière Films', in Fell, *Film before Griffith*, pp. 299–310; André Gaudreault, 'Film, Narrative, Narration: The Cinema of the Lumière Brothers', trans. Rosamund Howe, in Thomas Elsaesser and Adam Barker, eds, *Early Cinema: Space, Frame, Narrative*, London: British Film Institute, 1990, pp. 68–75; Dai Vaughan, 'Let There be Lumière', in ibid., *Early Cinema*, pp. 63–7; and Alan Williams, 'The Lumière Organization and Documentary Realism', in Fell, *Film before Griffith*, pp. 153–61.

51 There is limited information on the complex question of film distribution in its early years. Some general material on the Lumière company is given in Barnouw, *Documentary*. My thanks to Luke McKernan of the British Universities Film and Video Council for sharing his outstanding knowledge of the early film industry with me.

52 Allen, 'Vitascope/Cinématographe', p. 151. For discussion of the relationships between the Lumière Cinématographe and their earlier experiments with instantaneous photography see Tom Gunning, 'New Thresholds of Vision: Instantaneous Photography and the Early Cinema of Lumière', in Terry Smith, ed., *Impossible Presence: Surface and Screen in the Photogenic Era*, Chicago: Chicago University Press, 2001, pp. 71–99.

53 A list of Lumière films photographed in the United Kingdom between 1896–7 is given in Appendix 2 of Barnes, *Beginnings*. The choice of London subjects from the Warwick Trading Company, a British film company of the period, can be seen in Barnes's Appendix 3.

54 For tourist itineraries of London in the late 1890s see editions of *Cook's Handbook for London*, London and New York: Thomas Cook and Son, and K. Baedecker, *London and its Environs: Handbook for Travellers*, Leipzig and London: Karl Baedecker.

55 *Era*, 1 August 1896, p. 16. John Barnes discusses the Lumière local actuality films including this one in 'Filming Scenes in the United Kingdom', pp. 60–62.

56 The interior space of the Empire Theatre was the subject of intense fantasy and social debate in precisely this period. Mrs Ormiston Chant, a leading figure in the women's social purity movement, led an attack on

the moral behaviour of individuals in the promenade at the Empire and forced its closure for a period. See Sally Ledger and Roger Luckhurst, eds, *The Fin de Siècle: A Reader in Cultural History, c. 1880–1900*, Oxford and New York: Oxford University Press, 2000, pp. 69–72.

57 Roland Barthes, *Camera Lucida: Reflections on Photography* (*La chambre claire*, 1980), trans. Richard Howard, London: Flamingo, 1984, p. 26 and *passim*.

58 Mark-Paul Meyer, 'Moments of Poignancy: The Aesthetics of the Accidental and the Casual in Early Nonfiction Film', in Daan Hertogs and Nico de Klerk, eds, *Uncharted Territory: Essays on Early Nonfiction Film*, Amsterdam: Stichting Nederlands Filmmuseum, 1997, pp. 51–60. My thanks to Stephen Herbert for his helpful comments on the significance of the punctum in early silent film.

59 G. R. Baker quoted in Steve Humphries, *Victorian Britain through the Magic Lantern: Illustrated by Lear's Magic Lantern Slides*, London: Sidgwick and Jackson, 1989, p. 170.

60 See Burch, *Life to Those Shadows*, p. 17: 'these images carry inscribed in them the need to be seen and reseen'.

61 Tarkovsky, *Sculpting in Time*, pp. 63, 113, 117; original emphasis.

62 Tom Gunning describes the relationship between the stability of the frame and the contingencies of the events depicted as mesmerising; see 'From the Kaleidoscope to the X-Ray: Urban Spectatorship, Poe, Benjamin and *Traffic in Souls* (1913)', *Wide Angle*, XIX, no. 4, October 1997, p. 35. See also his excellent discussion of framing and viewpoint in 'Before Documentary: Early Nonfiction Films and the "View" Aesthetic', in Hertogs and de Klerk, *Uncharted Territory*, pp. 9–24.

63 See Barnes, 'Filming Scenes in the United Kingdom', p. 60.

64 Cook, *Highways*, p. 285.

65 'With a hand camera', *BJP*, 1 August 1902, p. 606.

66 Cecil M. Hepworth, *Animated Photography: The ABC of the Cinematograph. A Simple and Thorough Guide to the Projection of Living Photographs, with Notes on the Production of Cinematograph Negatives*, London: Hazell, Watson and Viney Ltd, 1897, p. 97. On the aesthetics of actuality films in this period see Stephen Bottomore, 'Shots in the Dark: The Real Origins of Film Editing', in Elsaesser and Barker, *Early Cinema*, pp. 104–13.

67 For Henri Bergson's work on time as continuity see *Creative Evolution* (*L'évolution créative*, 1907), trans. Arthur Mitchell, London: Macmillan and Co., 1911, and *Matter and Memory* (*Matière et mémoire*, 1896), trans. Nancy Margaret Paul and W. Scott Palmer, London: Swann Sonnenschein and Co., 1911. For discussion of Bergson in relation to moving photography see Marta Braun, *Picturing Time: The Work of Etienne-Jules Marey (1830–1904)*, Chicago and London: Chicago University Press, 1992, pp. 278–81.

68 Gaston Bachelard, *The Dialectic of Duration* (*La dialectique de la durée*, 1950), trans. and annotated by Mary McAllester Jones, introduction by Cristina Chimisso, Manchester: Clinamen Press, 2000, pp. 19–20. For different workings of the notion of rhythm analysis see Henri Lefebvre and Catherine Régulier, 'Le projet rythmanalytique', *Communications*, XLI, no. 2, 1985, pp. 191–9; Lefebvre, *Production of Space* (*La production de l'espace*, 1974); Henri Lefebvre, *Eléments de rythmanalyse: introduction à la connaissance des rythmes*, Paris: Editions Syllepse, 1992. A selection of essays from the last publication are translated in *Writings on Cities: Henri Lefebvre*, selected, trans. and introduced by Eleonore Kofman and Elizabeth Lebas, Oxford: Blackwell, 1996. See also Michel de Certeau, *The Practice of Everyday Life*, trans. Steven Rendall, Berkeley, Los Angeles, London: University of California Press, 1984.

69 See e.g. 'Through the Fire', *Answers*, 31 December 1898, p. 143, in which a film of a fire rescue enables the reconciliation of a son and father. My thanks to Dr Chris Willis for this reference. On the exposure of adultery through the cinematograph see 'The "Indiscretions" of a Cinematograph', *Photographic News*, 7 July 1899, p. 418.

70 Sigmund Freud, *The Standard Edition of the Complete Psychological Works of Sigmund Freud. Trans. from the German under the General Editorship of James Strachey. In collaboration with Anna Freud. Assisted by Alix Strachey and Alan Tyson. Volume VI* (1901): *The Psychopathology of Everyday Life*, London: Hogarth Press and the Institute of Psycho-Analysis, 1960, p. 176.

71 Contemporary responses to the lifelike qualities of actuality films are discussed in Richard Crangle, '"Astounding Actuality and Life": Early Film and the Illustrated Magazine in Britain', in Dupré la Tour, Gaudreault and Pearson, *Le Cinéma*, pp. 93–102. The deathly aspect of the photographic image is famously described in Barthes, *Camera Lucida*. Laura

Mulvey considers Barthes's work in relation to the uncanny in 'The Index and the Uncanny', in Carolyn Bailey Gill, ed., *Time and the Image*, Manchester and New York: Manchester University Press, 2000, pp. 139–48.

72 Maxim Gorky, review of the Lumière programme at the Nizhni-Novgorod Fair, as published in *Nizhegorodski listok*, 4 July 1896, trans. Leda Swan, in Jay Leyda, *Kino: A History of the Russian and Soviet Film*, 3rd edn, Princeton, N.J.: Princeton University Press, 1983, pp. 407–8.

4 paintings, films and fast cars

1 William Ernest Henley, *A Song of Speed*, London: David Nutt, 1903, p. 13.

2 Michel Serres and Bruno Latour, *Conversations on Science, Culture and Time*, trans. Roxanne Lapidus, Ann Arbor: University of Michigan Press, 1995. Hereafter, page references will be given in parentheses in the text.

3 This point has been well argued in Carolyn Marvin, *When Old Technologies were New: Thinking about Electric Communication in the Late Nineteenth Century*, Oxford and New York: Oxford University Press, 1988, p. 8 and *passim*.

4 For an extremely useful recent biography of Herkomer see Lee MacCormick Edwards, *Herkomer: A Victorian Artist*, Aldershot and Brookfield, Vt: Ashgate, 1999. Older biographies are also informative; see A. L. Baldry, *Hubert von Herkomer R. A.: A Study and a Biography*, London: George Bell and Sons, 1901; J. Saxon Mills, *Life and Letters of Sir Hubert Herkomer: A Study in Struggle and Success*, London: Hutchinson, 1923.

5 See Hubert von Herkomer, *The Herkomers*, 2 vols, London: Macmillan and Co. Ltd, 1911, and David Setford, 'Herkomer – A Passion for Work', in *A Passion for Work: Sir Hubert von Herkomer 1849–1914*, Watford Museum, Watford Borough Council, 1982, pp. 3–4.

6 Hubert von Herkomer, *Five Lectures delivered to the Students of the Royal Academy*, London: privately printed, 1900, cited in Setford, 'Herkomer', pp. 10–11.

7 See e.g. Julian Treuherz, *Hard Times: Social Realism in Victorian Art*, London: Lund Humphries, in association with Manchester City Art Galleries, 1987, for which Herkomer's painting provides the title and cover image.

8 For a well illustrated account of Lululaund see Baldry, *Herkomer*, pp. 102–14.

9 See Hubert von Herkomer, *My School and My Gospel*, London: Archibald Constable and Co. Ltd, 1908, pp. 1–5.

10 Herkomer, *The Herkomers*, II, p. 60. Hereafter, page references will be given in parentheses in the text.

11 Herkomer, *My School*, p. 15.

12 For a more detailed consideration of Herkomer's drama see John Stokes, *Resistible Theatres: Enterprise and Experiment in the Late Nineteenth Century*, London: Paul Elek Books Ltd, 1972, pp. 69–110.

13 Herkomer, *My School*, pp. 155–6. For Herkomer's principles of theatrical staging see also 'The Pictorial Music-Play', *Magazine of Art*, XII, 1889, p. 316.

14 Herkomer, *My School*, pp. 151 and 210.

15 Herkomer, *The Herkomers*, II, p. 43. See Hubert von Herkomer, *An Idyl: A Pictorial-Music Play*, London and New York: Novello, Ewer and Co., n.d.

16 A. Wallace Rimington, *Colour-Music: The Art of Mobile Colour*, London: Hutchinson and Co., 1912. See Luke McKernan, 'From the Archive: A New Art: Colour-Music. A Paper Read at St. James's Hall on 6 June 1895 by A. Wallace Rimington', *Living Pictures*, II, no. 2, 2003, pp. 69–71, and Michael Pritchard, 'Correspondence regarding A. Wallace Rimington and Colour Music', *Early Popular Visual Culture*, XIII, no. 1, May 2005, p. 109.

17 Hubert von Herkomer, letter to the *Daily Telegraph*, 21 December 1912, p. 9.

18 The most detailed account of Herkomer's film-making is Michael Pritchard, *Sir Hubert von Herkomer and his Film-Making in Bushey 1912–1914*, Bushey: Bushey Museum Trust and ALLM Books, 1987; but see also the short section in Edwards, *Herkomer*, pp. 121–3. On Herkomer's film studio see Peter Pitt, 'The Oldest Studio', *Films and Filming*, no. 343, March 1983, p. 30.

19 'The Rise of the Film', *Sphere*, 2 August 1913, p. 138.

20 This figure is given in Low Warren, 'Herkomer's Last Work', *Kinematograph and Lantern Weekly*, 14 May 1914, p. 6. Edwards refers to seven completed films, *Herkomer*, p. 122.

21 J. Saxon Mills, *The Old Wood Carver from the Cinematograph Film conceived and produced by Sir Hubert von Herkomer, R.A. and Siegfried Herkomer*, London: Stanley Paul and Co., 1913 – a film narrative with more than fifty still photographs.

22 Low Warren, 'A Great Artist's Appreciation of the Kinematograph', *Kinematograph and Lantern Weekly*, 26 December 1912, pp. 904–5.

23 From an interview in 1912, cited in Warren, 'Herkomer's Last Work', p. 6.

24 On the growth of cinema in Britain in this period see Nicholas Hiley, '"Nothing More than a Craze": Cinema Building in Britain from 1909 to 1914', in Andrew Higson, ed., *Young and Innocent? The Cinema in Britain 1896–1930*, Exeter: Exeter University Press, 2002, pp. 111–27, and Luke McKernan, '"A Fury for Seeing": London Cinemas and their Audiences, 1905–1914', paper delivered at Postgraduate Research Series, Birkbeck College, 5 May 2005.

25 *Daily Telegraph*, 21 December 1912, p. 9.

26 These debates are discussed in Peter Bailey, *Leisure and Class in Victorian England: Rational Recreation and the Contest for Control 1830–1885*, London: Routledge and Kegan Paul, 1978.

27 On film censorship in this period see Lise Shapiro Sanders, '"Indecent Incentives to Vice": Regulating Films and Audience Behaviour from the 1890s to the 1910s', in Higson, *Young and Innocent?*, pp. 97–110. The 1909 Cinematograph Act dealt with safety regulations, although its scope was not limited to this area.

28 For a history of the BBFC see James C. Robertson, *The British Board of Film Censors: Film Censorship in Britain, 1896–1950*. London: Croom Helm, 1985.

29 *The Times*, 9 April 1913, p. 11. I am grateful to Luke McKernan's discussion of this article in '"A Fury for Seeing"'.

30 Advertisement (n.d.) for Herkomer Films by his agents, the Tyler Film Company. Collection of Bushey Museum Trust.

31 'The Old Wood Carver', *Bioscope*, 2 October 1913, p. 57.

32 *Kinematograph and Lantern Weekly*, 2 April 1914, p. 3, and 14 May 1914, p. 6.

33 *The Times*, 1 April 1914, p. 10.

34 On the pictorialism of British cinema see Andrew Higson, *Waving the Flag: Constructing a National Cinema in Britain*, Oxford: Clarendon Press, 1995, and Christine Gledhill, *Reframing British Cinema 1918–1928: Between Restraint and Passion*, London: British Film Institute, 2003.

35 Frederick A. Talbot, *Practical Cinematography and its Applications*, London: William Heinemann, 1913, p. 247.

36 See cuttings from the archives of the Bushey Museum Trust. My thanks to Bryen Wood and Grant Longman for their help with this material.

37 Kristin Ross, *Fast Cars, Clean Bodies: Decolonization and the Reordering of French Culture*, Cambridge, Mass., and London: M.I.T. Press, 1995, p. 38; original emphasis.

38 Ibid., p. 39. See also Stephen Kern, *The Culture of Time and Space 1880–1914*, London: Weidenfeld and Nicolson, 1983, p. 118.

39 'An Act to Amend the Law with respect to the use of Locomotives on Highways', *Public General Acts*, 59 & 60 Vict. (1896), ch. 36, pp. 343–5. See also Sean O'Connell, *The Car and British Society: Class, Gender and Motoring 1896–1939*, Manchester and New York: Manchester University Press, 1998.

40 A. B. Filson Young, *The Complete Motorist: Being an Account of the Evolution and Construction of the Modern Motor-Car; with Notes on the Selection, Use, and Maintenance of the Same; and on the Pleasures of Travel upon the Public Roads*, London: Methuen and Co., 1904, p. xxiii.

41 Ibid., p. 311.

42 Rudyard Kipling quoted in ibid., p. 286.

43 Lady Jeune, June 1902, quoted in ibid., p. 272.

44 Ibid., p. 317.

45 See A. B. Filson Young, *The Happy Motorist: An Introduction to the Use and Enjoyment of the Motor Car*, London: E. Grant Richards, 1906, p. 15, and James John Hissey, *Untravelled England*, London: Macmillan and Co., 1906, p. 104.

46 Alfred C. Harmsworth, *Motors and Motor-Driving*, London: Longmans, Green and Co., 1902, p. 348.

47 *Country Life Illustrated. The Journal for all Interested in Country Life and Pursuits*, 1, no. 1, January 1897.

48 Patrick Wright, *On Living in an Old Country: The National Past in Contemporary Britain*, London: Verso, 1985, p. 2. See also Michael Bommes and Patrick Wright, '"Charms of Residence": The Public and the Past', in Richard Johnson *et al.*, eds, *Making Histories: Studies in History-Writing and Politics*, London: Hutchinson in association with the Centre for Contemporary Cultural Studies, 1982, pp. 253–302; Higson, *Waving the Flag*, pp. 41–50; and O'Connell, *Car and British Society*, pp. 150–84.

49 Harmsworth, *Motors and Motor-Driving*, p. 344.

50 Hissey, *Untravelled England*, pp. 6 and 162.

51 James John Hissey, *An English Holiday with Car and Camera*, London: Macmillan and Co., 1908, p. 8. See also p. 55: 'we drove slowly in a sort of daydream, for though a motor car

can go faster than any horse, it can go as slowly as its owner wishes'.

52 Ibid., p. 337. For a cumbersome poem celebrating the thrill of motor speed see W. E. Henley's *A Song of Speed*, quoted at the beginning of this chapter and dedicated to Alfred Harmsworth.

53 Hissey, *English Holiday*, p. 162. See also his *The Road and the Inn*, London: Macmillan and Co., 1917, p. vii.

54 'Junius the Younger', 'The Motorist and Traveller Portraits: Hubert von Herkomer R.A.', *Motorist and Traveller*, 19 April 1905, p. 429.

55 Ibid. This description may bring to mind the later, but now more familiar, figure of the 'Spirit of Ecstasy', or 'Flying Lady', which was used as the figurehead for the Rolls-Royce from 1911; see Martin Bennett, *Rolls-Royce: The History of the Car*, Oxford: Oxford Illustrated Press, 1973, pp. 5–7.

56 Edwards reports that the design was also 'struck as a silver medal to be awarded as a trophy for the Motor Union of Great Britain and Ireland', *Herkomer*, p. 131. The car was identified as a 1905 Daimler limousine and 'impressed Daimlers enough to use it as a publicity poster'. Barry Pladdys, 'Art and Automobiles', *Driving Member*, XXXV, no. 8, January–February 1999, pp. 18–19.

57 Filson Young, *Complete Motorist*, p. 257. See also *The Autocar Handbook: A Guide to the Motor Car*, 2nd edn, London: Iliffe and Sons Ltd, 1908, pp. 173–4.

58 Herkomer, *The Herkomers*, p. 62.

59 Setford, 'Herkomer', p. 10. See also Lee MacCormick Edwards, '"The Moving Picture is *the* thing of the Future": Hubert von Herkomer, British Film Pioneer', paper delivered to the College Art Association Conference, Boston, Mass., February 2002.

60 Hubert von Herkomer, 'The Motorhood', *Globe*, 12 August 1904, cited in Setford, 'Herkomer', p. 10.

61 For further discussion of this metaphor see Tom Gunning, 'From the Kaleidoscope to the X-Ray: Urban Spectatorship, Poe, Benjamin and *Traffic in Souls* (1913)', *Wide Angle*, XIX, no. 4, 1977, pp. 25–61.

62 First published as Jean Baudrillard, *Le système des objets*, Paris: Editions Gallimard, 1968; *The System of Objects*, trans. James Benedict, London and New York: Verso, 1996, p. 66. The translation I cite here is from Ross, *Fast Cars*, p. 21.

63 See Baudrillard, *System of Objects*, p. 112.

64 On spectatorship in early film see Tom Gunning, 'The Cinema of Attraction: Early Film, its Spectator and the Avant Garde', *Wide Angle*, VIII, nos 3–4, 1986, pp. 63–70, and Miriam Hansen, *Babel and Babylon: Spectatorship in American Silent Film*, Cambridge, Mass., and London: Harvard University Press, 1994, esp. pp. 23–89.

65 Filson Young, *Complete Motorist*, p. 317.

66 Hissey, *Untravelled England*, p. 9. Hereafter, page references will be given in parentheses in the text.

67 Max Pemberton, *The Amateur Motorist*, London: Hutchinson and Co., 1907, p. 13.

68 Hissey, *Untravelled England*, p. 427.

69 Hissey, *The Road*, p. 84.

70 On Tate's 'Motoring' sketch see Raymond Mander and Joe Mitchenson, *British Music Hall: A Story in Pictures*, London: Studio Vista, 1965, fig. 166, and www.rfwilmut.clara.net/musichll/tate.

71 Cecil M. Hepworth, *Animated Photography: The ABC of the Cinematograph. A Simple and Thorough Guide to the Projection of Living Photographs, with Notes on the Production of Cinematograph Negatives*, London: Hazell, Watson and Viney Ltd, 1897, pp. 83–7. For a brief biography of Hepworth see Stephen Herbert and Luke McKernan, eds, *Who's Who of Victorian Cinema*, London: British Film Institute, 1996, pp. 64–5.

72 See John Barnes, *The Beginnings of the Cinema in England 1894–1901*. V, *1900*, Exeter: University of Exeter Press, 1997, p. 130, and *Cinema 1900–1906: Filmography*. II, Brussels: Fédération Internationale des Archives du Film, 1982, p. 24, F10.

73 Barnes, *Beginnings*, V, pp. 26 and 164, and *Cinema 1900–1906*, p. 26, F14.

74 See Barnes, *Beginnings*, V, p. 26.

75 See Rachel Low and Roger Manvell, *The History of the British Film*: I, *1896–1906*, London: George Allen and Unwin Ltd, 1948, p. 80, and *Cinema 1900–1906*, pp. 70–71, F118. John Barnes refers to another film by Paul, now lost, called *On a Runnaway Motor Car through Piccadilly Circus*, 1899, filmed from a motor cab as it negotiates the London streets, *The Beginnings of the Cinema in England 1894–1901*. IV, *1899*, Exeter: University of Exeter Press, 1996, p. 16.

76 This image was also disseminated in the illustrated press; see 'A Quiet Sunday in Our Village', *Punch, Or the London Charivari*, 6 June 1906, p. 412, pl. 27, in which all the motifs of obsessed drivers, wreckage, dust and pollution of rural life are present.

77 Figures taken from 'Notes of the Week', *Motorist and Traveller*, 9 August 1905, p. 7.
78 On Herkomer's film entertainments at Lululaund see Pritchard, *Hubert von Herkomer*, pp. 13–14.
79 Serres and Latour, *Conversations*, p. 58.

5 strip: moving bodies in the 1890s

1 Maurice Blanchot, *The Gaze of Orpheus and Other Literary Essays,* trans. Lydia Davis, New York: Station Hill, 1981, p. 75.
2 I discuss this in greater detail and in the context of changing attitudes to obscenity in *The Female Nude: Art, Obscenity and Sexuality*, London and New York: Routledge, 1992.
3 On photography and nineteenth-century prosecutions for obscenity see Simon Popple, 'Indecent Exposures: Photography, Vice and the Moral Dilemma in Victorian Britain', *Early Popular Visual Culture*, III, no. 2, September 2005, pp. 113–33.
4 For a meticulous consideration of this narrative see Stephen Bottomore, 'The Panicking Audience?: Early Cinema and the "Train Effect"', *Historical Journal of Film, Radio and Television*, XIX, no. 2, 1999, pp. 177–216. Bottomore has also traced the dissemination of this narrative in caricatures of the period; see *I Want to See This Annie Mattygraph: A Cartoon History of the Coming of the Movies*, Gemona: Le Giornate del cinema muto, *c.*1995.
5 Bottomore, *Annie Mattygraph*, p. 44.
6 See Tom Gunning, 'The Cinema of Attractions: Early Film, its Spectator and the Avant Garde' *Wide Angle*, VIII, nos 3–4, 1986, pp. 63–70; 'An Aesthetic of Astonishment: Early Film and the (In)credulous Spectator', *Art and Text*, no. 34, Spring 1989, pp. 31–45.
7 On the history of nineteenth-century optical devices see Deac Rossell, *Living Pictures: The Origins of the Movies*, Albany, N.Y.: State University of New York Press, 1998, and Virgilio Tosi, *Cinema before Cinema: The Origins of Scientific Cinematography*, London: British Universities Film and Video Council, 2006.
8 See Jonathan Crary, *Techniques of the Observer: On Vision and Modernity in the Nineteenth Century*, Cambridge, Mass., and London, M.I.T. Press, 1992.
9 Ibid., p. 150.
10 Albert E. Osborne, *Why Man has used Pictures and A Comparison between the Telephone and the Stereoscope*, New York and London: Underwood and Underwood, 1904, p. 4; original emphasis.
11 Oliver Wendell Holmes, 'The Stereoscope and Stereoscopic Photographs', cited in ibid., p. 30.
12 Osborne, *Why Man has used Pictures*, p. 33.
13 M. S. Emery, 'Russia through the Stereoscope', in *Articles on the Underwood Travel System as applied to Various Countries*, New York and London: Underwood and Underwood, 1905, p. 22.
14 Charles Baudelaire, 'The Modern Public and Photography', in A. Trachtenberg, ed., with notes by Amy Weinstein Meyers, *Classic Essays on Photography*, New Haven, Conn.: Leete's Island Books, 1980, p. 87; my emphasis.
15 'About Animated Photography', *Photographic Times*, XXX, no. 10, October 1898, p. 460.
16 Linda Williams, 'Corporealized Observers: Visual Pornographies and the "Carnal Density of Vision"', in Patrice Petro, ed., *Fugitive Images: From Photography to Video*, Bloomington and Indianapolis: Indiana University Press, 1995, p. 17.
17 For an excellent illustrated history of peepshows see Richard Balzer, *Peepshows: A Visual History*, New York: Harry N. Abrams, 1998.
18 Jean-Paul Sartre, *Being and Nothingness: An Essay on Phenomenological Ontology*, trans. Hazel E. Barnes, London: Methuen and Co. Ltd., 1958, p. 259. For a helpful commentary on this episode see www.bbk.ac.uk/english/skc.corridors.
19 As cited in Richard Brown and Barry Anthony, *A Victorian Film Enterprise: The History of the British Mutoscope and Biograph Company, 1897–1915*, Trowbridge: Flicks Books, 1999, p. 97.
20 Vivian Sobchak, *The Address of the Eye: A Phenomenology of Film Experience*, Princeton, N.J.: Princeton University Press, 1992, p. 133.
21 M. Merleau-Ponty, *The Phenomenology of Perception*, trans. Colin Smith, London and New York: Routledge, 1962, p. 235.
22 Linda Williams, *Hard Core: Power, Pleasure and the 'Frenzy of the Visible'*, London: Pandora, 1990, esp. ch. 2, and 'Corporealized Observers'; Gertrud Koch, 'The Body's Shadow Realm', *October*, no. 50, Fall 1989, pp. 3–29; Giuliana Bruno, 'Spectatorial Embodiments: Anatomies of the Visible and the Female Bodyscape', *Camera Obscura: A Journal of Feminism and Film Theory*, special issue, 'Imaging Technologies, Inscribing Science', ed. Paula

A. Treichler and Lisa Cartwright, no. 28, 1992, pp. 239–61.

23 Bruno, 'Spectatorial Embodiments', p. 242.

24 Compare Walter Benjamin's analogy of the painter and the magician with the cameraman and the surgeon in 'The Work of Art in the Age of Mechanical Reproduction', *Illuminations*, ed. and with an introduction by Hannah Arendt, trans. Harry Zohn, London: Fontana, 1973, pp. 235–6.

25 Williams, *Hard Core*. On Muybridge's sequence photography see Stephen Herbert, ed., *Eadweard Muybridge: The Kingston Museum Bequest*, Hastings: The Projection Box in association with Kingston Museum and Heritage Service, 2005, and Phillip Prodger, *Time Stands Still: Muybridge and the Instantaneous Photography Movement*, New York: Oxford University Press in association with the Iris and B. Gerald Cantor Center for Visual Arts at Stanford University, 2003.

26 Examples of sexually explicit films before *c.*1915 are rare. A selection of films made in 1905–25 was compiled in *Polissons et Galipettes* (France, 2002), shown at the London Film Festival in 2002, although few of the films included were made in the early years. See also Al Di Lauro and Gerald Rabkin, *Dirty Movies: An Illustrated History of the Stag Film 1915–1970*, New York and London: Chelsea House, 1976.

27 See Marta Braun, *Picturing Time: The Work of Etienne-Jules Marey (1830–1904)*, Chicago and London: University of Chicago Press, 1992, p. 241.

28 This film is now attributed to Esmé Collings. See Simon Brown, 'Early Cinema in Britain and the Smoking Concert Film', *Early Popular Visual Culture*, III, no. 2, September 2005, p. 173.

29 The essays in the special issue, 'Vice and Immorality in Popular Victorian Culture', *Early Popular Visual Culture*, III, no. 2, September 2005, are especially relevant to this subject.

30 *BJP*, 15 December 1899, p. 786.

31 'A Censor Needed', *Photographic News*, 8 December 1899, p. 790.

32 My thanks to Dr Vanessa Toulmin for drawing Race's journals to my attention and to Dr Ann Featherstone for sharing her material with me. See also Ann Featherstone, '"There is a peep-show in the market": Gazing at/in the journals of Sydney Race', *Early Popular Visual Culture*, III, no. 1, May 2005, pp. 43–57.

33 From the journal of Sydney Race, Nottingham Archives M24, 480/A/14. Thanks to Ann Featherstone for her transcription and permission to use this material.

34 See Brown, Early Cinema', and his lecture 'Victorian Erotic Cinema', Tate Britain, 21 November 2001. My thanks to Simon Brown for discussing this material with me.

35 R. W. Paul, C. M. Hepworth and W. G. Barker, 'Before 1910: Kinematograph Experiences', Proceedings of the British Kinematograph Society, no. 38, London, 1936, p. 8.

36 *Warwick Trading Company Ltd 1901 Catalogue*, London: Warwick Trading Company, 1901, p. 62.

37 Other films in this period drew on the strip for narrative structure; see *From Showgirl to Burlesque Queen* (American Mutoscope and Biograph Company, 1903), *Pull Down the Curtains, Susie* (American Mutoscope and Biograph Company, 1904) and *Trapeze Disrobing Act* (1901). See also Judith Mayne, 'Uncovering the Female Body', in John Fell, ed., *Before Hollywood: Turn-of-the-Century American Film*, New York: Hudson Hills Press in association with the American Federation of Arts, 1987, pp. 63–7. Cecil M. Hepworth refers to a film of this subject shot at the Alhambra in *Came the Dawn: Memories of a Film Pioneer*, London: Phoenix House, 1951, p. 61.

38 Roland Barthes, *Mythologies*, selected and trans. Annette Lavers, London: Jonathan Cape, 1972, p. 84.

39 There is a limited analytical literature on striptease. For general histories see Richard Wortley, *A Pictorial History of Striptease: 100 Years of Undressing to Music*, London: Octopus, 1976; Jessica Glasscock, *Striptease: From Gaslight to Spotlight*, New York: Harry N. Abrams, 2003; and, more interestingly, Franck Evrard, *Effeuillages romanesques: essai sur la representation littéraire et culturelle*, Saint-Genouph: A.-G. Nizet, 1997.

40 Peter Brooks, *Body Work: Objects of Desire in Modern Narrative*, Cambridge, Mass., and London: Harvard University Press, 1993, p. 19.

41 On the history of women's underclothes in this period see C. Willett and Phillis Cunnington, *The History of Underclothes*, London: Michael Joseph, 1951; Elizabeth Ewing, *Dress and Undress: A History of Women's Underwear*, London: B. T. Batsford, 1978; David Kunzle, *Fashion and Fetishism: A Social History of the Corset, Tight-Lacing and Other Forms of Body-Sculpture in the West*, Ottowa: Rowman and

Littlefield, 1982; Alain Corbin, 'Backstage', in Michelle Perrot, ed. *A History of Private Life: IV, From the Fires of Revolution to the Great War*, trans. Arthur Goldhammer, Cambridge, Mass., and London: Belknap Press of Harvard University Press, 1990, pp. 457–667; Marianne Thesander, *The Feminine Ideal*, London: Reaktion Books, 1997.

42 Mrs Eric Pritchard, *The Cult of Chiffon*, London: Grant Richards, 1902, pp. 20–22.

43 Jonathan Crary, *Suspensions of Perception: Attention, Spectacle, and Modern Culture*, Cambridge, Mass., and London, 1999, p. 93.

44 Kunzle, *Fashion and Fetishism*, p. 31.

45 Sigmund Freud, 'Three Essays on the Theory of Sexuality (1905)', in *The Standard Edition of the Complete Psychological Works*, trans. and gen. ed. James Strachey. In collaboration with Anna Freud, VII (1901–5), London: Hogarth Press and the Institute of Psycho-Analysis, 1964, p. 153.

46 Valerie Steele, *The Corset: A Cultural History*, New Haven and London: Yale University Press, 2001, p. 132.

47 See the description of reversal techniques in 'Lantern Mems.', *Lantern Record*, 6 January 1899, p. 1.

48 Steele, *Corset*, p. 129.

49 See, for instance, the experimental psychology of Hugo Münsterberg at Harvard University and in his published work from *Psychology and Life*, London: Archibald Constable and Co., 1899, to *The Photoplay: A Psychological Study*, New York and London: D. Appleton and Co., 1916, which are discussed in chapter 1 above.

50 Hepworth, *Came the Dawn*, p. 61.

51 'Kinetography', *Photogram*, IV, no. 39, March 1897, p. 79.

52 From *The Times*, 3 August 1899, p. 12, cited in Bottomore, *Annie Mattygraph*, p. 38.

53 See Antonia Lant's excellent and suggestive article 'Haptical Cinema', *October*, no. 74, Fall 1995, pp. 45–73.

54 Adolf von Hildebrand, *The Problem of Form in Painting and Sculpture* (1893), trans. and rev. with the author's cooperation by Max Meyer and R. M. Ogden, New York: G. E. Stechert and Co., 1907.

55 Alöis Riegl, *Problems of Style: Foundations for a History of Ornament* (1893), trans. E. Kain, with introduction by David Castriota and preface by Henri Zerner, Princeton, N. J: Princeton University Press, 1992; 'Late Roman or Oriental?', in Gert Schiff, ed., *German Essays on Art History: Winckelmann, Burckhardt, Panofsky, and Others*, New York: Continuum, 1988, pp. 173–90. See also Margaret Iverson, *Alöis Riegl: Art History and Theory*, Cambridge, Mass., and London: M.I.T. Press, 1993. For an interesting recent reformulation of 'haptic visuality' see Laura U. Marks, *The Skin of the Film: Intercultural Cinema, Embodiment and the Senses*, Durham, N.C., and London: Duke University Press, 2000.

56 James Sully, *The Human Mind: A Text-Book of Psychology*, 2 vols, London: Longmans, Green and Co., 1892, I, p. 244.

6 lumen and the celestial archive of images

1 [Felix Eberty], *The Stars and the Earth: Or, Thoughts upon Space, Time and Eternity*, 2 parts, London: H. Baillière 1846, Part 1, pp. 27–8 and 36.

2 This painting is a smaller version of the picture shown at the New Gallery in 1903 and now in the Art Gallery of Ontario, Toronto.

3 For recent literature on G. F. Watts see Veronica Franklin Gould, *G. F. Watts: The Last Great Victorian*, New Haven and London: Yale University Press, 2004; Veronica Franklin Gould, ed., *The Vision of G. F. Watts (1817–1904)*, Compton, Surrey: Watts Gallery, 2004; Colin Trodd and Stephanie Brown, eds, *Representations of G. F. Watts: Art Making in Victorian Culture*, Aldershot: Ashgate, 2004.

4 'Astro-Photography', *Photographic Notes*, 15 November 1857, p. 417.

5 Alfred H. Fison, *Recent Advances in Astronomy*, London: Blackie and Son Ltd, 1898, pp. 13 and 15. See also Walter W. Bryant, *A History of Astronomy*, London: Methuen and Co., 1907, p. 323. On the discovery of the spiral structure of the stars see David Dewhirst and Michael Hoskin, 'The Message of Starlight: The Rise of Astrophysics', in Michael Hoskin, ed., *The Cambridge Illustrated History of Astronomy*, Cambridge: Cambridge University Press, 1997, pp. 256–343.

6 Mary Seton Watts cited in *The Age of Rossetti, Burne-Jones and Watts: Symbolism in Britain 1860–1910*, London: Tate Gallery, 1997, p. 280, cat. no. 134; Gould, *Vision of G. F. Watts*, p. 89, cat. no. 115.

7 Ibid. and Gould, *G. F. Watts*, p. 328.

8 Marcel Proust, *In Search of Lost Time*. I, *Swann's Way* (1913), trans. C. K. Scott Mon-

crieff and Terence Kilmartin, rev. D. J. Enright, London: Vintage, 2002, pp. 8 and 9.

9 For a 'long history' of 'technomancy' see Barbara Maria Stafford's excellent essay 'Revealing Technologies/Magical Domains', in Barbara Maria Stafford and Frances Terpak, *Devices of Wonder: From the World in a Box to Images on a Screen*, Los Angeles: Getty Research Institute, 2001, pp. 1–142.

10 Seton Watts cited in Gould, *G. F. Watts*, p. 328; Gould, *Vision of G. F. Watts*, p. 89; *Age of Rossetti*, p. 280.

11 Ann Thomas, 'Capturing Light: Photographing the Universe', in Ann Thomas, ed., *Beauty of Another Order: Photography in Science*, New Haven and London: Yale University Press in association with the National Gallery of Canada, Ottawa, 1997, p. 187. See also Jennifer Tucker, *Nature Exposed: Photography as Eyewitness in Victorian Science*, Baltimore and London: Johns Hopkins University Press, 2006.

12 R. M. McCreary, 'Newspaper Astronomy', *Popular Astronomy*, VI, no. 2, April 1898, p. 103.

13 E. E. Barnard, 'The Development of Photography in Astronomy', *Popular Astronomy*, VI, no. 8, October 1898, pp. 425–55.

14 See Thomas, *Beauty*, p. 191; Dewhirst and Hoskin, 'Message of Starlight', p. 271.

15 On the *Carte du Ciel* project see Peter Whitfield, *The Mapping of the Heavens*, London: British Library, 1995.

16 On the history of spectroscopy from Newton to Herschel, Huggins and the late nineteenth century see Michael J. Crowe, *Modern Theories of the Universe from Herschel to Hubble*, New York: Dover, 1994, esp. pp. 178–87.

17 E. Walter Maunder, 'The Spectra of Bright Stars', *Knowledge*, XXI, 1 February 1898, p. 40.

18 Richard A. Proctor, *The Spectroscope and its Work*, London: Society for Promoting Christian Knowledge, 1877. For a similar view of astronomy as a reminder of God's majesty see H. A. Howe, 'The Place and Function of Astronomy in Education', *Popular Astronomy*, VI, no. 7, September 1898, pp. 369–76.

19 Agnes Clerke, *The System of the Stars*, London: Longmans, Green and Co., 1890, p. 23.

20 Ibid., pp. 30, 23; original emphasis.

21 Camille Flammarion, *Popular Astronomy: A General Description of the Heavens*, London: Chatto and Windus, 1894, p. 156; original emphasis.

22 Ibid., p. 590; original emphasis.

23 Ibid; see also p. 676.

24 Robert S. Ball, *A Popular Guide to the Heavens*, London: George Philip and Son, 1905, p. 59. See also F. L. O. Wadsworth, 'A Comparison of the Photographic and of the Hand and Eye Methods of Delineating the Surface Markings of Celestial Objects', *Popular Astronomy*, V, no. 4, August 1897, pp. 200–06.

25 Robert S. Ball, *The Story of the Heavens*, rev. edn, London, Paris, Melbourne: Cassell and Co., 1897, pp. 465–6.

26 Thomas Hardy, *Two on a Tower* (1882), ed. with an introduction by Sally Shuttleworth, Harmondsworth: Penguin, 1999, p. 28. My thanks to Sally Shuttleworth for bringing this reference to my attention.

27 Camille Flammarion, *Astronomy for Amateurs*, London: T. Fisher Unwin, 1905, p. 205. See also fig. 44, 'The Earth Viewed from Mars', p. 144, and other illustrations in this volume.

28 James Nasmyth and James Carpenter, *The Moon: Considered as a Planet, a World, and a Satellite*, 4th edn, London: John Murray, 1903, pp. 256–7. The range of reproductive technologies used to illustrate their book is discussed in Carol Armstrong, 'From Microbes to the Moon: Experiments, Instruments, and Photographs I', *Scenes in a Library: Reading the Photograph in the Book*, Cambridge, Mass., and London: M.I.T. Press, 1998, pp. 56–80.

29 Nasmyth and Carpenter, *The Moon*, p. 276.

30 Richard A. Proctor, *The Moon: Her Motions, Aspect, Scenery and Physical Condition*, 3rd edn, London: Longmans, Green and Co., 1886, p. 233.

31 The performance is described in Albert A. Hopkins, *Magic: Stage Illusions and Scientific Diversions including Trick Photography*, London: Sampson Low, Marston and Co. Ltd, 1897, pp. 348–53. It is briefly discussed in John L. Fell, *Film and the Narrative Tradition*, University of Oklahoma Press, 1974, pp. 142–4, and Frank H. Winter, 'The "Trip to the Moon" and Other Early Spaceflight Simulation Shows ca. 1901–1915: Part I', in Donald C. Elder and Christophe Rothmund, eds, *History of Rocketry and Astronautics*, A.A.S. History Series, XXIII, I.A.A. History Symposia, XV, San Diego, Cal.: American Astronautical Society, 2001, pp. 135–6.

32 See Henry V. Hopwood, *Living Pictures: Their History, Photo-Production and Practical Working. With a Digest of British Patents and Annotated Bibliography*, London: Optician and Photographic Trades Review, 1899, p. 220.

33 On the Palace of Optics and the Giant Tele-

scope see *Harper's Guide to Paris and the Exposition of 1900: A Comprehensive Map and Guide to the City of Paris; A Complete Guide to the Exposition; French Phrases Translated; and Maps, Diagrams and Illustrations*, London and New York: Harper and Bros, 1900, p. 181, and 'Le Palais de l'Optique', in *L'Exposition de Paris (1900) publiée avec la collaboration d'écrivains spéciaux et des meilleurs artistes*, 3 vols, Paris: Libraire Illustré, 1900, I, pp. 3–6, 41–4, 76–8; II, pp. 121–2; 'La lune à un mètre', *L'Illustration*, 31 March 1900, pp. 198–201.

34 On the Celestial Globe see *Harper's Guide*, p. 184.

35 For an excellent account of this project and Flammarion's wider engagement with optical devices see Danielle Chaperon, 'Le cinématographe astronomique Camille Flammarion: un parcours de 1864 à 1898', *1895*, no. 18, eté 1995, pp. 53–64.

36 H. G. Wells, *The First Men in the Moon* (1901), London: Gollancz, 2001, p. 40.

37 John F. Kasson, *Amusing the Million: Coney Island at the Turn of the Century*, New York: Hill and Wang, 1978, pp. 8 and 61. On 'A Trip to the Moon' shows at World Fairs and amusement parks in this period see Winter, 'The "Trip to the Moon"', pp. 133–61. Robert Paul's 1895 invention of a mechanism based on H. G. Wells's *The Time Machine*, which combined film projection and kinaesthetic attraction, should be mentioned in this context, although since it drew on the narrative of time, rather than space travel, it will not be discussed in detail. See Terry Ramsaye, *A Million and One Nights: A History of the Motion Picture*, 2 vols, New York: Simon and Schuster, 1926, I, pp. 152–61; Ian Christie, *The Time Traveller: Robert Paul and the Early Film Business in Britain*, Chicago and London: University of Chicago Press, forthcoming.

38 Flammarion, *Astronomy for Amateurs*, p. 238.

39 *The Astronomer's Dream* was the title given to the film by Warwick Trading, Méliès's British distribution company. The French title, *La lune à un mètre*, deliberately recalls the popular press coverage and songs relating to the Giant Telescope in the years leading up to the 1900 Paris World's Fair.

40 See David Robinson, *Georges Méliès: Father of Film Fantasy*, London: British Film Institute, 1993, pp. 39–42; Phil Hardy, ed., *The Aurum Film Encyclopaedia: Science Fiction*, 3rd edn, London: Aurum Press, 1995, p. 23.

41 Flammarion, *Popular Astronomy*, pp. 616–17; original emphasis.

42 Flammarion, *Astronomy for Amateurs*, pp. 11 and 14.

43 For helpful and concise biographies of Flammarion see Brian Stableford, 'Introduction', Camille Flammarion, *Lumen*, trans. with an introduction by Brian Stableford, Middletown, Conn.: Wesleyan University Press, 2002, pp. ix–xxxv; Stephen Herbert and Luke McKernan, *Who's Who of Victorian Cinema*, London: British Film Institute, 1996, p. 51.

44 Camille Flammarion, *The Unknown*, New York and London: Harper and Bros, 1900, p. 14.

45 Ibid., p. 309.

46 For a full discussion of Flammarion's engagement with film see Chaperon, *1895*, pp. 53–64, and Danielle Chaperon, *Camille Flammarion: Entre astronomie et littérature*, Paris: Editions Imago, 1998.

47 On eighteenth-century orreries and the magic lantern see Günther Holzhey, 'World Machines and World Views', *New Magic Lantern Journal*, IX, no. 4, Summer 2003, pp. 54–7. The *Oxford English Dictionary* definition of 'planetarium' also traces the development from a machine with moving parts to a projection arrangement.

48 'Astronomy and the Cinematograph', *Amateur Photographer*, XXVII, 25 February 1898, p. 142, reported in the *Photographic Times*, XXX, no. 5, May 1898, p. 226; 'Kinetography of the Heavens', *Photogram*, V, no. 58, October 1898, p. 330; Hopwood, *Living Pictures*, pp. 231–2.

49 Flammarion, *Popular Astronomy*, p. 617.

50 Ibid., p. 676.

51 [Eberty], *Stars and the Earth*, rev. and enlarged with notes by Richard A. Proctor, London: Ballière, Tindall and Cox, 1880, repr. 1882 and 1895.

52 [Eberty], *Stars and the Earth*, Part 1, p. 37.

53 Ibid., pp. 41–2.

54 Ibid., Part 2, p. 12; original emphasis.

55 Ibid., p. 40; Part 1, p. 41.

56 Ibid., Part 2, pp. 54–5; see also [Eberty], *Stars and the Earth*, rev. Proctor, 1895, pp. 57–60.

57 Hopwood, *Living Pictures*, p. 234.

58 The *St Louis Post*, quoted in Ramsaye, *Million and One Nights*, I, pp. 159–160.

59 Camille Flammarion, *Lumen*, authorised trans. A. A. M. and R. M., London: William Heinemann, 1897, p. 38.

60 Ibid., p. 135.

61 Ibid., p. 95.

62 Ibid., pp. 119–20.

63 'Le Palais de l'électricité', *L'Exposition de Paris*, I, p. 100.

64 My thanks to Luke McKernan for sharing his information concerning the Mercury logo with me. The National Archives has a copyright registration for a logo for a Fine Arts Printer, dated 16 November 1900, that uses a '[female] Figure on a Winged Wheel' (plate 32). Although there is no evidence that this was the source for Urban's design, it does suggest that this striking motif may have been more common in this period than might initially be expected.

65 See Charles Urban, *The Cinematograph in Science, Education, and Matters of State*, London: Charles Urban, 1907.

66 For an excellent discussion of the relationship between Fuller's dance and early film see Tom Gunning, 'Loïe Fuller and the Art of Motion', *La decima musa: the tenth muse*, Udine: Forum, 2001, VI DOMITOR Conference VII International Film Studies Conference Proceedings, pp. 25–34.

67 Ibid., p. 32.

68 See Chaperon, *Flammarion*, pp. 179–82. Catherine Pedley-Hindson has suggested that Fuller took lunar photographs with a magnifying lens that she then had projected during her show. See 'The Female Illusionist – Loïe Fuller: Fairy or Magician?', paper given at 'Visual Delights III: Magic, Illusion and Popular Culture before 1914', University of Sheffield, July 2005, published in revised form in Catherine Hindson, 'The Female Illusionist: Loïe Fuller: Fairy or Wizardress?', *Early Popular Visual Culture*, IV, no. 2, July 2006, pp. 161–74.

69 Chaperon, *Flammarion*, p. 180.

70 Flammarion, *Lumen*, p. 47.

71 On historiography and film see Philip Rosen, 'Traces of the Past: From Historicity to Film', in David E. Klemm and William Schweiker, eds, *Meanings in Texts and Actions: Questioning Paul Ricoeur*, Charlottesville and London: University Press of Virginia, 1993, pp. 67–89, and in the same collection André Gaudreault, 'The Cinematograph: A Historiographical Machine', pp. 90–97.

72 *New York Mail and Express*, 25 September 1897, cited in *Biograph Bulletins 1896–1908*, compiled with an introduction and notes by Kemp R. Niver, Los Angeles: Locare Research Group, 1971, p. 28.

73 On Percival Lowell see Hoskin, *Cambridge Illustrated History*, pp. 284–7. The markings on the surface of Mars had been mapped by Giovanni Schiaparelli in 1877, on the last occasion of the planet's closest approach to Earth. Schiaparelli had referred to them as *canali*, which he regarded as natural, topographic formations. These 'canals' were subsequently reinterpreted as artificially constructed waterways, suggesting the presence of intelligent life on the planet. For discussion of the controversy see Michael J. Crowe, *The Extraterrestrial Life Debate 1750–1900: The Idea of a Plurality of Worlds from Kant to Lowell*, Cambridge: Cambridge University Press, 1986.

74 H. G. Wells, 'War of the Worlds', *Pearson's Magazine*, April–December 1897. See October 1897, 'London Under the Martians', p. 453: 'during that terrible June.' In December 1897, in the final instalment, following the defeat of the Martians, Wells's narrator wonders whether the returned London crowds are 'but the ghosts of the past, haunting the streets that I have seen silent and wretched, going to and fro, phantasms in a dead city, the mockery of life in a galvanised body'.

works cited

archival sources

British Library
  Map Library
  Rare Books and Manuscripts
British Film Institute
  National Film and Television Archive
Bushey Museum and Art Gallery
Bill Douglas Centre, University of Exeter
Hyman Kreitman Research Centre, Tate Library and Archive
Library of Congress, Washington, D.C.
Magic Circle Library
Museum of London
National Archives, Kew, Surrey
National Fairground Archive, University of Sheffield
National Museum of Photography, Film and Television, Bradford
Nederlands Filmmuseum
  Werner Nekes Collection
Pacific Film Archives, San Francisco
Harry Price Collection, University of London Library
South East Film and Television Archive

statutes and parliamentary papers

'An Act to Amend the Law with respect to use of Locomotives on Highways', *Public General Acts* 59 & 60 Vict. (1896), Ch. 36, pp. 343–5.
Hansard's Parliamentary Debates

newspapers and periodicals

Amateur Photographer
Bioscope
British Journal of Photography
Country Life Illustrated. The Journal for all Interested in Country Life and Pursuits
Daily News
Daily Telegraph
Early Popular Visual Culture
Era
Graphic
Illustrated London News
L'Illustration
Kinematograph and Lantern Weekly
Knowledge
Lantern Record
Living Pictures: The Journal of the Popular and Projected Image before 1914
Magazine of Art
Mind: A Quarterly Review of Psychology and Philosophy
Motorist and Traveller
New Magic Lantern Journal
New York Mail and Express
Pearson's Magazine
Photogram
Photographic News
Photographic Notes
Photographic Times
Photography
Popular Astronomy
Punch
Sphere
Strand Magazine
The Times
Wide Angle

unpublished theses and papers

Codling, Philip. 'The Road becomes Alive: Moving towards an Understanding of the Phantom Ride'. MA diss., British Film Institute and Birkbeck College, London, 1995.

Edwards, Lee MacCormick. '"The Moving Picture is *the* thing of the Future": Hubert von Herkomer, British Film Pioneer', paper delivered at College Art Association Conference, Boston, Mass., February 2002.

Jöttkandt, S. 'Image, Metaphor, Action: Representing Walter Pater's "Sebastian van Storck"', paper delivered at 'Image and Text', Research Society for Victorian Periodicals 2004 Conference, University of Ghent, Belgium, July 2004.

McKernan, Luke. '"A Fury for Seeing": London Cinemas and their Audiences, 1905–1914', paper delivered at Postgraduate Research Series, Birkbeck College, London, 5 May 2005.

North, Dan. '"Exceedingly amusing, and in no way repulsive": Showmanship, Magic and Early Film', paper delivered at AHRB Centre for Film and Television Studies, University of Exeter, conference, September 2002.

—. 'Special Effects and the Aesthetics of Illusion'. PhD thesis, University of Exeter, 2003.

Satz, Aura. 'Off the Pedestal; On the Stage: Animation and De-animation in Art and Theatre'. PhD thesis, Slade School of Fine Art, University College London, 2002.

online sources

www.bbk.ac.uk/english/skc/topologies

www.bbk.ac.uk/english/skc/corridors

www.chriswillis.freeserve.co.uk/georgesims

www.ex.ac.uk/bill.douglas/Houdini

www.inventors.about.com/library/inventors/blescalator

www.otis.com/aboutotis/elevatorsinfo

rfwilmut.clara.net/musichll/tate

www.victorianlondon.org/entertainment/magicians

printed sources

Abel, Richard. *The Ciné goes to Town: French Cinema 1896–1914*. Berkeley, Los Angeles, London: University of California Press, 1994.

Age of Rossetti, Burne-Jones and Watts, The: Symbolism in Britain 1860–1910. London: Tate Gallery, 1997.

Allen, Grant. *Physiological Aesthetics*. London: Henry S. King and Co., 1877.

Allen, Robert C. 'Contra the Chaser Theory', 105–15. 'Vitascope/Cinématographe: Initial Patterns of American Film Industrial Practice', 144–52. In *Film before Griffith*. Ed. John L. Fell. Berkeley, Los Angeles, London: University of California Press, 1983.

Altick, Richard D. *The Shows of London*. Cambridge, Mass., and London: Belknap Press of Harvard University Press, 1978.

Anderson, Joseph and Barbara. 'Motion Perception in Motion Pictures', 76–95. In *The Cinematic Apparatus*. Ed. Teresa de Lauretis and Stephen Heath. London and Basingstoke: Macmillan, 1980.

Anderson, Norman D. *Ferris Wheels: An Illustrated History*. Bowling Green, Ohio: Bowling Green State University Popular Press, 1992.

Armstrong, Carol. *Scenes in a Library: Reading the Photograph in the Book*. Cambridge, Mass., and London: M.I.T. Press, 1998.

Armstrong, Tim. *Modernism, Technology and the Body: A Cultural Study*. Cambridge: Cambridge University Press, 1998.

Arnheim, Rudolph. *Film as Art*. London: Faber and Faber, 1958.

Arnwine, Clark, and Jesse Lerner, eds. 'Cityscapes: Introduction', *Wide Angle* 19:4 (October 1997): 1–7.

Arscott, Caroline. 'Venus as Dominatrix: Nineteenth-Century Artists and their Creations', 109–25. In *Manifestations of Venus: Art and Sexuality*. Ed. Caroline Arscott and Katie Scott. Manchester and New York: Manchester University Press, 2000.

Articles on the Underwood Travel System as applied to Various Countries. New York and London: Underwood and Underwood, 1905.

Autocar Handbook, The: A Guide to the Motor

Car. 2nd edn. London: Iliffe and Sons Ltd, 1908.

Bachelard, Gaston. *The Dialectic of Duration*. Trans. and annotated by Mary McAllester Jones. Introduction by Cristina Chimisso. Manchester: Clinamen Press, 2000.

Baedecker, K. *London and its Environs: Handbook for Travellers*. Leipzig and London: Karl Baedecker, various edns.

Bailey, Peter. *Leisure and Class in Victorian England: Rational Recreation and the Contest for Control 1830–1885*. London: Routledge and Kegan Paul, 1978.

Bain, Alexander. *The Senses and the Intellect*. 4th edn. London: Longmans, Green and Co., 1894.

Baldry, A. L. *Hubert von Herkomer R.A.: A Study and a Biography*. London: George Bell and Sons, 1901.

Ball, Robert S. *The Story of the Heavens*. Rev. edn. London, Paris and Melbourne: Cassell and Co., 1897.

—. *A Popular Guide to the Heavens*. London: George Philip and Son, 1905.

Balzer, Richard. *Peepshows: A Visual History*. New York: Harry N. Abrams, 1998.

Barnes, John. *The Rise of the Cinema in Great Britain: The Beginnings of the Cinema in England 1894–1901*. II, *Jubilee Year 1897*. London: Bishopsgate Press, 1983.

—. 'Filming Scenes in the United Kingdom for the Cinématographe Lumiére', 60–62. In *Cinema: The Beginnings and the Future. Essays marking the Centenary of the First Film Show projected to a Paying Audience in Britain*. Ed. Christopher Williams. London: University of Westminster Press, 1996.

—. *The Beginnings of the Cinema in England 1894–1901*. IV, *1899*. Exeter: University of Exeter Press, 1996.

—. *The Beginnings of the Cinema in England 1894–1901*. V, *1900*. Exeter: University of Exeter Press, 1997.

—. *The Beginnings of the Cinema in England 1894–1901*. I, *1894–1896*. Exeter: University of Exeter Press, 1998.

Barnouw, Erik. *Documentary: A History of the Non-Fiction Film*. Oxford and New York: Oxford University Press, 1974.

—. *The Magician and the Cinema*. New York and Oxford: Oxford University Press, 1981.

Barr, John H. *Kinematics of Machinery: A Brief Treatise on Constrained Motions of Machine Elements*. New York: John Wiley and Sons; London: Chapman and Hall, 1899.

Barsam, Richard M. *Non-Fiction Film: A Critical History*. Bloomington and Indianapolis: Indiana University Press, 1992.

Barthes, Roland. *Mythologies*. Selected and trans. Annette Lavers. London: Jonathan Cape, 1972.

—. *Image–Music–Text*. Selected and trans. Stephen Heath. London: Fontana, 1977.

—. *Camera Lucida: Reflections on Photography*. Trans. Richard Howard. London: Flamingo, 1984.

Baudelaire, Charles. 'The Modern Public and Photography', 83–9. In *Classic Essays on Photography*. Ed. A.Trachtenberg with notes by Amy Weinstein Meyers. New Haven, Conn.: Leete's Island Books, 1980.

Baudrillard, Jean. *The System of Objects*. Trans. James Benedict. London and New York: Verso, 1996.

Beckmann, Karen. *Vanishing Women: Magic, Film and Feminism*. Durham, N.C.: Duke University Press, 2000.

Benjamin, Walter. 'The Work of Art in the Age of Mechanical Reproduction', 219–53. In *Illuminations*. Ed. with an introduction by Hannah Arendt, trans. Harry Zohn. London: Fontana, 1973.

Bennett, Martin. *Rolls-Royce: The History of the Car*. Oxford: Oxford Illustrated Press, 1973.

Berenson, Bernhard. *The Florentine Painters of the Renaissance: With an Index to their Works*. New York and London: G. P. Putnam's Sons, 1896.

Bergson, Henri. *Creative Evolution*. Trans. Arthur Mitchell. London: Macmillan and Co., 1911.

—. *Matter and Memory*. Trans. Nancy Margaret Paul and W. Scott Palmer. London: Swann Sonnenschein and Co., 1911.

Blanchot, Maurice. *The Gaze of Orpheus and Other Literary Essays*. Trans. Lydia Davis. New York: Station Hill, 1981.

Blühn, Andreas, and Louise Lippincott. *Light!*

The Industrial Age 1750–1900: Art and Science, Technology and Society. London: Thames and Hudson, 2000.

Bolter, Jay David, and Richard Grusin. *Remediation: Understanding New Media*. Cambridge, Mass., and London: M.I.T. Press, 1999.

Bommes, Michael, and Patrick Wright. '"Charms of Residence": The Public and the Past', 253–302. In *Making Histories: Studies in History-Writing and Politics*. Ed. Richard Johnson *et al*. London: Hutchinson in association with the Centre for Contemporary Cultural Studies, 1982.

Bottomore, Stephen. 'Dreyfus and Documentary', *Sight and Sound* 53 : 4 (autumn 1984): 290–93.

—. 'Shots in the Dark: The Real Origins of Film Editing', 104–13. In *Early Cinema: Space, Frame, Narrative*. Ed. Thomas Elsaesser and Adam Barker. London: British Film Institute, 1990.

—. *I want to see this Annie Mattygraph: A Cartoon History of the Coming of the Movies*. Gemona: Le Giornate del cinema muto, *c*.1995.

—. 'The Panicking Audience?: Early Cinema and the "Train Effect"', *Historical Journal of Film, Radio and Television* 19 : 2 (1999): 177–216.

Brake, Laurel. *Walter Pater*. Plymouth: Northcote House, 1994.

Braun, Marta. *Picturing Time: The Work of Etienne-Jules Marey (1830–1904)*. Chicago and London: University of Chicago Press, 1992.

Brewster, David. *The Stereoscope: Its History, Theory and Construction*. London: John Murray, 1856.

Briggs, Asa. *Mass Entertainment: The Origins of a Modern Industry*. Adelaide: Griffin Press, 1960.

British Journal Photographic Almanac and Photographer's Daily Companion. London: H. Greenwood, 1889.

Brooks, Peter. *Body Work: Objects of Desire in Modern Narrative*. Cambridge, Mass., and London: Harvard University Press, 1993.

Brown, Richard, and Barry Anthony. *A Victorian Film Enterprise: The History of the British Mutoscope and Biograph Company, 1897–1915*. Trowbridge: Flicks Books, 1999.

Brown, Simon. 'Early Cinema in Britain and the Smoking Concert Film', *Early Popular Visual Culture* 3 : 2 (September 2005): 165–78.

Bruno, Giuliana. 'Spectatorial Embodiments: Anatomies of the Visible and the Female Bodyscape', *Camera Obscura: A Journal of Feminism and Film Theory*, special issue, 'Imaging Technologies, Inscribing Science'. Ed. Paula A. Treichler and Lisa Cartwright, 28 (1992): 239–61.

—. *Streetwalking on a Ruined Map: Cultural Theory and the City Films of Elvira Notari*. Princeton, N.J.: Princeton University Press, 1993.

Bryant, Walter W. *A History of Astronomy*. London: Methuen and Co., 1907.

Burch, Noël. *Life to Those Shadows*. Trans. and ed. Ben Brewster. London: British Film Institute, 1990.

de Cauter, Lieven. 'The Panoramic Ecstasy: On World Exhibitions and the Disintegration of Experience', *Theory, Culture and Society* 10 : 4 (1993): 1–23.

de Certeau, Michel. *The Practice of Everyday Life*. Trans. Steven Rendall. Berkeley, Los Angeles, London: University of California Press, 1984.

Chaperon, Danielle. 'Le cinématographe astronomique Camille Flammarion: un parcours de 1864 à 1898', *1895* 18 (Eté 1995): 53–64.

—. *Camille Flammarion: Entre astronomie et littérature*. Paris: Editions Imago, 1998.

Chapman, Mary. '"Living Pictures": Women and *Tableaux Vivants* in Nineteenth-Century American Fiction and Culture', *Wide Angle* 18 : 3 (July 1996): 22–52.

Charney, Leo. 'In a Moment: Film and the Philosophy of Modernity', 279–94. In *Cinema and the Invention of Modern Life*. Ed. Leo Charney and Vanessa Schwartz. Berkeley, Los Angeles, London: University of California Press, 1995.

Cinema 1900–1906. Filmography. II. Brussels: Fédération Internationale des Archives du Film, 1982.

Clark, Kenneth. *The Nude: A Study in Ideal Art*. London: John Murray, 1956.

Clerke, Agnes. *The System of the Stars*. London: Longmans, Green and Co., 1890.

Cobbold, Charles S. W. 'Observations on Certain Optical Illusions of Motion', *Brain* 4 (April 1881): 75–81.

Connor, Steven. 'Topologies: Michel Serres and the Shapes of Thought', *Anglistik* 15 (2004): 105–17.

Cook, Mrs E. T. *Highways and Byways in London*. London: Macmillan and Co. Ltd, 1902.

Cook's Handbook for London. London and New York: Thomas Cook and Son, various edns.

Copinger, Walter Arthur. *The Law of Copyright in Works of Literature and Art: Including that of the Drama, Music, Engraving, Sculpture, Painting, Photography, and Designs*. 4th edn. Ed. J. M. Easton. London: Stevens and Haynes, 1904.

Corbin, Alain. 'Backstage', 457–667. In *A History of Private Life: IV, From the Fires of Revolution to the Great War*. Trans. Arthur Goldhammer, ed. Michelle Perrot. Cambridge, Mass., and London: Belknap Press of Harvard University Press, 1990.

Crafton, Donald. 'Animation Iconography: The "Hand of the Artist"', *Quarterly Review of Film Studies* 4:4 (fall 1979): 409–28.

Crangle, Richard. '"Astounding Actuality and Life": Early Film and the Illustrated Magazine in Britain', 93–102. In *Le Cinéma au tournant du siècle (Cinema at the Turn of the Century)*. Ed. Claire Dupré la Tour, André Gaudreault and Roberta Pearson. Quebec: Editions nota bene, 1999.

Crary, Jonathan. *Techniques of the Observer: On Vision and Modernity in the Nineteenth Century*. Cambridge, Mass., and London: M.I.T. Press, 1992.

—. *Suspensions of Perception: Attention, Spectacle and Modern Culture*. Cambridge, Mass., and London: M.I.T. Press, 1999.

Crompton, Dennis, Richard Franklin and Stephen Herbert, eds. *Servants of Light: The Book of the Lantern*. London: Magic Lantern Society, 1997.

Crowe, Michael J. *The Extraterrestrial Life Debate 1750–1900: The Idea of a Plurality of Worlds from Kant to Lowell*. Cambridge: Cambridge University Press, 1986.

—. *Modern Theories of the Universe from Herschel to Hubble*. New York: Dover, 1994.

Cunnington, C. Willett and Phillis. *The History of Underclothes*. London: Michael Joseph, 1951.

Danto, Arthur C. 'Moving Pictures', *Quarterly Review of Film Studies* 4.1 (winter 1979): 1–21.

Danziger, Kurt. 'Mid-Nineteenth-Century British Psycho-Physiology: A Neglected Chapter in the History of Psychology', 119–46. In *The Problematic Science: Psychology in Nineteenth-Century Thought*. Ed. William R. Woodward and Mitchell G. Ash. New York: Praeger, 1982.

Deutelbaum, Marshall. Structural Patterning in the Lumière Films', 299–310. In *Film before Griffith*. Ed. John L. Fell. Berkeley, Los Angeles, London: University of California Press, 1983.

Devant, David. 'My Illusions', *Strand Magazine* 45 (January 1913): 24–33.

—. *Secrets of My Magic*. London: Hutchinson and Co., 1936.

Dewhirst, David, and Michael Hoskin, 'The Message of Starlight: The Rise of Astrophysics', 256–343. In *The Cambridge Illustrated History of Astronomy*. Ed. Michael Hoskin. Cambridge: Cambridge University Press, 1997.

Doane, Mary Ann. *The Emergence of Cinematic Time: Modernity, Contingency and the Archive*. Cambridge, Mass., and London: Harvard University Press, 2002.

[Eberty, Felix]. *The Stars and the Earth: Or, Thoughts upon Space, Time and Eternity*, 2 parts. London: H. Baillière, 1846. Revised and enlarged with notes by Richard A. Proctor. London. Baillière, Tindall and Cox, 1880.

Eden, David. 'The Ancestors' Ancestor', 39–42. In *Ruddygore: A Booklet to Commemorate the Centenary of the First Performance. 22 January 1887*. London: Sir Arthur Sullivan Society, 1987.

Edwards, Lee MacCormick. *Herkomer: A Victo-*

rian Artist. Aldershot and Brookfield, Vt: Ashgate, 1999.

Ellis, Havelock. *Studies in the Psychology of Sex.* IV, *Sexual Selection in Man. I. Touch. II. Smell. III. Hearing. IV. Vision.* 7 vols. Philadelphia: F. A. Davis, 1905.

Elsner, John, 'Visual Mimesis and the Myth of the Real: Ovid's Pygmalion as Viewer', *Ramus: Critical Studies in Greek and Roman Literature* 20 : 2 (1991): 154–68.

Evrard, Franck. *Effeuillages romanesques: essai sur la representation littéraire et culturelle.* Genouph: A.-G. Nizet, 1997.

Ewing, Elizabeth. *Dress and Undress: A History of Women's Underwear.* London: B. T. Batsford, 1978.

L'Exposition de Paris (1900) publiée avec la collaboration d'écrivains spéciaux et des meilleurs artistes. 3 vols. Paris: Libraire Illustré, 1900.

Ezra, Elizabeth. *Georges Méliès: The Birth of the Auteur.* Manchester and New York: Manchester University Press, 2000.

Featherstone, Ann. '"There is a peep-show in the market": Gazing at/in the Journals of Sydney Race', *Early Popular Visual Culture* 3 : 1 (May 2005): 43–57.

Featherstone, Mike, ed. *Georg Simmel (A Theory, Culture and Society Special Issue).* London: Sage, 1991.

Fell, John L. *Film and the Narrative Tradition.* Oklahoma: University of Oklahoma Press, 1974.

Fielding, Raymond. 'Hale's Tours: Ultrarealism in the Pre-1910 Motion Picture', 116–30. In *Film before Griffith.* Ed. John L. Fell. Berkeley, Los Angeles, London: University of California Press, 1983.

Filson Young, A. B. *The Complete Motorist: Being an Account of the Evolution and Construction of the Modern Motor-Car; with Notes on the Selection, Use, and Maintenance of the Same; and on the Pleasures of Travel upon the Public Roads.* London: Methuen and Co., 1904.

—. *The Happy Motorist: An Introduction to the Use and Enjoyment of the Motor Car.* London: E. Grant Richards, 1906.

Fischer, Lucy. 'The Lady Vanishes: Women, Magic, and the Movies', 339–54. In *Film before Griffith.* Ed. John L. Fell. Berkeley, Los Angeles, London: University of California Press, 1983.

Fison, Alfred H. *Recent Advances in Astronomy.* London: Blackie and Son Ltd, 1898.

Flammarion, Camille. *Lumen* (1872). Trans. and with an introduction by Brian Stableford. Middletown, Conn.: Wesleyan University Press, 2002.

—. *Popular Astronomy: A General Description of the Heavens.* London: Chatto and Windus, 1894.

—. *Lumen.* Authorised trans. A. A. M. and R. M. London: Willliam Heinemann, 1897.

—. *The Unknown.* New York and London: Harper and Bros, 1900.

—. *Astronomy for Amateurs.* London: T. Fisher Unwin, 1905.

Flint, Kate. *The Victorians and the Visual Imagination.* Cambridge: Cambridge University Press, 2000.

Flukinger, Roy, Larry Schaaf and Standish Meacham. *Paul Martin: Victorian Photographer.* London: Gordon Fraser, 1978.

Fraser, Hilary. 'Women and the Ends of Art History: Vision and Corporeality in Nineteenth-Century Critical Discourse', *Victorian Studies* 42 : 1 (autumn 1998): 77–100.

Frazer, John. *Artificially Arranged Scenes: The Films of Georges Méliès.* Boston, Mass.: G. K. Hall and Co., 1979.

Freedberg, David. *The Power of Images: Studies in the History and Theory of Response.* Chicago and London: University of Chicago Press, 1989.

Freud, Sigmund. 'The Uncanny', 219–52. In *The Standard Edition of the Complete Psychological Works of Sigmund Freud.* XVII, trans. and ed. James Strachey. London: Hogarth Press and the Institute of Psycho-Analysis, 1955.

—. *The Standard Edition of the Complete Psychological Works of Sigmund Freud. Trans. from the German under the General Editorship of James Strachey. In collaboration with Anna Freud. Assisted by Alix Strachey and Alan*

Tyson. Volume VI (1901): *The Psychopathology of Everyday Life*. London: Hogarth Press and the Institute of Psycho-Analysis, 1960.

—. 'Three Essays on the Theory of Sexuality (1905)', 135–243. In *The Standard Edition of the Complete Psychological Works*. VII (1901–5), trans. and gen. ed. James Strachey. In collaboration with Anna Freud. London: Hogarth Press and the Institute of Psycho-Analysis, 1964.

Frisby, David. *Fragments of Modernity: Theories of Modernity in the Work of Simmel, Kracauer and Benjamin*. London: Polity Press, 1985.

—. *Simmel and Since: Essays on Georg Simmel's Social Theory*. London and New York: Routledge, 1992.

—, and Mike Featherstone. *Simmel on Culture: Selected Writings*. London: Sage, 1997.

Gardner, Burdett. *The Lesbian Imagination (Victorian Style): A Psychological and Critical Study of 'Vernon Lee'*. New York and London: Garland, 1987.

Gaudreault, André. 'Showing and Telling', 274–81. 'Film, Narrative, Narration: The Cinema of the Lumière Brothers', trans. Rosamund Howe, 68–75. In *Early Cinema: Space, Frame, Narrative*. Ed. Thomas Elsaesser and Adam Barker. London: British Film Institute, 1990.

—. 'The Cinematograph: A Historiographical Machine', 90–97. In *Meaning in Texts and Actions: Questioning Paul Ricoeur*. Ed. David E. Klemm and William Schweiker. Charlottesville and London: University Press of Virginia, 1993.

Gernsheim, Helmut, in collaboration with Alison Gernsheim. *The History of Photography from the Earliest Use of the Camera Obscura in the Eleventh Century up to 1914*. London, New York, Toronto: Oxford University Press, 1995.

Gilbert, W. S. *Pygmalion and Galatea: An Entirely Original Mythological Comedy in Three Acts*. London: Judd and Co., 1872.

—. *Iolanthe and Other Operas*. With Illustrations by W. Russell Flint. London: G. Bell and Sons Ltd, 1910.

Glasscock, Jessica. *Striptease: From Gaslight to Spotlight*. New York: Harry N. Abrams, 2003.

Gledhill, Christine *Reframing British Cinema 1918–1928: Between Restraint and Passion*. London: British Film Institute, 2003.

Gombrich, E. H. 'Moment and Movement in Art', *Journal of the Warburg and Courtauld Institutes* 27 (1964): 293–306.

Gomme, Laurence. *London in the Reign of Queen Victoria 1837–1897*. London: Blackie and Son Ltd, 1898.

Goodrick, G. J. *Tableaux Vivants and Living Waxworks, with Directions for Stage Management*. London: Dean and Son, 1895.

Goodwin, Jason. *Otis: Giving Rise to the Modern City*. Chicago: Ivan R. Dee, 2001.

Gordon, Lesley. *Peepshow into Paradise: A History of Children's Toys*. London: George G. Harrap and Co. Ltd, 1953.

Gould, Veronica Franklin. *G. F. Watts: The Last Great Victorian*. New Haven and London: Yale University Press, 2004.

—, ed. *The Vision of G. F. Watts (1817–1904)*. Compton, Surrey: Watts Gallery, 2004.

Gray, Frank. 'Robert Paul in 1896: Innovation, Success and Wonder', 337–45. In *Le cinéma au tournant du siècle (Cinema at the Turn of the Century)*. Ed. Claire Dupré la Tour, André Gaudreault and Roberta Pearson. Quebec: Editions nota bene, 1999.

—. 'George Albert Smith's Visions and Transformations: The Films of 1898', 170–80. In *Visual Delights: Essays on the Popular and Projected Image in the 19th Century*. Ed. Simon Popple and Vanessa Toulmin. Trowbridge: Flicks Books, 2000.

Gross, Kenneth. *The Dream of the Moving Statue*. Ithaca, N.Y., and London: Cornell University Press, 1992.

Gunn, Peter. *Vernon Lee: Violet Paget 1856–1935*. London: Oxford University Press, 1964.

Gunning, Tom. 'The Cinema of Attractions: Early Cinema, its Spectator and the Avant Garde', *Wide Angle* 8 : 3–4 (1986): 63–70.

—. 'An Aesthetic of Astonishment: Early Film and the (In)credulous Spectator', *Art and Text* 34 (spring 1989): 31–45.

—. '"Now You See It, Now You Don't": The

Temporality of the Cinema of Attractions', *Velvet Light Trap* 32 (fall 1993): 3–12.

—. 'Phantom Images and Modern Manifestations: Spirit Photography, Magic Theater, Trick Films, and Photography's Uncanny', 42–71. In *Fugitive Images: From Photography to Video*. Ed. Patrice Petro. Bloomington and Indianapolis: Indiana University Press, 1995.

—. 'From the Kaleidoscope to the X-Ray: Urban Spectatorship, Poe, Benjamin and *Traffic in Souls* (1913)', *Wide Angle* 19:4 (October 1997): 25–61.

—. 'Before Documentary: Early Nonfiction Films and the "View" Aesthetic', 9–24. In *Uncharted Territory: Essays on Early Nonfiction Film*. Ed. Daan Hertogs and Nico de Klerk. Amsterdam: Stichting Nederlands Filmmuseum, 1997.

—. 'Embarrassing Evidence: The Detective Camera and the Documentary Impulse', 46–64. In *Collecting Visible Evidence*. Ed. Jane M. Gaines and Michael Renov. Minneapolis and London: University of Minnesota Press, 1999.

—. 'The Ghost in the Machine: Animated Pictures at the Haunted Hotel of Early Cinema', *Living Pictures: The Journal of the Popular and Projected Image before 1914* 1:1 (2001): 3–17.

—. 'New Thresholds of Vision: Instantaneous Photography and the Early Cinema of Lumière', 71–99. In *Impossible Presence: Surface and Screen in the Photogenic Era*. Ed. Terry Smith. Chicago: University of Chicago Press, 2001.

—. 'Loïe Fuller and the Art of Motion', 25–34. In *La decima musa: the tenth muse*. Udine: Forum, 2001, VI DOMITOR Conference, VII International Film Studies Conference Proceedings.

Hale Jr, Matthew. *Human Science and Social Order: Hugo Münsterberg and the Origins of Applied Psychology*. Philadelphia: Temple University Press, 1980.

Hansen, Miriam. *Babel and Babylon: Spectatorship in American Silent Film*. Cambridge, Mass., and London: Harvard University Press, 1991.

Harding, Colin, and Simon Popple, eds. *In the Kingdom of Shadows: A Companion to Early Cinema*. London: Cygnus Arts; Carbury, N.J.: Fairleigh Dickinson University Press, 1996.

Hardy, Phil, ed. *The Aurum Film Encyclopaedia: Science Fiction*. 3rd edn. London: Aurum Press, 1995.

Hardy, Thomas. *Two on a Tower* (1882). Ed. with an introduction by Sally Shuttleworth. Harmondsworth: Penguin, 1999.

Harmsworth, Alfred C. *Motors and Motor-Driving*. London: Longmans, Green and Co., 1902.

Harper's Guide to Paris and the Exposition of 1900: A Comprehensive Map and Guide to the City of Paris; A Complete Guide to the Exposition; French Phrases Translated; and Maps, Diagrams and Illustrations. London and New York: Harper and Bros, 1900.

Helmoltz, Hermann von. *Treatise on Physiological Optics* (1867). Rev. and enlarged 1910–11. Ed. and trans. James P. C. Southall. 3 vols. Rochester, N.Y: Optical Society of America, 1924–5.

Henley, William Ernest. *A Song of Speed*. London: David Nutt, 1903.

Hepworth, Cecil M. *Animated Photography: The ABC of the Cinematograph. A Simple and Thorough Guide to the Projection of Living Photographs, with Notes on the Production of Cinematograph Negatives*. London: Hazell, Watson and Viney Ltd, 1897.

—. *Came the Dawn: Memories of a Film Pioneer*. London: Phoenix House, 1951.

Hepworth, T. C. *The Camera and the Pen*. London: Percy Lund Humphries and Co. Ltd, 1897.

Herbert, Stephen. *Eadweard Muybridge: The Kingston Museum Bequest*. Hastings: The Projection Box in association with Kingston Museum and Heritage Service, 2005.

— and Luke McKernan, eds. *Who's Who of Victorian Cinema*. London: British Film Institute, 1996.

Herkomer, Hubert von. *Five Lectures delivered to the Students of the Royal Academy*. London: privately printed, 1900.

—. *My School and My Gospel*. London: Archibald Constable and Co. Ltd, 1908.

—. *The Herkomers*. 2 vols. London: Macmillan and Co. Ltd, 1911.

—. *An Idyl: A Pictorial-Music Play*. London and New York: Novello, Ewer and Co., n.d.

Higson, Andrew. *Waving the Flag: Constructing a National Cinema in Britain*. Oxford: Clarendon Press, 1995.

Hildebrand, Adolf von. *The Problem of Form in Painting and Sculpture* (1893). Trans. and rev. with the author's co-operation by Max Meyer and R. M. Ogden. New York: G. E. Stechert and Co., 1907.

Hiley, Nicholas. '"Nothing More than a Craze": Cinema Building in Britain from 1909 to 1914', 111–27. In *Young and Innocent? The Cinema in Britain 1896–1930*. Ed. Andrew Higson. Exeter: Exeter University Press, 2002.

Hindson, Catherine. 'The Female Illusionist – Loïe Fuller: Fairy or Wizardess?', *Early Popular Visual Culture* 4 : 2 (2006): 161–74.

Hissey, James John. *Untravelled England*. London: Macmillan and Co., 1906.

—. *An English Holiday with Car and Camera*. London: Macmillan and Co., 1908.

—. *The Road and the Inn*. London: Macmillan and Co., 1917.

Hoffmann, Professor. *Modern Magic: A Practical Treatise on the Art of Conjuring*. London: G. Routledge and Sons, 1874.

Holzhey, Günther. 'World Machines and World Views', *New Magic Lantern Journal* 9 : 4 (summer 2003): 54–7.

Hopkins, Albert A. *Magic: Stage Illusions and Scientific Diversions including Trick Photography*. London: Sampson, Low, Marston and Co. Ltd, 1897.

Hopwood, Henry V. *Living Pictures: Their History, Photo-Production and Practical Working. With a Digest of British Patents and Annotated Bibliography*. London: Optician and Photographic Trades Review, 1899.

Huggett, Nick, ed. *Space from Zeno to Einstein: Classic Readings with a Contemporary Commentary*. Cambridge, Mass., and London: M.I.T. Press, 1999.

Humphries, Steve. *Victorian Britain through the Magic Lantern: Illustrated by Lear's Magic Lantern Slides*. London: Sidgwick and Jackson, 1989.

Iverson, Margaret. *Alöis Riegl: Art History and Theory*. Cambridge, Mass., and London: M.I.T. Press, 1993.

James, Henry. *Essays in London and Elsewhere*. London: James R. Osgood, McIlvaine and Co., 1893.

James, William. *The Principles of Psychology*. 2 vols. London: Macmillan and Co., 1890.

Jay, Bill. *Cyanide and Spirits: An Inside-Out View of Early Photography*. Munich: Nazraeli Press, 1991.

Jeffries, B. Joy. *The Eye in Health and Disease. Being a Series of Articles on the Anatomy and Physiology of the Human Eye, and its Surgical and Medical Treatment*. Boston: Alexander Moore, 1871.

Jenkins, C. Francis. *Animated Pictures: An Exposition of Chronophotography, its Present Scientific Applications and Future Possibilities and of the Methods and Apparatus employed in the Entertainment of Large Audiences by Means of Projecting Lanterns to give the Appearance of Objects in Motion*. Washington, D.C.: C. Francis Jenkins, 1898.

Jenkins, I., and K. Sloan. *Vases and Volcanoes: Sir William Hamilton and his Collection*. London: British Museum, 1996.

Jenness, George A. *Maskelyne and Cooke: Egyptian Hall, London, 1873–1904*. Enfield: George A. Jenness, 1967.

Jöttkandt, S. 'Effectively Equivalent: Walter Pater, "Sebastian van Storck", and the Ethics of Metaphor', *Nineteenth-Century Literature* 60 : 2 (2005): 163–98.

Kasson, John F. *Amusing the Million: Coney Island at the Turn of the Century*. New York: Hill and Wang, 1978.

Kennedy, J. B. *Space, Time and Einstein: An Introduction*. Chesham: Acumen, 2003.

Kern, Stephen. *The Culture of Time and Space 1880–1914*. London: Weidenfeld and Nicolson, 1983.

Kirby, Lynne. *Parallel Tracks: The Railroad and Silent Cinema*. Exeter: University of Exeter Press, 1997.

Koch, Gertrud. 'The Body's Shadow Realm', *October* 50 (fall 1989): 3–29.

Kunzle, David. *Fashion and Fetishism: A Social History of the Corset, Tight-Lacing and Other Forms of Body-Sculpture in the West.* Ottawa: Rowman and Littlefield, 1982.

Lant, Antonia. 'Haptical Cinema', *October* 74 (fall 1995): 45–73.

Lauretis, Teresa de, and Stephen Heath, eds. *The Cinematic Apparatus.* London and Basingstoke: Macmillan, 1980.

Lauro, Al Di, and Gerald Rabkin. *Dirty Movies: An Illustrated History of the Stag Film 1915–1970.* New York and London: Chelsea House, 1976.

Law, Ernest. *A Short History of Hampton Court.* London: George Bell and Sons, 1897.

—. *The Royal Gallery at Hampton Court Illustrated.* London: George Bell and Sons, 1898.

—. *The New Historical Guide to Hampton Court with a New Historical Catalogue of the Pictures.* London: George Bell and Sons, 1900.

—. *The Haunted Gallery at Hampton Court and its Associations with Shakespeare.* London: Hugh Rees Ltd, 1918.

Ledger, Sally, and Roger Luckhurst, eds. *The Fin de Siècle: A Reader in Cultural History, c. 1880–1900.* Oxford and New York: Oxford University Press, 2000.

Lee, Vernon. *Hauntings: Fantastic Stories.* London: William Heinemann, 1890.

—. *Pope Jacynth and Other Fantastic Tales.* London: Grant Richards, 1904.

—. *Beauty and Ugliness and Other Studies in Psychological Aesthetics.* London: John Lane, Bodley Head, 1912.

—, and C. Anstruther-Thomson. *Le rôle de l'élément moteur dans la perception esthétique visuelle: mémoire et questionnaire soumis au quatrième congrès de psychologie.* Imola: Coopérative Typographique Edit, 1901.

Lefebvre, Henri. *The Production of Space.* Trans. Donald Nicholson-Smith. Oxford: Basil Blackwell, 1991.

—. *Eléments de rythmanalyse: introduction à la connaissance des rythmes.* Paris: Editions Syllepse, 1992.

—. *Writings on Cities: Henri Lefebvre.* Selected, trans. and introduced by Eleonore Kofman and Elizabeth Lebas. Oxford: Blackwell, 1996.

—, and Catherine Régulier, 'Le project rythmanalytique', *Communications* 41:2 (1985): 191–9.

Leyda, Jay. *Kino: A History of the Russian and Soviet Film.* 3rd edn. Princeton, N.J.: Princeton University Press, 1983.

Livre des expositions universelles 1851–1989, le. Paris: Union Centrale des Arts Décoratifs, 1983.

Low, Rachel, and Roger Manvell. *The History of the British Film: 1, 1896–1906.* London: George Allen and Unwin Ltd, 1948.

MacCord, Charles William. *Kinematics: A Treatise on the Modification of Motion, as Affected by the Forms and Modes of Connection of the Moving Parts of Machines.* New York: John Wiley and Sons, 1883.

—. *Velocity Diagrams: Their Construction and their Uses. Intended for All who are interested in Mechanical Movements.* New York: John Wiley and Sons; London: Chapman and Hall Ltd, 1901.

Mandell, Richard D. *Paris 1900: The Great World's Fair.* Toronto: University of Toronto Press, 1967.

Mander, Raymond, and Joe Mitchenson. *British Music Hall: A Story in Pictures.* London: Studio Vista, 1965.

Marks, Laura U. *The Skin of the Film: Intercultural Cinema, Embodiment and the Senses.* Durham, N.C., and London: Duke University Press, 2000.

Marshall, Gail. *Actresses on the Victorian Stage: Feminine Performance and the Galatea Myth.* Cambridge: Cambridge University Press, 1998.

Martin, Paul. 'Blocked-Out Lantern Slides', *Amateur Photographer* (6 November 1896): 374–5.

—. *Victorian Snapshots: Illustrated from Contemporary Photographs.* London: Country Life Ltd, 1939.

Marvin, Carolyn. *When Old Technologies were New: Thinking about Electric Communication in the Late Nineteenth Century.* New York and Oxford: Oxford University Press, 1988.

Maskelyne, Nevil, and David Devant. *Our Magic: The Art in Magic. The Theory of Magic. The Practice of Magic.* London: George

Routledge and Sons Ltd, 1911.

Mayne, Judith. 'Uncovering the Female Body', 63–7. In *Before Hollywood: Turn-of-the-Century American Film*. Ed. John Fell. New York: Hudson Hills Press in association with the American Federation of Arts, 1987.

McCauley, Elizabeth Anne. *Industrial Madness: Commercial Photography in Paris 1848–1871*. New Haven and London: Yale University Press, 1994.

McCullogh, Jack W. *Living Pictures on the New York Stage*. Epping, Essex: Bowker Publishing, 1981.

McKernan, Jay. 'From the Archive: A New Art: Colour-Music. A Paper Read at St. James's Hall on 6 June 1895 by A. Wallace Rimington', *Living Pictures* 2 : 2 (2003): 69–71.

Mensel, Robert E. '"Kodakers Lying in Wait": Amateur Photography and the Right of Privacy in New York, 1885–1915', *American Quarterly* 43 : 1 (March 1991): 24–45.

Merleau-Ponty, M. *The Phenomenology of Perception*. Trans. Colin Smith. London and New York: Routledge, 1962.

Meyer, Mark-Paul. 'Moments of Poignancy: The Aesthetics of the Accidental and the Casual in Early Nonfiction Film', 51–60. In *Uncharted Territory: Essays on Early Nonfiction Film*. Ed. Daan Hertogs and Nico de Klerk. Amsterdam: Stichting Nederlands Filmmuseum, 1997.

Miles, Geoffrey, ed. *Classical Mythology in English Literature: A Critical Anthology*. London and New York: Routledge, 1999.

Mills, J. Saxon. *The Old Wood Carver from the Cinematograph Film conceived and produced by Sir Hubert von Herkomer, R.A. and Siegfried Herkomer*. London: Stanley Paul and Co., 1913.

—. *Life and Letters of Sir Hubert Herkomer: A Study in Struggle and Success*. London: Hutchinson, 1923.

Mulvey, Laura. 'The Index and the Uncanny', 139–48. In *Time and the Image*. Ed. Carolyn Bailey Gill. Manchester and New York: Manchester University Press, 2000.

Münsterberg, Hugo. *Psychology and Life*. London: Archibald Constable and Co., 1899.

—. *The Photoplay: A Psychological Study*. New York and London: D. Appleton and Co., 1916.

Musser, Charles. 'The Travel Genre in 1903–1904: Moving towards Fictional Narrative', *Iris* 2 : 1 (1984): 47–59.

—. 'Rethinking Early Cinema: Cinemas of Attraction and Narrativity', *Yale Journal of Criticism* 7 : 2 (1994): 203–33.

Nasmyth, James, and James Carpenter. *The Moon: Considered as a Planet, a World, and a Satellite*. 4th edn. London: John Murray, 1903.

Nead, Lynda. *The Female Nude: Art, Obscenity and Sexuality*. London and New York: Routledge, 1992.

—. 'Seductive Canvases: Visual Mythologies of the Artist and Artistic Creativity', *Oxford Art Journal* 18 : 2 (1995): 59–69.

—. *Victorian Babylon: People, Streets and Images in Nineteenth-Century London*. New Haven and London: Yale University Press, 2000.

Nesbit, Edith. *Fear*. London: Stanley Paul and Co., 1910.

Newhall, Beaumont. *The History of Photography from 1839 to the Present*. London: Secker and Warburg, 1982.

Nichols, Bill, and Susan J. Lederman. 'Flicker and Motion in Film', 96–105. In *The Cinematic Apparatus*. Ed. Teresa de Lauretis and Stephen Heath. London and Basingstoke: Macmillan, 1980.

Niver, Kemp R. *Motion Pictures from the Library of Congress Paper Print Collection*. Berkeley and Los Angeles: University of California Press, 1967.

—. *Biograph Bulletins 1896–1908*. Compiled with an introduction and notes by Kemp R. Niver. Los Angeles: Locare Research Group, 1971.

North, Dan. 'Magic and Illusion in Early Cinema', *Studies in French Cinema* 1 : 2 (2001): 70–79.

O'Connell, Sean. *The Car and British Society: Class, Gender and Motoring 1896–1939*. Manchester and New York: Manchester University Press, 1998.

Osborne, Albert E. *Why Man has used Pictures*

and A Comparison between the Telephone and the Stereoscope. New York and London: Underwood and Underwood, 1904.

Overy, Paul. 'Re-inventing the Wheel – Speed in Slow Motion: The London Eye (Millennium Wheel)', *Visual Culture in Britain* 4:2 (2003): 21–40.

Ovid. *Metamorphoses.* Ed. with an introduction, trans. and notes by D. E. Hill. Warminster: Aris and Phillips Ltd, 1999.

Owen, Alex. *The Darkened Room: Women, Power and Spiritualism in Late 19th-Century England.* London: Virago, 1989.

Pater, Walter. *Studies in the History of the Renaissance.* London: Macmillan and Co., 1873.

—. *Imaginary Portraits.* London: Macmillan and Co., 1887.

Paul, Robert. *The Hundred Best Animated Photography Films, in Every Variety of Subject.* London, 1900–01.

Paul, R. W., C. M. Hepworth and W. G. Barker. 'Before 1910: Kinematograph Experiences', Proceedings of the British Kinematograph Society, no. 38. London: 1936.

Pemberton, Max. *The Amateur Motorist.* London: Hutchinson and Co., 1907.

Penny, Nicholas. 'Goddesses and Girls', *London Review of Books* 2:29 (December 1982): 20.

Pennybacker, Susan. '"It was not what she said but the way in which she said it": The London County Council and the Music Halls', 120–40. In *Music Hall: The Business of Pleasure.* Ed. Peter Bailey. Milton Keynes: Open University Press, 1986.

Peucker, Brigitte. *Incorporating Images: Film and the Rival Arts.* Princeton, N.J.: Princeton University Press, 1995.

Pitt, Peter. 'The Oldest Studio', *Films and Filming* 343 (March 1983): 30.

Pladdys, Barry. 'Art and Automobiles', *Driving Member* 38:8 (January–February 1999): 18–19.

Poe, Edgar Allen. *Three Tales by Edgar Allen Poe.* London: S. Wellwood, 1907.

Popple, Simon, 'Indecent Exposures: Photography, Vice and the Moral Dilemma in Victorian Britain', *Early Popular Visual Culture* 3:2 (September 2005): 113–33.

Pritchard, Mrs Eric. *The Cult of Chiffon.* London: Grant Richards, 1902.

Pritchard, Michael. *Sir Hubert von Herkomer and his Film-Making in Bushey 1912–1914.* Bushey Museum Trust and ALLM Books, 1987.

—. 'Correspondence regarding A. Wallace Rimington and Colour Music', *Early Popular Visual Culture* 13:1 (May 2005): 109.

Proctor, Richard A. *The Spectroscope and its Work.* London: Society for Promoting Christian Knowledge, 1877.

—. *The Moon: Her Motions, Aspect, Scenery and Physical Condition.* 3rd edn. London: Longmans, Green and Co., 1886.

Prodger, Philip. *Time Stands Still: Muybridge and the Instantaneous Photography Movement.* New York: Oxford University Press in association with the Iris and B. Gerald Cantor Center for Visual Arts at Stanford Unversity, 2003.

Proust, Marcel. *In Search of Lost Time:* I, *Swann's Way* (1913). Trans. C. K. Scott Moncrieff and Terence Kilmartin, rev. D. J. Enright. London: Vintage, 2002.

Ramsaye, Terry. *A Million and One Nights: A History of the Motion Picture.* 2 vols. New York: Simon and Schuster, 1926.

Reuleaux, F. *The Kinematics of Machinery: Outlines of a Theory of Machines.* Trans. and ed. Alex B. W. Kennedy. London: Macmillan and Co., 1876.

Richards, Graham. *Putting Psychology in its Place: An Introduction from a Critical Historical Perspective.* London and New York: Routledge, 1996.

Riegl, Alöis. *Problems of Style: Foundations for a History of Ornament* (1893). Trans. E. Kain with introduction by David Castriota and preface by Henri Zerner. Princeton, N.J.: Princeton University Press, 1992.

—. 'Late Roman or Oriental?', 173–90. In *German Essays on Art History: Winckelmann, Burckhardt, Panofsky, and Others.* Ed. Gert Schiff. New York: Continuum, 1988.

Rimington, A. Wallace. *Colour-Music: The Art of Mobile Colour.* London: Hutchinson and Co., 1912.

Robertson, James C. *The British Board of Film Censors: Film Censorship in Britain, 1896–1950*. London: Croom Helm, 1985.

Robichon, François. 'L'attraction, parergon des expositions universelles', 315–28. In *Le livre des expositions universelles 1851–1989*. Paris: Union Centrale des Arts Décoratifs, 1983.

Robinson, David. *Georges Méliès: Father of Film Fantasy*. London: British Film Institute, 1993.

—. *From Peep Show to Palace: The Birth of American Film*. New York: Columbia University Press, 1996.

—, ed. *The Lantern Image: Iconography of the Magic Lantern 1420–1880. Supplement No. 1*. London: Magic Lantern Society, 1997.

Robinson, Henry Peach. *Picture-Making by Photography*. London: Hazell, Watson and Viney Ltd, 1902.

Rosen, Philip. 'Traces of the Past: From Historicity to Film', 67–89. In *Meanings in Texts and Actions: Questioning Paul Ricoeur*. Ed. David E. Klemm and William Schweiker. Charlottesville and London: University Press of Virginia, 1993.

Ross, Kristin. *Fast Cars, Clean Bodies: Decolonization and the Reordering of French Culture*. Cambridge, Mass., and London: M.I.T. Press, 1995.

Rossell, Deac. *Living Pictures: The Origins of the Movies*. Albany.: State University of New York Press, 1998.

Roterberg, A. *The Modern Wizard*. Chicago: A. Roterberg, 1896.

Sanders, Lise Shapiro. '"Indecent Incentives to Vice": Regulating Films and Audience Behaviour from the 1890s to the 1910s', 97–110. In *Young and Innocent? The Cinema in Britain 1896–1930*. Ed. Andrew Higson. Exeter: University of Exeter Press, 2002.

Sartre, Jean-Paul. *Being and Nothingness: An Essay on Phenomenological Ontology*. Trans. Hazel E. Barnes. London: Methuen and Co. Ltd, 1958.

Satz, Aura. 'Puppets and Prosthesis', *New Formations*, special issue 'The Prosthetic Aesthetic' 46 (spring 2002): 103–18.

Saxon, A. H. *The Life and Art of Andrew Ducrow and the Romantic Age of the English Circus*. Hamdon, Conn.: Archon Books, 1978.

Schivelbusch, Wolfgang. *The Railway Journey: The Industrialization of Time and Space in the 19th Century*. Leamington Spa, Hamburg, New York: Berg, 1986.

Schulz, Juergen. 'Michelangelo's Unfinished Works', *Art Bulletin* 57 (1975): 366–73.

A Selected Catalogue of the Best and Most Interesting 'Hepwix' Films Manufactured Only by Hepworth & Co.. London: 1903.

Sennett, Richard. *The Fall of Public Man*. New York: W. W. Norton, 1976.

Serres, Michel. *Atlas*. Paris. Editions Juilliard, 1994.

—, and Bruno Latour. *Conversations on Science, Culture and Time*. Trans. Roxanne Lapidus. Ann Arbor: University of Michigan Press, 1995.

Setford, David. 'Herkomer – A Passion for Work', 3–18. In *A Passion for Work – Sir Hubert von Herkomer 1849–1914*. Watford Museum, Watford Borough Council, 1982.

Sharpe, S. H. *Devant's Delightful Delusions*. Pasadena, Cal.: Magical Publications, 1990.

Sharrock, A. R. 'The Love of Creation', *Ramus: Critical Studies in Greek and Roman Literature* 20:2 (1991): 169–82.

Simmel, Georg. 'The Metropolis and Mental Life', 409–24. In *The Sociology of Georg Simmel*. Ed. Kurt H. Wolff. New York: Free Press, 1964.

Sims, George R., ed. *Living London: Its Work and its Play, its Humour and its Pathos, its Sights and its Scenes*. 3 vols. London: Cassell and Co., 1901–3.

Singer, Ben. 'Modernity, Hyperstimulus, and the Rise of Popular Sensationalism', 72–99. In *Cinema and the Invention of Modern Life*. Ed. Leo Charney and Vanessa Schwartz. Berkeley, Los Angeles, London: University of California Press, 1995.

Smith, Alison, ed. *Exposed: The Victorian Nude*. London: Tate Publishing, 2001.

Sobchak, Vivian. *The Address of the Eye: A Phenomenology of Film Experience*. Princeton, N.J.: Princeton University Press, 1992.

Sokalski, J. A. 'Living Motion Pictures: The

Panoramic Stage and Pre-Cinematic Show Technology', *Living Pictures: The Journal of the Popular and Projected Image Before 1914* 1 : 2 (2001): 59–68.

Sorensen, Colin. *London on Film: 100 Years of Filmmaking in London*. London: Museum of London, 1996.

Spencer, Herbert. *The Principles of Psychology*. 3rd edn. 2 vols. London: Williams and Norgate, 1890.

Stallybrass, Peter, and Allon White. *The Politics and Poetics of Transgression*. London: Methuen, 1986.

Stafford, Barbara Maria, and Frances Terpak. *Devices of Wonder: From the World in a Box to Images on a Screen*. Los Angeles: Getty Research Institute, 2001.

Steele, Valerie. *The Corset: A Cultural History*. New Haven and London: Yale University Press, 2001.

Stokes, John. *Resistible Theatres: Enterprise and Experiment in the Late Nineteenth Century*. London: Paul Elek Books Ltd, 1972.

—. *In the Nineties*. New York and London: Harvester Wheatsheaf, 1989.

Sully, James. *Sensation and Intuition: Studies in Psychology and Aesthetics*. London: Henry S. King and Co., 1874.

—. 'Pleasure of Visual Form', *Mind: A Quarterly Review of Psychology and Philosophy*, n.s., 20 (18 April 1880): 181–201.

—. *Illusions: A Psychological Study*. London: C. Kegan Paul and Co., 1881.

—. *The Human Mind: A Text-Book of Psychology*. 2 vols. London: Longmans, Green and Co., 1892.

Summers, Montague, ed. *Victorian Ghost Stories*. London: Fortune Press, 1933.

Talbot, Frederick A. *Practical Cinematography and its Applications*. London: William Heinemann, 1913.

Tarkovsky, Andrey. *Sculpting in Time: Reflections on the Cinema*. Trans. Kitty Hunter-Blair. London and Boston, Mass.: Faber and Faber, 1989.

Tarnowsky, Benjamin. *The Sexual Instinct and its Morbid Manifestation from the Double Standpoint of Jurisprudence and Psychiatry* (1885). Trans. W. C. Costello and Alfred Allinson. Paris: Charles Carrington, 1898.

Thesander, Marianne. *The Feminine Ideal*. London: Reaktion Books, 1997.

Thomas, Ann. *Beauty of Another Order: Photography in Science*. New Haven and London: Yale University Press in association with the National Gallery of Canada, Ottawa, 1997.

Thompson, Silvanus P. 'Optical Illusions of Movement'. *Brain* 3 (October 1880): 289–98.

Thomson, Robert. *The Pelican History of Psychology*. Harmondsworth: Penguin, 1968.

'Through the Fire', *Answers* (31 December 1898): 143.

Toulmin, Vanessa, Patrick Russell and Simon Popple, eds. *The Lost World of Mitchell and Kenyon: Edwardian Britain on Film*. London: British Film Institute, 2004.

Tosi, Virgilio. *Cinema before Cinema: The Origins of Scientific Cinematography*. London: British Universities Film and Video Council, 2006.

Treuherz, Julian. *Hard Times: Social Realism in Victorian Art*. London: Lund Humphries, in association with Manchester City Art Galleries, 1987.

Trodd, Colin, and Stephanie Brown, eds. *Representations of G. F. Watts: Art Making in Victorian Culture*. Aldershot: Ashgate, 2004.

Tucker, Jennifer. *Nature Exposed: Photography as Eyewitness in Victorian Science*. Baltimore and London: Johns Hopkins University Press, 2006.

Turner, R. Steven. 'Helmoltz, Sensory Physiology and the Disciplinary Development of German Psychology', 147–66. In *The Problematic Science: Psychology in Nineteenth-Century Thought*. Ed. William R. Woodward and Mitchell G. Ash. New York: Praeger, 1982.

Uglow, J., ed. *Walter Pater: Essays on Literature and Art*. London: Dent, 1973.

Urban, Charles. *The Cinematograph in Science, Education, and Matters of State*. London: Charles Urban, 1907.

Urban and Eclipse Films. London: Charles Urban Trading Co. Ltd.

Vaughan, Dai. 'Let There Be Lumière', 63–7.

In *Early Cinema: Space, Frame, Narrative*. Ed. Thomas Elsaesser and Adam Barker. London: British Film Institute, 1990.

Vere, Arprey. *Ancient and Modern Magic: With Explanations of Some of the Best Known Tricks performed by Messrs. Maskelyne and Cooke*. London: George Routledge and Sons, 1879.

Wagner, Peter, ed. *Icons – Texts – Iconotexts: Essays on Ekphrasis and Intermediality*. Berlin and New York: Walter de Gruyter, 1996.

Walpole, Horace. *The Castle of Otranto: A Gothic Story*. 2nd edn, London: William Bathoe and Thomas Lownds, 1765.

Warwick Trading Company Ltd Catalogues. London: Warwick Trading Company.

Welford, Walter D. *Photographer's Indispensable Handbook: A Complete Cyclopaedia upon the Subject of Photographic Apparatus, Material and Processes*, compiled by Walter D. Welford. London: Iliffe and Sons, 1887.

—. 'Detective and Hand Cameras. Issued as a Supplement to *Photography*, compiled and written by Walter D. Welford', *Photography* (23 May 1889): 3–11.

—. *The Hand Camera Manual: A Beginner's Guide to Photography in its Connection with the Hand Camera*. London: L. Upcott Gill, 1893.

—. *The Hand Camera and how to use it*. London: Iliffe, Sons and Sturmey Ltd, 1899.

Wells, H. G. 'War of the Worlds', *Pearson's Magazine* (April–December 1897).

—. *The First Men in the Moon* (1901). London: Gollancz, 2001.

Whitfield, Peter. *The Mapping of the Heavens*. London: British Library, 1995.

Wilde, Oscar. *The Picture of Dorian Gray* (1891). London: Penguin, 1994.

Wildman, Stephen. *Visions of Love and Life: Pre-Raphaelite Art from Birmingham Museums and Art Gallery*. Alexandria, Va: Art Services International, 1995.

Williams, Alan. 'The Lumière Organization and Documentary Realism', 153–61. In *Film before Griffith*. Ed. John L. Fell. Berkeley, Los Angeles, London: University of California Press, 1983.

Williams, Linda. 'Film Body: An Implantation of Perversions', 507–34. In *Narrative, Apparatus, Ideology: A Film Theory Reader*. Ed. Philip Rosen. New York: Columbia University Press, 1986.

—. *Hard Core: Power, Pleasure and the 'Frenzy of the Visible'*. London: Pandora, 1990.

—. 'Corporealized Observers: Visual Pornographies and the "Carnal Density of Vision"', 3–41. In *Fugitive Images: From Photography to Video*. Ed. Patrice Petro. Bloomington: Indiana University Press, 1995.

Winter, Frank H. 'The "Trip to the Moon" and Other Early Spaceflight Simulation Shows ca. 1901–1915: Part I', 133–61. In *History of Rocketry and Astronautics*. Ed. Donald C. Elder and Christophe Rothmund. AAS History Series, XXIII, IAA History Symposia, XV. San Diego, Cal.: American Astronautical Society, 2001.

Woodbury, Walter E. *Photographic Amusements: Including a Description of a Number of Novel Effects obtainable with the Camera*. New York: Scovill and Adams, 1898.

Woodward, William R., and Mitchell G. Ash, eds. *The Problematic Science: Psychology in Nineteenth-Century Thought*. New York: Praeger, 1982.

Wortley, Richard. *A Pictorial History of Striptease: 100 Years of Undressing to Music*. London: Octopus, 1976.

Wright, Patrick. *On Living in an Old Country: The National Past in Contemporary Britain*. London: Verso, 1985.

Yonge, C. D., ed. *Letters of Horace Walpole*. 2 vols. London: Swan Sonnenschein and Co., 1891.

Ziolkowski, Theodore. *Disenchanted Images: A Literary Iconology*. Princeton, N.J.: Princeton University Press, 1977.

photograph credits

In most cases, illustrations have been made from photographs, transparencies or digital scans kindly supplied by the owners or custodians of the works. Those plates for which further credit is due are listed below:

Stephen Bottomore 87
The Bridgeman Art Library 76, 77, 78
The British Library, London 3, 9, 10, 13, 14, 39, 74
The Trustees of the British Museum, London page viii, 2, 124
Bushey Museum and Art Gallery 58, 61, 62, 69, 71, 72, 73, 75, 98, 99, 103, 104, 105, 106, 107, 108, 109, 110, 113, 114, 115, 116
© The Metropolitan Museum of Art, New York 21
The Museum of London 4
Roger-Viollet, Paris 119
Sefton MBC Leisure Services Department, Arts and Cultural Services, Atkinson Art Gallery 28
Lawrence Steigrad Fine Arts, New York 48

index

Index by Christine Shuttleworth